AMERICAN
CERAMICS
BEFORE
1930

AMERICAN CERAMICS BEFORE 1930

A Bibliography

Compiled by
RUTH IRWIN WEIDNER

ART REFERENCE COLLECTION, NUMBER 2

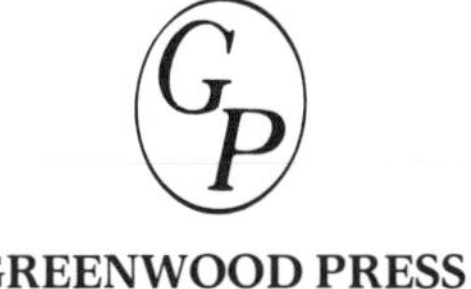

GREENWOOD PRESS

WESTPORT, CONNECTICUT • LONDON, ENGLAND

Library of Congress Cataloging in Publication Data

Weidner, Ruth Irwin.
   American ceramics before 1930.

   (Art reference collection, ISSN 0193-6867 ; no. 2)
   Includes indexes.
   1. Pottery, American—Bibliography. 2. Porcelain,
American—Bibliography. I. Title. II. Series.
Z7179.W43 [NK4005] 016.738'0973   82-6117
ISBN 0-313-22831-0 (lib. bdg.)   AACR2

Library of Congress Catalog Card Number: 82-6117
ISBN: 0-313-22831-0
ISSN: 0193-6867

First published in 1982

Greenwood Press
A division of Congressional Information Service, Inc.
88 Post Road West, Westport, Connecticut 06881

Printed in the United States of America

10 9 8 7 6 5 4 3 2 1

For Donna, David, and Meg

CONTENTS

Preface   ix
Notes on the Use of This Bibliography   xiii
Suggestions for Additional Research   xvii

A.   Books and Pamphlets   1
B.   Conference Proceedings and
     Chapters from Books   25
C.   Catalogs of Exhibitions,
     Collections, and Sales   37
D.   Theses and Dissertations   44
E.   Federal, State, and
     Municipal Publications   47
F.   Trade Publications   53
G.   Periodical Articles   62

Appendix: Guide to Selected American Clayworking,
    Ceramics, China Painting, and Crockery
    Journals Before 1930   216
Author Index   223
Subject Index   239

PREFACE

Pottery making, an important trade in the colonies from the first years of settlement, grew rapidly in the United States after the Civil War and especially in the last two decades of the nineteenth century—and so did the literature related to the art, science, and history of American ceramic production. Although the focus here is on American ceramics from the Civil War through World War I, this bibliography covers the history of pottery making from the earliest colonial manufacture through about 1930, when styles, production methods, and terminology changed as the activities of folk potters and pottery companies gave way to the pre-eminence of the studio potter. The literature included is that published from the early nineteenth century through the end of 1980, this compiler's arbitrary cut-off date. The rich and abundant literature of the 1970s reflects the growing interest of researchers and collectors in pre-1930 American ceramic wares.

Ceramic products were a necessity in seventeenth-century America. Scarcely had our first colonists put down tentative roots, when the clay-workers among them began producing material goods needed for survival: bricks, tiles, and simple containers for various domestic uses. Most wares produced throughout the eighteenth and first half of the nineteenth century were rather similar in character—solidly constructed and essentially utilitarian, although some, for example Pennsylvania–German sgraffito wares, were highly decorative as well. From the pre-Civil War period, we have few extensive written records about the making of American ceramic wares: only a few substantive publications before 1860 were noted by this bibliographer. Today archaeologists and ceramic historians are literally piecing together the evidence offered by shards at kiln sites.

After 1865, the pottery industry grew by leaps and bounds, not only in number of establishments but also in types of wares produced. These wares were of an infinite variety of forms and types, from roofing tiles and sanitary wares to delicate molded eggshell Belleeks. Although the artistic philosophies of the Arts and Crafts Movement were an important guiding spirit for turn-of-the-century art wares, the rapid growth in United States pottery production may also be attributed to the development of the factory system and the faster and more profitable production methods made possible by new sophisticated machinery and energy sources.

Spawned by the Arts and Crafts Movement was a fad for pottery making and china painting as an avocation. This widespread popular interest, in which women were the major participants, set the stage for both the American art pottery movement and a new concern for writing about pottery, both past and present. In the early 1880s, articles about pottery production began to appear in general literature, for example, *Harper's New Monthly Magazine* and *Century Magazine*. By the late 1890s articles in the popular literature were quite common. In 1899, the first annual *Transactions* of the newly founded American Ceramic Society were compiled, heralding a more scientific and scholarly emphasis in the literature. During the same year, the first issue of *Keramic Studio*, an important periodical devoted to china painting and art pottery, also appeared. Two years later, *Old China*, a journal with a historical slant, began publication, a clear indication of a growing American interest in the history of pottery. These new publications joined several clayworking trade journals, which had previously been the major vehicles for historical and artistic studies about American ceramics. They included *Brick*, *Brickmaker*, *Brickbuilder*, and *Clay-Worker*.

By the early twentieth century, articles about the history and progress of the pottery industry abounded in general, art, and trade literature. These articles were written by ceramists, artists, business personnel, scholars, local historians, collectors, afficionados, and raconteurs. Each documented a part, large or small, of the burgeoning industry of American ceramics, and almost every piece of this voluminous record is important—for the unique information it contains, for its viewpoint, for its acquaintance with some part of the industry now unknown to us, or for its photographs and descriptions of individual pieces, some of which are now lost.

The study of ceramics embraces many disciplines, including artistic history and theory, business and technological history, economics, geology, chemistry, and popular culture. A renewed interest in American history and culture, especially our material culture, has increased the need for access to the rich literature of American ceramics, much of which appears in relatively inaccessible local publications and unindexed periodicals. It is the purpose of this bibliography to make this literature more easily available to researchers, collectors, librarians, and ceramists.

Acknowledgments

Gathering together the bibliographic information for nearly three thousand publications related to American ceramics was a project with which many individuals and institutions have assisted. Two libraries have been particularly helpful. Henry Francis du Pont Winterthur Library's rich collection of materials in American decorative arts was invaluable, as was the advice of its librarian, Neville Thompson. The Free Library of Philadelphia, especially the Art Department, provided hundreds of volumes—turn-of-the-century art and ceramic journals—from their impressive collections. I should like to acknowledge the help given to me over a period of more than a year by the Art Department staff: Miriam L. Lesley, Head; Barbara J. Ickes; Jewel Phelps; Joann Stewart; and Irena Uknalis. I am grateful for Barbara Ickes's advice about organization of the bibliography and its index.

For assistance given by the following libraries and their staff I am most appreciative: Library of Congress; Eleutherian Mills Historical Library; New York Public Library; Trenton Public Library; Smithsonian Institution libraries; Philadelphia Museum of Art Library; Newark Public Library; Yale University Library; Massachusetts Historical Society Library; Library Company of Philadelphia; and Pennsylvania Historical Society Library. A faculty research grant from West Chester State College made it possible for me to spend several days in the Boston Public Library in August 1980.

The following individuals graciously answered my pleas for information: Harold M. Forbes, Associate Curator, West Virginia and Regional History Collection, West Virginia University; Susan Strong, New York State College of Ceramics Library, Alfred University; Betty Barker, Archives Department, New Jersey State Library; Hester Rich, Maryland Historical Society; Garth Clark, Institute of Ceramic History; Margie Hughto, Everson Museum of Art; Marjorie Uren, Keramos; Amy Barnum, Special Collections Librarian, New York State Historical Association; Eva Slezak, Reference Librarian, Maryland Department, Enoch Pratt Free Library; E. S. Carson, Homer Laughlin China Company; Michael Voors, Art Librarian, East Carolina University; Louise Henning, Kohler Art Library, Elvehjem Museum of Art, University of Wisconsin; Marshall J. Becker, Professor of Anthropology, West Chester State College; LaVonne R. Leary, Adult Services Librarian, Ohio County Public Library, Wheeling; Jessie J. Poesch, Professor, History of Art, Newcomb College, Tulane University; and David M. Ment, Director of Research, Brooklyn Rediscovery.

Dr. Kenneth L. Ames, Henry Francis du Pont Winterthur Museum, and Dr. Pamela Hemphill, Professor, Department of Art, West Chester State College, kindly read the introductory material.

Pamela Jeffcott Parry, Series Editor, *The Art Reference Collection*, and Marilyn Brownstein, Acquisitions Editor, Greenwood Press, offered well-considered solutions to difficult problems, as well as much time and constant encouragement. Their broad experience, specialized expertise, and good judgment have enhanced this volume immeasurably.

But it is to friends and family that the greatest debt is owed. Suzanna Barucco, my research assistant, carefully checked many sources and tirelessly assisted with indexing and proofreading. Ann Barnett Schloss, a friend and colleague in New York City, indexed several volumes available only in that city's libraries. Beth Haw has been much more than the expert typist whose work may be admired on the pages following. She has brought to her part of the work a discerning eye, excellent judgment, editorial expertise, and a cheerful spirit. To her must go a large share of the credit for the preparation of this volume.

Finally, my immediate family have given much more than the ''patient understanding and support'' for which authors frequently thank loved ones. Donna Weidner, David Weidner, and Margaret Weidner have each actively participated in the preparation of copy or bibliographic searching. I should especially like to acknowledge David's contribution to the final indexing, a segment of the work that took several months. In many respects this book is the product of family teamwork, my most valuable, and most treasured, asset.

West Chester, Pa.

NOTES ON THE USE
OF THIS BIBLIOGRAPHY

Purpose, Scope, and Arrangement

The purpose of this book is to draw together in one volume a comprehensive listing of materials relating to the production of pottery and porcelain in America before 1930. Approximately 90 percent of the nontechnical literature published between the early nineteenth century and the end of 1980 is listed herein. For each of the 2,921 citations included, full bibliographic description are given.

In subject content, the emphasis is on decorative ceramics such as fine porcelain, art pottery, dinnerware, and architectural terra cotta. However, literature relating to essentially utilitarian ceramics like roofing tiles and sanitary wares has been included, as have writings about many related considerations, for example, clays, machinery and equipment, ceramic societies and clubs, and tariffs and wages. In general, coverage has been determined by the subject content of materials published rather than by editorial decision, and is purposely broad so as to fill many research needs. (Ceramics is defined here as the art and technology of producing materials from fired clay, or products made from fired clay. American glass and glassware will be covered in a subsequent volume, currently in preparation for this series.)

The bibliography is arranged by type of research material in seven sections as follows: (A) ''Books and Pamphlets'' (265 entries); (B) ''Conference Proceedings and Chapters from Books'' (104 entries); (C) ''Catalogs of Exhibitions, Collections, and Sales'' (56 entries); (D) ''Theses and Dissertations'' (25 entries); (E) ''Federal, State, and Municipal Publications'' (45 entries); (F) ''Trade Publications'' (101 entries); and (G) ''Periodical Articles'' (2,325 entries from 232 journals). Within each of the major sections, entries have been arranged alphabetically by author. (Please note that in section G, anonymous periodical articles have been entered under the title of the journal in which they appear.) If a work might logically fall in either of two sections, as in the case of a book published with an exhibition, reference has been made from one section to the other. Each entry is fully indexed in the author and subject indices, which appear at the end of the volume. An appendix provides information about thirty-seven selected clayworking, ceramics, china painting, and crockery journals published before 1930.

"American" wares are defined as having been constructed or decorated by those residing in the area that constituted the United States up to 1930. Please note the exclusion of Staffordshire and other English wares made for the American market, especially china with American views. Because it is a different genre, and because bibliographic coverage is available elsewhere, ceramics made by the American Indian have been excluded.[1] Also excluded is literature of a highly scientific or technical nature, especially that containing extensive formulae.[2]

Material included is that published in the United States or abroad through December 1980, excluding newspaper accounts, book reviews, news notes and similar short contributions in journals, unpublished manuscripts and typescripts, articles from most weekly publications, and writings of an extremely rare or local nature, which would not be generally available for research use.

Explanation of Bibliographic Citations

Each entry is preceded by its own unique code letter/number, a combination of the letter for the section within which it appears and its number within that section. (These entry codes are used to guide the reader in both indexing and cross-referencing.) Full bibliographic descriptions have been given to provide the reader with an idea of the length and character of each entry and to facilitate use of interlibrary loan. Where titles are vague or not sufficiently descriptive, a few words in brackets have been provided to clarify the meaning.

In notations about illustrations (specified by "illus"), "col" refers to full-color photographs or other color illustrations; "b&w" indicates that illustrative material is comprised of black and white photographs, halftones, or sketches. Although illustrations are most frequently of pottery products, they may also be portraits of personnel, photographs of pottery buildings, or diagrams and maps. Numbers before "b&w" and "col" in section G, "Periodical Articles," refer to the number of such illustrations in a given article rather than to the number of objects illustrated. (If there is only one illustration, and it is a frontispiece or cover design, it has not been noted because of the frequency of loss in binding.) For readers primarily interested in illustrations, knowing how many an article contains may be useful. On the other hand, if a reader needs textual information, he/she may conclude that a two-page article with many illustrations would not be worth locating.

"Bibliog" refers to the presence of bibliographic references that will lead the reader to more specialized materials not within the purview of this volume, such as local histories and newspaper accounts. In citations for books, the page number on which the bibliography appears have been provided in most cases. ("Bibliog" may also refer to footnotes in the text.)

The notations "index" and "glossary" have been used for books that contain same. It certain instances, notes about appendices and other special features have been included, as have notes about earlier or subsequent editions, if full information is not available for those editions. Reprint editions are given as separate entries, with references to the original editions.

Indexing

The Author Index lists in one alphabet all authors, joint authors, and corporate authors, as well as auxiliary personnel such as general editors or persons who contributed to exhibition catalogs. Full names have been given if known.

The detailed Subject Index provides access by names of potteries, potters, trade names, geographical areas (for example, New York State potteries; Bennington (Vt.) potteries); types of wares (for example, Slip-decorated wares; Belleek; Stoneware); and by subjects (for example, China painting; Glazes and glazing; Health conditions in potteries; Wartime uses of ceramics). In certain cases, similar subjects have been grouped together under general terms, for example, "Motifs," "Influences," and "Exhibitions and expositions." Cross-referencing has been provided in this index as desirable. Whenever possible, as a guide to the reader, geographical locations for potters and potteries have been provided, as have dates of birth and death for potters and other personnel. It has not been within the scope of this bibliography to verify each of these dates; however, they have been confirmed whenever possible.

Notes

1. See, for example, William Farrington, *Prehistoric and Historic Pottery of the Southwest: A Bibliography* (Santa Fe, N. Mex.: Sunstone Press, 1975).

2. Many highly technical articles have appeared in the American Ceramic Society *Journal* and *Bulletin*. These are indexed (through 1955) in Lola Schell Bigler et al., *Indexes to Publications of the American Ceramic Society* (Columbus, Ohio: American Ceramic Society, 1957).

SUGGESTIONS FOR ADDITIONAL RESEARCH

The present bibliography will provide access to most of the materials already published about American potteries before 1930. Although there is a great wealth of literature available, many American potters and potteries have never been seriously studied, and of those that have, certain aspects of the operation or specialized types of wares frequently have been left undocumented. The following suggestions have been compiled to assist the researcher or collector to obtain further information about a potter, pottery, type of ware, or manufacturing technique. Additional information can be obtained from several types of sources: (1) local resources; (2) federal, state, and municipal records; (3) trade journals; (4) directories; and (5) physical remains.

Local Resources

For additional information about a chosen pottery or type of ware, the first step in further research should be to contact—or, preferably, visit—the historical society closest to the area in which the potter resided or the wares were made.[1] Libraries of local historical societies or museums usually contain any or all of the following, all invaluable in ceramics research: clipping files, collections of trade and advertising material, photographs, local histories and genealogies, city directories, copies of speeches given in the community, and local publications. Be on the lookout for publications issued in conjunction with city or county celebrations, for example, a special issue of the local newspaper commemorating a town centennial; these frequently describe the histories of local businesses. In some instances library collections include records of potteries, such as account books, day books, and shape books. If a pottery's contents have been sold at auction or sheriff's sale, extensive records of facilities and equipment should be available. Scanning long runs of local newspapers for news notes and advertisements is tedious and time consuming, but if reliable clipping files are not available, the effort can be rewarding. In local newspapers the researcher can often find announcements of new lines, notices of changes in ownership of pottery companies or expansion of facilities, and so on.

In most communities knowledgeable collectors or antique dealers may be found; often these persons are able to provide many facts about potteries and wares from their long experience in the field. It would indeed by shortsighted to overlook this potential source of information. Collectors and dealers frequently have made extensive studies of their own, and might even have known and interviewed personnel who once worked in a particular pottery. Most dealers and collectors have seen and handled hundreds of pieces of pottery over a period of many years, and are familiar with marks, glazes, and design types.

Federal, State, and Municipal Records

If a particular potter cannot be located in the appropriate city directory or other local records, it is often worthwhile to search census or tax records. Unless such records have been destroyed by fire or other calamity, most municipalities have annual tax records, which should include lists of all adult residents. In searching such records, be aware that they were often compiled hastily, and that names may be misspelled or not in correct alphabetical order. Be careful to check under any possible variant spelling of each name sought. For a potter known to have immigrated to this country, federal immigration records may establish date of arrival here. In addition, births, marriages, and deaths are part of the official record and may be useful.

The federal *Census of Manufactures* is a valuable source, which provides a picture of methods of production. This census, begun in 1820, lists such factors as numbers of employees, capital, types of equipment, kinds of energy ("water" or "horse"), and types of wares marketed. Moreover, certain states have on file periodical reports of factory inspectors or others responsible for licensing.

Trade Journals

For pottery companies in operation after 1880, the many trade journals of the period 1880-1930 (see Appendix) offer a treasure trove of information about business history and products. These journals contain advertisements, editorial comment, and news notes, which reveal many small details of company history. Included are reports of fires with notes on the extent of damage, notices of hiring, illnesses, and deaths of pottery personnel, announcements of new lines and products, and comments about major changes in production methods. A thorough search of the following will yield a wealth of detail: "Echoes from the Trade," a regular feature in *China, Glass & Pottery Review*; "Among the

Potteries,'' in *Crockery and Glass Journal*; ''Editorial Notes and Clippings,'' in *Clay-Worker*; ''Flying Notes,'' in *Pottery and Glassware Reporter*; ''Trenton News,'' in *Pottery, Glass & Brass Salesman*; and ''Pottery Pointers,'' in *American Potters' Journal*.

Directories

Aside from directories of a purely local nature, there are several that address the pottery industry at large. See, for example, *Clay Products Cyclopedia* (A59) or *Directory of Plants in the White Ware Branches of the Ceramic Industries* (A79). In addition, *Thomas' Register of American Manufactures*,[2] available in most large public libraries, may be useful in determining exactly when a pottery company was in operation, its capital, type of wares, or officers.

Physical Remains

Occasionally the study of a potter or pottery can be augmented by what physical evidence remains. Familiarity with the full range of output of a business is an asset to the researcher, who should take measurements and careful notes for each piece examined. If it is not possible to photograph all pieces examined, detailed sketches of shapes and designs, with rubbings or careful descriptions of potters' marks, should be made.

Aside from the wares themselves, other information may be gleaned from the foundations of the pottery building,[3] from tools or equipment known to have been used at the pottery, from shards at the pottery site (especially those from other potteries, from which designs may have been borrowed), or from samples or ''lunch hour'' pieces which elucidate new or experimental artistic directions. Or, for example, the researcher might be interested in knowing about the location of local clay fields, or in finding out how close a railroad line ran to a late nineteenth-century pottery company. Even the discovery of a mold or marking device may provide a meaningful clue to the work of a particular pottery.

Research in American ceramics before 1930 is a complicated and tedious undertaking, but can yield rich rewards in our understanding of American history and material culture. It is hoped that the present bibliography, by drawing together in one volume a list of most of the published materials in the field, will point the way to further research and will lighten the work of the researcher—without spoiling the fun!

Notes

1. Always call or write before visiting a historical society library. This will allow you to plan a visit when the library is certain to be open and the staff best

able to assist you, and may give the staff lead time to assemble materials pertinent to your research.

2. First issued in 1905–1906, this directory was originally called *Thomas' Wholesale Grocery and Kindred Trades Register*.

3. In no instance should excavation or other disruption of sites of former potteries be undertaken without official permission and the supervision of an archaeologist working in an official capacity.

AMERICAN
CERAMICS
BEFORE
1930

A
BOOKS AND PAMPHLETS

A1.   ADAMSON, Jack E. Illustrated Handbook of Ohio Sewer
     Pipe Folk Art. Barberton, Ohio: Author, 1973. 88p.
     illus (b&w).

A2.   ALEXANDER, Donald E. Roseville Pottery for Collectors.
     Richmond, Ind.: Author, 1970. 78p. illus (b&w).

A3.   ALTMAN, Violet, and ALTMAN, Seymour. The Book of Buffalo
     Pottery. New York: Bonanza Books, 1969. 192p. illus
     (b&w, col); index; glossary; bibliog.
       Includes List of Commercial Service Clients, 5p.

A4.   AMERICAN CERAMIC SOCIETY. Art Division Symposium:
     Complete Proceedings of Sessions of the Art Division
     . . . February 1930. [Easton, Pa.: The Society]
     1930. 66p.

A5.   [ANDERSON, Mary F.] The White House China. Trenton,
     N.J.: Lenox, Inc. [1940?] 31p. illus.
       Originally published in Americana. See G138.

A6.   [BALLUFF, George Erhart] China Painter Instruction
     Book. Chicago: Thayer & Chandler, 1914. 58p. illus
     (b&w).

A7.   BARBER, Edwin AtLee. The Ceramic Collectors' Glossary.
     New York: Printed for the [Walpole] Society, 1914.
     119p. illus (b&w).

A8.   __________. The Ceramic Collectors' Glossary. New York:
     Da Capo Press, 1976. 119p. illus (b&w).
       Reprint of A7.

A9.   __________. Historical Sketch of the Green Point (N.Y.)
     Porcelain Works of Charles Cartlidge & Co. Indian-
     apolis, Ind.: Clay-Worker, 1895. 59p. illus (b&w).
       Also published as G227-231.

A10.   BARBER, Edwin AtLee. Marks of American Potters, with
        Facsimiles of 1,000 Marks, and Illustrations of Rare
        Examples of American Wares. Philadelphia: Patterson
        and White, 1904. 174p. illus (b&w); index.

A11.   _______. Marks of American Potters, with Facsimiles
        of 1,000 Marks and Illustrations of Rare Examples of
        American Wares. Southampton, N.Y.: Cracker Barrel
        Press [1971?] 174p. illus (b&w); index.
            Reprint of A10.

A12.   _______. Marks of American Potters. Ann Arbor, Mich.:
        Ars Ceramica, 1976. 174p. illus (b&w); index.
            Reprint of A10.

        _______. Marks of American Potters.
            (Feingold reprint edition), see A17.

A13.   _______. The Pottery and Porcelain of the United
        States: An Historical Review of American Ceramic Art
        from the Earliest Times to the Present Day [1st ed.]
        New York: G. P. Putnam, 1893. 446p. illus (b&w);
        index.

A14.   _______. The Pottery and Porcelain of the United
        States: An Historical Review of American Ceramic Art
        from the Earliest Times to the Present Day. 2d ed.
        rev. and enl. New York: G. P. Putnam, 1901. 539p.
        illus (b&w); index.

A15.   _______. The Pottery and Porcelain of the United
        States: An Historical Review of American Ceramic Art
        from the Earliest Times to the Present Day. 3d ed.
        rev. and enl. New York: G. P. Putnam, 1909. 621p.
        illus (b&w); index.

A16.   _______. The Pottery and Porcelain of the United
        States: An Historical Review of American Ceramic Art.
        With a New Introduction and Bibliography. Watkins
        Glen, N.Y.: Century House Americana, 1971. 450p.
        illus (b&w); index; bibliog (pp. 407-435).
            Reprint of A13.

A17.   _______. The Pottery and Porcelain of the United
        States: An Historical Review of American Ceramic Art
        from the Earliest Times to the Present Day . . . Com-
        bined with Marks of American Potters. New York:
        Feingold & Lewis, 1976. 621p., 174p. illus (b&w);
        indices.
            Reprint of A15 and A10.

A18.   _______. Tulip Ware of the Pennsylvania-German Potters:
        An Historical Sketch of the Art of Slip-Decoration in
        the United States. Philadelphia: [Patterson & White]
        1903. 233p. illus (b&w, col); index.
            "Only 300 copies printed on large paper [24.3 x
            17cm]"

A19. BARBER, Edwin AtLee. Tulip Ware of the Pennsylvania-
      German Potters: An Historical Sketch of the Art of
      Slip-Decoration in the United States. Art Handbook
      of the Pennsylvania Museum and School of Industrial
      Art. Philadelphia: Printed for the Museum, 1903.
      233p. illus (b&w, col); index.

A20. ________. Tulip Ware of the Pennsylvania-German Potters:
      An Historical Sketch of the Art of Slip-Decoration in
      the United States. Art Handbook of the Pennsylvania
      Museum and School of Industrial Art. Philadelphia:
      Printed for the Museum, 1926. 233p. illus (b&w);
      index.

A21. ________. Tulip Ware of the Pennsylvania-German Potters:
      An Historical Sketch of the Art of Slip-Decoration in
      the United States. With a New Introduction by Henry
      J. KAUFFMAN. New York: Dover, 1970. 233p. illus
      (b&w); index.
         Reprint of A20.

A22. ________. The Work of the Potteries of New Jersey from
      1685 to 1876. Newark, N.J.: Newark Museum Associa-
      tion, 1914. [39]p. illus (b&w).
         Extracts from A15 and A166.

A23. BARGLOFF, Elva Zesiger. The Potteries of Fort Dodge,
      Iowa: A Price Guide Identification. Spencer, Iowa:
      Author, 1980. 32p. illus (b&w).

A24. BARNARD, Julian. Victorian Ceramic Tiles. Greenwich,
      Conn.: New York Graphic Society, 1972. 184p. illus
      (b&w, col); index; glossary.
         List of American Tile Manufacturers: pp. 165-167.

A25. BARNES, Benjamin H. The Moravian Pottery: Memories of
      Forty-Six Years. Doylestown, Pa.: Bucks County His-
      torical Society, 1970. 25p.

A26. BARR, Margaret Libby, MILLER, Donald, and BARR, Robert.
      University of North Dakota Pottery: The Cable Years.
      Fargo, N.D.: Printed by Knight Printing Co., 1977.
      51p. illus (b&w, col); bibliog (p. 37).

A27. BARRET, Richard Carter. Bennington Pottery and Porce-
      lain: A Guide to Identification. New York: Bonanza
      Books, 1958. 342p. illus (b&w, col); index.
         Guide to Marks: pp. 13-14.

A28. ________. A Color Guide to Bennington Pottery. Man-
      chester, Vt.: Forward's Color Productions, 1966.
      30p. illus (col); index.

A29. ________. How to Identify Bennington Pottery. Brattle-
      boro, Vt.: Stephen Greene Press, 1964. 71p. illus
      (b&w); index.

A30.   BEARD, James C. Painting on China: What to Paint and
         How to Paint It: A Hand-Book of Practical Instruction
         in Overglaze Painting for Amateurs in the Decoration
         of Hard Porcelain. New York: Dick & Fitzgerald,
         1882. 95p. illus (b&w, col).

A31.   BECKWITH, Arthur. International Exhibition, London,
         1871: Pottery--Observations on the Materials and
         Manufacture of Terra-Cotta, Stone-Ware, Fire-Brick,
         Porcelain, Earthen-Ware, Brick, Majolica and Encaustic
         Tiles, with Remarks on the Products Exhibited. New
         York: D. Van Nostrand, 1872 [103]p. index.

A32.   BENJAMIN, Marcus. American Art Pottery. Washington,
         1907. 57p. illus (b&w).
            Originally published in Glass and Pottery World,
            Vol. 15: February 1907, pp. 28-31; March 1907,
            pp. 13-18; April 1907, pp. 35-40; May 1907, pp.
            35-39.

A33.   BERKY, Andrew S. The Passmore Pottery, 1828-1911.
         Pennsburg, Pa.: Schwenkfelder Library, 1953. 20p.
         illus (b&w).

A34.   BINNS, Charles F., Ed. The Manual of Practical Potting,
         Specially Compiled by Experts. 3d ed. rev. and enl.
         New York: D. Van Nostrand, 1901. 204p. index.
         Earlier editions published in London.

A35.   ________. The Potter's Craft: A Practical Guide for
         the Studio and Workshop. 1st ed. New York: D. Van
         Nostrand, 1910. 171p. illus (b&w); index.

A36.   ________. The Potter's Craft: A Practical Guide for
         the Studio and Workshop. 2d ed. rev. and enl. New
         York: D. Van Nostrand, 1922. 206p. illus (b&w);
         index.
            Two later editions: (3d ed., 1947; 4th ed., 1967).

A37.   BIVINS, John, Jr. The Moravian Potters in North
         Carolina. Old Salem Series. Chapel Hill, N.C.:
         University of North Carolina Press, 1972. 300p.
         illus (b&w, col); index; glossary; bibliog (pp. 289-
         290).

A38.   BLAIR, C. Dean. The Potters and Potteries of Summit
         County, 1828-1915. Akron, Ohio: Summit County
         Historical Society, 1965. 59p. illus (b&w); bibliog
         (pp. 35-36).

A39.   BLASBERG, Robert W. George E. Ohr and His Biloxi Art
         Pottery. Port Jervis, N.Y.: J. W. Carpenter, 1973.
         40p. illus (b&w); bibliog (pp. 23-24).

A40.   BLEICHER, Fred, HU, William C., and UREN, Marjorie E.
         Pewabic Pottery: An Official History. Ann Arbor,
         Mich.: Ars Ceramica, 1977.

A41. BOGUE, Dorothy McGraw. The Van Briggle Story. Colorado
      Springs, Col.: Printed by Century One Press, 1968,
      1976. 60p. illus (b&w); bibliog (pp. 50-52).
         Two printings.

A42. BRANIN, M[anlif] Lelyn. The Early Potters and Potteries
      of Maine. Middletown, Conn.: Wesleyan University
      Press, 1978. 262p. illus (b&w); index; bibliog
      (pp. 194-218).
         Marks of Early Maine Potteries: pp. 222-224.

A43. __________. The Early Potters and Potteries of Maine.
      Maine Heritage Series, No. 3. Augusta, Me.: Maine
      State Museum, 1978. 262p. illus (b&w); index; bibliog
      (pp. 194-218).
         Identical to A42.

A44. BRASIER de la VAUGUYON, (Mme.) L. H. Guide to Painting
      on Porcelain and Earthen-Ware. Boston: E. Farwell,
      1877. 31p.

A45. BREININGER, Lester P., Jr. Potters of the Tulpehocken.
      Myerstown, Pa.: Ron's Printing Service, 1979. 56p.
      illus (b&w, col).
         List of Tulpehocken Potters: pp. 53-54.

A46. BRUNK, Thomas W. Pewabic Pottery: Marks and Labels.
      Detroit: Historic Indian Village Press, 1978. 35p.
      illus (b&w); bibliog.

A47. [BUCKS COUNTY HISTORICAL SOCIETY] Henry Chapman Mercer,
      Born June 24, 1856, Died March 9, 1930: Memorial
      Services, Saturday, May Third, Nineteen Hundred and
      Thirty. Doylestown, Pa.: The Society, 1930. 40p.
      illus (b&w).
         See also G431.

A48. __________. The Mercer Mile: The Story of Dr. Henry
      Chapman Mercer and His Concrete Buildings. Doyles-
      town, Pa.: The Society, 1972. 28p. illus (b&w).

A49. BURGEON, Adelbert Joseph. China Painting (With Glaze
      Colours). Chicago, 1892. 31p.

A50. BURT, Stanley G. 2,292 Pieces of Early Rookwood Pot-
      tery in the Cincinnati Art Museum in 1916. Foreword
      by Herbert PECK. Cincinnati, Ohio: Cincinnati His-
      torical Society, 1978. 192p.
         From a ms.: "Rookwood Pottery in Cin'ti Art
         Museum Listed by S. G. Burt, 1916."

A51. BUXTON, Virginia Hillway. Roseville Pottery for Love or
      Money. Nashville, Tenn.: Tymbre Hill, 1977. 320p.
      illus (b&w, col); index; bibliog (pp. 306-309).

A52. CAMPANA, Domenic Mathews. Enamel Decorations for Por-
      celain and Glass. Chicago: Printed by Post Printing
      Shop, 1921. 16p. illus (b&w).

A53.   CAMPANA, Domenic Mathews. The Teacher of China Paint-
        ing. 3d ed. rev. and enl. Chicago [192-?] 147p.
        illus (b&w).

A54.   Catalog of Rookwood Art Pottery Shapes. Kingston, N.Y.:
        P-B Enterprises, 1971-1973. 2 v. illus (b&w).
           Vol. 1: 1880-1907; vol. 2: 1907-1967.

        Ceramic Data Book, see Clay Products Cyclopedia.

        China Painter Instruction Book, see BALLUFF, George
        Erhart.

A55.   CHRISTENSEN, Edwin O. Early American Designs: Ceramics.
        New York: Pitman, 1952. 48p. illus (b&w); index.
        From Index of American Design.

A56.   CLARK, Garth, Ed. Transactions of the Ceramics Sympo-
        sium: 1979. Los Angeles, Calif.: Institute for
        Ceramic History, 1980. 122p. bibliog.
           For contents see: B6, B11, B16, B31, B33, B47, B70-
           71, B73, B92.

A57.   CLARK, Garth, and HUGHTO, Margie. A Century of Ceramics
        in the United States, 1878-1978: A Study of Its Devel-
        opment. New York: E. P. Dutton, in association with
        Everson Museum of Art, 1979. 372p. illus (b&w, col);
        index; bibliog (pp. 345-361).
           Biographies of Potters, pp. 269-343. Published in
           conjunction with an exhibition first shown at the
           Everson Museum of Art.

A58.   CLARKE, John M. The Swiss Influence on the Early Penn-
        sylvania Slip Decorated Majolica. Albany, N.Y.: J.
        B. Lyon, 1908. 18p. illus (b&w).

A59.   Clay Products Cyclopedia, Containing Important Informa-
        tion for Every Executive from President to Foreman of
        Every Branch of the Clay Products Industry Including
        Both Pottery and Heavy Clay Products. 1st ed.
        Chicago: Industrial Publications, 1922. 252p. illus
        (b&w).
           Biennial through 1930; Later editions entitled
           Ceramic Data Book.

A60.   CLEMENT, Arthur W. More Early New Jersey Potteries.
        Notes on American Pottery, Part 2. New York: Court
        Press, 1942?

A61.   ________. Notes on American Ceramics, 1607-1943.
        Brooklyn, N.Y.: Brooklyn Museum, 1944. 36p. illus
        (b&w); bibliog (pp. 35-36).
        "An aid to the appreciation and study of the collec-
        tion of American earthenware and porcelain which the
        Brooklyn Museum placed on exhibition in January 1944."

CLEMENT, Arthur W. Notes on American Pottery, see his
Some Early New Jersey Potteries and More Early New
Jersey Potteries.

A62.   CLEMENT, Arthur W. Notes on Early American Porcelain,
1738-1838. New York: Court Press, 1946. 38p.

A63.   ________. Our Pioneer Potters. New York, 1947. 94p.
illus (b&w); index; bibliog (pp. 89-91).

A64.   ________. Some Early New Jersey Potteries. Notes on
American Pottery, Part 1. New York: Court Press,
1942. 11p.

A65.   COATES, Pamela. The Real McCoy. Cherry Hill, N.J.:
Reynolds Publishers, 1971. 86p. illus.

A66.   ________. The Real McCoy, Volume 2. Indianapolis,
Ind.: Author, 1974. 72p. illus (b&w, col).

A67.   CONNELLY, John. A Century-Old Concern: Business of
Jones, McDuffee & Stratton Co.: The Largest Whole-
sale and Retail Crockery, China, and Glassware
Establishment in the Country Has Kept Pace with the
Changing Needs and Tastes of the American People.
Boston: George H. Ellis, Printers, 1910. 52p.
illus (b&w).

A68.   CONWAY, Bob. Traditional Pottery of North Carolina.
Waynesville, N.C.: Printed by the Mountaineer, 1974.
36p. illus (b&w).

A69.   COUNTS, Charles. Common Clay. Indiana, Pa.: Halldin,
1977. 102p. illus (b&w).

A70.   COX, George J[ames]. Pottery, for Artists, Craftsmen &
Teachers. Technical Art Series. New York: Macmillan,
1914. 200p. illus (b&w); glossary; bibliog (pp. 198-
199).
Republished in 1923 and 1926.

A71.   CRAWFORD, Jean. Jugtown Pottery: History and Design.
Winston-Salem, N.C.: John F. Blair, 1964. 127p.
illus (b&w, col); bibliog (pp. 120-127).

A72.   CUMMINS, Virginia Raymond. Rookwood Pottery Potpourri.
Silver Spring, Md.: C. R. Leonard and D. Coleman,
1980. 136p. illus (b&w, col); index; bibliog
(p. 108).

A73.   DARLING, Sharon S. Chicago Ceramics and Glass: An
Illustrated History, 1871-1933. Chicago: Chicago
Historical Society/University of Chicago Press, 1979.
221p. illus (b&w, col); index; bibliog (pp. 211-213).
Published in conjunction with an exhibit at The
Chicago Historical Society.

A74.   DAVENPORT, S. W. The Nation's Obligations and Duty to
        Its Domestic Manufacturers, A Protectionist's Reply
        to Some Recent Criticisms by a Foreign Importer, to
        Which is Appended an Article on the Tariff on Earth-
        enware: The Pottery Industry--Domestic Competition
        Reduces Prices. New York: Commercial World Print,
        1882. 23p.

A75.   DAVIS, Charles Thomas. A Practical Treatise on the
        Manufacture of Bricks, Tiles, Terra-Cotta, Etc. . . .
        Philadelphia: Henry Carey Baird, 1884. 472p. illus
        (b&w); index.

A76.   ________. A Practical Treatise on the Manufacture of
        Bricks, Tiles, Terra Cotta, Etc. . . . 2d ed. rev.
        Philadelphia: Henry Carey Baird, 1889. 501p. illus
        (b&w); index.

A77.   ________. A Practical Treatise on the Manufacture of
        Brick, Tiles and Terra-Cotta, Etc. . . . 3d ed. rev.
        and enl. Philadelphia: Henry Carey Baird, 1895.
        628p. illus (b&w); index.

A78.   DIETER, Gerald W., and CUMMINGS, John. The Bible in
        Tile: The Story of the Mercer Biblical Tile in the
        Sanctuary of Salem Church. Doylestown, Pa.: The
        Consistory, Salem United Church of Christ, 1957.
        [32]p. illus (b&w, col).

A79.   Directory of Plants in the White Ware Branches of the
        Ceramic Industries in the United States and Canada.
        1st ed. Newark, N.J.: Ceramics Publishing Co.,
        1929. 171p. illus (b&w, col).

A80.   DOAT, Taxile. Grand Feu Ceramics: A Practical Treatise
        on the Making of Fine Porcelain and Grès. Translated
        from the French by Samuel E. ROBINEAU. Syracuse, N.Y.:
        Keramic Studio Publishing Co., 1905. 207p. illus
        (b&w).
            Includes "American Clays for Grand Feu Wares" by
            Charles F. BINNS. Originally published in Keramic
            Studio. See G913-929.

A81.   DONHAUSER, Paul S. History of American Ceramics: The
        Studio Potter. Dubuque, Iowa: Kendall Hunt, 1978.
        260p. illus (b&w, col); index; bibliog (pp. 237-241).

A82.   DUFFY, Thomas J. History of the National Brotherhood
        of Operative Potters from 1890 to 1901. Pittsburgh,
        Pa.: Commoner & Glassworker, 1901. 43p. illus
        (b&w).

A83.   DUKE, Harvey. Superior Quality: Hall China, A Guide
        for Collectors. Otisville, Mich.: Depression Glass
        Daze, 1977. 100p. illus (b&w, col).

A84.   DÜMMLER, Karl. Die Ziegel- und Thonwaaren-Industrie in
        den Vereinigten Staten und auf der Columbus-Weltaus-
        stellung in Chicago, 1893. Halle a. Salle: K. W.
        Knapp, 1894. 180p. illus (b&w).

A85.   EARTHENWARE ASSOCIATION OF BOSTON. The Earthenware
        Association of Boston. [Boston?]: The Association,
        1871. 12p.

A86.   [EARTHENWARE TRADE OF NEW YORK CITY] The Tariff on
        Earthenware. New York: Croker & Telfer, Printers,
        1872. 13p.

A87.   EAST LIVERPOOL SCHOOL OF CHINA PAINTING. Lessons in
        China Painting. East Liverpool, Ohio: The School
        [1905] 68p. illus (col).

A88.   EVANS, Paul. Art Pottery of the United States: An
        Encyclopedia of Producers and Their Marks. New York:
        Charles Scribner, 1974. 353p. illus (b&w, col);
        index; bibliog.
           Geographical Listing of Art Potteries: pp. 343-344.

A89.   EWAN, N. R. Early Brickmaking in the Colonies: A
        Common Fallacy Corrected. Camden, N.J.: Camden
        County Historical Society, 1938. 15p.

A90.   FILKINS, (Mrs.) Clarabel (Childs). The China Painters
        A-B-C: A Primer for Beginners, with Many Hints for
        the Advanced Student and Teacher. Buffalo, N.Y.:
        Printed by Courier Co., 1915. 147p. illus (b&w,
        col).

A91.   FINKE, Hans-Joachim. The Pottery and Metal Working
        Complex in 18th Century Bethlehem. Bethlehem, Pa.:
        Historic Bethlehem [1976] 8p.

A92.   FRACKELTON, Susan Stuart. Tried by Fire: A Work on
        China Painting. New York: D. Appleton, 1886. 110p.
        illus (b&w, col).

A93.   ________. Tried by Fire: A Work on China Painting.
        2d ed.? New York: D. Appleton, 1892.

A94.   ________. Tried by Fire: A Work on China Painting.
        3d ed., enl. and rev. New York: D. Appleton, 1895.
        138p. illus (b&w, col).

A95.   GALL, Irma M., and VAN ETTA, Vivian M. The Art of
        Pottery. New York: Bruce, 1930. 80p. illus (b&w);
        bibliog (p. 79).

A96.   GARVE, T. W. Factory Design and Equipment and Manu-
        facture of Clay Wares. Indianapolis, Ind.: T. A.
        Randall, 1929. 304p. illus (b&w).

A97.   GEER, Walter. The Story of Terra Cotta [Companies
        and Personnel] New York: Tobias A. Wright, 1920.
        303p. illus (b&w).

A98.   GILFILLEN, Statler, Ed. The American Terra Cotta
        Index [Northwest Architectural Archives] Palos Park,
        Ill.: Prairie School Press [1972?] 486p.

A99.   GOODYEAR, Clarissa. A Message to China Decorators.
        New York: J. B. Colt, 1890. 41p. illus (b&w).

A100.   GRALEY, Helen F. American Vitrified China. Washing-
        ton: Vitrified China Association, 1946. 31p.
        illus (b&w).

A101.   GREER, Georgeanna H., and BLACK, Harding. The Meyer
        Family: Master Potters of Texas. San Antonio, Tex.:
        San Antonio Museum Association/Trinity University
        Press, 1971. 97p. illus (b&w, col).
            Published in conjunction with an exhibit at Witte
        Memorial Museum.

A102.   GUAPPONE, Carmen A. New Geneva and Greensboro Pottery,
        Illustrated and Priced. McClellandtown, Pa.:
        Guappone Publishers, 1975. 48p. illus (b&w).

A103.   ________. New Geneva & Greensboro Pottery: Illustra-
        ted Price Guide No. 11. McClellandtown, Pa.: Guap-
        pone Publishers, 1980. 36p. illus (b&w).

A104.   ________. United States Utilitarian Folk Pottery: A
        Pictorial Price Guide. McClellandtown, Pa.: Guap-
        pone Publishers, 1977. 64p. illus (b&w).

A105.   GUILLAND, Harold F. Early American Folk Pottery.
        Philadelphia: Chilton, 1971. 322p. illus (b&w,
        col); bibliog (pp. 293-309).

A106.   HALL, Fanny E. A Lesson in the Art of China Firing
        Applicable to the Portable Keramic Kiln and Other
        Kilns Designed for Use of Amateurs. Catskill, N.Y.:
        Author, 1888. 10p.

A107.   HARBIN, Edith. Blue & White Stoneware, Pottery &
        Crockery. Paducah, Ky.: Collector Books, 1977.
        63p. illus (col).

A108.   HARPER, George. Please Don't Call Us Bennington [S.
        Wilson Pottery] [Troy, Ind.?] Author, 1980. 84p.
        illus (b&w); bibliog (p. 83).

A109.   HARRIS, W. S. The Potters Wheel and How It Goes
        Around: A Complete Description of the Manufacture
        of Pottery in America. Trenton, N.J.: Burroughs &
        Mountford [1886] 63p. illus (b&w).

A110.   HAWES, Lloyd E. The Dedham Pottery and The Earlier
        Robertson's Chelsea Potteries. Dedham, Mass.:
        Dedham Historical Society, 1968. 52p. illus (b&w);
        bibliog (p. 52).
            Published in conjunction with an exhibit at the
        Dedham Historical Society.

A111.   HENZKE, Lucile. American Art Pottery. Camden, N.J.:
        Thomas Nelson, 1970. 336p. illus (b&w, col); index;
        glossary.

A112.   Highlights Of Pewabic Pottery. Ann Arbor, Mich.: Ars
        Ceramica/Michigan State University, 1977. [30]p.
        illus (b&w, col).
            Adapted from A40.

A113.   HILL, F. Stanhope. Practical Hints for Amateurs in
        Porcelain Painting Based Upon the Dresden Method for
        Figures and Flowers. New York: Judson Printing Co.,
        1883. 44p.

A114.   HOLMES, George Sanford. Lenox China: The Story of
        Walter Scott Lenox. Pt. 1: "The Story of Walter
        Scott Lenox." Pt. 2: "The Making of Lenox China."
        Trenton, N.J.: Lenox, Inc., 1924. 72p. illus
        (b&w).
            Also published as A115. Pt. 1 also published as
        G1260.

A115.   [_____]. Lenox China: The Story of Walter Scott
        Lenox. Trenton, N.J.: Lenox, Inc., 1924. 32p.

A116.   HOOD, Graham. Bonnin and Morris of Philadelphia: The
        First American Porcelain Factory, 1770-1772. Chapel
        Hill, N.C.: University of North Carolina Press,
        1972. 78p. illus (b&w); index; bibliog.

A117.   HORNEY, Wayne B. Pottery of the Galena Area [Illinois,
        1843-1899] East Dubuque, Ill.: Printed by the
        Telegraph-Herald Commercial Printing Division, 1965.
        48p. illus (b&w, col); bibliog.

A118.   HUXFORD, Sharon, and HUXFORD, Bob. The Collectors
        Encyclopedia of Brush McCoy Pottery. 1st ed.
        Paducah, Ky.: Collector Books, 1978. 190p. illus
        (b&w, col); index; bibliog (pp. 188-189).

A119.   _________. The Collectors Encyclopedia of McCoy Pot-
        tery. 1st ed. Paducah, Ky.: Collector Books, 1978.
        239p. illus (b&w, col); index; bibliog (p. 238).

A120.   _________. The Collectors Encyclopedia of Roseville
        Pottery. 1st ed. Paducah, Ky.: Collector Books,
        1976. 184p. illus (b&w, col); index; bibliog
        (p. 179).

A121. HUXFORD, Sharon, and HUXFORD, Bob. The Collectors
       Encyclopedia of Roseville Pottery. 2d. Series.
       Paducah, Ky.: Collector Books, 1980. 191p. illus
       (b&w, col); index; bibliog (p. 190).

A122. __________. The Collectors Encyclopedia of Weller Pot-
       tery. 1st ed. Paducah, Ky.: Collector Books, 1979.
       375p. illus (b&w, col); index; bibliog (p. 371).

A123. JAMES, Arthur E. The Potters and Potteries of Chester
       County, Pennsylvania. 1st ed. West Chester, Pa.:
       Chester County Historical Society, 1945. 116p.
       illus (b&w); bibliog (pp. 115-116).
            Checklist of Chester County Potters: pp. 111-114.

A124. __________. The Potters and Potteries of Chester County,
       Pennsylvania. 2d ed. Exton, Pa.: Schiffer, 1978.
       208p. illus (b&w). bibliog (pp. 205-208).
            Checklist of Chester County Potters: pp. 199-204.

A125. JOHNSON, Deb, and JOHNSON, Gini. Beginner's Book of
       American Pottery. Des Moines, Iowa: Wallace-Home-
       stead, 1974. 119p. illus (b&w, col).

A126. __________ and __________. Beginner's Book of American Pot-
       tery: Price Guide Plus. North Newton, Kan.: Men-
       nonite Press, 1974. 45p. illus (b&w).

A127. KENDALL, A. Harold. The Story of Hampshire Pottery.
       [Keene, N.H.?]: Author?, 1963. [5]p.

A128. KERAMIC STUDIO. The Art of Teaching a Color Palette
       and Its Use; Ground Laying; Lustres. The Class
       Room, No. 1. Syracuse, N.Y., 1909. 47p. illus
       (b&w, col).

A129. __________. The Book of Roses: Studies for the China
       Painter and the Student of Water Colors. Syracuse,
       N.Y., 1903. 41p. illus (b&w).

A130. __________. The Conventional Decoration of Porcelain
       and Glass. The Class Room, No. 4. Syracuse, N.Y.,
       1911. 50p. illus (b&w, col).

A131. __________. Cups and Saucers from Keramic Studio.
       Syracuse, N.Y., 1913. 26p. illus (b&w).

A132. __________. Figure Painting on Porcelain; Firing. The
       Class Room, No. 3. Syracuse, N.Y., 1910. 48p.
       illus (b&w, col).

A133. __________. Flower Painting on Porcelain. The Class
       Room, No. 2. Syracuse, N.Y., 1908. 43p. illus
       (b&w, col).

A134.   KERAMIC STUDIO. The Fruit Book: Studies for the
         Painter of China and the Student of Water Colors.
         Syracuse, N.Y., 1906. 43p. illus (b&w, col).

A135.   ________. Little Things to Make. Syracuse, N.Y.,
         1913. 41p. illus (b&w, col).

A136.   ________. The Second Rose Book: Studies for the
         Painter of China and the Student of Water Colors.
         Syracuse, N.Y., 1907. 48p. illus (b&w, col).

A137.   KERSEY, Jesse. A Narrative of the Early Life, Travels,
         and Gospel Labors of Jesse Kersey, Late of Chester
         County, Pennsylvania. Philadelphia: T. Ellwood
         Chapman, 1851. 288p.

A138.   KETCHUM, William C., Jr. Early Potters and Potteries
         of New York State. New York: Funk & Wagnalls,
         1970. 278p. illus (b&w); index; bibliog (pp. 254-
         269).
           List of New York Potters and Their Marks: pp. 203-
           251.

A139.   ________. The Pottery and Porcelain Collector's Hand-
         book: A Guide to Early American Ceramics from Maine
         to California. New York: Funk & Wagnalls, 1971.
         204p. illus (b&w); index.
           List of Early American Potteries: pp. 159-193.

A140.   KIRCHER, Edwin J. Rookwood Pottery: An Explanation
         of Its Marks and Symbols. [Terrace Park, Ohio]:
         Author, 1962. [19]p. illus (b&w).

A141.   KIRCHER, Edwin J., AGRANOFF, Barbara, and AGRANOFF,
         Joseph. Rookwood: Its Golden Age of Art Pottery,
         1880-1929. Cincinnati, Ohio: Authors, 1969. [29]p.
         illus (b&w, col).

A142.   KOVEL, Ralph, and KOVEL, Terry. The Kovels' Collector's
         Guide to American Art Pottery. New York: Crown,
         1974. 368p. illus (b&w, col); index; bibliog.

A143.   LAMSON, Everett C., Jr. The Old Exeter Pottery Works.
         Barre, Vt.: Modern Printing Co., 1978. 84p. illus
         (b&w); bibliog (p. 83).

A144.   LANGENBECK, Karl. The Chemistry of Pottery. Easton,
         Pa.: Chemical Publishing Co., 1895. 195p. illus
         (b&w); index; bibliog.

A145.   LASANSKY, Jeanette. Central Pennsylvania Redware Pot-
         tery, 1780-1904. Lewisburg, Pa.: Union County Oral
         Traditions Projects, 1979. 60p. illus (b&w);
         index; bibliog (pp. 54-56).

A146.   LASANSKY, Jeanette. Made of Mud: Stoneware Potteries
        in Central Pennsylvania 1834-1929. Lewisburg, Pa.:
        J. Lasansky/Union County Bicentennial Commission,
        1977. 59p. illus (b&w); index; bibliog (p. 58).

A147.   ________. Made of Mud: Stoneware Potteries in Central
        Pennsylvania 1834-1929. University Park, Pa.:
        Pennsylvania State University Press, 1979. 59p.
        illus (b&w); index; bibliog (p. 58).
           Republication of A146.

A148.   LAURENCE, Frederick S. Color in Architecture. New
        York: National Terra Cotta Society, 1924. 64p.
        illus (b&w, col).

A149.   LEHNER, Lois. Complete Book of American Kitchen and
        Dinner Wares. Des Moines, Iowa: Wallace-Homestead,
        1980. 240p. illus (b&w); bibliog (pp. 220-228).

A150.   ________. Ohio Pottery and Glass Marks and Manufac-
        turers. Des Moines, Iowa: Wallace-Homestead, 1978.
        113p. illus (b&w); index; bibliog (pp. 109-113).

A151.   LEWIS, Florence. China Painting. New York: Cassell,
        1883. 52p. illus (b&w, col).

A152.   LOVEJOY, Ellis. Burning Clay Wares. Indianapolis,
        Ind.: T. A. Randall, 1920. 322p. illus (b&w).

A153.   ________. Fundamentals and Economies in the Clay
        Industries. 1st ed. Wellsville, N.Y.: Randall,
        1935. 361p.

A154.   McCABE, David A. National Collective Bargaining in
        the Pottery Industry. Baltimore: Johns Hopkins
        Press, 1932. 449p. bibliog.

A155.   McCOLLAM, C. Harold. The Brick and Tile Industry in
        Stark County, 1809-1976. Canton, Ohio: Stark
        County Historical Society/Kent State University
        Press, 1976. 337p. index; bibliog.

A156.   McKEE, Floyd W. The Second Oldest Profession: A
        Century of American Dinnerware Manufacture. Salem,
        Ohio: Printed by Lyle, 1966. 63p. index.

A157.   McLAUGHLIN, M[ary] Louise. The China Painters' Hand-
        book. The Practical Series, I. Cincinnati, Ohio:
        Author, 1917. 30p. illus (b&w).

A158.   ________. China Painting: A Practical Manual for the
        Use of Amateurs in the Decoration of Hard Porcelain.
        Cincinnati, Ohio: Robert Clarke, 1877. 69p. illus
        (b&w).
           Republished in 1878, 1880, 1882, and 1883(?)

A159. McLaughlin, M[ary] Louise. China Painting: A Practical
       Manual for the Use of Amateurs in the Decoration of
       Hard Porcelain. Cincinnati, Ohio: Robert Clarke,
       1889. 103p. illus (b&w).
          Republished in 1890, 1894.

A160. ________. China Painting: A Practical Manual for the
       Use of Amateurs in the Decoration of Hard Porcelain.
       New ed. Cincinnati, Ohio: Robert Clarke, 1904.
       140p. illus (b&w); index.
          Republished in 1911.

A161. ________. China Painting: A Practical Manual for the
       Use of Amateurs in the Decoration of Hard Porcelain.
       Cincinnati, Ohio: Stewart & Kidd, 1914. 140p.
       illus (b&w).

A162. ________. Pottery Decoration Under the Glaze. Cin-
       cinnati, Ohio: Robert Clarke, 1880. 95p.

A163. ________. Pottery Decoration Under the Glaze. Cincin-
       nati, Ohio: Robert Clarke, 1881. 101p.

A164. ________. Suggestions to China Painters. Cincinnati,
       Ohio: Robert Clarke, 1884. 96p. illus (b&w).

A165. MADDOCK, Archibald M., II. The Polished Earth: A
       History of the Plumbing Fixture Industry in the
       United States. Trenton, N.J., 1962. 382p. illus
       (b&w); index; bibliog.

A166. MADDOCK'S, THOMAS, SONS CO. Pottery: A History of the
       Pottery Industry and Its Evolution as Applied to
       Sanitation with Unique Specimens and Facsimile Marks
       from Ancient to Modern Foreign and American Wares.
       Philadelphia: Printed by Dando, 1910. 224p. illus
       (b&w).

A167. MERCER, Henry C. Guide Book to the Tiled Pavement in
       the Capitol of Pennsylvania. [Doylestown, Pa.: B.
       McGinty, 1908] 95p. illus (b&w); index.

A168. ________. The Tiled Pavement in the Capitol of Penn-
       sylvania. Rev. and ed. by Ginger DUEMLER. State
       College, Pa.: Pennsylvania Guild of Craftsmen,
       1975. 83p. illus (b&w); index.
          Originally published as A167.

A169. MILLER L[eslie] W[illiam]. The Lesson of the Hour
       for American Potters: An Address Delivered by Invi-
       tation of the Committee on Design before the U.S.
       Potters Association at Its Annual Meeting Held in
       Washington, D.C., Jan. 22, 1890. East Liverpool,
       Ohio: The Association, Printed by J. H. Simms,
       1890. 24p.
          Also published as Appendix of A249.

A170.   MILLER, [Noda May Senter] (Mrs. W. H. Miller, Jr.)
        Text Book of China Painting, Being a Complete Ency-
        clopaedia of All Methods of Decorating China and
        Firing. Also, Notes Concerning What Should Be
        Avoided by the Beginner in Order to Become Successful.
        Chicago and Kansas City: Anglo-French Art Co., 1912.
        30p.

A171.   MONACHESI, (Mrs.) N[icola] di R[ienzi] A Manual for
        China Painters. Boston: Lee and Shepherd, 1897.
        286p. illus (b&w, col); index.

A172.   NATIONAL MERCANTILE PUBLISHING CO. How and Where to
        Purchase Anything in the Crockery and Glassware
        Trade to the Best Advantage. New York: The Company,
        1883. 40p.

A173.   NATIONAL TERRA COTTA SOCIETY. Architectural Terra
        Cotta: Standard Construction. New York: The
        Society, 1914. 3p., 70 plates (b&w).

A174.   ________. Architectural Terra Cotta. Vol. 1: The
        School. Brochure Series. New York: The Society,
        1914. 32p. illus (b&w).

A175.   ________. Architectural Terra Cotta. Vol. 2: The
        Theatre. Brochure Series. New York: The Society,
        1915. 32p. illus (b&w, col).

A176.   ________. Terra Cotta: Standard Construction. Rev.
        ed. New York: The Society, 1927. 3p., 67 plates
        (b&w).
           Revision of A173.

A177.   [NEW JERSEY CLAYWORKERS' ASSOCIATION] Papers Read
        Before the New Jersey Clay Workers' Association at
        the Meetings Held at Rutgers College, June 25 and
        26, 1914 [and] December 28 and 29, 1914. Trenton,
        N.J.: MacCrellish & Quigley, Printers, 1915. 149p.

A178.   NEWARK MUSEUM. The China and Pottery of New Jersey
        from 1685 to 1876: A Plan and an Appeal to the
        Members of the Women's Clubs of New Jersey, from the
        Newark Museum Association. [Newark, N.J.: The
        Museum, 1914?] [11]p. illus (b&w).

A179.   NEWCOMB, Rexford. Ceramic Whitewares: History, Tech-
        nology, Applications. New York: Pitman, 1947.
        313p. illus (b&w); bibliog.

A180.   NEWKIRK, David A. A Guide to Red Wing Markings.
        Monticello, Minn.: Printed by Monticello Printing,
        1979. 40p. illus (b&w).

A181. NICHOLS, George Ward. Pottery: How It Is Made, Its
       Shape and Decoration. Practical Instructions for
       Painting on Porcelain and All Kinds of Pottery with
       Vitrifiable and Common Oil Colors. New York: G. P.
       Putnam, 1878. 142p. illus (b&w); index.

A182. NORWOOD, John Nelson. Fifty Years of Ceramic Educa-
       tion: New York State College of Ceramics at Alfred
       University. Alfred, N.Y.: The University, 1950.
       80p. illus (b&w).

A183. O'HARA, Dorothea Warren. The Art of Enameling on Por-
       celain. [New York: Madison Square Press] 1912.
       32p. illus (b&w).

A184. "ONE WHO HAS SUCCEEDED." China Painting as a Business.
       New York: Montague Marks [1896?] 8p.

A185. ORMOND, Suzanne, and IRVINE, Mary E. Louisiana's Art
       Nouveau: The Crafts of the Newcomb Style. Foreword
       by John Canaday. Gretna, La.: Pelican, 1976. 182p.
       illus (b&w, col); index; bibliog (pp. 175-177).

A186. [OSGOOD, Adelaide Harriet] How to Apply Gold, Royal
       Worcester, Bronze and Matt Colors to China: A Prac-
       tical Handbook for Amateurs. New York: Osgood Art
       School, 1888. 30p. illus (b&w).
       At least 17 later editions; 18th ed., 1905.

A187. OSGOOD, Cornelius. The Jug and Related Stoneware of
       Bennington. Rutland, Vt.: Charles E. Tuttle, 1971.
       222p. illus (b&w, col); index; bibliog (pp. 207-212).

A188. PAIST, Henrietta Barclay. Design and the Decoration
       of Porcelain. Syracuse, N.Y.: Keramic Studio Pub-
       lishing Co., 1916. 103p. illus (b&w).

A189. PAPPAS, Joan, and KENDALL, Harold. Hampshire Pottery
       Manufactured by J. S. Taft & Company, Keene, N.H.
       Manchester, Vt.: Forward's Color Productions, 1971.
       44p. illus (b&w, col).

A190. PEAR, Lillian Myers. The Pewabic Pottery: A History
       of Its Products and Its People. Des Moines, Iowa:
       Wallace-Homestead, 1976. 295p. illus (b&w, col);
       index; bibliog (pp. 263-265).
       Major Installations and Collections: pp. 282-290.

A191. PECK, Herbert. The Book of Rookwood Pottery. New
       York: Bonanza Books, 1968. 184p. illus (b&w, col);
       index; bibliog (p. 177).

A192. Pewabic Pottery Commemorative Exhibit (To Honor the
       Pottery's 70th Anniversary) Souvenir Brochure--June
       4, 1977--Private Showing. Ann Arbor, Mich.: Ars
       Ceramica, 1977. [6]p. illus (b&w, col).
       Includes G2106.

A193.   PITKIN, Albert Hastings. Early American Folk Pottery
         Including the History of the Bennington Pottery.
         Hartford, Conn.: [Case, Lockwood & Brainard] 1918.
         144p. illus (b&w); index.
             Includes a Catalogue of the Pitkin Collection of
             Early American Folk Pottery in the Morgan Memorial,
             Hartford, Conn.

A194.   PITON, Camile. A Complete Practical Treatise on China
         Painting in America, with Some Suggestions as to
         Decorative Art. New York: J. Wiley, 1878-1800.
         3 vols. (vol. 1: 69p; vols. 2-3: Plates) illus
         (b&w).

A195.   PLATT, Dorothy Pickard. The Story of Pickard China.
         Hanover, Pa.: Everybody's Press, 1970. 85p. illus
         (b&w, col).

A196.   [PORTER, George Richardson] A Treatise on the Origin,
         Progressive Improvement, and Present State of the
         Manufacture of Porcelain and Glass. Dr. Lardner's
         Cabinet Cyclopaedia [of] Useful Arts. Philadelphia:
         Carey & Lee, 1832. 252p. illus (b&w); index.

A197.   POSTLE, Kathleen R. The Chronicle of the Overbeck
         Pottery. Indianapolis: Indiana Historical Society,
         1978. 109p. illus (b&w, col); index; bibliog
         (pp. 101-106).
             Overbeck Contributions to Keramic Studio: pp. 97-
             100.

A198.   POWELL, Elizabeth A. Pennsylvania Pottery: Tools and
         Processes. Doylestown, Pa.: Bucks County Historical
         Society, 1972. 20p. illus (b&w).

A199.   POWELL, Robert Blake. Antique Shaving Mugs of the
         United States. Hurst, Tex.: Author, 1972. 272p.
         illus (b&w); index.

A200.   ________. Occupational & Fraternal Shaving Mugs of
         the United States. Hurst, Tex.: Author, 1978.
         211p. illus (b&w).

A201.   PURVIANCE, Evan, and PURVIANCE, Louise. Zanesville
         Art Tile in Color. Des Moines, Iowa: Wallace-
         Homestead, 1972. [48]p. illus (b&w, col).

A202.   PURVIANCE, Louise, PURVIANCE, Evan, SCHNEIDER, Norris
         F. Roseville Art Pottery in Color. Des Moines,
         Iowa: Wallace-Homestead, 1970. 48p. illus (b&w,
         col).

A203.   ________, ________, ________. Weller Art Pottery in
         Color. Des Moines, Iowa: Wallace-Homestead, 1971.
         [62]p. illus (b&w, col).

A204.   PURVIANCE, Louise, PURVIANCE, Evan, and SCHNEIDER,
        Norris F. Zanesville Art Pottery in Color. Leon,
        Iowa: Mid-America Book Co., 1968. [48]p. illus
        (col).

A205.   RADFORD, Fred W. A. Radford Pottery: His Life and
        Works. Columbia, S.C.: Author, 1973. 50 p. illus
        (b&w).

A206.   RAMSAY, John. American Potters and Pottery. [Boston]:
        Hale, Cushman & Flint, 1939. 304p. illus (b&w);
        index; bibliog (pp. 244-251.).
           Checklist of American Potters, 1611-1900: pp. 161-
        243. Marks: pp. 252-285.

A207.   ________. American Potters and Pottery. New York:
        Tudor, 1947. 304p. illus (b&w); index; bibliog
        (pp. 244-251).
           Reprint of A206.

A208.   ________. American Potters and Pottery. With a New
        Introduction. Ann Arbor, Mich.: Ars Ceramica, 1976.
        304p. illus (b&w); index; bibliog (pp. 244-251).
           Reprint of A206.

A209.   RAYCRAFT, Don, and RAYCRAFT, Carol. American Country
        Potter. Des Moines, Iowa: Wallace-Homestead, 1975.
        [53]p. illus (col).

A210.   REHL, Norma. The Collectors Handbook of Stangl Pottery.
        [Milford, N.J.?]: Author, 1979. 120p. illus (b&w,
        col).

A211.   RHEAD, Frederick H. Studio Pottery. St. Louis, Mo.:
        Peoples University Press, 1910. 83p. illus (b&w).

A212.   RIES, Heinrich, and LEIGHTON, Henry. History of the
        Clay-Working Industry in the United States. New
        York: John Wiley, 1909. 270p. illus (b&w).

A213.   RINGO, Fredonia Jane. China and Glassware [Manual for
        Salespersons] Chicago and New York: A. W. Shaw,
        1925. 166p. index; bibliog (p. 159).

A214.   ROBERTSON, Sarah. How I Made Money at China Painting.
        By a Self Made Girl. New York: A. C. Baker, 1900.
        59p.

A215.   ROBINSON, Dorothy, with FEENY, Bill. The Official
        Price Guide to American Pottery and Porcelain.
        [Trenton, N.J., potteries, especially Lenox] Ed. by
        Thomas E. Hudgeons III. 1st ed. Orlando, Fla.:
        House of Collectibles, 1980. 390p. illus (b&w, col);
        bibliog (p. 390).
           Marks: pp. 6-21. Biographies: pp. 32-45.

A216.   ROCKY RIVER PUBLIC LIBRARY. Cowan Pottery Museum.
        Rocky River, Ohio: The Library, 1978. 14p. illus
        (b&w).

A217.   ROSE, Arthur Veel. S. A. Weller's Sicardo Ware. [New
        York?: Tiffany & Co.?], n.d. [11]p. illus (b&w).
           Originally published in Crockery and Glass Journal
        (September 10, 1903). See also G1961.

A218.   ST. GAUDENS, Paul. Clay Craft. Camp Fire Girls, Li-
        brary of the Seven Crafts, Book No. 7. New York:
        Camp Fire Outfitting Co., 1931. 35p. illus (b&w).

A219.   SAMMIS, Romanah. The Pottery at Huntington, New York.
        Huntington, N.Y.: Huntington Historical Society,
        1939? 7p. illus (b&w).
           Originally published in Long Island Forum. See
        G1976.

A220.   SATURDAY EVENING GIRLS. The Story of the Saturday Eve-
        ning Girls . . . Especially Written for the Reunion,
        December 12, 1929. [Articles in Verse] Boston, 1929.
        16p.

A221.   SCHALTENBRAND, Phil. Old Pots: Salt-Glazed Stoneware
        of the Greensboro-New Geneva Region. Hanover, Pa.:
        Everybodys Press [1977]. 89p. illus (b&w); bibliog
        (p. 89).

A222.   SCHNEIDER, Norris F. Zanesville Art Pottery. Zanes-
        ville, Ohio: Author, 1963. 29p. illus (b&w).

A223.   SCHWARTZ, Marvin D. Collectors' Guide to Antique
        American Ceramics. Garden City, N.Y.: Doubleday,
        1969. 134p. illus (b&w); index.

A224.   SCHWARTZ, Marvin D., and WOLFE, Richard. A History of
        American Art Porcelain. New York: Renaissance
        Editions, 1967. 93p. illus (b&w, col); bibliog
        (p. 93).

A225.   SCHWARTZ, Stuart C. North Carolina Pottery: A Bibliog-
        raphy. Charlotte, N.C.: Mint Museum, 1978. 23p.

A226.   ________. The North State Pottery Company, 1924-1959.
        Charlotte, N.C.: Mint Museum, 1977. [14]p. illus
        (b&w); bibliog.
           Published in conjunction with an exhibit at the
        Mint Museum. See also F65 and F67.

A227.   SEARLE, Alfred B. Clay and What We Get From It. New
        York: Macmillan, 1925. 178p. index.

A228.   SHOEMAKER, Henry Wharton. Early Potters of Clinton
         County, With Special Reference to the Work Done In
         Sugar Valley by the Pioneer Pennsylvania Potters--John
         Gerstung, Joseph Kemmerer, Joseph Eilert and Reuben
         McKee. Altoona, Pa.: Altoona Tribune Publishing Co.,
         1916. 37p. illus (b&w).

A229.   SMITH, Elmer L. Pottery: A Utilitarian Folk Craft.
         Lebanon, Pa.: Applied Arts Publishers, 1972. 32p.
         illus (b&w).

A230.   SNOOK, Josh, and SNOOK, Anna. Roseville Donatello Pot-
         tery. Lebanon, Pa.: Author, 1975. [49]p. illus
         (b&w, col).

A231.   SPARGO, John. The A.B.C. of Bennington Pottery Wares:
         A Manual for Collectors and Dealers. Bennington His-
         torical Museum Publications, No. 3. Bennington, Vt.:
         Bennington Historical Museum, 1938. 38p. illus (b&w).

A232.   __________. The A.B.C. of Bennington Pottery Wares: A
         Manual for Collectors and Dealers. New and rev. ed.
         Bennington, Vt.: Bennington Historical Museum, 1948.
         38p. illus (b&w).

A233.   __________. Early American Pottery and China. New York:
         Century, 1926. 393p. illus (b&w); index.
            Chronological List of Potteries from 1850 to 1876:
            pp. 337-344. Marks: pp. 359-372.

A234.   __________. Early American Pottery and China. Garden
         City, N.Y.: Garden City Publishing Co., 1948. 393p.
         illus (b&w); index.
            Reprint of A233.

A235.   __________. Early American Pottery and China. Rutland,
         Vt.: C. E. Tuttle, 1974. 393p. illus (b&w); index.
            Reprint of A233.

A236.   __________. The Potters and Potteries of Bennington.
         Boston: Houghton Mifflin and Antiques, 1926. 265p.
         and 44 Plates. illus (b&w, col); index; bibliog.

A237.   __________. The Potters and Potteries of Bennington.
         New York: Dover, 1972. 265p. and 44 Plates. illus
         (b&w, col); index; bibliog.
            Reprint of A236.

A238.   __________. The Potters and Potteries of Bennington.
         Southampton, N.Y.: Cracker Barrel Press [1969?] 265p.
         and 44 Plates. illus (b&w); index; bibliog.
            Reprint of A236.

A239.   SPARKES, John C. L. A Hand-Book to the Practice of Pot-
         tery Painting. Harper's Half-Hour Series, Vol. 76.
         New York: Harper, 1878. 79p.

A240. SQUIRES, Frederick. The Hollow-Tile House. New York:
       William T. Comstock, 1913. 208p. illus (b&w).

A241. STEVENS, A. Made in USA [Marks] New Paltz, N.Y.:
       Franklin Printing, 1978. 36p. illus (b&w); bibliog
       (p. 36).

A242. STEWARD, [Florence Pratt] (Mrs. LeRoy T.) Flat Enamel
       Decoration on China with Suggestions for Color Schemes
       and Designing. Chicago: Author?, 1907. 37p. bibli-
       og (pp.36-37).

A243. STEWART, Regina, and COSENTINO, Geraldine. Stoneware.
       A Golden Handbook of Collectibles. New York: Golden
       Press, 1977. 128p. illus (b&w, col); index; bibliog
       (p. 127).

A244. STILES, Helen E. Pottery in the United States. Fore-
       word by R. Guy COWAN. New York: E. P. Dutton, 1941.
       329p. illus (b&w); index; bibliog (pp. 317-324).

A245. STRADLING, Diana, and STRADLING, J. Garrison, Eds. The
       Art of the Potter: Redware and Stoneware. Antiques
       Magazine Library. New York: Main Street/Universe
       Books, 1977. 158p. illus (b&w); index.
          Compilation of articles originally published in
       Antiques.

A246. STRATTON, Mary Chase. Ceramic Processes. Ann Arbor,
       Mich.: Edwards, 1941. 77p. illus (b&w).

A247. TALBOT, James J. The Use of Terra Cotta in Architec-
       ture. New York: Printed by American Bank Note Co.
       for Perth Amboy Terra Cotta Co., 1879. 16p.
       "Excerpted from the author's Ceramic Art and Art
       Education."

       TALBOT, Mary White, see WHITE, Mary.

A248. [TILTON, Stephen Willis]. Designs and Instructions for
       Decorating Pottery in Imitation of Greek, Roman, Egyp-
       tian, and Other Styles of Vases. Boston: S. W.
       Tilton, 1876. 49p. illus (col).

A249. U.S. POTTERS' ASSOCIATION. Proceedings of the Four-
       teenth Convention . . . January 21st and 22nd, 1890.
       East Liverpool, Ohio: The Association, Printed by
       J. H. Simms, 1890. 32p., 24p.
          Appendix: "The Lesson of the Hour for American Pot-
       ters," by L. W. MILLER, pp. 1-24. See also A169.

A250. __________. Shall the Pottery Industry of the United
       States Be Destroyed? Washington: The Association,
       1888.

A251. VANCE-PHILLIPS, L. Book of the China Painter: A Complete Guide for the Keramic Decorator. Art Amateur Handbooks. New York: Montague Marks, 1896. 311p. illus (b&w, col); index.
          Includes "Hints by Mr. Charles VOLKMAR on Underglaze": pp. 229-233.

A252. VAN WINKLE, William Mitchell. The Brooks Pottery, Goshen, Connecticut. [New York?] 1937. [14]p. illus (b&w).
          Originally published in Walpole Society Note Book.

A253. VIEL, Lyndon C. The Clay Giants: The Stoneware of Red Wing, Goodhue County, Minnesota. Des Moines, Iowa: Wallace-Homestead, 1977. 128p. illus (b&w, col).

A254. __________. Clay Giants: The Stoneware of Red Wing, Goodhue County, Minnesota. Book 2. Des Moines, Iowa: Wallace-Homestead, 1980. 168p. illus (b&w, col).

A255. WAITT, Madalaine. China Painting for Beginners, With Colored Studies. Boston: Perry Mason, 1890. 23p. illus (col).

A256. WARE, W. Porter. Price List of Occupational and Society Emblems Shaving Mugs. Chicago: Lightner, 1949. 96p. illus (b&w).
          List of Shaving Mug Collectors: pp. 77-84.

A257. WATKINS, Lura Woodside. Early New England Potters and Their Wares. Cambridge, Mass.: Harvard University Press, 1950. 291p. illus (b&w); index; bibliog (pp. 271-276).
          Checklist of New England potters: pp. 249-270.

A258. __________. Early New England Potters and Their Wares. [Hamden, Conn.] Archon Books, 1968. 291p. illus (b&w); index; bibliog (pp. 271-276).
          Reprint of A257.

A259. __________. Early New England Pottery. Old Sturbridge Village Booklet Series, No. 10. Sturbridge, Mass.: Old Sturbridge Village, 1959. 22p. illus (b&w).

A260. WEBB, Judson Thomas. Pottery Making: An Illustrated Text Book on Art Pottery Making for Teachers and Artists. Chicago: Lewis Institute, 1914. 72p. illus (b&w).

A261. WEBSTER, Donald Blake. Decorated Stoneware Pottery of North America. Rutland, Vt.: Charles E. Tuttle, 1971. 232p. illus (b&w); index; glossary; bibliog (pp. 229-230).
          Checklist of potteries: pp. 215-226.

A262.   WHITE, Charles E., Jr. Architectural Terra Cotta.
         Scranton, Pa.: International Textbook Co., 1925.
         78p. illus (b&w, col).
           "Instruction paper . . . for International Corres-
         pondence Schools."

         The White House China. See ANDERSON, Mary F.

A263.   WHITE, Mary. How to Make Pottery. New York: Double-
         day, Page, 1904. 179p. illus (b&w).
           "Modern American Pottery": pp. 167-179.

A264.   WILTSHIRE, William E. Folk Pottery of the Shenandoah
         Valley. New York: E. P. Dutton, 1975. 127p. illus
         (col); bibliog.

A265.   WIRES, E. Stanley, SCHNEIDER, Norris F., and MESRE,
         Moses. Zanesville Decorative Tiles. Zanesville,
         Ohio: Authors, 1972. 32p. illus (b&w); bibliog
         (p. 32).

B

CONFERENCE PROCEEDINGS AND CHAPTERS FROM BOOKS

B1.   ANTHONY, Ronald W. "Descriptive Analysis and Replica-
      tion of Historic Earthenware: Colono Wares from the
      Spiers Landing Site, Berkeley County, South Carolina."
      In: South, Stanley, ed. Conference on Historic Site
      Archaeology Papers, Vol. 13, 1978. Columbia, S.C.:
      Institute of Archaeology and Anthropology, University
      of South Carolina, 1979, pp. 253-268. illus (b&w);
      bibliog.

B2.   BARBER, Edwin AtLee. "Stoneware of the United States."
      In: Salt Glazed Stoneware. Pennsylvania Museum and
      School of Industrial Art, Art Primer, Ceramic Series,
      No. 6. Philadelphia: The Museum, 1906, pp. 21-25.
      illus (b&w).

B3.   ________. "The United States." In: Lead Glazed Pottery.
      Part First (Common Clays) Plain Glazed, Sgraffito and
      Slip-Decorated Ware. Pennsylvania Museum and School of
      Industrial Art, Art Primer, Ceramic Series, No. 3.
      Philadelphia: The Museum, 1907, pp. 11-18. illus (b&w).

B4.   BARKA, Norman F. "The Kiln and Ceramics of the 'Poor
      Potter' of Yorktown: A Preliminary Report." In:
      Quimby, Ian M. G., ed. Ceramics in America. Winter-
      thur Conference Report, 1972. Charlottesville, Va.:
      University Press of Virginia for the Henry Francis du
      Pont Winterthur Museum, 1973, pp. 291-318. illus (b&w);
      bibliog.

B5.   BARKA, Norman F., and SHERIDAN, Chris. "The Yorktown
      Pottery Industry, Yorktown, Virginia." In: Michael,
      Ronald L., ed. Northeast Historical Archaeology, Vol.
      6. California, Pa.: Center for Prehistoric and His-
      toric Site Archaeology, California State College, 1977,
      pp. 21-32. illus (b&w); bibliog.
         Paper presented at a conference, Rochester Museum
      and Science Center, 1977.

B6.   BERNSTEIN, Melvin. "To Think for Industry and the A.C.S.
       [Abstract]" In: Clark, Garth, ed. Transactions of
       the Ceramics Symposium, 1979 [Syracuse University].
       Los Angeles, Calif.: Institute for Ceramic History,
       1980, pp. 7-9.

B7.   BISHOP, Robert. "Pottery." In: American Folk Sculp-
       ture. New York: E. P. Dutton, 1974, pp. 214-225.
       illus (b&w, col).

B8.   BISHOP, Robert, and COBLENTZ, Patricia. "Ceramics."
       In: The World of Antiques, Art, and Architecture in
       Victorian America. New York: E. P. Dutton, 1979,
       pp. 190-223. illus (b&w); bibliog (p. 482).

B9.   BIVINS, John F., Jr. "The Moravian Potters in North
       Carolina, 1756-1821." In: Quimby, Ian M. G., ed.
       Ceramics in America. Winterthur Conference Report,
       1972. Charlottesville, Va.: University Press of
       Virginia for the Henry Francis du Pont Winterthur
       Museum, 1973, pp. 255-290. illus (b&w); bibliog.

B10.   BROWN, Joshua, and MENT, David. "Porcelain." In:
       Factories, Foundries, and Refineries: A History of
       Five Brooklyn Industries. Brooklyn, N.Y.: Brooklyn
       Educational and Cultural Alliance, 1980, pp. 21-31.
       illus (b&w); bibliog (p. 73).

B11.   BRUNK, Thomas W. "The Pewabic Pottery." In: Clark,
       Garth, ed. Transactions of the Ceramic Symposium,
       1979 [Syracuse University]. Los Angeles, Calif.:
       Institute for Ceramic History, 1980, pp. 10-14.
       bibliog.

B12.   BULLEN, Ripley P. "Comments on Greer's Paper on Alka-
       line Glaze." In: South, Stanley, ed. Conference on
       Historic Site Archaeology Papers, Vol. 5, 1970.
       Columbia, S.C.: Institute of Archaeology and Anthro-
       pology, University of South Carolina, 1971, pp. 186-
       187.

B13.   BURRISON, John A. "The Living Tradition: A Comparison
       of Three Southern Folk Potters [G. Stewart, B. Craig,
       L. Meaders]" In: Cotz, JoAnn, ed. Northeast Histor-
       ical Archaeology, Vol. 7, 8, 9, 1978-1980. Midland
       Park, N.J.: Council for Northeast Historical Archae-
       ology [1980?] pp. 33-38. illus (b&w); bibliog.
          Paper presented at a conference, Rochester Museum
       and Science Center, 1977.

B14.   BUTLER, Joseph T. "Ceramics." In: The Arts in America:
       The Nineteenth Century. New York: C. Scribner, 1969,
       pp. 358-371. illus (b&w).

B15.   CLARK, Edna Maria. "Ceramics." In: Ohio Art and
       Artists. Richmond, Va.: Garrett and Massie, 1932,
       pp. 153-178. illus (b&w).

B16.   CLARK, Garth. "Robineau and Ohr: A Study in Polarities."
       In: Clark, Garth, ed. Transactions of the Ceramics
       Symposium, 1979 [Syracuse University]. Los Angeles,
       Calif.: Institute for Ceramic History, 1980, pp. 15-
       22. bibliog.

B17.   COX, Warren E. "American Colonial to 19th Century
       Wares." In: The Book of Pottery and Porcelain.
       New York: Crown, 1944, pp. 979-1008. illus (b&w).

B18.   CRAIG, James H. "Potters [Newspaper Reports]" In:
       The Arts and Crafts in North Carolina, 1699-1840.
       Winston-Salem, N.C.: Museum of Early Southern Decor-
       ative Arts, 1966, pp. 87-94.

B19.   CUNNINGHAM, John T. "Ceramics." In: Made in New
       Jersey: The Industrial Story of a State. New Bruns-
       wick, N.J.: Rutgers University Press, 1954, pp. 96-
       103. illus (b&w).

B20.   CURTIS, Philip H. "The Production of Tucker Porcelain,
       1826-1838: A Reevaluation." In: Quimby, Ian M. G.,
       ed. Ceramics in America. Winterthur Conference
       Report, 1972. Charlottesville, Va.: University Press
       of Virginia for the Henry Francis du Pont Winterthur
       Museum, 1973, pp. 339-374. illus (b&w); bibliog.

B21.   DENKER, Ellen Paul. "The Kirkpatricks' Pottery, Anna,
       Illinois." In: Cotz, JoAnn, ed. Northeast Histori-
       cal Archaeology, Vol. 7, 8, 9, 1978-1980. Midland
       Park, N.J.: Council for Northeast Historical Archae-
       ology [1980?], pp. 27-32. illus (b&w); bibliog.
       Paper presented at a conference, Rochester Museum
       and Science Center, 1977.

B22.   DOW, George Francis. "Potters." In: The Arts & Crafts
       in New England, 1704-1775: Gleanings from Boston
       Newspapers. Topsfield, Mass.: Wayside Press, 1927,
       pp. 81-82.

B23.   DYER, Walter A. "Early American Potters." In: Early
       American Craftsmen. New York: Century, 1915, pp.
       273-297. illus (b&w).

B24.   _________. "The Potters of Bennington." In: Early
       American Craftsmen. New York: Century, 1915, pp.
       298-319. illus (b&w).

B25.   EARLE, Alice Morse. "Early Fictile Art in America."
       In: China Collecting in America. New York: C.
       Scribner, 1892, pp. 70-101. illus (b&w).

B26.   EATON, Allen H. "New England Pottery." In: Handicrafts
        of New England. 1st ed. New York: Harper, 1949, pp.
        152-167. illus (b&w).

B27.   ________. "Pottery and the Uses of Clay." In: Handi-
        crafts of the Southern Highlands. New York: Russell
        Sage Foundation, 1939, pp. 209-219. illus (b&w).

B28.   EBERLEIN, Harold Donaldson, and McCLURE, Abbot. "Early
        American Slip-Decorated Pottery." In: The Practical
        Book of American Antiques, Exclusive of Furniture.
        Rev. ed. Philadelphia: J. B. Lippincott, 1927, pp.
        217-238. illus (b&w).
            Same as B29.

B29.   ________ and ________. "Early American Slip-Decorated
        Pottery." In: The Practical Book of Early American
        Arts and Crafts. Philadelphia: J. B. Lippincott,
        1916, pp. 217-238. illus (b&w).
            Same as B28.

B30.   EBERLEIN, Harold Donaldson, and RAMSDELL, Roger Wearne.
        "American Chinaware." In: The Practical Book of
        Chinaware. Rev. ed. Philadelphia: J. B. Lippincott,
        1948, pp. 293-306. illus (b&w).

B31.   EIDELBERG, Martin. "The American Pottery Movement--A
        Critical Analysis [Abstract]" In: Clark, Garth, ed.
        Transactions of the Ceramics Symposium, 1979 [Syracuse
        University]. Los Angeles, Calif.: Institute for
        Ceramic History, 1980, pp. 30-32.

B32.   ELLIOTT, Charles Wyllys. "Pottery and Porcelain in the
        United States." In: Pottery and Porcelain from
        Early Times down to the Philadelphia Exhibition of
        1876. New York: D. Appleton, 1878, pp. 331-342.
        illus (b&w).

B33.   EVANS, Paul. "Art Pottery in California: An American
        Era in Microcosm." In: Clark, Garth, ed. Trans-
        actions of the Ceramics Symposium, 1979 [Syracuse
        University]. Los Angeles, Calif.: Institute for
        Ceramic History, 1980, pp. 33-37. bibliog.

B34.   GOTTESMAN, Rita Susswein. "Potters." In: The Arts
        and Crafts in New York, 1726-1776: Advertisements and
        News Items from New York City Newspapers. New York:
        New-York Historical Society, 1938, pp. 84-85.

B35.   ________. "Potters." In: The Arts and Crafts in New
        York, 1777-1799: Advertisements and News Items from
        New York City Newspapers. New York: New-York Histor-
        ical Society, 1954, pp. 95-96.

B36.   GOTTESMAN, Rita Susswein. "Potters and Pottery." In:
       The Arts and Crafts in New York, 1800-1804: Adver-
       tisements and News Items from New York City Newspapers.
       New York: New-York Historical Society, 1965, pp. 127-
       129.

B37.   GREER, Georgeanna. "Basic Forms of Historic Pottery
       Kilns Which May Be Encountered in the United States."
       In: South, Stanley, ed. Conference on Historic Site
       Archaeology Papers, Vol. 13, 1978. Columbia, S.C.:
       Institute of Archaeology and Anthropology, University
       of South Carolina, 1979, pp. 133-147. illus (b&w);
       bibliog.

B38.   __________. "Groundhog Kilns--Rectangular American Kilns
       of the Nineteenth and Early Twentieth Centuries." In:
       Michael, Ronald L., ed. Northeast Historical Archae-
       ology, Vol. 6. California, Pa.: Center for Prehis-
       toric and Historic Site Archaeology, California State
       College, 1977, pp. 42-54. illus (b&w); bibliog.
          Paper presented at a conference, Rochester Museum
       and Science Center, 1977.

B39.   __________. "Preliminary Information on the Use of the
       Alkaline Glaze for Stoneware in the South, 1800-1970."
       In: South, Stanley, ed. Conference on Historic Site
       Archaeology Papers, Vol. 5, 1970. Columbia, S.C.:
       Institute of Archaeology and Anthropology, University
       of South Carolina, 1971, pp. 155-170. illus (b&w).

B40.   GUILD, Lurelle Van Arsdale. "Pottery and Porcelain."
       In: The Geography of American Antiques. Garden City,
       N.Y.: Doubleday, Page, 1927, pp. 195-208. illus
       (b&w).

B41.   HAMELL, George R. "Earthenwares and Salt-Glazed Stone-
       wares of the Rochester-Genesee-Valley Region: An
       Overview." In: Cotz, JoAnn, ed. Northeast Historical
       Archaeology, Vol. 7, 8, 9, 1978-1980. Midland Park,
       N.J.: Council for Northeast Historical Archaeology.
       [1980?] pp. 1-14. illus (b&w); bibliog.
          Paper presented at a conference, Rochester Museum
       and Science Center, 1977.

B42.   HARK, Ann. "The Last of the Old-Time Potters [Stahl
       Family]" In: Blue Hills and Shoofly Pie. Philadel-
       phia: J. B. Lippincott, 1952, pp. 189-196.

B43.   HASLAM, Malcolm. "American Ceramics [Marks]" In:
       Marks and Monograms of the Modern Movement, 1875-1930.
       New York: C. Scribner, 1977, pp. 23-33. illus (b&w).

B44.   HAZEN, Edward. "The Potter." In: The Panorama of
       Professions and Trades. Philadelphia: Uriah Hunt,
       1839, pp. 236-240. illus (b&w).

B45.   JERVIS, W. P. "Rookwood Pottery." In: Rough Notes on
        Pottery. Newark, N.J.: Author, 1896, pp. 94-95.
        illus (b&w).

B46.   ________. "United States." In: A Pottery Primer.
        New York: O'Gorman, 1911, pp. 168-186. illus (b&w).
        Also published in Pottery, Glass & Brass Salesman.
        See G1329-1330.

B47.   KEEN, Kirsten H. "Art Pottery in Context [Abstract]"
        In: Clark, Garth, ed. Transactions of the Ceramics
        Symposium, 1979 [Syracuse University]. Los Angeles,
        Calif.: Institute for Ceramic History, 1980, pp. 44-
        45.

B48.   KETCHUM, William C., Jr. "Pottery." In: The New and
        Revised Catalog of American Antiques. New York:
        Rutledge Books, 1980, pp. 98-119. illus (b&w).

B49.   KLAMKIN, Marian. "Woodrow Wilson, 1913-1921 [Presiden-
        tial China by Lenox]" In: White House China. New
        York: C. Scribner, 1972, pp. 113-119. illus (b&w).

B50.   LICHTEN, Frances. "From the Earth Itself--Clay." In:
        Folk Art of Rural Pennsylvania. New York: C. Scrib-
        ner, 1946, pp. 9-45. illus (b&w).

B51.   LUCAS, Dorothy F. "Pottery and Glass." In: Myers,
        William Starr, ed. The Story of New Jersey. New York:
        Lewis Historical Publishing Co., 1945, pp. 162-199.
        illus (b&w).

B52.   McCLINTON, Katharine M. "Country Pottery." In: The
        Complete Book of American Country Antiques. New York:
        Coward-McCann, 1967, pp. 100-130. illus (b&w).

B53.   ________. "Pottery and Porcelain." In: Collecting
        American Victorian Antiques. New York: C. Scribner,
        1966, pp. 220-247. illus (b&w).

B54.   MacDOWELL, Marsha, and DEWHURST, C. Kurt. "The Sewer
        Tile Clay Pottery of Grand Ledge, Michigan." In:
        Cotz, JoAnn, ed. Northeast Historical Archaeology,
        Vol. 7, 8, 9, 1978-1980. Midland Park, N.J.: Council
        for Northeast Historical Archaeology [1980?] pp. 39-43.
        illus (b&w); bibliog.
            Paper presented at a conference, Rochester Museum
        and Science Center, 1977.

B55.   MADDEN, Betty I. "Jug Towns." In: Art, Crafts, and
        Architecture in Early Illinois. Urbana, Ill.: Uni-
        versity of Illinois Press, in cooperation with the
        Illinois State Museum, 1974, pp. 181-194. illus (b&w,
        col); bibliog.

B56. MICHAEL, George. "Earthenware and Porcelain." In: The
      Treasury of New England Antiques. New York: Hawthorn
      Books: 1969, pp. 80-98. illus (b&w).

B57. MICHAEL, Ronald L. "Stoneware from Fayette, Greene, and
      Washington Counties, Pennsylvania." In: Michael,
      Ronald L., ed. Northeast Historical Archaeology, Vol.
      6. California, Pa.: Center for Prehistoric and His-
      toric Site Archaeology, California State College, 1977,
      pp. 33-41. illus (b&w); bibliog.
          Paper presented at a conference, Rochester Museum
      and Science Center, 1977.

B58. MITCHELL, James R. "Industrial Pottery of the United
      States." In: Michael, Ronald L., ed. Northeast
      Historical Archaeology, Vol. 6. California, Pa.:
      Center for Prehistoric and Historic Site Archaeology,
      California State College, 1977, pp. 14-20. illus
      (b&w); bibliog.
          Paper presented at a conference, Rochester Museum
      and Science Center, 1977.

B59. __________. The Potters of Cheesequake, New Jersey." In:
      Quimby, Ian M. G., ed. Ceramics in America. Winter-
      thur Conference Report, 1972. Charlottesville, Va.:
      University Press of Virginia for the Henry Francis
      du Pont Winterthur Museum, 1973, pp. 319-338. illus
      (b&w); bibliog.

B60. MORROW, Frank C. "The Ceramic Industry." In: A History
      of Industry in Jackson County, Ohio. [Athens, Ohio:
      Lawhead Press]: 1956, pp. 125-138. illus (b&w).

B61. MOSES, John. "American Potteries." In: Depew, Chaun-
      cey M., ed., One Hundred Years of American Commerce,
      1795-1895. New York: D. O. Haynes, 1895, Vol. 1,
      pp. 285-294. illus (b&w).

B62. MYERS, Susan H. "A Survey of Traditional Pottery Manu-
      facture in the Mid-Atlantic and Northeastern United
      States." In: Michael, Ronald L., ed. Northeast
      Historical Archaeology, Vol. 6. California, Pa.:
      Center for Prehistoric and Historic Site Archaeology,
      California State College, 1977, pp. 1-13. illus (b&w);
      bibliog.
          Paper presented at a conference, Rochester Museum and
      Science Center, 1977.

B63. NOEL HUME, Ivor. "Ceramics, American." In: A Guide
      to Artifacts of Colonial America. New York: Alfred
      A. Knopf, 1970, pp. 98-101. bibliog.

B64.   OLIN, Jacqueline S.   "Comments on Dr. Georgeanna H.
       Greer's Preliminary Information on the Use of the
       Alkaline Glaze for Stoneware in the South, 1800-1970."
       In: South, Stanley, ed. Conference on Historic Site
       Archaeology Papers, Vol. 5, 1970. Columbia, S.C.:
       Institute of Archaeology and Anthropology, University
       of South Carolina, 1971, pp. 194-197. illus (b&w).

B65.   ONONDAGA POTTERY CO. "Onondaga Pottery Company, Makers
       of Syracuse China." In: Little Romances of China.
       Syracuse, N.Y.: The Company, 1919, pp. 43-56.

B66.   PELICHET, Edgar. "Les U.S.A." In: La céramique art
       nouveau. Lausanne: Éditions du Grand-Pont, Jean-
       Pierre Laubscher, [1976] pp. 132-136.

B67.   PRIME, Alfred Coxe. "Pottery and Porcelain [Newspaper
       Reports]" In: The Arts and Crafts in Philadelphia,
       Maryland, and South Carolina, 1721-1785. [Topsfield,
       Mass.]: Walpole Society, 1929, pp. 112-133. illus
       (b&w).

B68.   _________. "Pottery and Porcelain [Newspaper Reports]"
       In: The Arts & Crafts in Philadelphia, Maryland, and
       South Carolina, 1786-1800. [Topsfield, Mass.]: Walpole
       Society, 1932, pp. 146-150.

B69.   RAUCHENBERG, Brad. "A Sprigg Mould for 'Flowers for
       the Fine Pottery'." In: South, Stanley, ed. Confer-
       ence on Historic Site Archaeology Papers, Vol. 2,
       Part 1, 1967. Raleigh, N.C.: Institute of Archae-
       ology and Anthropology, 1968, pp. 107-122. illus
       (b&w); bibliog.

B70.   REED, Cleota. "Henry Chapman Mercer and the Moravian
       Pottery." In: Clark, Garth, ed. Transactions of the
       Ceramics Symposium, 1979 [Syracuse University]. Los
       Angeles, Calif.: Institute for Ceramic History, 1980,
       pp. 66-72. bibliog.

B71.   SCHERMA, George W. "R. Guy Cowan and His Associates."
       In: Clark, Garth, ed. Transactions of the Ceramics
       Symposium, 1979 [Syracuse University]. Los Angeles,
       Calif.: Institute for Ceramic History, 1980, pp. 77-
       82. bibliog.

B72.   SCHIFFER, Margaret. "Ceramics." In: Arts and Crafts
       of Chester County, Pennsylvania. Exton, Pa.:
       Schiffer, 1980, pp. 31-49. illus (b&w).

B73.   SELVAGE, Nancy. "Art versus Craft: The Issue of Crafts-
       manship in 20th Century Art." In: Clark, Garth, ed.
       Transactions of the Ceramics Symposium, 1979 [Syracuse
       University]. Los Angeles, Calif.: Institute for
       Ceramic History, 1980, pp. 83-89. bibliog.

B74. SHERMAN, Frederic Fairchild. "Potters." In: Early
      Connecticut Artists & Craftsmen. New York: Author,
      1925, pp. 51-52.

B75. SHULL, Thelma. "The Pauline Pottery." In: Victorian
      Antiques. Rutland, Vt.: Charles E. Tuttle, 1963,
      pp. 155-160. illus (b&w).

B76. _________. "Pottery Jugs, Mugs, and Shoes." In: Vic-
      torian Antiques. Rutland, Vt.: Charles E. Tuttle,
      1963, pp. 221-225. illus (b&w).
         Originally published in Hobbies. See G2033.

B77. _________. "The Robertson Family and Dedham Pottery."
      In: Victorian Antiques. Rutland, Vt.: Charles E.
      Tuttle, 1963, pp. 132-136. illus (b&w).
         Republished, slightly abridged, from Hobbies. See
         G2034.

B78. _________. "Rookwood Pottery." In: Victorian Antiques.
      Rutland, Vt.: Charles E. Tuttle, 1963, pp. 137-147.
      illus (b&w).
         Republished, with additions, from Hobbies. See
         G2035.

B79. _________. "The Stockton Art Pottery." In: Victorian
      Antiques. Rutland, Vt.: Charles E. Tuttle, 1963,
      pp. 148-154. illus (b&w).

B80. SIM, Robert J. "Cake, Pudding and Jelly Molds." In:
      Pages from the Past of Rural New Jersey. Trenton,
      N.J.: New Jersey Agricultural Society, 1949, pp.
      37-39. illus (b&w).

B81. _________. "An Old Bridge Pottery [Bissett?]" In:
      Pages from the Past of Rural New Jersey. Trenton,
      N.J.: New Jersey Agricultural Society, 1949, pp.
      22-25. illus (b&w).

B82. _________. "Spouted Pitchers or Cruses." In: Pages
      from the Past of Rural New Jersey. Trenton, N.J.:
      New Jersey Agricultural Society, 1949, pp. 18-19.
      illus (b&w).

B83. _________. "A Trenton Pie Dish [J. S. McCully]" In:
      Pages from the Past of Rural New Jersey. Trenton,
      N.J.: New Jersey Agricultural Society, 1949, pp.
      20-21. illus (b&w).

B84. SOUTH, Stanley. "The Ceramic Forms of the Potter Gott-
      fried Aust at Bethabara, North Carolina, 1755 to 1771."
      In: South, Stanley, ed. Conference on Historic Site
      Archaeology Papers, Vol. 1, 1965-1966. [Raleigh, N.C.:
      Institute of Archaeology and Anthropology] 1967, pp.
      33-52. illus (b&w); bibliog.

B85.   SOUTH, Stanley. "The Ceramic Ware of the Potter Rudolph
        Christ at Bethabara and Salem, North Carolina, 1786-
        1821." In: South, Stanley, ed. Conference on His-
        toric Site Archaeology Papers, Vol. 3, 1968. Columbia,
        S.C.: Institute of Archaeology and Anthropology, Uni-
        versity of South Carolina, 1970, pp. 70-72. illus
        (b&w).

B86.   _________. "A Comment on Alkaline Glazed Stoneware."
        In: South, Stanley, ed. Conference on Historic Site
        Archaeology Papers, Vol. 5, 1970. Columbia, S.C.:
        Institute of Archaeology and Anthropology, University
        of South Carolina, 1971, pp. 171-185. illus (b&w);
        bibliog.

B87.   _________. "Comment on Alkaline Glazed Stoneware from
        Various States." In: South, Stanley, ed. Conference
        on Historic Site Archaeology Papers, Vol. 5, 1970.
        Columbia, S.C.: Institute of Archaeology and Anthro-
        pology, University of South Carolina, 1971, pp. 188-
        193. illus (b&w).

B88.   SPRINGSTED, Brenda Lockhart. "Ringoes: An Eighteenth
        Century Pottery Site." In: Michael, Ronald L., ed.
        Northeast Historical Archaeology, Vol. 6. California,
        Pa.: Center for Prehistoric and Historic Site Archae-
        ology, California State College, 1977, pp. 55-71.
        illus (b&w); bibliog.
            Paper presented at a conference, Rochester Museum
        and Science Center, 1977.

B89.   STOUDT, John Joseph. "The Potter's Craft." In: Early
        Pennsylvania Arts and Crafts. New York: A. S. Barnes,
        1964, pp. 206-220. illus (b&w).

B90.   SUDBURY, Byron. "A Preliminary Report on the R. Banner-
        man Eagle Tobacco Pipe Manufactory, Rouses Point, New
        York." In: Historic Clay Tobacco Pipe Studies, Vol.
        1. [Ponca City, Okla.?, Sudbury?] 1980, pp. 3-22.
        bibliog.

B91.   THOMAS, B. B. (Ted), and BURNETT, Richard M. "A Study
        of Clay Smoking Pipes Produced at a Nineteenth Century
        Kiln at Point Pleasant, Ohio." In: South, Stanley,
        ed., Conference on Historic Site Archaeology Papers,
        Vol. 6, 1971. Columbia, S.C.: Institute of Archae-
        ology and Anthropology, University of South Carolina,
        1972, pp. 1-31. illus (b&w); bibliog.

B92.   TRAPP, Kenneth R. "The Japanese Influence on Rookwood
        Pottery [Abstract]" In: Clark, Garth, ed. Trans-
        actions of the Ceramics Symposium, 1979 [Syracuse
        University]. Los Angeles, Calif.: Institute for
        Ceramic History, 1980, pp. 94-96.

B93. WALKER, Iain C. "Note on the Bethabara, North Carolina, Tobacco Pipes." In: South, Stanley, ed. Conference on Historic Site Archaeology Papers, Vol. 4, 1969. Columbia, S.C.: Institute of Archaeology and Anthropology, University of South Carolina, 1971, pp. 26-31. bibliog.

B94. WATKINS, C. Malcolm. "Ceramics in the Seventeenth-Century English Colonies." In: Quimby, Ian M. G., ed. Arts of the Anglo-American Community in the Seventeenth Century. Winterthur Conference Report, 1974. Charlottesville, Va.: University Press of Virginia, published for the Henry Francis du Pont Winterthur Museum, 1975, pp. 275-299. illus (b&w); bibliog.

B95. WEYGANDT, Cornelius. "The Last of the Old Potters." In: The Red Hills: A Record of Good Days, Outdoors and In, With Things Pennsylvania Dutch. Philadelphia: University of Pennsylvania Press, 1929, pp. 181-191.

B96. ________. "The Last of the Potters [J. Medinger]" In: The Dutch Country: Folks and Treasures in the Red Hills of Pennsylvania. New York: D. Appleton-Century, 1939, pp. 19-30. illus (b&w).

B97. ________. "Sundry Sorts of Earthen Ware [Redware]" In: The Red Hills: A Record of Good Days, Outdoors and In, With Things Pennsylvania Dutch. Philadelphia: University of Pennsylvania Press, 1929, pp. 91-116. illus (b&w).

B98. WHITE, Margaret F. "The Potter and His Clay." In: The Decorative Arts of Early New Jersey. New Jersey Historical Series, Vol. 25. Princeton, N.J.: D. Van Nostrand, 1964, pp. 27-50. illus (b&w).

B99. WILLIAMSON, Scott Graham. "Craftsmen in Clay." In: The American Craftsman. New York: Crown, 1940, pp. 48-68. illus (b&w).

B100. WOODHOUSE, Charles Platten. "Colonial North America." In: The World's Master Potters: Their Techniques and Art. [New York]: Pitman, 1974, pp. 199-209. illus (b&w).

B101. ________. "The United States." In: The World's Master Potters: Their Techniques and Art. [New York]: Pitman, 1974, pp. 210-223. illus (b&w).

B102. WORK PROJECTS ADMINISTRATION. NEW HAMPSHIRE. WRITERS' PROGRAM. "Clay Kiln and Potter's Wheel." In: Hands That Built New Hampshire. Brattleboro, Vt.: Stephen Daye Press, 1940, pp. 90-104. illus (b&w).

B103.   YOUNG, Jennie J. "United States." In: The Ceramic
        Art: A Compendium of the History and Manufacture of
        Pottery and Porcelain. New York: Harper, 1878, pp.
        442-487. illus (b&w).

B104.   ZUG, Charles G., III. "The Alkaline-Glazed Stoneware
        of North Carolina." In: Cotz, JoAnn, ed. Northeast
        Historical Archaeology, Vol. 7, 8, 9, 1978-1980.
        Midland,Park, N.J.: Council for Northeast Historical
        Archaeology [1980?] pp. 15-20. illus (b&w); bibliog.
          Paper presented at a conference, Rochester Museum
          and Science Center, 1977.

C

CATALOGS OF EXHIBITIONS, COLLECTIONS, AND SALES

N.B. Books published in conjunction with exhibits are noted here with reference to their full citations in Section A, "Books and Pamphlets."

C1. AMERICAN LIFE FOUNDATION. Blue Decorated Stoneware: One Hundred Crocks. Watkins Glen, N.Y.: The Foundation, 1966. [16]p. illus (b&w); bibliog.

C2. ARTS RESOURCES OF CONNECTICUT. "Pottery and Potters." In: Three Centuries of Connecticut Folk Art. Organized by Alexandra GRAVE. New Haven: Printed by Eastern Press, 1979, pp. 30-34. illus (b&w).

BROOKLYN INSTITUTE OF ARTS AND SCIENCES, see BROOKLYN MUSEUM.

C3. BROOKLYN MUSEUM. "Ceramics." In: Victoriana: An Exhibition of the Arts of the Victorian Era in America. Brooklyn, N.Y.: The Museum, 1960, pp. [5-10]. illus (b&w).

___________. Notes on American Ceramics, 1607-1943 (Clement). See A61.

C4. ___________. Preliminary Notes for a Catalogue of Made-in-America Pottery and Porcelain Assembled for Exhibition at the Brooklyn Museum. Foreward by A[rthur] W. C[LEMENT]. Brooklyn, N.Y., [1942]. [35]p. illus (b&w); bibliog (p. 32).

CHICAGO HISTORICAL SOCIETY. Chicago Ceramics and Glass (Darling). See A73.

C5. CINCINNATI ART MUSEUM. The Ladies, God Bless 'Em: The Women's Art Movement in Cincinnati in the Nineteenth Century. Introduction by Carol MACHT. Cincinnati, Ohio: The Museum, 1976. 69p. illus (b&w); bibliog (pp. 61-62).

C6.   CLEVELAND MUSEUM OF ART. "Pottery." In: American
       Folk Art from the Traditional to the Naive. By
       Lynette I. RHODES. Cleveland, Ohio: Cleveland
       Museum of Art, 1978, pp. 60-66. illus (b&w).

C7.   COLORADO SPRINGS FINE ARTS CENTER. Van Briggle Pottery:
       The Early Years. Barbara M. ARNEST, Editor; Robert
       E. MORRIS, Editorial Associate; Robert Wyman NEWTON,
       the catalogue; Lois K. CROUCH and Euphemia B. DEMMIN,
       Research Assistants. Colorado Springs, Col.: The
       Center, 1975. 70p. illus (b&w, col); bibliog (p. 37).
          Catalogue of Van Briggle designs, 1900-1912, by
          R. W. NEWTON: pp. 37-70.

       DEDHAM HISTORICAL SOCIETY. The Dedham Pottery and the
       Earlier Robertson's Chelsea Potteries (Hawes).
       See A110.

C8.   DELAWARE ART MUSEUM. American Art Pottery, 1875-1930.
       Exhibition and catalogue by Kirsten Hoving KEEN.
       Wilmington, Del.: The Museum, 1978. 84p. illus
       (b&w); bibliog (pp. 83-84).

C9.   EASTERN MENNONITE COLLEGE. Heatwole and Suter Pottery.
       Text and catalog by Stanley A. KAUFMAN. Harrisonburg,
       Va.: Good Printers, 1978. 47p. illus (b&w, col);
       bibliog (pp. 8, 13).

       EVERSON MUSEUM OF ART. A Century of Ceramics in the
       United States, 1878-1978 (Clark). See A57.

C10.   EVERSON MUSEUM OF ART. Onondago Pottery. Text by
       Richard G. CASE. Syracuse, N.Y.: The Museum, 1973.
       10p. illus (b&w).

C11.   GEORGIA COUNCIL FOR THE ARTS AND HUMANITIES. "Folk
       Pottery of Georgia," by John A. BURRISON. In:
       Missing Pieces: Georgia Folk Art, 1770-1976. Exhi-
       bition organized by Anna WADSWORTH. [Atlanta?]:
       The Council, 1976, pp. 24-29, 86-103. illus (b&w);
       bibliog.

C12.   GEORGIA STATE UNIVERSITY ART GALLERY. The Meaders
       Family of Mossy Creek: Eighty Years of North Georgia
       Folk Pottery, A Retrospective Exhibit. By John A.
       BURRISON. Atlanta: The University, 1976? 32p.
       illus.

C13.   GREENVILLE COUNTY MUSEUM OF ART. Early Decorated Stone-
       ware of the Edgefield District, South Carolina. By
       Stephen T. FERRELL and T. M. FERRELL. Greenville,
       S.C.: The Museum, 1976. [25]p. illus (b&w);
       bibliog (p. [17]).

C14.   HISTORICAL SOCIETY OF YORK COUNTY. Regional Aspects of
       American Folk Pottery. Introduction by William C.
       KETCHUM, Jr. York, Pa.: The Society, 1974. [56]p.
       illus (b&w, col); bibliog.

C15.   INDIANAPOLIS MUSEUM OF ART. Indiana Stoneware. By
       Peggy A. LOAR, with a Foreword by Carl J. WEINHARDT,
       Jr., and an Introduction by Don D. MOORE. Indianap-
       olis: The Museum, 1974. 48p. illus (b&w, col);
       bibliog (pp. 47-48).

C16.   INTERNATIONAL ANTIQUES EXPOSITION. Loan Exhibition of
       Early American Pottery and Early American Glass . . .
       From the Private Collection of George S. McKearin.
       By George S. McKEARIN. [Hoosick Falls, N.Y.]
       Printed by D. L. Hall, 1931. 56p. illus (b&w).

C17.   JORDAN-VOLPE GALLERY. Fulper Art Pottery: An Aesthetic
       Appreciation, 1909-1929. Text by Robert W. BLASBERG,
       with Carol L. BOHDAN. New York: The Gallery, 1979.
       88p. illus (b&w, col); bibliog (pp. 78-79).

C18.   ________. Ode to Nature: Flowers and Landscapes of
       the Rookwood Pottery, 1880-1940. Text by Kenneth R.
       TRAPP. New York: The Gallery, 1980. 88p. illus
       (b&w, col); bibliog (pp. 69-70).

       McKEARIN, George S., Collection, see INTERNATIONAL
       ANTIQUES EXPOSITION.

C19.   MARYLAND HISTORICAL SOCIETY. Edwin Bennett and the
       Products of His Baltimore Pottery. Baltimore: The
       Society, 1973. 44p. illus (b&w, col); bibliog.

C20.   ________. The Potter's Craft in Maryland: An Exhibi-
       tion of Nearly 200 Examples of Pottery Manufactured
       1793 to 1890. Baltimore: The Society, 1955. 14p.

C21.   METROPOLITAN MUSEUM OF ART. A Memorial Exhibition of
       Porcelain and Stoneware by Adelaide Alsop Robineau,
       1865-1929. Text by Joseph BRECK. New York: The
       Museum, 1929. [11]p. illus (b&w).

C22.   MILWAUKEE ART CENTER. Susan S. Frackelton and the
       American Arts and Crafts Movement: A Collection of
       Ceramic Art by Susan S. Frackelton and Her Contempor-
       aries. Organized by George WEEDON. Milwaukee, Wisc.:
       The Center, 1974. 10 leaves.

       MINT MUSEUM. The North State Pottery Company. See A226
       and F65, F67.

C23.   MINT MUSEUM. Potters of the Catawba Valley. Edited
       and compiled by Daisy Wade BRIDGES. Charlotte, N.C.:
       The Museum, 1980. 94p. illus (b&w); bibliog (p. 92).
       Published as Vol. 4, Ceramic Circle of Charlotte
       Journal of Studies. See also G423, 879, 1658, 2003,
       2047, 2325, which serve as catalogue preface.

C24.   MINT MUSEUM. The Pottery of Walter Stephen. Charlotte,
        N.C., 1978. [24]p. illus (b&w).
           Published as Vol. 3, Ceramic Circle of Charlotte
        Journal of Studies (1978), 2-30.

C25.   MISSISSIPPI STATE HISTORICAL MUSEUM. The Biloxi Art
        Pottery of George Ohr. Text by Garth CLARK. [Jack-
        son, Miss.] Mississippi Department of Archives and
        History, 1978. [33]p. illus (b&w, col).

C26.   ________. "The Folk Pottery of Mississippi," by
        Georgeanna H. GREER. In: Made by Hand. Jackson,
        Miss.: Department of Archives and History, 1980,
        pp. 45-54, 81-85. illus (b&w).

C27.   MONMOUTH COUNTY HISTORICAL ASSOCIATION. New Jersey
        Stoneware. Freehold, N.J.: The Association, 1955.
        20p. illus (b&w).

C28.   MUNSON-WILLIAMS-PROCTOR INSTITUTE. "Pottery and Glass."
        In: Made in Utica. Utica, N.Y.: The Institute,
        1976, pp. 16-21. illus (b&w).

C29.   MUNSON-WILLIAMS-PROCTOR INSTITUTE, and ONEIDA HISTORI-
        CAL SOCIETY. White's Utica Pottery. Introduction by
        Barbara FRANCO. Utica, N.Y.: The Institute, 1969.
        19p. illus (b&w).

C30.   MUSEUM OF AMERICAN FOLK ART. The Pottery of the State
        [New York]. Catalogue and exhibition by William C.
        KETCHUM, Jr. New York: The Museum, 1974. [14]p.
        illus (b&w).

C31.   MUSEUM OF ART OF OGUNQUIT. A Catalogue of the Ceramic
        Sculpture of Carl Walters, 1883-1955. Publications
        on American Art, 1. Compiled by William I. HOMER.
        Ogunquit, Me.: The Museum; Printed by Princeton
        University Press, 1958. [8]p.

C32.   MUSEUM OF CONTEMPORARY CRAFTS. Forms from the Earth:
        1,000 Years of Pottery in America. New York: The
        Museum, 1962. 21p. and 25 plates. illus (b&w).

C33.   NATIONAL MUSEUM OF HISTORY AND TECHNOLOGY. The John
        Paul Remensnyder Collection of American Stoneware.
        By Susan H. MYERS. Washington: The Museum, 1978.
        [8]p. illus (b&w).

C34.   NEW JERSEY STATE MUSEUM. Early Arts of New Jersey:
        The Potter's Art, c.1680-c.1900. Trenton, N.J.: The
        Museum, 1956. 56p.

C35.   ________. An Exhibition of Pottery and Porcelain Made
        by Ott and Brewer at Etruria Works in Trenton, N.J.,
        1871-1892. Trenton: The Museum, 1971. [16]p.
        illus (b&w).

C36.   NEW JERSEY STATE MUSEUM. Herman Carl Mueller: Archi-
       tectural Ceramics and the Arts and Crafts Movement.
       By Lisa Factor TAFT. Edited by Suzanne CORLETTE and
       Ed GRUSHESKI. Trenton, N.J.: The Museum, 1979.
       48p. illus (b&w); bibliog.

C37.   __________. New Jersey Pottery to 1840. Trenton, N.J.:
       The Museum, 1972. [46]p. illus (b&w); bibliog.

C38.   NEWARK MUSEUM. The Clay Products of New Jersey at the
       Present Time. Newark, N.J.: The Museum, 1915. 20p.
       illus (b&w).

C39.   __________. "The Decorative Arts: Ceramics." In:
       Classical America, 1815-1845. [By Berry B. TRACY]
       [Newark, N.J.] The Museum, 1963, pp. 107-115. illus
       (b&w).

C40.   __________. New Jersey's Clay Products. Newark, N.J.:
       The Museum, 1915. 16p. illus (b&w); bibliog
       (pp. 15-16).
          Originally published in Newarker, December 1914 and
       January-March 1915.

C41.   __________. The Pottery and Porcelain of New Jersey
       Prior to 1876. Newark, N.J.: The Museum, 1915.
       32p.

C42.   __________. The Pottery and Porcelain of New Jersey,
       1688-1900. Newark, N.J.: The Museum, 1947. 100p.
       illus (b&w); bibliog (p. 76).

       NEWARK MUSEUM ASSOCIATION, see NEWARK MUSEUM.

       ONEIDA HISTORICAL SOCIETY, see MUNSON-WILLIAMS-PROCTOR
       INSTITUTE, and ONEIDA HISTORICAL SOCIETY.

C43.   PANAMA-PACIFIC INTERNATIONAL EXPOSITION. High Fire
       Porcelains: Adelaide Alsop Robineau, Potter, Syra-
       cuse, New York. San Francisco: The Exposition, 1915.
       [22]p. illus (b&w).

       PENNSYLVANIA MUSEUM AND SCHOOL OF INDUSTRIAL ART, see
       also PHILADELPHIA MUSEUM.

C44.   PENNSYLVANIA MUSEUM AND SCHOOL OF INDUSTRIAL ART.
       Pottery: Catalogue of American Potteries and Por-
       celains. By Edwin AtLee BARBER. Philadelphia:
       Printed by Allen, Lane & Scott, 1893. 43p. illus
       (b&w).

       PHILADELPHIA MUSEUM OF ART, see also PENNSYLVANIA
       MUSEUM AND SCHOOL OF INDUSTRIAL ART.

C45.   PHILADELPHIA MUSEUM OF ART. Tucker China, 1825-1838:
       An Exhibition of Examples of the Porcelain Made in
       Philadelphia by William Ellis Tucker, Tucker and
       Hulme, Tucker and Hemphill, Joseph Hemphill, and
       Thomas Tucker. By H[orace] H. F. J[AYNE]. Philadel-
       phia: The Museum, 1957. 36p. illus (b&w, col);
       bibliog.

C46.   PRINCETON UNIVERSITY ART MUSEUM. "Art Pottery," by
       Martin EIDELBERG. In: The Arts and Crafts Movement
       in America, 1876-1916. Ed. by Robert Judson CLARK.
       Princeton, N.J.: Princeton University Press, 1972,
       pp. 119-186. illus (b&w); bibliog (pp. 189-190).

C47.   R. W. NORTON ART GALLERY. The American Porcelain Tra-
       dition, 18th, 19th, and 20th Centuries. [Loan Exhi-
       bition from NEW JERSEY STATE MUSEUM] Shreveport, La.:
       Printed by C. Young, 1972. 34p. illus (b&w, col);
       bibliog (pp. 29-30).

C48.   RICE, A. H., COLLECTION. The Shenandoah Pottery [Cata-
       logue]. By A. H. RICE and John Baer STOUDT. Stras-
       burg, Va.: Shenandoah Publishing House, 1929. 227p.
       illus (b&w, col).

C49.   ROCHESTER MUSEUM AND SCIENCE CENTER. Clay in the Hands
       of the Potter: An Exhibition of Pottery Manufactured
       in the Rochester and Genesee Valley Region, c.1793-
       1900. Rochester, N.Y.: The Museum, 1974. 56p.
       illus (b&w); bibliog (p. 56).

       SAN ANTONIO MUSEUM ASSOCIATION. The Meyer Family
       (Greer). See A101.

C50.   SOTHEBY PARKE BERNET, INC. The Jacqueline D. Hodgson
       Collection of Important American Ceramics. Sale No.
       3594. New York: Sotheby Parke Bernet, 1974. 55p.
       illus (b&w, col).

C51.   STAR OF THE REPUBLIC MUSEUM. Texas Pottery: Caddo
       Indian to Contemporary. By Sherry B. HUMPHRIES and
       Johnell L. SCHMIDT. Washington, Tex.: The Museum,
       1976. 45p. illus (b&w, col); bibliog (p. 45).

C52.   STATE UNIVERSITY COLLEGE AT NEW PALTZ. An Exhibition
       of 18th and 19th Century American Folk Pottery.
       Introduction by Richard I. BARONS. New Paltz, N.Y.:
       The College, 1969. 35p. illus (b&w).

C53.   SYRACUSE MUSEUM OF FINE ARTS. A Collection of Robineau
       Porcelains [Etc.] Syracuse: The Museum, 1916? 11
       leaves.

C54.   TENNESSEE FINE ARTS CENTER. "Ceramics." In: Made in
       Tennessee: An Exhibition of Early Arts and Crafts.
       Comp. by Ellen BEASLEY. Nashville, Tenn.: The
       Center, 1971, pp. 42-45. illus (b&w).

C55.   WILLIAM BENTON MUSEUM OF ART. American Decorative
          Tiles, 1870-1930. Exhibition and catalogue by
          Thomas P. BRUHN. Storrs, Conn.: University of
          Connecticut, 1979. 48p. illus (b&w); bibliog.

       WITTE MEMORIAL MUSEUM. The Meyer Family (Greer).
          See A101.

C56.   WORCESTER HISTORICAL MUSEUM. The F. B. Norton Pottery:
          Stoneware of Every Description. Worcester, Mass.:
          The Museum, 1980. [11]p. illus (b&w).

D
THESES AND DISSERTATIONS

N.B. Complete bibliographic descriptions have been given
where possible. Lack of specific information regarding
illustrations and/or bibliography does not indicate that the
thesis or dissertation has none.

D1.   BRUNSMAN, Sue. "The European Origins of Early Cincin-
       nati Art Pottery, 1870-1900." M.A. Thesis, University
       of Cincinnati, 1973. 142p. illus; bibliog (pp. 137-
       142).

D2.   BURRISON, John A. "Georgia Jug Makers: A History of
       Southern Folk Pottery." Ph.D. Dissertation, Univer-
       sity of Pennsylvania, 1973. 458p. illus; bibliog
       (pp. 405-416).

D3.   CLAUSER, John W. "The Excavation of the Bethabara Pot-
       tery Kiln: An Analysis of Nineteenth Century Potting
       Techniques." M.A. Thesis, University of Florida, 1978.
       154p. illus; bibliog (pp. 149-153).

D4.   CURTIS, Philip H. "Tucker Porcelain, 1826-1838: A Re-
       appraisal." M.A. Thesis, University of Delaware,
       1972. 148p. illus (b&w); bibliog (pp. 96-104).

D5.   DENKER, Ellen Paul. "'Forever Getting Up Something New':
       The Kirkpatricks' Pottery at Anna, Illinois, 1859-1896."
       M.A. Thesis, University of Delaware, 1978. 129p.
       illus (b&w); bibliog (pp. 116-120).

D6.   DONHAUSER, Paul Stefan. "A History of the Development
       of American Studio-Pottery." Ed.D. Dissertation,
       Illinois State University, 1967. 341p.

D7.   HELMS, Charles Douglas. "An Historical Study of Folk
       Potters In and Around Alton Community of Union County,
       North Carolina, From 1800-1950 With Emphasis on the
       Pottery of 'Jug Jim' Broome." M.A. Thesis, East
       Carolina University, 1974.

D8.   LAU, William. "The American Tradition in Ceramics
       Since Colonial Times." M.F.A. Thesis, State Univer-
       sity of New York College at Alfred, 1966. 40p.
       bibliog (p. 39).

D9.   McBEATH, Stuart H. "Wisconsin Ceramics." M.A. Thesis,
       University of Wisconsin, 1939. [47]p. and Plates.

D10.   MITCHELL, Jerry J. "An Analysis of the Decorative
       Styles of Newcomb Pottery." M.A. Thesis, Louisiana
       State University, 1972. 71p. illus (col. slides);
       bibliog (pp. 58-64).

D11.   MYERS, Susan Helen. "Handcraft to Industry: Philadel-
       phia Ceramics in the First Half of the Nineteenth
       Century." M.A. Thesis, George Washington University,
       1977. 289p. illus (b&w); bibliog (pp. 279-289).
       Checklist of Philadelphia Potters, 1800-1850:
       pp. 113-220. Published in 1980. See E18.

D12.   PEARCE, John N. "The Early Baltimore Potters and Their
       Wares, 1763-1850." M.A. Thesis, University of Dela-
       ware, 1959. 150p. illus (b&w, col); bibliog (pp.
       141-150).

D13.   PERKINS, Dorothy Wilson. "Education in Ceramic Art in
       the United States." Ph.D. Dissertation, Ohio State
       University, 1956. 326p.

D14.   PERSICK, Roberta Stokes. "Arthur Eugene Baggs, American
       Potter." Ph.D. Dissertation, Ohio State University,
       1963. 232p.

D15.   PERSICK, William Thomas. "Three Concepts of Pottery
       [C. F. Binns, A. E. Baggs, B. H. Leach]" Ph.D. Dis-
       sertation, Ohio State University, 1964. 129p.

D16.   POCKRANDT, Florence Delores. "Lotus Ware: A Ceramic
       Product of the Nineties." M.A. Thesis, Ohio State
       University, 1942.

D17.   ROBERTS, Clarence Nelson. "The History of the Brick
       and Tile Industry in Missouri." Ph.D. Dissertation,
       University of Missouri, 1950.

D18.   ST. JOHN, Richard W. "Early American Pottery--With
       Illustrations from the Collection of R. W. St. John."
       M.F.A. Thesis, State University of New York College
       at Alfred, 1969. 55p. illus; bibliog (p. 55).

D19.   SHOTLIFF, Don Anthony. "The History of the Labor Move-
       ment in the American Pottery Industry: The National
       Brotherhood of Operative Potters-International Brother-
       hood of Operative Potters, 1890-1970." Ph.D. Disser-
       tation, Kent State University, 1977. 451p.

D20.   STRATTON, Herman John. "Factors in the Development of
        the American Pottery Industry, 1860-1929." Ph.D.
        Dissertation, University of Chicago, 1929. 360p.
        bibliog (pp. 355-360).

D21.   TYRRELL, George V., Jr. "New Ulm Potters and Pottery,
        1860-1900." M.A. Thesis, State University of New
        York College at Oneonta (Cooperstown Graduate Pro-
        gram), 1969. 156p. illus (b&w, col); bibliog (pp.
        152-156).

D22.   WEIDNER, Ruth Irwin. "The Majolica Wares of Griffen,
        Smith and Company." M.A. Thesis, University of Dela-
        ware, 1980. 89p. illus (b&w, col); bibliog (pp. 63-
        68).

D23.   WHITLATCH, George I. "The Clay Resources of Indiana."
        Ph.D. Dissertation, Indiana University, 1932. See E44.

D24.   ZAUG, Dawson D. "Form as Ornamental Objects: Newcomb
        Pottery, An Essay." M.F.A. Thesis, Tulane University,
        1965. 60p. illus (b&w); bibliog (p. 44-45).

D25.   ZSERDIN, (Sister) Mary Carmelle. "The Growth of Ameri-
        can Ceramic Art: A Brief Summary." M.A. Thesis,
        University of Iowa, 1962. 73p. illus.

E

FEDERAL, STATE, AND MUNICIPAL PUBLICATIONS

(Including publications of state colleges and universities)

E1. ALFRED UNIVERSITY. Charles Fergus Binns, D.Sc. [Memor-
     ial] University Bulletin 3, Vol. 11, November 1935.
     Alfred, N.Y.: The University, 1935. 24p. illus
     (b&w).

E2. BUCKLEY, Ernest Robertson. The Clays and Clay Industries
     of Wisconsin. Wisconsin Geological and Natural History
     Survey, Bulletin No. 7, Part 1, Economic Series, No. 4.
     Madison, Wisc.: State of Wisconsin, 1901. 304p.
     index.

E3. COX, Paul E. The Use of Iowa Clays in Small-Scale Pro-
     duction of Ceramic Art. Iowa State College Engineering
     Experiment Station, Vol. 35, No. 44, March 31, 1937;
     Bulletin 133, March 1937. Ames, Iowa: Iowa State
     College of Agriculture and Mechanic Arts, 1937. 48p.
     illus (b&w); bibliog (pp. 39-42).

E4. GARRISON, W. C. Health Conditions of the Pottery Indus-
     try: The Eight Hour Movement; Wages and Production
     in the Glass Industry. Trenton, N.J.: MacCrellish &
     Quigley, 1905. 163p.

E5. [HAMILTON, Alice] Lead Poisoning in Potteries, Tile
     Works, and Porcelain Enameled Sanitary Ware Facilities.
     U.S. Bureau of Labor, Bulletin No. 104; Industrial Ac-
     cidents and Hygiene Series, No. 1. Washington: GPO,
     1912. 95p. index.

E6. HOPKINS, Thomas C. Clays and Clay Industries of Pennsyl-
     vania. I: Clays of Western Pennsylvania. Pennsylva-
     nia State College Annual Report, 1897. Harrisburg,
     Pa.: W. S. Ray, State Printer, 1898. 183p. illus
     (b&w).

E7. ________. Clays and Clay Industries of Pennsylvania.
     II: Clays of Southeastern Pennsylvania. Pennsylvania
     State College Annual Report, 1898/1899. Harrisburg,
     Pa. W. S. Ray, State Printer, 1900. 76p. illus (b&w).

E8.   HOPKINS, Thomas C. Clays and Clay Industries of Pennsyl-
       vania. III: Clays of the Great Valley and South
       Mountain Areas. Pennsylvania State College Annual
       Report, 1899/1900. Harrisburg, Pa.: W. S. Ray, State
       Printer, 1900. 45p. illus (b&w).

E9.   HOUGH, Walter. An Early West Virginia Pottery [Morgan-
       town] Washington: GPO, 1901. [82]p. illus (b&w).
          From the Report of the U.S. National Museum of 1899.

E10.   IRELAN, Linna. "Pottery." In: Ninth Annual Report of
       the State Minerologist for the Year Ending December 1,
       1899. Sacramento, Calif: J. D. Young, 1890. Pub-
       lished as: California. Appendix to Journals, 29th
       Session, 1891, Vol. 4, pp. 240-261. illus (b&w).

E11.   KOEHLER, W. A. The Whiteware Industry of West Virginia:
       A Technical Survey with Descriptive Articles on "The
       Manufacture of Vitrified Hotel China" by E. K. KOOS
       and "The Manufacture of Ceramic Floor and Wall Tile"
       by Kenneth E. BUCK. Engineering Experiment Station
       Research Bulletin, No. 5; West Virginia University
       College of Engineering Bulletin, Series 7, No. 7,
       June 1929. Morgantown, W.Va.: West Virginia Univer-
       sity, 1929. 106p. illus (b&w).

E12.   LADD, George E. A Preliminary Report on a Part of the
       Clays of Georgia. Geological Survey of Georgia, Bul-
       letin No. 6-A. Atlanta, Ga.: George W. Harrison,
       1898. 204p. illus (b&w); index; bibliog (pp. 193-
       199).

E13.   LOUGHLIN, Gerald Francis. The Clays and Clay Industries
       of Connecticut. State of Connecticut Public Document,
       No. 47; State Geological and Natural History Survey,
       Bulletin No. 4. Hartford, Conn.: Case, Lockwood &
       Brainard Co., 1905. 121p. illus (b&w); index.

E14.   MALONE, James M., GREER, Georgeanna H., and SIMONS,
       Helen. Kirbee Kiln: A Mid-19th-Century Texas Stone-
       ware Pottery. Texas Historical Commission, Office of
       the State Archaeologist, Report 31. Austin, Tex.:
       Texas Historical Commission, 1979. 60p. illus (b&w):
       bibliog (pp. 59-60).

E15.   MAYNARD, T[homas] Poole. [Pottery Possibilities in
       Vicinity of Macon, Georgia]: Report of the Investi-
       gation in the Macon District of the Raw Materials
       Used in the Manufacture of Pottery Products. Macon,
       Ga.: Macon Chamber of Commerce and Central of Georgia
       Railway [1917?] 51p.

E16. MICHAEL, Ronald L., and JACK, Phil R. Stoneware of
      New Geneva [and] Greensboro, Pennsylvania. Archaeo-
      logical Informational Leaflet, No. 2. California, Pa.:
      California State College Center for Prehistoric and
      Historic Site Archaeology, 1973. 1 leaf. illus (b&w).

E17. MIDDLETON, Jefferson. Statistics of the Clay-Working
      Industries in the United States in 1903. Department
      of the Interior, U.S. Geological Survey. Washington:
      GPO, 1904. 96p.

E18. MYERS, Susan H. Handcraft to Industry: Philadelphia
      Ceramics in the First Half of the Nineteenth Century.
      Smithsonian Studies in History and Technology, No. 43.
      Washington: Smithsonian Institution Press, 1980.
      117p. illus (b&w); bibliog (pp. 111-117).
         Originally submitted as author's M.A. Thesis. See
      D11.

E19. OHIO STATE UNIVERSITY. Edward Orton, Jr.: A Memorial.
      Columbus, Ohio: Engineering Experiment Station, Ohio
      State University, 1932. 70p. illus (b&w); bibliog
      (pp. 67-70).

E20. ORTON, Edward, Jr. The Progress of the Ceramic Indus-
      try. University of Wisconsin, Bulletin No. 83;
      Engineering Series, Vol. 2, No. 9, pp. 277-299.
      Madison, Wisc.: University of Wisconsin, 1903. [21]p.

E21. PARMELEE, Cullen W. An Investigation of the Translu-
      cency of Porcelains. University of Illinois Engineer-
      ing Experiment Station, Bulletin No. 154. Urbana,
      Ill.: University of Illinois, 1926. 24p. bibliog.

E22. POTTER, A. D., and McKNIGHT, David, Jr. The Clays and
      the Ceramic Industries of Texas. University of Texas
      Bulletin No. 3120, May 22, 1931. Austin, Tex.: Uni-
      versity of Texas Press, 1931. 215p. illus (b&w).

E23. RIES, Heinrich. Clay Deposits and Clay Industry in
      North Carolina: A Preliminary Report. North Carolina
      Geological Survey, Bulletin No. 13. Raleigh, N.C.:
      Guy V. Barnes, 1897. 157p. index; bibliog (pp. 150-
      152).

E24. _________. The Clays of the United States East of the
      Mississippi River. Department of the Interior, United
      States Geologic Survey, Professional Paper, No. 11.
      Washington: GPO, 1903. 298p. illus (b&w); index.

E25. _________. The Pottery Industry of the United States.
      Department of the Interior, U.S. Geological Survey.
      Washington: GPO, 1896. [38]p.
         Extract from the 17th Annual Report of the Survey,
      1895-1896, Part 3, Mineral Resources of the U.S.

E26.   RIES, Heinrich. Preliminary Report on the Clays of
       Alabama. Survey of Alabama, Bulletin No. 6. Jack-
       sonville, Fla.: Vance Printing Co., 1900. 220p.
       index.

E27.   RIES, Heinrich, and KÜMMELL, Henry B. The Clays and
       Clay Industry of New Jersey. New Jersey Geological
       Survey. Final Report of the State Geologist, Vol. 6.
       Trenton, N.J.: MacCrellish & Quigley, 1904. 548p.

E28.   SCHURECHT, H. G. The Properties of Some Stoneware
       Clays. Department of the Interior, Bureau of Mines,
       Technical Paper No. 233. Washington: GPO, 1920.
       41p. illus (b&w); bibliog (pp. 39-41).

E29.   SHAW, Joseph B. The Ceramic Industries of Pennsylvania.
       Pennsylvania State College Mineral Industries Experi-
       ment Station, Bulletin 7, Vol. 24, No. 22, May 29,
       1930. State College, Pa.: Pennsylvania State College
       School of Mineral Industries, 1930. [205]p. illus
       (b&w); index; bibliog (pp. 200-203).
         Alphabetical Listing of Ceramic Producers: pp. 191-
         199.

E30.   SIM, Robert J. "New Jersey Stoneware." In: Some Van-
       ishing Phases of Rural Life in New Jersey. New Jersey
       Department of Agriculture, Circular 327. Trenton,
       N.J.: New Jersey Department of Agriculture, 1941,
       pp. 40-49. illus (b&w).

E31.   ________. "Red Earthenware." In: Some Vanishing
       Phases of Rural Life in New Jersey. New Jersey De-
       partment of Agriculture, Circular 327. Trenton, N.J.:
       New Jersey Department of Agriculture, 1941, pp. 50-53.
       illus (b&w).

E32.   SMITH, Samuel D., and ROGERS, Stephen T. A Survey of
       Historic Pottery Making in Tennessee. Tennessee
       Department of Conservation, Division of Archaeology,
       Research Series, No. 3. Nashville, Tenn., 1979.
       159p. illus (b&w); bibliog (pp. 151-159).

E33.   SNIDER, Luther C. Preliminary Report on the Clays and
       Clay Industries of Oklahoma. Oklahoma Geological Sur-
       vey, Bulletin No. 7. Norman, Okl., 1911. 270p.
       illus (b&w).

E34.   SOUTH, Stanley. The Ceramic Types and Forms of the
       Potter, Gottfried Aust of Bethabara, North Carolina,
       1755-1771. Raleigh, N.C.: North Carolina Department
       of Archives & History, 1965. 12p. illus (b&w).
         Cf. B84.

E35.   STOUT, Wilber. "History of the Clay Industry in Ohio."
       In: STULL, William, McCAUGHEY, William J., and
       DEMOREST, D. J. Coal Formation Clays of Ohio. Geo-
       logical Survey of Ohio, 4th Series, Bulletin 26.
       Columbus, Ohio: Printed by the Kelly-Springfield
       Printing Co., 1923, pp. 7-102. illus (b&w); bibliog.
       "Record of Pottery Industry, East Liverpool Dis-
       trict": pp. 74-81. "Art Pottery": pp. 89-97.

E36.   STOUT, Wilber, SHAW, Myril C., BOLE, G. A., and SCHAAF,
       Downs. The Lawrence Clay of Lawrence County. Geo-
       logical Survey of Ohio, 4th Series, Bulletin 36.
       Columbus, Ohio, 1931. 134p. illus (b&w).
       Also published as Bulletin 67 of the Engineering
       Experiment Station, Ohio State University.

E37.   THOMPSON, Erwin N. The Poor Potter of Yorktown: Colon-
       ial National Historical Park, Virginia. Historic
       Structure Report, National Park Service No. 836.
       Denver, Col.: Denver Service Center, Historic Preser-
       vation Team, National Park Service, U.S. Department
       of the Interior, 1974. 112p. illus (b&w); bibliog
       (pp. 83-89).

E38.   U.S. DEPARTMENT OF COMMERCE. Bureau of Standards.
       Ceramic Properties of Some White-Burning Clays.
       Bureau of Standards, Circular No. 325. Washington:
       GPO, 1927. 54p.

E39.   __________. Bureau of Standards. Dining-Car Chinaware.
       Simplified Practice Recommendation, No. 39. Washing-
       ton: GPO, 1926. 9p.

E40.   WATKINS, C. Malcolm, and NOEL HUME, Ivor. The "Poor
       Potter" of Yorktown. Contributions from the Museum
       of History and Technology, Paper 54; United States
       National Museum, Bulletin 249. Washington: GPO,
       1967. [38]p. illus (b&w); bibliog.

E41.   WATTS, Arthur S. Probable Effect of the War in Europe
       on the Ceramic Industries of the United States. U.S.
       Department of the Interior, Bureau of Mines, Mineral
       Technology Technical Paper, 99. Washington: GPO,
       1915. 15p.

E42.   __________. The Selection of Dinnerware for the Home.
       Ohio State University Studies, Engineering Series;
       Engineering Experiment Circular No. 21. Columbus,
       Ohio: Ohio State University, 1930. 14p.

E43.   WHITFORD, W. G., and WHITTEMORE, O. J. Possibilities of
       Pottery Manufacture from Iowa Clays. Iowa State Col-
       lege of Agriculture and Mechanic Arts, Bulletin 58,
       Vol. 19, No. 4, June 23, 1920. Ames, Iowa: Engineer-
       ing Experiment Station, 1920. 31p. illus (b&w);
       glossary.

E44.   WHITLATCH, George I. The Clay Resources of Indiana.
       Indiana Department of Conservation, Publication No.
       123. Indianapolis, Ind.: William B. Burford Printing
       Co., 1933. 298p. illus (b&w); index; bibliog (pp.
       263-267).
          "Submitted in Partial Fulfillment for the Degree,
       Ph.D., . . . Indiana University, June 1932."

E45.   WORCESTER, Wolsey Garnet, and ORTON, Edward, Jr. The
       Manufacture of Roofing Tiles. Geological Survey of
       Ohio, 4th Series, Bulletin No. 11. Columbus, Ohio:
       Printed by the Springfield Publishing Co., 1910.
       476p. illus (b&w); index.

─────────────── **F** ───────────────

TRADE
PUBLICATIONS

Few of the hundreds of editions of trade catalogues and other
promotional materials circulated by U.S. ceramic companies
before 1930 have survived. The list which follows is a rep-
resentative sampling of those which were published; it is not
intended to be a complete listing.

Measurements in centimeters have been given when known, height
preceding width. (Where one measurement is given, it is for
height.) Names of printers have been supplied when known.
Unless otherwise specified, the company is the publisher.
Information about the city and state in which each company
was located may be found in the subject index.

F1.   AMERICAN CLAY MACHINERY CO. [Clay Working Machinery]
        Catalogue No. 100. Bucyrus, Ohio, 1918. 441p. illus
        (b&w); 27x22cm.

F2.   AMERICAN ENCAUSTIC TILING CO. Designs for Tiles, Geo-
        metric and Encaustic. [New York: E. C. Miles, 19--?]
        17 Plates (col); 17x25.5cm.

F3.   _________. Lombardic Mosaic. Cleveland: Corday & Gross,
        1928. 39p. illus (col); 29cm.

F4.   _________. Tile Design: A Handbook Illustrating Effects
        Produced by Combining Various Ceramic Materials. New
        York, 1917. [10]p., Plates (b&w, col); 29cm.

F5.   ASSOCIATED TILE MANUFACTURERS. Beautiful Tiles, Never
        Renewed--Yet Ever New. Beaver Falls, Pa. [ca. 1928]
        [32]p. illus; 14x8.5cm.

F6.   _________. Casa Bonita: A House of Tiles Built at the
        Sesqui Centennial as an Educational Exhibit. Beaver
        Falls, Pa., 1926. 32p. illus (plans); 27.5cm.

F7.   ASSOCIATED TILE MANUFACTURERS. Ceramic Mosaic: Stand-
       ardized Sheets and Patterns Adopted by the Members of
       the Associated Tile Manufacturers. Publication K. 500.
       Beaver Falls, Pa., 1922. 32p. illus (b&w, col); 27cm.

F8.   _________. Glazed Tiles and Trimmers. Publication K.
       400. Beaver Falls, Pa., 1921. 86p. illus; 27.5cm.

F9.   _________. Swimming Pools. Beaver Falls, Pa., 1917.
       32p. illus (b&w); 27.5x21cm.

F10.   _________. Tile Floors and Walls for Hospitals. Beaver
       Falls, Pa., 1916. 40p. illus (b&w, col); 28cm.

F11.   _________. Tiled Swimming Pools. Rev. 2d ed. Beaver
       Falls, Pa., 1924. 32p. illus; 28cm.

F12.   _________. Tiles . . . Basic Information: Ingredients
       and Processes, Gradings, Sizes, Shapes, Colors, Fin-
       ishes, Nomenclature. Beaver Falls, Pa., 1921. [25]p.
       illus (b&w); 27x19cm.

F13.   ATLANTIC TERRA COTTA CO. Atlantic Architectural Terra
       Cotta, Buffalo and Vicinity. New York, 1913. 31p.
       illus; 16cm.

F14.   _________. Atlantic Terra Cotta: A 52 Story Facade
       [Woolworth Building] New York, 1913. 44p. illus;
       23cm.

F15.   _________. Garden Pottery. New York, 1911. 19p. illus
       (b&w).

F16.   BARTLEY, JONATHAN, CRUCIBLE CO. Graphite Crucibles for
       Foundry Practice. Trenton, N.J., 1925. 66p. illus
       (b&w); 22.8x15.2cm.

F17.   BATCHELDER-WILSON CO. Batchelder Tiles: A Catalog of
       Mantel Designs. Los Angeles, Calif. [1922-1923]
       2v. illus (b&w, col).

F18.   BELLMARK POTTERY CO. Sanitary Earthenware. [Trenton,
       N.J.?] 1899. 73p. illus (b&w); 16x24cm.
       Includes Price Lists.

F19.   BOSTON ARCHITECTURAL TERRA COTTA WORKS (H. A. LEWIS).
       Belt and Tile Courses, Panels, Lintels, Sills, Crest-
       ings, Finials, Mantels, and All Kinds of Plain and
       Ornamental Exterior and Interior Terra Cotta. South
       Boston, Mass., 1887. 1p., 16 Plates. illus (b&w);
       25x20cm.

F20.   BURLEY & TYRRELL CO. China for Decorating and Artists'
       Materials. Catalog No. 20. Chicago: Printed by
       Stevens, Maloney & Co. [ca. 1916] 48p. illus (b&w);
       19.5x25.4cm.

F21.   CHAMBERS BROTHERS CO. Brick Making Machinery. Cata-
       logue No. 24. Philadelphia? [ca. 1907] 136p.
       illus (b&w); 19.5x27.3cm.

F22.   CONKLING-ARMSTRONG TERRA COTTA CO. [Architectural
       Views and Details] Philadelphia, 1898. 3p., 78
       Plates (b&w); 31x24cm.

F23.   COORS PORCELAIN CO. The Evolution of a Lump o' Clay.
       Golden, Col., 1936. 56p. illus (b&w); 19x23.3cm.

F24.   CROSSLEY MACHINE (MANUFACTURING) CO. Clay Working
       Machinery: Pottery, Electrical Porcelain, Tile
       Making, Clay Washing Machinery. Trenton, N.J., 1906.
       158p. illus (b&w); 20.2x12.5cm.

F25.   _________ . . . . . Clay Working Machinery: Pottery,
       Electrical Porcelain, Tile Making, Clay Washing and
       Crucible Machinery . . . . Trenton, N.J., 1918.
       198p. illus (b&w); 18.5x12cm.

F26.   DEDHAM POTTERY. Dedham Pottery, Formerly Known as
       Chelsea Pottery, U.S.A.: A Short History. Boston:
       D. B. Updike, Merrymount Press, 1898. [7]p. 16.5x11cm.
       Lettered in red on title page.

F27.   _________ . Dedham Pottery, Formerly Known as Chelsea
       Pottery, U.S.A.: A Short History. Boston: D. B.
       Updike, Merrymount Press, 1898. [7]p. 16.5x11cm.
       Same as F26, except lettered in black on title page
       and includes list of officers and agents.

F28.   _________ . Dedham Pottery, Formerly Known to the Trade
       and to the Public as Chelsea Pottery, U.S., But Now
       Newly Established Under the Style of Dedham Pottery
       at Dedham, Massachusetts, U.S.A. Dedham, Mass., 1896.
       [3]p. illus (b&w); 31.5x20cm.

F29.   DENVER FIRE CLAY CO. Keramic Kilns for Pottery and
       China Firing and Development Work. Introduction,
       "Elementary Ceramic Procedure," by Hewitt WILSON.
       Denver, 1930. 45p. illus (b&w); 26.5x17.8cm.

F30.   DICKEY, W. S., CLAY MANUFACTURING CO. Everlasting Clay
       Products. Kansas City, Mo.? 1921. 74p. 26.4x19.4cm.

F31.   ENFIELD POTTERY AND TILE WORKS. Enfield Pottery and
       Tile Works: Hand-Made Terra Cotta, Faience and
       Majolica. [Laverock, Pa.?] 1907. [38]p. illus
       (b&w); 24x15.8cm.
       Includes Price List.

       FAIR HILL TERRA COTTA & LAVA WORKS, see STEAVENSON &
       CASSEL.

F32.   FEUSTEL, WALZ & CO. Palestine Pottery . . . Manufac-
        turers of Rockingham, Yellow and White Lined Ware,
        Terra Cotta Hanging Baskets and Flower Pots: Standard
        Price List. East Palestine, Ohio: Printed by Valley
        Echo Printing and Engraving House [ca. 1890] 8p.
        16.2x11cm.

F33.   FULPER POTTERY CO. Fulper Pottery & Porcelaines.
        Flemington, N.J., n.d. 28p. illus (b&w); 26.5x12.3cm.
        Includes prices.

F34.   GALLOWAY & GRAFF CO. Art and Horticultural Terra Cotta.
        Philadelphia [1876] 15p. illus (b&w); 23x30cm.

F35.   . Art Terra Cotta, Horticultural Terra Cotta.
        Philadelphia [1876?] 3p. illus (b&w); 32.5x25cm.

F36.   GALLOWAY TERRA COTTA CO. Galloway Pottery for Garden &
        Interior. Catalog No. 24. Philadelphia? [ca. 1906-
        1912?] 24p. illus (b&w); 31x23.8cm.

F37.   . Galloway Pottery for Garden & Interior.
        Catalog No. 27. Philadelphia? [ca. 1915?] 24p.
        illus (b&w); 30.5x23.5cm.

F38.   . Terra Cotta and Pottery for Garden and
        Interior. Catalog No. 15. Philadelphia: Edward
        Stern & Co., Printers [1904 or after] 48p. illus
        (b&w); 26.8x21.4cm.
        Includes Prices.

F39.   . Terra Cotta and Pottery, for Garden, Terrace
        and Interior Decoration. Philadelphia: Press of
        Alfred M. Slocum [1904 or after] 40p. illus (b&w);
        22.8x19cm.
        Includes Price List.

F40.   GLADDING, McBEAN & CO. Latin Tiles. San Francisco:
        Printed by Taylor & Taylor, 1923. 87p. illus (b&w);
        31x23.5cm.

F41.   . Pottery. San Francisco: Printed by Taylor
        & Taylor [ca. 1905?] [13]p. illus (b&w); 28x21.5cm.

F42.   GRIFFEN, SMITH & CO. Majolica: Catalogue of Majolica.
        New York: Printed by Hatch Lithographic Co. [ca.
        1880-1884] 14 leaves. illus (col); 28.5x24cm.

F43.   . Majolica: Catalogue of Majolica. Phoenix-
        ville, Pa.: Brooke Weidner, 1960. [13]p. illus
        (col); 22.7x15.1cm.
        Reprint of leaves 1-11 of F42.

        GRUNEWALD & BUSHER, see WESTERN DECORATING WORKS.

F44. HAVILAND & CO. The White House Porcelain Service:
      Designs by an American Artist Illustrating Exclusively
      American Fauna and Flora [T. R. DAVIS, designer] New
      York, 1879. 88p. illus (b&w); 24.6x17.2cm.

F45. JEFFORDS, J. E., & CO. Philadelphia City Pottery:
      Manufacturers of Yellow, Rockingham, and Lava Ware,
      White Lined Fire Proof Ware [Etc.]: Prices Current
      for 1874. Philadelphia, [1874] 12p. 15x9cm.

F46. LANCASTER IRON WORKS (BRICK MACHINERY DEPT.) Clay Pre-
      paring Machinery. Lancaster, Pa., 1925. 15p. illus
      (b&w); 28.4x21.6cm.

F47. LAUGHLIN, HOMER, CHINA CO. The China Book. Newell,
      W.Va., 1912. 24p. illus (b&w, col); 23x15.5cm.

F48. LENOX, INC. Lenox-China. Trenton, N.J., 1922. loose-
      leaf binder. illus (b&w); 29.5cm.

      LENOX, INC. Lenox China: The Story of Walter Scott
      Lenox (Holmes). See A114-115.

      LENOX, INC. The White House China ([Anderson]). See
      A5.

      LEWIS, H. A., see BOSTON ARCHITECTURAL TERRA COTTA
      WORKS.

F49. LOW, J. AND J.G. Plastic Sketches. Boston: C. A.
      Wellington, 1882? 1p., 14 Plates; 24x14.5cm.

F50. LOW, J. G. and J. F. Illustrated Catalogue of Art Tiles
      Made by J. G. & J. F. Low, Chelsea, Mass., U.S.A.
      [Chelsea, Mass.?] 1884? 5p., 30 Plates (b&w);
      34x27cm.

F51. ________. Plastic Sketches. Boston: Lee and Shepard/
      New York: Charles T. Dillingham, 1887. 12p., 47
      Plates (b&w); 30x24cm.

      MADDOCK'S, THOMAS, SONS, CO. Pottery. See A166.

F52. MERCER POTTERY CO. Mercer Lowestoft, Decorated Under
      the Glaze. Trenton, N.J., 1926. 15p. illus (b&w);
      17.4x12cm.

F53. MORAVIAN POTTERY AND TILE WORKS. Directions for Set-
      ting, Pointing and Finishing Moravian Tiles and Pave-
      ments. Doylestown, Pa., n.d. [4]p.

F54. ________. Everlasting Tree Labels Made at the Moravian
      Pottery and Tile Works, Doylestown, Pennsylvania,
      U.S.A. Doylestown, Pa., n.d. [4]p.

F55. MORAVIAN POTTERY AND TILE WORKS. _Moravian Tiles Made at the Moravian Pottery and Tile Works, Doylestown, Pennsylvania, U.S.A._ Doylestown, Pa., n.d. [4]p. illus (b&w); 29.7x21.6cm.

F56. ________. _Moravian Tiles Made at the Moravian Pottery and Tile Works, Doylestown, Pennsylvania, U.S.A. Catalogue No. 2._ Doylestown, Pa. [ca. 1900-1904?] 16p. illus (b&w).
        Includes prices.

F57. ________. _Moravian Tiles Made at the Moravian Pottery and Tile Works, Doylestown, Pennsylvania, U.S.A. Catalogue No. 4._ Doylestown, Pa., [after 1912?] 16p. illus (b&w).

F58. MORGAN, A. R., CO. _Hawley's Patent Kiln and Drying-House for Burning Brick, Tile, Pottery, Queen's Ware, &c., &c._ New York: Printed by George F. Nesbitt, 1871. 18p. illus (b&w); 14.3x11cm.

F59. MOSAIC TILE COMPANY. _Mosaic Faience Tiles: One of the Signal Achievements in the Renaissance of Color._ Zanesville, Ohio, 1929. 79p. illus (b&w, col); 28x21.5cm.

F60. MUELLER MOSAIC CO. _Mueller Tile: Faience, Rusta, Mosaics, Flemish . . . For Exterior and Interior Application._ Trenton, N.J. [ca. 1920] 20p. illus (b&w); 27.8x21.5cm.

F61. NEW YORK BLOWER CO. _The New York Blower Company's Hot Blast and Waste Heat Dryer, for the Drying of Brick, Terra Cotta, Pottery, and All Other Clay Products. Catalogue No. 56._ Chicago: Printed by Continental Colortype Co., 1906. 23p. illus (b&w); 23x15.2cm.

F62. NILOAK POTTERY. _The Niloak Pottery._ [Benton, Ark.? ca. 1920] [15]p. illus.
        Includes prices.

F63. ________. _Niloak Pottery Catalog._ Dumas, Ark.: Kenneth Mauney, 1971. [15]p. illus (b&w); 17.6x11.6cm.
        Reprint of F62.

F64. NORTH STATE POTTERY CO. _Hand Made Pottery by North State._ Sanford, N.C., n.d. [8]p. illus.

F65. ________. _Hand Made Pottery by North State._ Charlotte, N.C.: Mint Museum, 1977. [8]p. illus (b&w); 21.5x14cm.
        Facsimile Reproduction of F64; Printed to Accompany an Exhibition, "The North State Pottery Company, 1924-1959." See also A226.

F66.   NORTH STATE POTTERY CO. Hand Made Pottery by North
       State. Sanford, N.C., n.d. [14]p. illus.
       Includes Price List.

F67.   _________. Hand Made Pottery by North State. Charlotte,
       N.C.: Mint Museum, 1977. [14]p. illus (b&w);
       21.5x14cm.
       Facsimile Reproduction of F66; Printed to Accompany
       an Exhibition, "The North State Pottery Company,
       1924-1959." See also A226.

F68.   _________. The North State Pottery, Creators of Artistic
       North Carolina Pottery. Southern Pines, N.C.: Printed
       by Foss and Morris, n.d. [6]p.

F69.   NORTHWESTERN TERRA COTTA WORKS (TRUE, BRUNKHORST & CO.)
       Architectural Catalogue. Chicago, 1882. 20p.
       (23.5x40cm); 26 Plates (26.5x40cm).

F70.   OSGOOD ART SCHOOL. Complete Price List of Materials
       for China Decoration Including the Osgood Art School
       Specialities: Gold, Royal Worcester, Matt and Bronze
       Colors, Mediums, Etc. Rev. & enl. ed. New York,
       [ca. 1900] 44p. illus (b&w); 15.5x22cm.

       PALESTINE POTTERY, see FEUSTEL, WALZ & CO.

F71.   PERTH AMBOY TERRA-COTTA CO. Catalogue and Price List.
       Philadelphia: Printed by George S. Harris & Sons,
       1895. 56p. illus (b&w); 23.5x29.5cm.

       PERTII AMBOY TERRA-COTTA CO. The Use of Terra Cotta in
       Architecture (Talbot). See A247.

F72.   PHILADELPHIA CHINA AND TILE WORKS. Prospectus of China
       and Tile Works in Philadelphia, Pa., in Connection
       with a School of Ceramic Art, Where Designing, Model-
       ling, Decorating and Painting May Be Practically
       Learned in All Their Branches. Philadelphia: Printed
       by Edward Stern & Co., 1879. 24p. 17.5x11.2cm.

       PHILADELPHIA CITY POTTERY, see JEFFORDS, J. E. & CO.

F73.   ROBINSON CLAY PRODUCT CO. Stoneware and All Clay
       Products. New York, [1907] 36p. 23x11cm.

F74.   ROOKWOOD POTTERY CO. Points of Superior Merit in Rook-
       wood Faience. Cincinnati, Ohio [190-?] 5p. illus;
       20.5cm.

F75.   _________. The Rookwood Book: Rookwood, an American
       Art. Cincinnati, Ohio, 1904. [33]p. illus (b&w,
       col); 19x14.2cm.

F76.   _________. Rookwood Book-Ends. [Cincinnati, Ohio? ca.
       1920?] 3p. illus (b&w); 15.5x9cm.

F77. ROOKWOOD POTTERY CO. Rookwood Bowls. [Cincinnati, Ohio,
      ca. 1920?] 1 leaf. illus (b&w); 16x24cm.

F78. ________. Rookwood Candlesticks. [Cincinnati, Ohio,
      ca. 1920?] 1 leaf. illus (b&w); 16x24cm.

F79. ________. Rookwood Pottery. Cincinnati, Ohio [190-?]
      47p. illus; 22cm.

F80. ________. Rookwood Pottery at the Paris Exhibition.
      Cincinnati, Ohio: Press of the Procter & Collier
      Co. [1900?] 32p. illus (b&w); bibliog.

F81. ________. The Rookwood Pottery Company. [Cincinnati,
      Ohio, ca. 1920] 7p. illus (b&w); 22.5x15.5cm.

F82. ROSEVILLE POTTERY CO. Rozane Ware. Zanesville, Ohio,
      1906. [24]p. illus.

F83. ________. Rozane Ware. Zanesville, Ohio, 1970. [24]p.
      illus. 23cm.
        Reprint of F82.

F84. STANDARD SANITARY MANUFACTURING CO. "Standard" Baths
      and Plumbing Fixtures. Catalog "P." Pittsburgh, Pa.,
      1911. 674p. illus (b&w, col); 30.1x23cm.

F85. ________. "Standard" Modern Lavatories. Pittsburgh,
      Pa., 1912. 64p. illus (b&w).

F86. STANGL POTTERY. Stangl: A Portrait of Progress in
      Pottery. Trenton, N.J., 1965. [31]p. illus (b&w);
      glossary; 21.5x14cm.

F87. STEAVENSON & CASSEL. Fair Hill Terra Cotta & Lava Works.
      [Philadelphia? 1876?] 1 leaf. 30x23.8cm.

F88. TIFFANY & CO. Porcelains from the Robineau Pottery,
      Adelaide Alsop-Robineau, Potter. New York [1906]
      26p. illus (b&w); 17.5x14.5cm.

F89. TRENT TILE CO. Floor, Wall and Trim Tile of Every
      Description. Trenton, N.J., n.d. [72]p. illus
      (b&w, col); 23.4x14cm.

F90. ________. Illustrated Catalogue. New York: Printed
      by N.Y. Photo Gravure Co., n.d. 61 Plates. illus
      (b&w); 30x22.5cm.

F91. ________. Tiles for Everywhere and Anywhere. Catalogue
      "B." Philadelphia: Printed by Edw. Stern, 1907.
      98p. illus (b&w, col); 29x18cm.

F92. TRENTON POTTERIES CO. The Blue Book of Plumbing. Cata-
      logue R, July 1921. Trenton, N.J., 1921. 321p.
      illus (b&w); 20x13.5cm.

TRUE, BRUNKHORST & CO., see NORTHWESTERN TERRA COTTA WORKS.

F93.   VAN BRIGGLE TILE AND POTTERY CO. Van Briggle Pottery. Denver, Col.: Welch-Haffner, n.d. 12p. illus (b&w).

F94.   WELLSVILLE CHINA CO. . . . Manufacturers of Semi-Vitreous Porcelain, Plain and Decorated. [Wellsville, Ohio? 1911?] 16p. illus (b&w, col); 23.1x31.2cm.

F95.   WESTERN DECORATING WORKS (GRUNEWALD & BUSHER). [China Bodies, Including Those Made by Ceramic Art Co., Ott & Brewer, Willet's, American Art China Works, Rittenhouse, Evans & Co.] Chicago: n.d. [99]p. illus (b&w); 15x32.5cm.

F96.   WHEATLEY POTTERY CO. Garden Pottery. Anderson, Ind.: Herald Publishing Co., 1922. 36p. illus (b&w).

F97.   WHITMAN, J. FRANKLIN, CO. Garden Pottery. Philadelphia, 1903. 68p. illus (b&w).

F98.   WILLETS MANUFACTURING CO. Willets Egg Shell, Belleek, White Art Porcelain. [Trenton, N.J.? 1893?] [48]p. illus (b&w); 15x23.5cm.
        Includes Price List for September 1, 1893.

F99.   WRIGHT, TYNDALE & VAN RODEN. Illustrated Catalogue and Price List of White China and Materials for China Painting. [Philadelphia? ca. 1895?] [29]p. illus (b&w); 26.5x34.6cm.

F100.   ZANE POTTERY CO. Zane Ware. Catalog No. 22. South Zanesville, Ohio, n.d. [14]p. illus.

F101.   ________. Zane Ware. Catalog No. 22. South Zanesville, Ohio? [197-?] [14]p. illus (b&w); 28.2x21.7cm.
        Reprint of F100.

G

PERIODICAL ARTICLES

N.B. In this section, anonymous articles are entered under
the name of the journal in which they appear.

G1.   ABRAHAM, Evelyn. "The Pottery of Greensboro and New
           Geneva." Antiquarian 17 (September 1931), 25-29.
           illus (17 b&w).

G2.   ADAMS, Ella L. "Firing a Gasoline Kiln." Keramic
           Studio 8 (May 1906), 8-9.

G3.   _______. "Firing Charcoal Kilns." Keramic Studio 8
           (May 1906), 8.

G4.   ADAMS, John. "The Four Sages Discuss Dinnerware Deco-
           ration." American Pottery Gazette 10 (December 1909),
           38-41.

G5.   ADLER, Hazel H. "Exhibition of the Keramic Society of
           Greater New York." Keramic Studio 18 (July 1916),
           19-44. illus (38 b&w).

G6.   _______. "Modern Tableware for the Modern Home." Arts
           & Decoration 6 (July 1916), 436-437, 444. illus
           (7 b&w).

G7.   ALBERY, Duane F. "Grog for Terra Cotta." American Cer-
           amic Society Bulletin 5 (July 1926), 316-319.

G8.   _______. "A Terra Cotta Defect [Green Spots Caused by
           Copper, Brass]" Ceramist 2 (June 1922), 44-45.

G9.   ALBRIGHT, Frank P. "Clay Pipe Making at Salem, North
           Carolina." Early American Industries Association
           Chronicle 11 (June 1958), 18-20, 24. illus (5 b&w).

G10.   ALEXANDER, Julia S. "New York Society of Craftsmen."
           Art Center New York Bulletin 2 (May 1924), 289-290.
           illus (1 b&w).

G11.   ALEXANDER, Letitia H. "A New Potter: The Work of Miss
       Fayette Barnum." House Beautiful 15 (March 1904),
       238-239. illus (2 b&w).

G12.   ALLEN, Frederick W. "More About Dedham Pottery."
       Hobbies 57 (September 1952), 80-81, 99, 104. illus
       (3 b&w).

G13.   ALLISON, Grace. "A Rare Bone China of the 1890s--Lotus
       Ware from Ohio." American Antiques 6 (January 1978),
       26-29. illus (4 b&w).

G14.   ALLISON, LeRoy W. "Theodore A. Randall, 1857-1926
       [Obituary]" Ceramist 8 (August 1926), 352, 354.
       illus (1 b&w).

       ALSOP-ROBINEAU, Adelaide, see ROBINEAU, Adelaide Alsop.

G15.   AMERICAN ANTIQUES. "Shenandoah Valley Pottery Exhibited
       at Williamsburg." Vol. 3 (August 1975), 24. illus
       (4 b&w).

G16.   AMERICAN ARCHITECT AND BUILDING NEWS. "American Pot-
       teries." Vol. 5 (January 11, 1879), 15.

G17.   _________. "The Manufacture of Terra Cotta in Chicago."
       Vol. 1 (December 30, 1876), 420-421.

G18.   _________. "The New Central Music Hall--Artistic Work
       in Terra Cotta." Vol. 6 (November 8, 1879), 151.

G19.   _________. "The School of Pottery and Painting on Por-
       celain [Boston]" Vol. 8 (October 30, 1880), 215.

G20.   _________. "A Terra-Cotta Company's Loss [Boston Terra-
       Cotta Co.]" Vol. 16 (December 13, 1884), 277.

G21.   _________. "Terra-Cotta Lumber." Vol. 11 (January 14,
       1882), 22.

G22.   _________. "Terra-Cotta Stable Decorations." Vol. 8
       (November 6, 1880), 225.

G23.   AMERICAN CERAMIC SOCIETY BULLETIN. "A. E. Baggs to
       Lecture During Annual Meeting." Vol. 15 (March 1936),
       99. illus (1 b&w).

G24.   _________. "A. V. Bleininger, Honorary Member." Vol.
       20 (May 1941), 177.

G25.   _________. "Adelaide Alsop-Robineau [Obituary]" Vol.
       8 (May 1929), 121-124. illus (3 b&w).

G26.   _________. "Albert Victor Bleininger [Obituary]" Vol.
       25 (June 15, 1946), 241-242. illus (1 b&w).

G27.   AMERICAN CERAMIC SOCIETY BULLETIN. "Alice Annie Ayars,
        Master Potter [Obituary]" Vol. 25 (December 15,
        1946), 490-491. illus (1 b&w).

G28.   ________ . "Another Honorary Member Has Passed Away:
        Mary Louise McLaughlin." Vol. 18 (February 1939),
        66-67.

G29.   ________ . "Arthur Frederick Greaves-Walker [Retires]"
        Vol. 25 (September 15, 1946), 315-320. illus (4 b&w);
        bibliog.

G30.   ________ . "Arthur Simeon Watts [Retires]" Vol. 25
        (July 15, 1946), 243-247. illus (4 b&w); bibliog.

G31.   ________ . "Charles A. Bloomfield [Obituary]" Vol. 8
        (November 1929), 336-337. illus (1 b&w).

G32.   ________ . "Charles Fergus Binns, D.Sc." Vol. 4 (July
        1925), 331-334. illus (3 b&w).

G33.   ________ . "Charles Fergus Binns [Obituary]" Vol. 14
        (January 1935), 24-25. illus (1 b&w).

G34.   ________ . "Charles Howell Cook [Obituary]" Vol. 6
        (February 1927), 61-62. illus (1 b&w).

G35.   ________ . "Charles W. Franzheim." Vol. 20 (May 1941),
        185-186. illus (1 b&w).

G36.   ________ . "Clara Chipman Newton, Pioneer Secretary,
        Rookwood Pottery Company." Vol. 18 (November 1939),
        443-445.

G37.   ________ . "Collegiate Study of Ceramic Arts [Ohio State
        U.]" Vol. 7 (September 1928), 286-297.

G38.   ________ . "The Craft Potters of North Carolina." Vol.
        21 (June 1942), 79-87. illus (11 b&w).

G39.   ________ . "Dr. Cullen Warner Parmelee." Vol. 21 (July
        1942), 117-121. illus (1 b&w); bibliog.

G40.   ________ . "Edward Orton, Jr. Defines His Platform for
        Service if Elected President." Vol. 8 (December
        1929), 358-359.

G41.   ________ . "Elizabeth Gray Overbeck [Obituary]" Vol.
        16 (February 1937), 67. illus (1 b&w).

G42.   ________ . "Ellsworth Woodward [Obituary]" Vol. 18
        (May 1939), 179-180.

G43.   ________ . "F. A. Sebring [Obituary]" Vol. 16 (Janu-
        ary 1937), 23-24. illus (1 b&w).

G44.   AMERICAN CERAMIC SOCIETY BULLETIN. "Francis William
       Walker." Vol. 18 (June 1939), 227-229.

G45.   _________. "Frederick Hurten Rhead [Obituary]" Vol. 21
       (December 1942), 305-307. illus (1 b&w); bibliog.

G46.   _________. "General Edward Orton, Jr. [Obituary, Etc.]"
       Vol. 11 (March 1932), 43-68. illus (1 b&w).

G47.   _________. "Genuine Pennsylvania German Ware: Powder
       Valley Men Who Produce This Ware." Vol. 19 (January
       1940), 22-24. illus (4 b&w).

G48.   _________. "George F. Young: A Story of Roseville Pot-
       tery." Vol. 23 (July 1944), 219-222. illus (4 b&w).

G49.   _________. "Get Acquainted with Your Own Folk: Mary
       Elizabeth Cook." Vol. 9 (August 1930), 246-253.
       illus (10 b&w).

G50.   _________. "Gustav Hottinger." Vol. 18 (December 1939),
       476.

G51.   _________. "Gustav Hottinger [Obituary]" Vol. 8 (Octo-
       ber 1929), 324. illus (1 b&w).

G52.   _________. "H. Ries Receives Honorary Degree." Vol. 24
       (July 1945), 274. illus (1 b&w).

G53.   _________. "H. A. Wheeler, Charter Member of the Ameri-
       can Ceramic Society." Vol. 18 (February 1939), 73.

G54.   _________. "Heinrich Ries." Vol. 17 (December 1938),
       490-491. bibliog.

G55.   _________. "Herman Mueller." Vol. 21 (January 1942),
       1-3. illus (2 b&w).

G56.   _________. "History of Norton Company." Vol. 15 (August
       1936), 295-296. illus (1 b&w).

G57.   _________. "History of the Bowmans: O. O. Bowman and
       His Sons, W. J. J. and R. K. Bowman--Activities in
       Manufacturing a Full Line of Plumbing Fixtures."
       Vol. 19 (May 1940), 175-177. illus (1 b&w).

G58.   _________. "History of the Haeger Potteries, Inc." Vol.
       24 (October 1945), 355-357. illus (2 b&w).

G59.   _________. "History of the Hall China Company, East
       Liverpool, Ohio." Vol. 24 (August 1945), 280-281.

G60.   _________. "Identification of Cincinnati Pottery Club
       and Porcelain League Gifts to the American Ceramic
       Society." Vol. 19 (September 1940), 353. illus
       (1 b&w).

G61.   AMERICAN CERAMIC SOCIETY BULLETIN. "James Macmath
        Smith, President of Shenango Pottery Company." Vol.
        20 (May 1941), 163-164.

G62.   ________. "James Tams, Dean Among Potters." Vol. 17
        (January 1938), 35-36. bibliog.
        Originally published in Pottery, Glass and Brass
        Salesman. See G1833.

G63.   ________. "John Maddock [Obituary]" Vol. 17 (August
        1937), 340. bibliog.

G64.   ________. "Joseph Mayer [Obituary]" Vol. 9 (December
        1930), 336. illus (1 b&w).

G65.   ________. "Karl Langenbeck [Obituary]" Vol. 17 (Octo-
        ber 1938), 429-430.

G66.   ________. "Leon Irwin Shaw." Vol. 25 (November 15,
        1946), 435-437. illus (1 b&w).

G67.   ________. "Leon Victor Solon Awarded Charles Fergus
        Binns Medal." Vol. 15 (June 1936), 230. illus
        (1 b&w).

G68.   ________. "Mary Elizabeth Cook, Sculptor and Potter:
        Our Own WAC in World War I." Vol. 23 (December 1944),
        451-456. illus (9 b&w).

G69.   ________. "Mary Louise McLaughlin." Vol. 17 (May
        1938), 217-225. illus (4 b&w); bibliog.

G70.   ________. "Membership Roster of American Ceramic
        Society." Vol. 8 (July 1929), 187-254.

G71.   ________. "Moses Golding." Vol. 19 (June 1940), 205-
        206.

G72.   ________. "Mrs. Bellamy Storer [Obituary]" Vol. 11
        (June 1932), 157-159.

G73.   ________. "Notes on Early American Porcelain [Tucker]"
        Vol. 17 (April 1938), 177-178.
        Originally published in American Journal of Science
        and Arts. See G105 and G106.

G74.   ________. "Ohio State University Ceramic Men Honor
        Professor Edward Orton, Jr." Vol. 4 (April 1925),
        195-196.

G75.   ________. "Orton: Helmsman of Ceramics [E. Orton,
        Jr.]" Vol. 31 (January 1952), 1-3 illus (2 b&w).

G76.   ________. "The Overbeck Pottery." Vol. 23 (May 1944),
        155-158. illus (7 b&w).

G77.   AMERICAN CERAMIC SOCIETY BULLETIN. "Passing of W. D.
       Gates." Vol. 14 (February 1935), 93. illus (1 b&w).

G78.   __________. "Permanent Exhibit at Society's Executive
       Offices: Crystalline Glazes Cone 11 Porcelain."
       Vol. 6 (January 1927), 33. illus (2 b&w).

G79.   __________. "Peter McGil McBean, Co-Founder, The Gladding,
       McBean, and Company." Vol. 16 (July 1937), 314-315.
       illus (1 b&w).

G80.   __________. "Porcelain League of Cincinnati." Vol. 19
       (September 1940), 351-352. illus (1 b&w).

G81.   __________. "Ray Thomas Stull [Obituary]" Vol. 23 (Febu-
       ary 1944), 41-43. illus (1 b&w); bibliog.

G82.   __________. "Robertson Art Tile Company." Vol. 20 (Novem-
       ber 1941), 413-414. illus (2 b&w).

G83.   __________. "Rookwood Living Proof of Profit in Nonprofi-
       teering Industry." Vol. 13 (January 1934), 7-8.

G84.   __________. "Ross Coffin Purdy Passes Away at the Age of
       73." Vol. 28 (January 15, 1949), 24-25. illus
       (1 b&w).

G85.   __________. "Ross Coffin Purdy Retires." Vol. 25 (April
       15, 1946), 147-150. illus (1 b&w).

G86.   __________. "Samuel A. Weller [Obituary]" Vol. 4 (Novem-
       ber 1925), 625-627. illus (2 b&w).

G87.   __________. "Two Notable Events Mark Progress in Ceramic
       Engineering: Edward Orton, Jr. Made Doctor of Science;
       New Jersey Ceramic Research Station Building Dedica-
       ted." Vol. 1 (July 1922), 63-67. illus (5 b&w).

G88.   __________. "W. E. Wells [Obituary]" Vol. 10 (October
       1931), 326-328. illus (1 b&w).

G89.   __________. "W. H. Fulper [Obituary]" Vol. 7 (December
       1928), 380-381. illus (1 b&w).

G90.   __________. "William H. Bloor." Vol. 16 (January 1937),
       25-31. illus (7 b&w); bibliog.

G91.   __________. "William J. Miller." Vol. 25 (January 15,
       1946), 1-4. illus (1 b&w).

G92.   __________. "Theodore Amasa Randall, 1857-1926." Vol.
       19 (February 1940), 71-73.

G93.   __________. "University of Illinois Recipient of Heinrich
       Ries Collection." Vol. 24 (February 1945), 70-71.
       illus (1 b&w); bibliog.

G94.   AMERICAN CERAMIC SOCIETY BULLETIN. "Who Began Vitri-
        fied Porcelain Sanitary Ware Making? [T. Maddock]"
        Vol. 16 (September 1937), 384-386. bibliog.

G95.   AMERICAN CERAMIC SOCIETY JOURNAL. "[American Ceramic
        Society]: Charter Members." Vol. 6 (January 1923),
        23-35. illus (19 b&w).

G96.   ________. "[American Ceramic Society Yearbook, 1918]"
        Vol. 1 (December 1918), 813-877.

G97.   ________. "[American Ceramic Society Yearbook, 1918-
        1919; 1919-1920]" Vol. 3 (August 1920, Pt. 2),
        3-112.

G98.   ________. "[American Ceramic Society Yearbook, 1920-
        1921]" Vol. 4 (June 1921, Pt. 2), 3-150.

G99.   ________. "American Ceramic Society Yearbook, 1921-
        22." Vol. 5 (April 1922, Pt. 2), 5-234.

G100.   ________. "An Art Division." Vol. 3 (April 1920),
        263-264.

G101.   ________. "Edward Orton, Jr." Vol. 1 (January 1918),
        6-7. illus (1 b&w).

G102.   ________. "Necrology: George F. Young." Vol. 3 (July
        1920), 608.

G103.   ________. "Officers of the American Ceramic Society
        from 1899 to 1922-2[3]" Vol. 6 (January 1923), 35-
        61. illus (53 b&w).

G104.   ________. "School of Industrial Art, City of Trenton."
        Vol. 6 (January 1923), 115-116. illus (7 b&w).

G105.   AMERICAN JOURNAL OF SCIENCE AND ARTS. "American Por-
        celain [Tucker & Hulme]" Vol. 14 (July 1828), 198-
        199.

G106.   ________. "Porcelain of Philadelphia [W. E. Tucker]"
        Vol. 18 (July 1830), 384-385.

G107.   AMERICAN MAGAZINE OF ART. "The Work of an American
        Potter [C. Poillon]" Vol. 7 (January 1916), 111.
        illus (1 b&w).

G108.   AMERICAN POTTERY GAZETTE. "About Decalcomania." Vol.
        8 (December 1908), 30. illus (1 b&w).

G109.   ________. "American Art Pottery." Vol. 5 (June 10,
        1907), 39-40, 42.

G110.   ________. "American Art Pottery." Vol. 5 (July 10,
        1907), 40-42, 45-47.

G111.   AMERICAN POTTERY GAZETTE. "American Art Pottery."
        Vol. 5 (August 1907), 41-45.

G112.   ________. "American Art Ware Potteries." Vol. 9
        (June 1909), 34, 37.

G113.   ________. "American Potters Building up Industry."
        Vol. 4 (October 10, 1906), 24, 26.

G114.   ________. "The Centennial Vase." Vol. 8 (September
        1908), 13, 20. illus (2 b&w).

G115.   ________. "Charles H. L. Smith [Obituary]" Vol. 8
        (September 1908), 23-24.

G116.   ________. "Domestic vs. Foreign: Pottery and Glass-
        ware Arguments as Presented to the Ways and Means
        Committee." Vol. 8 (December 1908), 35, 37, 38, 41,
        43-44, 47, 49-50.

G117.   ________. "English 'Bone-China' Made in America
        [Lenox]" Vol. 1 (April 5, 1905), 21.

G118.   ________. "John Smith Goodwin: Obituary." Vol. 8
        (January 1909), 37-38.

G119.   ________. "Lenox China." Vol. 1 (August 1905), 22,
        26.

G120.   ________. "Lenox, Incorporated." Vol. 2 (February 5,
        1906), 18, 20. illus (2 b&w).

G121.   ________. "Master and Operative Potters' Committees."
        Vol. 9 (August 1909), 16, 19, 21, 41.

G122.   ________. "Mycenean Ware--A New Haynes Product."
        Vol. 7 (July 1908), 21. illus (2 b&w).

G123.   ________. "An Old Pennsylvania Pottery [J. G. Glase]"
        Vol. 4 (October 10, 1906), 43.

G124.   ________. "Operative Potters' Annual Convention."
        Vol. 9 (July 1909), 9-10, 13.

G125.   ________. "A Plea for a Plain Toilet Shape." Vol. 10
        (October 1909), 19, 21. illus (2 b&w).

G126.   ________. "The Possibilities of a Plain Dinner Shape."
        Vol. 10 (January 1910), 34.

G127.   ________. "S. A. Weller's New 'Mat Glazes'." Vol. 1
        (April 5, 1905), 41.

G128.   ________. "St. Louis Has a Pottery [R. P. Bringhurst]"
        Vol. 10 (November 1909), 33, 34.

G129.   AMERICAN POTTERY GAZETTE. "A Satisfactory Kiln [Excel-
         sior]" Vol. 8 (January 1909), 28.

G130.   ________. "Some Opinions on the New Tariff Bill."
         Vol. 9 (March 1909), 10, 13, 15, 19.

G131.   ________. "Thirtieth Annual Convention of the United
         States Potters' Association." Vol. 8 (December
         1908), 10, 13, 15-16, 19, 21.

G132.   ________. "Thirty-first United States Potters' Con-
         vention." Vol. 10 (December 1909), 19, 21-22, 25,
         27-28, 31, 33-34.

G133.   ________. "Trenton as a Pottery Center." Vol. 8
         (February 1909), 25, 27.

G134.   ________. "Trenton's Art School Gets Handsome Gift."
         Vol. 9, (May 1909), 21.

G135.   AMERICANA. "Underground Gallery--Art in a 75-Year Old
         Subway." Vol. 7 (November-December 1979), 72-73.
         illus (1 b&w, 7 col).

G136.   ANDERSON, Alexandra. "American Art Pottery."
         Portfolio 2 (February-March 1980), 94-97. illus
         (10 col).

G137.   ________. "George Ohr's 'Mud Babies'." Art in
         America 67 (January-February 1979), 60-61, 63.
         illus (4 b&w, 1 col).

G138.   ANDERSON, Mary F. "Dishes for the White House."
         Americana (American Historical Society) 31 (April
         1937), 221-244. illus (4 b&w).

G139.   ANTIQUARIAN. "Tulip Ware: Quaint Pottery Made in
         Pennsylvania." Vol. 3 (August 1924), 24-25. illus
         (1 b&w).

G140.   ANTIQUE COLLECTING. "Pottery on Exhibit in Alexandria,
         Va." Vol. 1 (August 1977), 12. illus (4 b&w).

G141.   ________. "Whately and Ashfield Pottery, Historic
         Deerfield, Deerfield, Massachusetts." Vol. 2
         (April 1979), 16. illus (1 b&w).

G142.   ANTIQUES. "Ceramics [Old Northwest Territory]" Vol.
         87 (March 1965), 324-326. illus (8 b&w).

G143.   ________. "Found! Bonnin and Morris Porcelain."
         Vol. 59 (February 1954), 139. illus (2 b&w).

G144.   ________. "The Jug and the Ring [Anna Pottery]"
         Vol. 34 (November 1938), 238-239. illus (2 b&w).

G145.   ANTIQUES. "More About Pottery Pigs [Anna Pottery]"
        Vol. 35 (March 1939), 115.

G146.   _________. "More Anna and More Serpent [Anna Pottery]"
        Vol. 23 (June 1933), 204. illus (1 b&w).

G147.   _________. "Potter and Potter's Wheel [Greenwich House
        Pottery]" Vol. 19 (January 1931), 23-25. illus
        (11 b&w).

G148.   _________. "A Pottery Pig [Anna Pottery]" Vol. 35
        (January 1939), 27. illus (1 b&w).

G149.   _________. "Rarities in Tucker Porcelain in the Col-
        lection of Philip H. Hammerslough." Vol. 74 (Sep-
        tember 1958), 240-241. illus (4 b&w; 1 col).

G150.   ARCHITECTURAL RECORD. "Tile Resources in Surface
        Embellishment." Vol. 36 (November 1914), 421-430.
        illus (24 b&w).

G151.   ARMSTRONG, Henry R. "The Norwich Pottery Works."
        Antiques 4 (October 1923), 170-172. illus (5 b&w).

G152.   ARMSTRONG, Irene. "An Old Art Serves a New Age [Paul
        Revere]" Recreation 27 (February 1934), 515-516,
        539-540. illus (2 b&w).

G153.   _________. "The Paul Revere Pottery: A School of
        Pottery." Our Boston 3 (September 1928), 17-20.
        illus (2 b&w).

G154.   ART CENTER NEW YORK BULLETIN. "[Leon Volkmar]" Vol.
        7 (December 1928), 41-42. illus (3 b&w).

G155.   ART EDUCATION. "An Experiment with Applied Art in
        Newcomb College, New Orleans." Vol. 4 (May 1898),
        166-168. illus (5 b&w).

G156.   ART INTERCHANGE. "American Belleek Ware." Vol. 36
        April 1896), 98.

G157.   _________. "Art Gossip [Cincinnati Pottery Club]"
        Vol. 8 (May 25, 1882), 123.

G158.   _________. "Boston Exhibition of Decorated China
        [Mineral Art League]" Vol. 42 (April 1899), 99.

G159.   _________. "Exhibition of National League of Mineral
        Painters." Vol. 34 (January 1895), 25.

G160.   _________. "Keramic Exhibition [N.Y. Society of Keram-
        ic Arts]" Vol. 44 (January 1900), 25-26.

G161.   _________. "Keramic Exhibition [N.Y. Society of Keram-
        ic Arts]" Vol. 46 (January 1901), 22-23.

G162.   ART INTERCHANGE. "The New Revelation China Kiln."
         Vol. 35 (July 1895), 23-24.

G163.   ________. "New York Ceramics [N.Y. Society of Keramic
         Arts]" Vol. 42 (January 1899), 22.

G164.   ART WORLD. "Modern American Pottery." Vol. 1 (Janu-
         ary 1917), xii. illus (6 b&w).

G165.   ________. "The Oldest Pottery in America [Fulper]"
         Vol. 3 (December 1917), 252-254. illus (7 b&w).

G166.   ARTIST. "Grueby Faience." Vol. 23 (December 1898),
         xxxix-xl. illus (3 b&w).

G167.   ARTS & DECORATION. "A Logical Decoration for Modern
         Architectural Needs: The Growing Popularity of
         Moravian Tiles." Vol. 1 (September 1911), 435-437.
         illus (4 b&w).

G168.   ________. "Ombroso Pottery: A Recent Rookwood Pro-
         duct." Vol. 1 (September 1911), 449. illus (1 b&w).

G169.   ________. "The Pottery at Marblehead: The Exquisite
         Work Produced on the Massachusetts Coast." Vol. 1
         (September 1911), 448-449. illus (2 b&w).

G170   ________. "Who's Who in American Art [G. DeF. Brush]"
         Vol. 6 (February 1916), 187.

G171.   ASHBERY, John. "Feelin' Grueby." New York 13 (March
         17, 1980), 56-57. illus (3 col).

G172.   ASHBY, Geo. J. M. "New St. Louis--World's Fair City,
         1904: Some Splendid Specimens of Brick Architec-
         ture." Clay-Worker 38 (October 1902), 317-320.
         illus (3 b&w).

G173.   ________. "Winkle Terra Cotta Works." Clay-Worker 41
         (May 1904), 598-601. illus (3 b&w).

G174.   ASHLEY, Harrison Everett. "A Trip through a Modern
         Pottery--Its Construction, Operation and Products
         [H. Laughlin China Co.]" Clay-Worker 53 (June 1910),
         834-836. illus (7 b&w).

G175.   ATHERTON, Carlton. "Adelaide Alsop Robineau--Master
         Potter." Ceramic Age 19 (May 1932), 208-210, 234.
         illus (7 b&w).

G176.   AUMAN, Dorothy Cole and ZUG, Charles G. III. "Nine
         Generations of Potters: The Cole Family." Southern
         Exposure 5 (Summer-Fall 1977), 166-174. illus
         (11 b&w); bibliog.

G177.   AVERY, C. Louise. "A Memorial Exhibition of the Works
        of Charles F. Binns." Metropolitan Museum of Art
        Bulletin 30 (May 1935), 106-108. illus (1 b&w).

G178.   AYE, James H. "Chicago as a Center of Ceramic Art."
        Pottery, Glass & Brass Salesman 2 (December 22,
        1910), 51-52. illus (4 b&w).

G179.   BACH, Richard F. "Art in Industry [Lenox]" American
        Ceramic Society Bulletin 3 (August 1924), 277-288.
        illus (13 b&w).

G180.   ________. "Art in Industry: What is the Value of
        Design?" Ceramist 8 (July 1926), 213-226. illus
        (9 b&w).

G181.   BACK, Robert. "The Manufacture of Leads for the
        Mechanical Pencil." American Ceramic Society Bul-
        letin 4 (November 1925), 571-579. illus (7 b&w).

G182.   BACKLUND, Herman. "History Set in Tile [Moravian Pot-
        tery and Tile Works]" Today Magazine in Eastern
        Pennsylvania 2 (March 1972), 16-19. illus (9 b&w).

G183.   ________. "History Set In Tile [Part 2]" Today Maga-
        zine in Eastern Pennsylvania 2 (April 1972), 13-15,
        20. illus (5 b&w).

G184.   BAGGS, Arthur E. "The Story of a Potter [A. E. Baggs]"
        Handicrafter 1 (April-May 1929), 8-10. illus
        (3 b&w).

G185.   BAGGS, Arthur E. and FOSDICK, Marion L. "Design
        Problems of the Tableware Industry." American
        Ceramic Society Journal 13 (May 1930), 11-23.

G186.   ________ and ________. "Design Problems of the Table-
        ware Industry." Design 32 (February 1931), 193-195.
        illus (2 b&w).
          Originally published in American Ceramic Society
          Journal. See G185.

G187.   ________ and ________. "Preparing Designers in
        Schools for the Ceramic Industry." Design 32
        (April 1931), 249, 253.

G188.   BAILEY, Worth. "Concerning Jamestown Pottery--Past
        and Present." Ceramic Age 30 (October 1937), 101-
        104. illus (7 b&w).

G189.   BAKER, A. C. "China Painting is Growing in Favor."
        Ceramic Monthly 3 (May 1896), 82-85. illus (2 b&w).

G190.   BAKER, Gordon C. "Checklist of Potteries and Pottery
        Owners in Greensboro, Pennsylvania." Spinning Wheel
        34 (November 1978), 12-14. illus (8 b&w).

G191.   BAKER, Gordon C. "Checklist of Potteries and Pottery
         Owners in New Geneva, Pennsylvania." Spinning Wheel
         34 (June 1978), 29-31. illus (6 b&w).

G192.   ________. "Debolt and Atchison: Early New Geneva
         Stoneware Potters." Spinning Wheel 35 (May 1979),
         17-18. illus (5 b&w).

G193.   ________. "Early Potteries of Morgantown, West
         Virginia." Spinning Wheel 36 (November-December
         1980), 47-50. illus (12 b&w).

G194.   ________. "The Hamilton Family Potters of Greensboro,
         Pennsylvania." Spinning Wheel 35 (January-February
         1979), 42-44. illus (11 b&w).

G195.   ________. "New Geneva Tanware." Spinning Wheel 36
         (March-April 1980), 64-65. (11 b&w).

G196.   ________. "Pottery of Greensboro and New Geneva, Pa."
         Spinning Wheel 29 (November 1973), 14-17. illus
         (9 b&w).

G197.   ________. "Robert T. Williams, New Geneva, Pa. Potter."
         Spinning Wheel 34 (April 1978), 12-14. illus
         (5 b&w).

G198.   ________. "Samuel R. Dilliner and the Dilliner Potters
         of New Geneva, Pennsylvania." Spinning Wheel 35
         (July-August 1979), 29. illus (3 b&w).

G199.   ________. "Union Pottery, Point Marion, Pennsylvania."
         Spinning Wheel 36 (May-June 1980), 42. illus
         (2 b&w).

G200.   BAKER, Mary F. "The Newcomb Art School and Its
         Achievements." Sketch Book 4 (June 1905), 264-265.
         illus (3 b&w).

G201.   BALL, Berenice M. "Ceramic Heritage of Chester County,
         Pennsylvania." Hobbies 58 (September 1953), 80-81.
         illus (3 b&w).

G202.   ________. "Chester County Collectibles [Tucker;
         Etruscan Majolica]" Spinning Wheel 12 (October
         1956), 24, 35. illus (2 b&w).

G203.   ________. "Etruscan Majolica." Antiques Journal 19
         (September 1964), 24-25. illus (4 b&w).

G204.   ________. "Majolica on Parade [Etruscan]" Hobbies 65
         (October 1960), 70. illus (2 b&w).

G205.   ________. "Tucker Ware: Pennsylvania Porcelain."
         Antiques Journal 16 (November 1961), 9, 27. illus
         (4 b&w).

G206.   BALL, Berenice. "You and Your Antiques . . . Etruscan
         Majolica." National Antiques Review 4 (January
         1973), 17-19, 40. illus (4 b&w).

G207.   ________. "You and Your Antiques . . . Those Collect-
         ible Shaving Mugs." National Antiques Review 7
         (July 1975), 31-32. illus (4 b&w).

G208.   BALL, F. Carlton. "Strictly Stoneware: Introduction
         to Salt Glaze." Ceramics Monthly 10 (January 1962),
         11, 37. illus (1 b&w).

G209.   ________. "Strictly Stoneware: Salt-Glazed Stone-
         ware." Ceramics Monthly 10 (February 1962), 26-27.
         illus (4 b&w).

G210.   BALLARD, Margaret. "A Fresh Appraisal of Old Shaving
         Mugs." Spinning Wheel 35 (January-February 1979),
         16-18. illus (7 b&w).

G211.   BANE, Reynolds. "Artus Van Briggle: Man and Artist."
         Antiques Journal 30 (August 1975), 30-33. illus
         (13 b&w).

G212.   BARBER, Edwin AtLee.   "The American China Factory:
         An Interesting Chapter on an Early American Pottery
         [Tucker]" American Pottery Gazette 9 (August 1909),
         33-34, 37, 39.

G213.   ________. "The American China Factory: An Interesting
         Chapter on an Early American Pottery, Part II."
         American Pottery Gazette 10 (September 1909), 28, 31,
         33, 34, 37.

G214.   ________. "American 'Majolica' [Etruscan]" Pennsyl-
         vania Museum Bulletin 5 (July 1907), 46-49. illus
         (6 b&w).

G215.   ________. "Artistic Tableware." Keramic Studio 3
         September 1901), 105-106.

G216.   ________. "The Beginning of a National Ceramic Art in
         America." Clay-Worker 21 (June 1894), 653-654.
         illus (4 b&w).

G217.   ________. "Ceramic Embellishment in Architecture
         [Mosaic Tile Co.]" Clay-Worker 27 (June 1897),
         511-515. illus (8 b&w).

G218.   ________. "Ceramic Relics of the Confederate States
         of America." Art Interchange 35 (September 1895),
         64. illus (2 b&w).

G219.   ________. "Cincinnati Women Art Workers." Art Inter-
         change 36 (February 1896), 29-31. illus (4 b&w).

G220.   BARBER, Edwin AtLee. "The Earliest Decorative Pottery
        of the White Settlers in America [Pennsylvania
        German]" House & Garden 2 (June 1902), 233-239.
        illus (8 b&w, 1 col).

G221.   ________. "Early Ceramic Printing and Modeling in the
        United States. I--The Origin of Some Well-Known
        Game Jugs. II--The Beginning of Ceramic Printing in
        America." Old China 3 (December 1903), 50-55. illus
        (4 b&w).

G222.   ________. "Early Potting Moulds in America." Clay-
        Worker 22 (July 1894), 20-22. illus (3 b&w).

G223.   ________. "Hints on China Painting, First Paper."
        Clay-Worker 22 (October 1894), 331-333. illus
        (4 b&w).

G224.   ________. "Hints on China Painting, Second Paper."
        Clay-Worker 22 (November 1894), 428-431. illus
        (11 b&w).

G225.   ________. "Hints on China Painting, Third Paper."
        Clay-Worker 22 (December 1894), 531-532. illus
        (9 b&w).

G226.   ________. "Historical Designs on Tucker Porcelain."
        Art Interchange 34 (April 1895), 106. illus (3 b&w).

G227.   ________. "Historical Sketch of the Green Point Por-
        celain Works. I: Charles Cartlidge and William
        Ridgway." Clay-Worker 23 (June 1895), 688-691.
        illus (7 b&w).

G228.   ________. "Historical Sketch of the Green Point Por-
        celain Works. II: Establishment of Works and First
        Products." Clay-Worker 24 (July 1895), 23-25.
        illus (6 b&w).

G229.   ________. "Historical Sketch of the Green Point Por-
        celain Works. III: Decorators and Their Work."
        Clay-Worker 24 (August 1895), 120-123. illus
        (8 b&w).

G230.   ________. "Historical Sketch of the Green Point Por-
        celain Works. IV: Josiah Jones, Modeler." Clay-
        Worker 24 (September 1895), 226-229. illus (5 b&w).

G231.   ________. "Historical Sketch of the Green Point Por-
        celain Works. V: Portrait Modeling." Clay-Worker
        24 (October 1895), 330-333. illus (4 b&w).
          G227-231 also published as A9.

G232.   BARBER, Edwin AtLee. "Historical Sketch of the
        Phoenixville (Pa.) Pottery." Clay-Worker 28
        (August 1897), 96-101. illus (11 b&w).

G233.   ________. "Historical Sketch of the Phoenixville
        (Pa.) Pottery. Second Paper." Clay-Worker 28
        (October 1897), 266-268. illus (6 b&w).

G234.   ________. "Inscribed Pottery of the Pennsylvania
        Germans." New England Magazine n.s. 12 (March 1895),
        34-39. illus (4 b&w).

G235.   ________. "Interesting Work of a Noted China Painter.
        --'Monitor' China.--'Murrhines' [E. Lycett]" Clay-
        Worker 28 (November 1897), 362-364. illus (3 b&w).

G236.   ________. "The Modern Dinner Plate." Clay-Worker 22
        (September 1894), 238. illus (1 b&w).

G237.   ________. "New Style in Mosaic Tiling [Mosaic Tile
        Co.]" Clay-Worker 25 (January 1896), 15-17. illus
        (3 b&w).

G238.   ________. "An Old American China-Manufactory [Tucker]"
        Lippincott's Monthly Magazine 50 (December 1892),
        766-774. illus (10 b&w).

G239.   ________. "Old American Cream Ware and Yellow Ware."
        Old China 2 (June 1903), 171-174. illus (3 b&w).

G240.   ________. "Old German Tulip Ware in Pennsylvania."
        Clay-Worker 32 (August 1899), 106-108. illus
        (5 b&w).

G241.   ________. "Old German Tulip Ware in Pennsylvania
        [Part 2]" Clay-Worker 32 (September 1899), 188-189.
        illus (5 b&w).

G242.   ________. "An Old Pennsylvania Potter--David Spinner."
        Keramic Studio 2 (October 1900), 135-136. illus
        (2 b&w).

G243.   ________. "An Old Pennsylvania Potter--David Spinner,
        Continued." Keramic Studio 2 (November 1900), 159-
        160. illus (4 b&w).

G244.   ________. "Old Tulip Ware of the Pennsylvania
        Germans." Old China 1 (May 1902), 112-114. illus
        (3 b&w).

G245.   ________. "The Oldest American China [Bonnin &
        Morris]" Clay-Worker 24 (November 1895), 439-440.
        illus (1 b&w).

G246.   BARBER, Edwin AtLee. "The Oldest Known Example of
         American Transfer Printing [Jersey City Pottery]"
         Pennsylvania Museum Bulletin 3 (October 1, 1905),
         61-62. illus (2 b&w).

G247.   __________. "The Pioneer of China Painting in America
         [E. Lycett]" American Pottery Gazette 2 (December 5,
         1905), 19, 21-23. illus (5 b&w).

G248.   __________. "The Pioneer of China Painting in America
         [Part 2]" American Pottery Gazette 2 (January 5,
         1906), 17-18, 22-24. illus (8 b&w).

G249.   __________. "The Pioneer of China Painting in America
         [E. Lycett]" Ceramic Monthly 2 (September 1895),
         5-20. illus (24 b&w).

G250.   __________. "The Pioneer of China Painting in America
         [E. Lycett]" New England Magazine n.s. 13 (Septem-
         ber 1895), 33-48. illus (24 b&w).

G251.   __________. "A Rare Piece of American Pottery [R. B.
         Beech]" Old China 1 (August 1902), 174-176. illus
         (1 b&w).

G252.   __________. "Recent Advances in the Pottery Industry."
         Popular Science Monthly 40 (January 1892), 289-322.
         illus (52 b&w).

G253.   __________. "Recent Progress in Tile Modeling." Clay-
         Worker 23 (January 1895), 20-22. illus (2 b&w).

G254.   __________. "Recent Progress of American Potters
         [Chelsea Keramic Art Works; Columbian Art Pottery;
         Knowles, Taylor & Knowles]" Clay-Worker 23 (May
         1895), 580-581. illus (3 b&w).

G255.   __________. "The Rise of the Pottery Industry." Popular
         Science Monthly 40 (December 1891), 145-170. illus
         (17 b&w).

G256.   __________. "Some American 'Tobys'." Art Interchange
         33 (September 1894), 61-62. illus (3 b&w).

G257.   __________. "Some Curious Old Water Coolers Made in
         America." Clay-Worker 34 (November 1900), 352-353.
         illus (3 b&w).

G258.   __________. "Some Recent German-American Stoneware [C.
         Wingender]" Clay-Worker 25 (February 1896), 125-127.
         illus (6 b&w).

G259.   __________. "Some Recently Discovered American Porce-
         lains [Smith, Fife & Co.; Kurlbaum & Schwartz]"
         Old China 3 (November 1903), 22-24. illus (3 b&w).

G260.   BARBER, Edwin AtLee. "Tile Modeling in America."
         Clay-Worker 22 (August 1894), 134-136. illus
         (5 b&w).

G261.   ________. "Transfer Printing in America." Clay-Worker
         23 (February 1895), 123-125. illus (6 b&w).

G262.   ________. "The Tucker and Hemphill Hard Porcelain
         Manufactory, Philadelphia, 1825-1838." Pennsylvania
         Museum Bulletin 4 (April 1906), 17-23. illus
         (5 b&w).

G263.   ________. "A Typical American Pottery [Rookwood]"
         Art Interchange 34 (January 1895), 2-5. illus
         (10 b&w).

G264.   ________. "Utility of Burned Clay. First Paper:
         Earthenware Tomb Stones." Clay-Worker 21 (March
         1894), 339. illus (1 b&w).

G265.   ________. "Utility of Burned Clay. Second Paper:
         Early American Roofing Tiles." Clay-Worker 21
         (April 1894), 442-444. illus (4 b&w).

G266.   BARBER, Daniel M., and HAMELL, George R. "The Red-
         ware Pottery Factory of Alvin Wilcox--At Mid-19th
         Century." Historical Archaeology 5 (1971), 18-37.
         illus (18 b&w); bibliog.

G267.   BARKER, Eva M. "Potters of Pottersville [Mass.]"
         American Collector 15 (February 1946), 8-9. illus
         (4 b&w).

G268.   BARKER, M. E. "Clay Resources in South Carolina."
         Ceramist 8 (July 1926), 249-252, 254-265. illus
         (7 b&w).

G269.   ________. "Clay Resources of South Carolina: Descrip-
         tion of Individual Mines, Aiken Area." Ceramist 8
         (September 1926), 378-391. illus (22 b&w); bibliog.

G270.   DELETED.

G271.   BARNARD, Charles. "The Rocks Tried by Fire."
         Chautauquan 7 (June 1887), 519-521.

G272.   BARRET, Richard Carter. "Little-Known Ceramic Treas-
         ures from the Bennington Potteries." Antiques 98
         (July 1970), 100-109. illus (23 b&w).

G273.   ________. "The Porcelain and Pottery of Bennington,
         Part I." Antiques 69 (June 1956), 528-531. illus
         (8 b&w).

G274.   BARRET, Richard Carter. "The Porcelain and Pottery of
        Bennington, Part II." Antiques 70 (August 1956),
        142-145. illus (11 b&w).

G275.   __________. "Treasure Hunting [Bennington]" National
        Antiques Review 3 (January 1972), 16-19. illus
        (10 b&w).

G276.   BAYER, Ralph E. "Van Briggle Pottery." Western Col-
        lector 7 (March 1969), 110-115. illus (7 b&w).

G277.   BECK, William O. "Earle Jay Babcock and North Dakota
        Lignite." North Dakota History 41 (Winter 1974),
        4-15. illus (14 b&w); bibliog.

G278.   BEECHER, M. F. "A Note on the Requirements of Sagger
        Bodies." American Ceramic Society Bulletin 2
        (August 1923), 251-253.

G279.   BEHRENDT, L. "Mining of Indiana Clay for Terra Cotta."
        American Ceramic Society Bulletin 3 (September 1924),
        331-332.

G280.   BELKNAP, Henry W. "Another American Pottery: Grueby
        Ware With Its Single Low Toned Colors and Convention-
        al Design Is Among the Best Art Pottery." Pottery &
        Glass 1 (November 1908), 12-14. illus (4 b&w).

G281.   BENNER, Russell L. "A Unique Pottery [S. Veyon]"
        Ceramic Age 10 (August 1927), 69. illus (2 b&w).

G282.   BENNETT, B. "Ceramics at the Eleventh Annual Exhibi-
        tion of Art Crafts of the Chicago Art Institute."
        Keramic Studio 14 (January 1913), 195-200. illus
        (10 b&w).

G283.   BENNETT, Charles A. "Newcomb School of Art: Its
        Relation to Art Industries." Vocational Education 3
        (November 1913), 119-125. illus (6 b&w).

G284.   BENNETT, J. A. W. "John Goodwin: Story of Pioneer
        Potter." American Ceramic Society Bulletin 23 (Octo-
        ber 1944), 393.

G285.   BENSEL, L. M. "Biloxi Pottery." Art Interchange 46
        (January 1901), 8-9. illus (1 b&w).

G286.   BERGENGREN, Ralph. "A Master Potter of Thoughts [H. C.
        Mercer]" House Beautiful 37 (May 1915), 179-181,
        xxviii. illus (6 b&w).

G287.   BERGMANS, Carl. "Modern Ceramics of Art." American
        Ceramic Society Bulletin 5 (February 1926), 161-163.

G288.   BERRILL, Jacquelyn. "The Past in My Hands [Etruscan
        Majolica]" Hobbies 52 (January 1948), 64, 68.
        illus (5 b&w).

G289.   BEYER, Nancy. "Work of the Duquesne Ceramic Club."
        Keramic Studio 11 (August 1909), 87-93. illus
        (20 b&w).

G290.   BIDDLE, Dorothy. "Birds in China Painting." Arts &
        Decoration 1 (December 1910), 81. illus (4 b&w).

G291.   ________. "Ceramic Work of Matilda Middleton." Arts &
        Decoration 1 (June 1911), 351-352. illus (5 b&w).

G292.   BILLINGER, R. D. "Early Pennsylvania Pottery."
        Journal of Chemical Education 17 (September 1940),
        407-413. illus (9 b&w); bibliog.

G293.   BINNS, Charles F. "An Adventure in Discontent."
        Brick and Clay Record 62 (June 12, 1923), 1051-1054.

G294.   ________. "American Clays for Porcelains and Kiln
        Use." Keramic Studio 5 (March 1904), 250-251.

G295.   ________. "American Grès." Keramic Studio 6 (October
        1904), 123-124.

G296.   ________. "The Art of Manufacture and the Manufacture
        of Art." American Ceramic Society Bulletin 2 (April
        1923), 55-59.

G297.   ________. "The Art of the Fire [A. A. Robineau]"
        Clay-Worker 44 (October 1905), 356-357. illus
        (2 b&w).
        Originally published in Craftsman. See G298.

G298.   ________. "The Art of the Fire [A. A. Robineau]"
        Craftsman 8 (May 1905), 205-210. illus (6 b&w).

G299.   ________. "Building in Clay." Craftsman 4 (July
        1903), 303-305.

G300.   ________. "The Burning of Clay Wares." Claycrafter 1
        (May 1910), 23-25.

G301.   ________. "Ceramic Schools and their Work." Glass
        and Pottery World 16 (August 20, 1908), 40-41.

G302.   ________. "Clay and the Craftsman." Pottery & Glass
        8 (March 1912), 13-14. illus (2 b&w).

G303.   ________. "Clay in the Potter's Hand." Craftsman
        (May 1904), 162-168.

G304.   ________. "Clay in the Studio." Keramic Studio 4
        (November 1902), 142-143.

G305.   BINNS, Charles F. "Clay in the Studio, Second Paper."
         Keramic Studio 4 (December 1902), 170-171.

G306.   ________. "Clay in the Studio, Third Paper." Keramic
         Studio 4 (January 1903), 189-190.

G307.   ________. "Clay in the Studio, Fourth Paper." Keramic
         Studio 4 (February 1903), 220-221.

G308.   ________. "Clay in the Studio, Fifth Paper." Keramic
         Studio 4 (March 1903), 244-245. illus (5 b&w).

G309.   ________. "Clay in the Studio, Sixth Paper." Keramic
         Studio 4 (April 1903), 269-271. illus (5 b&w).

G310.   ________. "Clay in the Studio, Seventh Paper."
         Keramic Studio 5 (May 1903), 13, 16. illus (8 b&w).

G311.   ________. "Clay in the Studio, Eighth Paper."
         Keramic Studio 5 (June 1903), 46-47. illus (10 b&w).

G312.   ________. "Clay in the Studio, Ninth Paper." Keramic
         Studio 5 (July 1903), 53-54. illus (1 b&w).

G313.   ________. "Clay in the Studio, Tenth Paper." Keramic
         Studio 5 (August 1903), 77-78. illus (1 b&w).

G314.   ________. "Clay in the Studio, Tenth Paper [Part 2]"
         Keramic Studio 5 (October 1903), 131-132.

G315.   ________. "Clay in the Studio, Eleventh Paper."
         Keramic Studio 5 (November 1903), 160-161.

G316.   ________. "Clay in the Studio, Twelfth Paper."
         Keramic Studio 5 (January 1904), 202-204.

G317.   ________. "Color Scheme." Ceramic Monthly 6 (Novem-
         ber 1897), 171-172.

G318.   ________. "A Contrast." Ceramic Monthly 4 (November
         1896), 57-58.

G319.   ________. "The Craft of the Potter." Craftsman 9
         (March 1906), 854-856.

G320.   ________. "The Cycle of Ceramics." Clay-Worker 43
         (January 1905), 58-59.

G321.   ________. "Design in Printed Table Ware." American
         Ceramic Society Bulletin 7 (April 1928), 75-77.

G322.   ________. "Diaper Work." Ceramic Monthly 5 (February
         1897), 3-4.

G323.   ________. "A Dictionary of Ceramic Terms." Pottery &
         Glass 12 (June 1914), 17-18.

G324.   BINNS, Charles F. "A Dictionary of Ceramic Terms
         [Part 2]" Pottery & Glass 13 (July 1914), 17-18.

G325.   ________ . "A Dictionary of Ceramic Terms [Part 3]"
         Pottery & Glass 13 (August 1914), 17-18.

G326.   ________ . "A Dictionary of Ceramic Terms [Part 4]"
         Pottery & Glass 13 (September 1914), 17-18.

G327.   ________ . "E Concrematione Confirmatio." American
         Ceramic Society Bulletin 4 (July 1925), 334-339.

G328.   ________ . "Education in Clay." Clay-Worker 40
         (August 1903), 140-143. illus (3 b&w).
           Originally published in Craftsman. See G329.

G329.   ________ . "Education in Clay." Craftsman 4 (June
         1903), 160-168. illus (4 b&w).

G330.   ________ . "The Elements of Beauty in Ceramics."
         Ceramic Monthly 3 (May 1896), 79-82.

G331.   ________ . "The Elements of Beauty in Ceramics [Part
         2]" Ceramic Monthly 3 (June 1896), 103-106.

G332.   ________ . "The Extent of the Ceramic Industry."
         Ceramist 6 (June 1925), 525-534.

G333.   ________ . "The Fire." Ceramic Monthly 4 (January
         1897), 93-94. illus (1 b&w).

G334.   ________ . "Foliage." Ceramic Monthly 6 (January
         1898), 9-11.

G335.   ________ . "The Future of Ceramics in America."
         Craftsman 7 (February 1905), 563-566.

G336.   ________ . "The History of the Ceramic Arts [Address,
         Dedication of Ceramics Building, U. of Illinois]"
         Clay-Worker 66 (December 1916), 532-535. illus
         (1 b&w).

G337.   ________ . "The History of the Ceramic Arts, Continu-
         ation." Clay-Worker 67 (January 1917), 40-41.

G338.   ________ . "How Roofing Tiles are Made." Clay-Worker
         41 (January 1904), 44-46. illus (6 b&w).

G339.   ________ . "An Idea from the Chinese." Ceramic Monthly
         4 (September 1896), 25-27.

G340.   ________ . "In Defence of Fire." Craftsman 3 (March
         1903), 369-372.

G341.   BINNS, Charles F. "Industrial Fellowships in Ceramic
         Research: A Plea for the Establishment of a Fund
         for the Advancement of Individual Research Work in
         the Pottery and Glass Fields." Pottery & Glass 8
         (April 1912), 11-12.

G342.   ________. "Inspiration in Material." Clay-Worker 44
         (September 1905), 234-235.

G343.   ________. "Jewel Work." Ceramic Monthly 4 (December
         1896), 73-74.

G344.   ________. "Light and Shade." Ceramic Monthly 6
         (August 1897), 104-105.

G345.   ________. "Matt Glazes at Low Temperatures." Keramic
         Studio 6 (November 1904), 148, 150.

G346.   ________. "The Mission of the School: The Reason for
         Existence of Schools of Ceramics . . ." Pottery &
         Glass 7 (August 1911), 11-12.

G347.   ________. "The Nature of Value." Clay-Worker 39
         (May 1903), 542.

G348.   ________. "The Need for Novelty." Ceramic Monthly 6
         (October 1897), 143-144.

G349.   ________. "New York School of Clay-Working and
         Ceramics." American Ceramic Society Journal 6
         (January 1923), 90-93. illus (2 b&w).

G350.   ________. "The New York Society of Keramic Arts:
         Annual Exhibition." Ceramic Monthly 6 (December
         1897), 207-211. illus (2 b&w).

G351.   ________. "The Possibilities of Clay." International
         Studio 32 (August 1907), lxvi-lxxii. illus (7 b&w).

G352.   ________. "The Possibilities of Porcelain." Clay-
         Worker 45 (January 1906), 90-92. illus (3 b&w).

G353.   ________. "The Potter and His Wheel." Clay-Worker 53
         (January 1910), 66-68. illus (7 b&w).

G354.   ________. "Pottery in America." American Magazine of
         Art 7 (February 1916), 131-138. illus (8 b&w).

G355.   ________. "Pottery-Making--American and English."
         Clay-Worker 57 (April 1912), 616-617. illus (1 b&w).

G356.   ________. "Pottery Making as a Field for Personal
         Enterprise." American Magazine of Art 10 (November
         1918), 18-23.

G357.   BINNS, Charles F.   "The Progress of the Ceramic Art."
         American Ceramic Society Transactions 4 (1902),
         19-24.

G358.   __________ .   "Search and Research." American Ceramic
         Society Bulletin 8 (June 1929), 129-134.

G359.   __________ .   "Some Ideals in Pottery Manufacture."
         Clay-Worker 57 (January 1912), 42-43. illus (1 b&w).
         Originally published in Pottery & Glass. See G360.

G360.   __________ .   "Some Ideals in Pottery Manufacture."
         Pottery & Glass 7 (December 1911), 35-37. illus
         (2 b&w).

G361.   __________ .   "Spitting Out." Pottery & Glass 2 (April
         1909), 194-195.

G362.   __________ .   "Tea and Coffee Cups." Keramic Studio 7
         (May 1905), 4. illus (2 b&w).

G363.   __________ .   "Tiles, Decorative and Structural."
         Architectural Record 22 (July 1907), 72-78. illus
         (5 b&w).

G364.   __________ .   "Tiles of All Kinds for All Places." Clay-
         Worker 55 (March 1911), 464-465. illus (1 b&w).

G365.   __________ .   "Tin-Enameled Ware." Keramic Studio 7
         (April 1906), 268, 270. illus (1 b&w).

G366.   __________ .   "Tin-Enameled Ware, Second Paper." Keramic
         Studio 8 (May 1906), 12-13.

G367.   __________ .   "Tin-Enameled Ware, Third Paper." Keramic
         Studio 8 (June 1906), 36, 39, 40. illus (1 b&w).

G368.   __________ .   "Tin-Enameled Ware, Fourth Paper." Keramic
         Studio 8 (August 1906), 86.

G369.   __________ .   "The Use of a 'Study'." Ceramic Monthly 6
         (November 1897), 161-163. illus (1 b&w).

G370.   __________ .   "The Use of American Wares by American
         Ceramic Decorators." Keramic Studio 1 (August 1899),
         81-82.

G371.   __________ .   "The Value of an Idea." Ceramic Monthly 4
         (October 1896), 41-42.

G372.   __________ .   "Winter in the Country [Weeds as Design
         Sources]" Ceramic Monthly 7 (February 1898), 10-14.
         illus (2 b&w).

G373.   BINNS, Norah W. "Twenty-Five Years of the American
         Ceramic Society." American Ceramic Society Journal
         6 (January 1923), 10-23.

G374.   BIVINS, John, Jr. "Old Salem Pottery: 1770 vs. 1970."
         Salem College Bulletin 12 (March 1970), 15-16, 40.

G375.   BLASBERG, Robert W. "American Art Porcelain--The Work
         of Adelaide Alsop-Robineau." Spinning Wheel 27
         (April 1971), 40-42. illus (8 b&w).

G376.   ________. "Arequipa Pottery." Western Collector 6
         (October 1968), 7-10. illus (3 b&w).

G377.   ________. "Grueby Art Pottery." Antiques 100 (August
         1971), 246-249. illus (9 b&w).

G378.   ________. "Moravian Tiles--Fairy Tales in Colored
         Clay." Spinning Wheel 27 (June 1971), 16-19. illus
         (8 b&w).

G379.   ________. "Newcomb Pottery." Antiques 94 (July 1968),
         73-77. illus (9 b&w).

G380.   ________. "Paul Revere Pottery." Western Collector 7
         (January 1969), 13-16. illus (3 b&w).

G381.   ________. "Reform Art for a Reform Era." Craft
         Horizons 30 (October 1970), 24-27. illus (8 b&w).

G382.   ________. "The Sadie Irvine Letters: A Further Note
         on the Production of Newcomb Pottery." Antiques 100
         (August 1971), 250-251. illus (2 b&w).

G383.   ________. "Twenty Years of Fulper." Spinning Wheel
         29 (October 1973), 14-18. illus (13 b&w).

G384.   BLASBERG, Robert W., and VOLPE, Todd M. "American Art
         Pottery." Nineteenth Century 5 (Summer 1979), 62-69.
         illus (4 b&w, 9 col).

G385.   BLATCHLEY, W. S. "The Clays and Clay Industries of
         North-Western Indiana." Clay-Worker 30 (July 1898),
         13-14.

G386.   ________. "The Clays and Clay Industries of North-
         Western Indiana [Part 2]" Clay-Worker 30 (August
         1898), 108-109. illus (1 b&w).

G387.   BLEININGER, A. V. "The Development of the Ceramic
         Industries in the United States." Franklin Institute
         Journal 183 (February 1917), 127-167. illus (22 b&w).

G388.   ________. "The Effect of Preliminary Heat Treatment
         Upon Clays." American Pottery Gazette 9 (April 1909),
         39, 41, 43.

G389. BLEININGER, A. V. "The Limits of Our Knowledge of
       Ceramic Materials." American Ceramic Society
       Bulletin 5 (May 1926), 225-229.

G390. ______. "Report of Research Committee, U.S. Potters
       Association." American Ceramic Society Bulletin 1
       (September 1922), 209-210.

G391. ______. "Saggers in the Earthenware Industry and
       Discussion." American Ceramic Society Bulletin 4
       (October 1925), 531-540.

G392. ______. "Sagger Symposium." American Ceramic
       Society Bulletin 5 (December 1926), 445-459. illus
       (1 b&w).

G393. ______. "Thirty Years of Progress in Ceramic Educa-
       tion." American Ceramic Society Bulletin 4 (March
       1925), 96-99.

G394. BLEININGER, A. V., and McDANEL, W. W. "The Use of
       American Raw Materials in the Manufacture of White
       Ware Pottery." American Ceramic Society Journal 3
       (February 1920), 134-148.

G395. BOGNAR, E. J. "The Roof Tiles of Zoar." Antiques 25
       (February 1934), 52-54. illus (10 b&w).

G396. BOICOURT, Jane. "For the Casual Collector: Design in
       American Pottery." Antiques 59 (February 1951),
       134-135. illus (8 b&w).

G397. BOND, Harold Lewis. "Hugh C. Robertson and His
       Pottery." American Collector 10 (August 1941), 12.
       illus (3 b&w).

G398. BOPP, H. F. "Art and Science in the Development of
       Rookwood Pottery." American Ceramic Society Bulletin
       15 (December 1936), 443-445. illus (1 b&w); bibliog.

G399. BOTT, Leo P., Jr. "The Niloak Pottery, Benton, Ark."
       Ceramic Age 11 (June 1928), 219-220.

G400. BOULDEN, Jane Long. "Rookwood." Art Interchange 46
       (June 1901), 129-131. illus (6 b&w).

G401. BOWDOIN, W. G. "Grueby Pottery." Art Interchange 45
       (December 1900), 136-137. illus (4 b&w).

G402. ______. "Some American Pottery Forms." Art Inter-
       change 50 (April 1903), 87-90. illus (11 b&w).

G403. BOWLES, Elsie Shannon. "Pioneer Pottery: Crockery
       Containers Dear to Housewives of the Past." House
       Beautiful 60 (December 1926), 732, 754, 756, 758.
       illus (4 b&w).

G404.   BOYERS, C. J. "The Story of a Mug." Lehigh County
         Historical Society Proceedings 25 (April 1964),
         221-225. illus (1 b&w).

G405.   BRACE, Ernest. "Carl Walters." Creative Art 10
         (June 1932), 431-436. illus (5 b&w).

G406.   BRADFORD, Emma F. "A Search for Local Pottery [North
         Orange, Mass.]" Early American Industries Associa-
         tion Chronicle 1 (November 1936), 1-2. illus
         (1 b&w).

G407.   BRANDENBURG, Marie. "Tragedy in the Ceramic Arts."
         Pottery & Glass 2 (May 1909), 239-243. illus
         (7 b&w).

G408.   BRANIN, M. Lelyn. "The Dodge Pottery in Portland,
         Maine." Old-Time New England 59 (January-March
         1969), 75-85. illus (3 b&w).

G409.   ________. "The Early Stoneware Potteries in Gardiner-
         Farmingdale, Maine." National Antiques Review 4
         (January 1973), 24-26. illus (6 b&w); bibliog.

G410.   ________. "The Lamson & Swasey Pottery in Portland,
         Maine." Old-Time New England 61 (January-March
         1971), 66-74. illus (3 b&w).

G411.   ________. "The Orcutt & Crafts Pottery in Portland
         Maine." Old-Time New England 60 (January-March
         1970), 94-103. illus (4 b&w); bibliog.

G412.   ________. "The Providence and Bay View Potteries in
         South Amboy, New Jersey." Spinning Wheel 31 (June
         1975), 13-17. illus (10 b&w).

G413.   ________. "The Saffords: Skilled Earthenware Potters
         of Monmouth, Maine." Spinning Wheel 29 (January-
         February 1973), 14-16. illus (5 b&w).

G414.   ________. "The Winslow Pottery in Portland, Maine."
         Old-Time New England 61 (April-June 1971), 95-104.
         illus (2 b&w).

G415.   BRANNER, George C. "The Commercial Clays of Arkansas."
         Ceramist 7 (January 1926), 250-253. illus (2 b&w).

G416.   ________. "Expansion in Arkansas Clay Industry, 1926
         and 1927." Ceramic Age 10 (July 1927), 22.

G417.   BREESE, Jessie Martin. "Jugtown, N. C." Country Life
         42 (October 1922), 64-65. illus (4 b&w).

G418.   BREININGER, Lester. "The Stahl Family of Potters."
         Antique Collecting 2 (February 1979), 21-25. illus
         (6 b&w, 6 col).

G419. BREWER, Harriet E. "American Belleek." New Jersey
       Historical Society Proceedings 52 (April 1934),
       96-108.

G420. BRICK AND CLAY RECORD. "The Panama-Pacific Clay
       Products Home." Vol. 45 (November 17, 1914),
       982-983. illus (3 b&w).

G421. BRICKBUILDER. "The Interesting Tile Work of 'Dream-
       wold'." Vol. 11 (October 1902), 205-209. illus
       (14 b&w).

G422. ________. "Terra Cotta Block Walls for Dwellings."
       Vol. 16 (March 1907), 50. illus (1 b&w).

G423. BRIDGES, Daisy Wade. "Burlon B. Craig." Ceramic
       Circle of Charlotte Journal of Studies 4 (1980),
       39-47. illus (18 b&w).
          Prefatory to C23.

G424. BRODBECK, John. "Cowan Pottery." Spinning Wheel 29
       (March 1973), 24-27. illus (11 b&w).

G425. BROWN, E. H. "Kaolin in Texas." Ceramist 8 (April
       1926), 34-37. illus (1 b&w).

G426. BROWN, George H. "The Ceramic Department at Rutgers
       College and the State University of New Jersey."
       American Ceramic Society Journal 6 (January 1923),
       93-97. illus (3 b&w).

G427. BROWN, Nell. "I, Too, Collect Majolica." Hobbies 44
       (March 1939), 72-73. illus (1 b&w).

G428. BRUSH AND PENCIL. "Newcomb Pottery." Vol. 6 (April
       1900), 15-17. illus (5 b&w).

G429. ________. "Pointers on American Pottery." Vol. 19
       (March 1907), 116-121. illus (5 b&w).

G430. BUCHER, Robert C. "Steep Roofs and Red Tiles."
       Pennsylvania Folklife 12 (Summer 1961), 18-25, 55.
       illus (15 b&w).

G431. BUCKS COUNTY HISTORICAL SOCIETY COLLECTIONS. "Memorial
       Services for Henry Chapman Mercer, Sc.D., LL.D."
       Vol. 6 (1932), 296-321. illus (1 b&w).
          See also A47.

G432. BUEHLER, H. A. "Ball Clays of Butler County, Missouri."
       Ceramic Age 9 (February 1927), 50-51. illus (4 b&w).

G433. ________. "Missouri Clays." Ceramist 7 (January 1926),
       261-266. illus (3 b&w).

G434.   BURBAGE, Beverly S. "The Remarkable Pottery of Charles
        Decker and His Sons." Tennessee Conservationist 37
        (November 1971), 6-8. illus (11 b&w).

G435.   BURBANK, Leonard F. "Lyndeboro Pottery." Antiques 13
        (February 1928), 124-126. illus (5 b&w).

G436.   BURRISON, John A. "Alkaline-Glazed Stoneware: A Deep-
        South Pottery Tradition." Southern Folklore Quar-
        terly 39 (December 1975), 377-403. illus (10 b&w);
        bibliog.

G437.   ________. "Clay Clans: Georgia's Pottery Dynasties
        [Ferguson family; Hewell family]" Family Heritage 2
        (June 1979), 70-77.

G438.   ________. "The Story of Southern Folk Pottery Has Yet
        to Be Written." Antique Monthly 2 (August 1978),
        16B, 18-19B. illus (3 b&w).
           Excerpted from G436.

G439.   BURSLEM, Alexander Young. "Development of the U.S.
        Pottery Industry." Bulletin of the Pan American
        Union 55 (August 1922), 139-160. illus (20 b&w).

G440.   BURT, Stanley G. "The Rookwood Pottery Company."
        American Ceramic Society Journal 6 (January 1923),
        232-234.

G441.   BURTON. "Notable Examples of Artistic Work in the Con-
        struction of Buildings with Brick and Terra Cotta
        [Long Island Cold Storage Warehouse, Brooklyn, N.Y.]"
        Clay-Worker 45 (April 1906), 601-602. illus (1 b&w).

G442.   BURTON, William. "Oriental Influence on 20th Century
        Pottery." American Pottery Gazette 1 (April 5, 1905)
        35-36.

G443.   BUSBEE. Jacques. "Jugtown Pottery." Ceramic Age 14
        (October 1929), 127-130. illus (7 b&w).

G444.   BUSBEE, Juliana Royster. "Jugtown Pottery--A New Way
        for Old Jugs. " American Ceramic Society Bulletin
        16 (October 1937), 415-418. illus (9 b&w).

G445.   ________. "New Ways for Old Jugs--Art in Jugtown
        Pottery." E.S.C. Quarterly 5 (Spring-Summer 1947),
        60-62. illus (3 b&w).

G446.   BUSKEY, Leo Albert. "John Harrison and His Bennington
        Parian Ware." Antiques Journal 9 (November 1954),
        7, 38. illus (1 b&w).

G447.   ________. "The Story of Lenox Pottery." Antiques
        Journal 10 (April 1955), 9-11, 22. illus (5 b&w).

G448.   BUTLER, Lorine Letcher. "Bennington Pottery." _Mentor_
        15 (September 1927), 54-55. illus (5 b&w).

G449.   BUTTERWORTH, Elsie Walker. "Tucker China." _Spinning_
        Wheel 5 (June 1949), 6, 16. illus (2 b&w).

G450.   BUXTON, Bessie W. "The Making of a Flower Pot [Paige
        Pottery.]" _Antiques_ 28 (August 1935), 62-63. illus
        (5 b&w).

G451.   BUXTON, Virginia Hillway. "The Other Roseville
        [Cornelian Ware]" _Spinning Wheel_ 31 (April 1975),
        28-30. illus (9 b&w).

G452.   ________. "Roseville." _Antiques Journal_ 28 (November
        1973), 10-12, 46. illus (11 b&w).

G453.   CABLE, Margaret Kelly. "The Development of Ceramic
        Work at the University of North Dakota." _American_
        Ceramic Society Journal 5 (March 1922), 140-145.
        illus (6 b&w).

G454.   ________. "Gloss Glazes and Indian Designs on North
        Dakota Pottery." _American Ceramic Society Journal_
        7 (June 1924), 489-493. illus (2 b&w).

G455.   ________. "Pots and Pines, a Decorative Problem for
        the Artist Potter." _American Ceramic Society Journal_
        8 (June 1925), 393-395. illus (1 b&w).

G456.   CALHOUN, F. H. H. "The High Grade Clays of South
        Carolina." _Ceramist_ 7 (January 1926), 224-231.
        illus (5 b&w).

G457.   CALKINS, S. Homer. "The Usefulness and Economy of
        Tile [U.S. Encaustic Tile Co.]" _Clay-Worker_ 38
        (August 1902), 123-125, illus (3 b&w).

G458.   CAMEHL, Ada Walker. "Mehwaldt, A Pioneer American
        Potter." _Antiques_ 2 (September 1922), 113-116.
        illus (7 b&w).

G459.   CAMP, Helen B. "A Craftsman of the Old School [O.
        Bachelder]" _International Studio_ 78 (October 1923),
        54-56. illus (5 b&w).

G460.   CAMPANA, Dominic M. "Art in Pottery." _Fine Arts_
        Journal 14 (December 1903), 503.

G461.   CANFIELD, Ruth. "Pottery Recently Shown in New York."
        Design 31 (July-August 1929), 47, 52. illus (2 b&w).

G462.   CARDWELL, Kenneth C. "Clayworking in Miniature
        [Wheatley Pottery]" _Clay-Worker_ 68 (November 1917),
        432. illus (2 b&w).

G463.   CARR, James. "Reminiscences of an Old Potter: A
         Series of Letters by James Carr." Crockery and Glass
         Journal 53 (March 21, 1901), 27-28. illus (1 b&w).

G464.   ________. "Reminiscences of an Old Potter: A Series
         of Letters by James Carr, No. II." Crockery and
         Glass Journal 53 (March 28, 1901), 23-24.

G465.   ________. "Reminiscences of an Old Potter: A Series
         of Letters by James Carr, No. III." Crockery and
         Glass Journal 53 (April 4, 1901), 17-18.

G466.   ________. "Reminiscences of an Old Potter: A Series
         of Letters by James Carr, No. IV." Crockery and
         Glass Journal 53 (April 11, 1901), 15-16.

G467.   ________. "Reminiscences of an Old Potter: A Series
         of Letters by James Carr, No. V." Crockery and Glass
         Journal 53 (April 18, 1901), 23-24.

G468.   ________. "Reminiscences of an Old Potter: A Series
         of Letters by James Carr, No. VI." Crockery and
         Glass Journal 53 (April 25, 1901), 15-16.

G469.   CARRICK, Alice Van Leer. "The Bennington Pottery Owned
         by Mark La Fountain." House Beautiful 67 (January
         1930), 62-63, 99-102. illus (12 b&w).

G470.   ________. "The Orchard Potteries." Country Life 49
         (January 1926), 48-50. illus (10 b&w).

G471.   CARROON, Robert G. "The Pottery Industry in 19th
         Century Milwaukee." Milwaukee County Historical
         Society Historical Messenger 26 (March 1970), 13-23.
         illus (2 b&w); bibliog.

G472.   CARRUTHERS, John L. "Economics of the Car Tunnel Kiln."
         American Ceramic Society Bulletin 4 (December 1925),
         668-676.

G473.   ________. "Notes on Shivering of Terra Cotta." Clay-
         Worker 78 (September 1922), 235-237. Bibliog.

G474.   CARSON, Courtenay. "Seven Generations of Pottery
         Makers [Bethune, S.C.]" Sandlapper 1 (August 1968),
         18-20. illus (5 b&w).

G475.   CASE, Richard G. "Onondago Pottery." York State
         Tradition 28 (Spring 1974), 32-36, 38. illus (7 b&w).

G476.   CERAMIC AGE. "Better Design Chief Topic of Art
         Sessions." Vol. 15 (March 1930), 152-153.

G477.   ________. "Betterment in Ceramic Design." Vol. 11
         (February 1928), 42-45. illus (1 b&w).

G478.   CERAMIC AGE. "Binns Memorial Exhibition of Art Ware at
        Metropolitan Museum of Art." Vol. 25 (June 1935),
        195. illus (3 b&w).

G479.   _________ . "Ceramic Department at Iowa State Keeps an
        Open House." Vol. 13 (June 1929), 217-220. illus
        (9 b&w).

G480.   _________ . "Ceramic Education Shows Fast Development."
        Vol. 16 (August 1930), 89-95.

G481.   _________ . "Ceramic Products of Trenton Prominent at
        American Fair [Atlantic City]" Vol. 16 (August 1930),
        76-78. illus (10 b&w).

G482.   _________ . "Charles A. Bloomfield [Obituary]" Vol. 14
        (October 1929), 157-158.

G483.   _________ . "Developments of the Clay Products Industry
        in 1926." Vol. 10 (September 1927), 113-116.

G484.   _________ . "Early Pottery at Trenton." Vol. 10 (July
        1927), 35-36.

G485.   _________ . "Exhibition of Pottery Closes School Year
        [Newark (N.J.) School of Fine and Industrial Arts]"
        Vol. 14 (July 1929), 16-17. illus (1 b&w).

G486.   _________ . "First Exposition of New Jersey Ceramic
        Wares Shows Merit and Diversity." Vol. 13 (April
        1929), 130-139. illus (18 b&w).

G487.   _________ . "Former Weller Artware Reflects Public
        Taste a Half Century Ago." Vol. 54 (August 1949),
        87-88. illus (3 b&w).

G488.   _________ . "General Edward Orton [Jr.], Inspiration and
        Guide, Passes." Vol. 19 (March 1932), 133. illus
        (1 b&w).

G489.   _________ . "Glazed Clay in a Modern Dairy [Mueller
        Tiles at Walker-Gordon Laboratories]" Vol. 18
        (August 1931), 75-77. illus (7 b&w).

G490.   _________ . "Guy Cowan." Vol. 17 (March 1931), 150.
        illus (3 b&w).

G491.   _________ . "The Holland Tunnel and Its Ceramic Tiling."
        Vol. 10 (July 1927), 3-10. illus (19 b&w).

G492.   _________ . "Honoring Washington in Ceramics [Scammell
        China Co.; Robertson Art Tile Co.]" Vol. 19 (April
        1932), 157. illus (2 b&w).

G493.   _________ . "In the Early Days of Terra Cotta." Vol.
        10 (November 1927), 184.

G494.   CERAMIC AGE. "International Exhibition of Contempor-
         ary Ceramic Art [Metropolitan Museum, NYC]" Vol. 12
         (October 1928), 127-135. illus (19 b&w).

G495.   ________. "Labor Report of W. E. Wells at United
         States Potters Association Convention." Vol. 13
         (March 1929), 114-116. illus (1 b&w).

G496.   ________. "Large Attendence at the Annual Meeting of
         the New Jersey Clay Workers Association." Vol. 9
         (January 1927), 22-27. illus (4 b&w).

G497.   ________. "Lenox Lighting Fixtures a Feature of New
         Naval Architecture." Vol. 17 (February 1931), 98.

G498.   ________. "A Master Potter of the Old School [O. L.
         Bachelder]" Vol. 25 (May 1935), 169. illus (1 b&w).

G499.   ________. "A Modern Wall Tile Plant at Keyport, N.J."
         Vol. 11 (January 1928), 11-14. illus (15 b&w).

G500.   ________. "New Jersey Ceramic Exhibit at Montclair
         Art Museum." Vol. 29 (April 1937), 121. illus
         (1 b&w).

G501.   ________. "New Jersey Clay Workers Association Annual
         Meeting." Vol. 15 (January 1930), 35-42. illus
         (5 b&w).

G502.   ________. "New Jersey Clay Workers' Association Holds
         Annual Meeting." Vol. 10 (December 1927), 204-208.
         illus (2 b&w).

G503.   ________. "New Jersey Clay Workers Association Meets
         at Asbury Park." Vol. 13 (June 1929), 207-209.
         illus (2 b&w).

G504.   ________. "New Jersey Clay Workers Association Meets
         at New Brunswick.'' Vol. 13 (January 1929), 21-27.
         illus (5 b&w).

G505.   ________. "New Jersey--The Pioneer Pottery State."
         Vol. 49 (May 1947), 237-241. illus (12 b&w).

G506.   ________. "Notable Industrial Progress Exhibit at
         Trenton." Vol. 14 (November 1929), 170-174. illus
         (16 b&w).

G507.   ________. "An Outstanding Monument in Terra Cotta:
         'Christ on the Rockies' [Denver Terra Cotta Co.]"
         Vol. 28 (October 1936), 118-119. illus (5 b&w).

G508.   ________. "A Pioneering American Pottery--Approaching
         the Century Mark [E. Bennett]" Vol. 25 (March 1935),
         89. illus (1 b&w).

G509. CERAMIC AGE. "Plant Cooperation and Simplified Prac-
       tice Discussed at Summer Meeting of New Jersey Clay
       Workers Association." Vol. 11 (June 1928), 205-211.
       illus (3 b&w).

G510. __________. "The Potter and His Wheel--Still Thriving
       at Old Lyme, Connecticut [H. W. Austin]" Vol. 29
       (February 1937), 44-45. illus (3 b&w).

G511. __________. "Pottery at New Brunswick Produces Bathroom
       Fixtures [Willette Corp.]" Vol. 11 (March 1928), 91-
       92. illus (4 b&w).

G512. __________. "The Pottery Industry in Iowa." Vol. 29
       (January 1937), 13.

G513. __________. "Prize Awards for Ceramic Art at Cleveland
       Museum of Art." Vol. 12 (September 1928), 96-97.
       illus (2 b&w).

G514. __________. "Production of Ceramic Products." Vol. 13
       (June 1929), 244-247.

G515. __________. "Putting Flower Pots into Modern Production
       [Florence Pottery Co.]" Vol. 16 (October 1930),
       209-210. illus (5 b&w).

G516. __________. "Rookwood Pottery." Vol. 39 (April 1942),
       116-118. illus (4 b&w).

G517. __________. "Ross C. Purdy Dies Suddenly." Vol. 53
       (January 1949), 30-31. illus (1 b&w).

G518. __________. "Sanitary Ware in the United States: Brief
       Historical Review of the Development of an Industry."
       Vol. 56 (September 1950), 14-16. illus (8 b&w).

G519. __________. "Sanitary Ware in the United States: Brief
       Historical Review of the Development of an Industry
       (Second Installment)" Vol. 56 (October 1950), 30-31.
       illus (7 b&w).

G520. __________. "Terra Cotta Mantel at Rutgers University
       [Federal Terra Cotta Co.]" Vol. 10 (December 1929),
       229. illus (1 b&w).

G521. __________. "Thirty-three Years of Ceramic Progress
       [N.Y. State School, Alfred]" Vol. 22 (July 1933),
       14-15. illus (7 b&w).

G522. __________. "Tioughnioga Pottery: Early Manufacture of
       Stoneware in New York." Vol. 26 (October 1935),
       145, 164-165. illus (1 b&w).

G523. __________. A Touch of Old Mexico in a California Roof-
       ing Tile Plant [International Clay Products, Inc.]"
       Vol. 14 (August 1929), 50-52. illus (7 b&w).

G524.   CERAMIC AGE.   "Trenton--The Pottery City."   Vol. 11
        (January 1928), 7-8.   illus (3 b&w).

G525.   ________.   "Trenton Tile to be Used in New Antiquarian
        Home at Los Angeles [Mueller Mosaic Co.]"   Vol. 9
        (June 1927), 200.

G526.   ________.   "Tunnel Kiln Installation and Tile Setters
        at Plant of Architectural Tile Company."   Vol. 13
        (May 1929), 189-190.

G527.   ________.   "Tunnel Kilns Operate Continuously for More
        Than Three Years [T. Maddock Sons Co.]"   Vol. 12
        (August 1928), 56-58.   illus (4 b&w).

G528.   ________.   "University of North Dakota."   Vol. 33
        (June 1939), 183-184.   illus (3 b&w).

G529.   ________.   "Upward Trend in Ceramic Design."   Vol. 13
        (February 1929), 49-51.   illus (1 b&w).

G530.   ________.   "The Use of Terra Cotta in the Philadelphia
        Museum of Art."   Vol. 9 (May 1927), 139-141.   illus
        (6 b&w).

G531.   ________.   "W. E. Wells."   Vol. 17 (May 1931), 261.
        illus (1 b&w).

G532.   ________.   "Where Color Development in Tile is Foremost
        [Architectural Tile Co.]"   Vol. 13 (April 1929),
        123-127.   illus (11 b&w).

G533.   ________.   "A Year's Service Shows No Deterioration of
        Ceramic Tile in Hudson River Tunnels [Holland Tunnel]"
        Vol. 13 (February 1929), 75-76.   illus (2 b&w).

G534.   CERAMIC MONTHLY.   "The Companion of Rookwood [H. B.
        Wright]"   Vol. 8 (January 1899), [2].   illus (1 b&w).

G535.   ________.   "Frederick L. Grunewald."   Vol. 2 (August
        1895), 16-17.   illus (1 b&w).

G536.   ________.   "George R. Busher."   Vol. 2 (September
        1895), 28.   illus (2 b&w).

G537.   ________.   "A Great Keramic Exhibition [Western Decor-
        ating Works]"   Vol. 4 (October 1896), 43-46.   illus
        (1 b&w).

G538.   ________.   "Have You No Rookwood?"   Vol. 2 (January
        1896), 4-5.   illus (1 b&w).

G539.   ________.   "Helen M. Topping."   Vol. 4 (September
        1896), 27-28.   illus (1 b&w).

G540.   ________.   "Mr. Binns in New York."   Vol. 6 (October
        1897), 139-140.   illus (1 b&w).

G541.   CERAMIC MONTHLY.   "Mrs. Frackelton."   Vol. 2 (August
         1895), 20-21.

G542.   __________.   "Nina E. Lumbard."   Vol. 4 (September 1896),
         36-37.   illus (1 b&w).

G543.   __________.   "Suit Against Rookwood Pottery [L. Fry]"
         Vol. 8 (January 1899), [9].

G544.   __________.   "Won Our Gold Medal [H. B. Wright]"   Vol. 4
         (October 1896), 48-49.   illus (1 b&w).

G545.   CERAMICS MONTHLY.   "Early American Ceramics at Yale."
         Vol. 24 (May 1976), 21-23.   illus (6 b&w).

G546.   __________.   "Fulper Art Pottery."   Vol. 28 (May 1980),
         47-49.   illus (5 b&w, 2 col).

G547.   __________.   "Pre-Industrial Salt-Glazed Ware."   Vol. 28
         (February 1980), 44-47.   illus (7 b&w).

G548.   __________.   "The Saturday Evening Girls."   Vol. 23
         (December 1975), 32-33.   illus (4 b&w).

G549.   CERAMIST.   "Annual Meeting of the New Jersey Clay
         Workers Association."   Vol. 7 (February 1926), 302-
         318.   illus (6 b&w).

G550.   __________.   "Annual Meeting of the New Jersey Clay
         Workers Association and Eastern Section of the
         American Ceramic Society."   Vol. 2 (Winter 1922-
         1923), 249-269.   illus (4 b&w).

G551.   __________.   "The Ceramic Age."   Vol. 8 (December 1926),
         553-554.

G552.   __________.   "The Ceramist as a Monthly."   Vol. 3
         (Winter 1924), 222-226.   illus (5 b&w).

G553.   __________.   "Dedication of the New Ceramics Building,
         Rutgers College, New Brunswick."   Vol. 2 (June 1922),
         78-115.   illus (26 b&w).

G554.   __________.   "Degree Conferred on the Dean of the Ceramic
         Profession [E. Orton, Jr.]"   Vol. 2 (June 1922),
         146-147.   illus (1 b&w).

G555.   __________.   "New Ceramics Building, Rutgers College,
         State University of New Jersey."   Vol. 2 (June 1922),
         116-135.   illus (13 b&w).

G556.   __________.   "New China Clay Plant in North Carolina:
         Pollard Clay Co."   Vol. 8 (November 1926), 500-503.
         illus (4 b&w).

G557.   CERAMIST. "New Jersey Clay Workers Association Holds
         Annual Meeting." Vol. 5 (December 1924), 151-169.
         illus (7 b&w).

G558.   ________. "New Jersey Clay Workers Association Meets
         at Trenton." Vol. 3 (Summer 1923), 123-132. illus
         (1 b&w).

G559.   ________. "New Jersey Clay Workers Hold Summer Con-
         vention." Vol. 8 (July 1926), 227-248. illus
         (3 b&w).

G560.   ________. "New Jersey Clay Workers Meet at Trenton."
         Vol. 4 (July 1924), 243-250. illus (1 b&w).

G561.   ________. "Ohio Ceramic Industries Association Holds
         Meeting." Vol. 8 (November 1926), 517-523.

G562.   ________. "Pioneer Potter Honored [James Bennett]"
         Vol. 8 (September 1926), 414-415.

G563.   ________. "Portrait of Charles A. Bloomfield in the
         Ceramics Building, Rutgers College." Vol. 3
         (Spring 1923), 56-61. illus (1 b&w).

G564.   ________. "The Potteries of the Knowles China Co. [E.
         M. Knowles]" Vol. 2 (Fall 1922), 242-243. illus
         (1 b&w).

G565.   ________. "Pottery Industries to be Represented at the
         Paris Exposition." Vol. 6 (April 1925), 409-410.

G566.   ________. "Summer Meeting of the New Jersey Clay
         Workers Association at Trenton." Vol. 6 (June 1925),
         516-524. illus (1 b&w).

G567.   ________. "Technical Education in Clay Working."
         Vol. 8 (May 1926), 107-111.

G568.   ________. "United States Potters Association Holds
         Golden Jubilee Meeting." Vol. 5 (December 1924),
         170-176.

G569.   CHACE, Paul G. "'Many Worthy Young Men': Nathan
         Clark's Potters in New York State." _Spinning Wheel_
         27 (November 1971), 16-18. illus (8 b&w).

G570.   ________. "'Many Worthy Young Men': Nathan Clark's
         Potters in New York State, Part 2." _Spinning Wheel_
         27 (December 1971), 58-59. illus (4 b&w).

G571.   ________. "'Many Worthy Young Men': Nathan Clark's
         Potters in New York State, Part 3." _Spinning Wheel_
         28 (January-February 1972), 44-45. illus (1 b&w).

G572.   CHADWICK, J. H. "Chryso-Ceramics." _Art Interchange_ 32
         (April 1894), 109-110.

G573.   CHADWICK, J. H. "Women as Ceramic Workers, Second
        Paper." Art Interchange 31 (December 1893), 163.

G574.   CHAMBERLAIN, Georgia S. "The Story of a Sunbonnet
        Babies' Mug." Hobbies 59 (July 1954), 80-81.
        illus (2 b&w).

G575.   CHAMBERLAIN, Jacqueline. "American Stoneware."
        Western Collector 4 (May 1966), 8-10. illus (9 b&w).

G576.   CHANDLER, Reginald. "The Methods of Early American
        Potters." Antiques 5 (April 1924), 174-178. illus
        (30 b&w).

G577.   CHAPPELL, Edward A. "Morgan Jones and Dennis White:
        Country Potters in Seventeenth-Century Virginia."
        Virginia Cavalcade 2[5] (Spring 1975), 148-155.
        illus (9 b&w, 1 col).

G578.   CHARD, Louise C. "A Sculptor as Potter." Craftsman 3
        (January 1903), 244-246. illus (4 b&w).

G579.   CHERRY, Kathryn E. "Four Winds Summer School Work."
        Keramic Studio 15 (March 1914), 194-199. illus
        (14 b&w).

G580.   CHINA, GLASS AND POTTERY REVIEW. "The Crockery City
        [East Liverpool]" Vol. 14 (June 20, 1904), 9-11.
        illus (3 b&w).

G581.   CHIOLINO, Barbara B. "Folk Art on Utilitarian Stone-
        ware." Spinning Wheel 24 (April 1968), 16-18.
        illus (9 b&w).

G582.   CINCINNATI HISTORICAL SOCIETY BULLETIN. "Overture of
        Cincinnati Ceramics." Vol. 25 (January 1967), 70-84.
        illus (3 b&w).
        From a handwritten ms. of unknown authorship, 1890.

G583.   CLARK, Garth. "From the Potter's Wheel: An American
        Art." Antiques World 1 (September 1979), 82-87.
        illus (6 b&w, 4 col.).

G584.   __________. "George Ohr: Clay Prophet." Craft Horizons
        38 (October 1978), 44-49, 65. illus (4 b&w, 12 col).

G585.   CLARK, Ivan Stowe. "An Isolated Industry: Pottery of
        North Carolina." Journal of Geography 25 (September
        1926), 222-228. illus (4 b&w).

G586.   CLARK, William H. "Pottery and Potters." Americana
        (American Historical Society) 32 (July 1938), 425-
        460.

G587.   CLARKE, D. S. "Tucker Porcelain." Antiques Journal 9
        (May 1954), 11. illus (3 b&w).

G588.   CLARKE, J. F. Gates. "Rebekah at the Well Teapots,
        Part One." Spinning Wheel 34 (July-August 1978),
        17-20. (6 b&w).

G589.   ________. "Rebekah at the Well Teapots, Part Two."
        Spinning Wheel 34 (September 1978), 11-15. illus
        (13 b&w).

G590.   ________. "Rebekah at the Well Teapots, Part Three."
        Spinning Wheel 34 (November 1978), 27-30. illus.
        (17 b&w).

G591.   ________. "Rebekah at the Well Teapots, Part Four."
        Spinning Wheel 34 (December 1978), 35-37. illus
        (9 b&w).

G592.   CLAY RECORD. "Ceramics Their Fad [Chicago Ceramic Art
        Association Preparing Exhibit for World's Fair]"
        Vol. 1 (August 12, 1892), 84-85.

G593.   ________. "The Clays of Kentucky." Vol. 16 (May 14,
        1900), 17.

G594.   ________. "Fire Clay Roofing Tile." Vol. 1 (November
        12, 1892), 338-339. illus (1 b&w).

G595.   ________. "Florida Kaolin." Vol. 3 (October 27, 1893),
        16-17.

G596.   ________. "The Pottery Industry [Wilson Bill]" Vol.
        3 (December 14, 1893), 14-15.

G597.   ________. "The Standard Dry Kiln Company." Vol. 2
        (January 24, 1893), 12-14. illus (6 b&w).

G598.   CLAY-WORKER. "Advantages of Enameled Brick and Terra
        Cotta for Exterior Walls [Schlesinger & Mayer,
        Chicago]" Vol. 40 (August 1903), 125-127. illus
        (3 b&w).

G599.   ________. "The Alpine Peak in Burned Clay: New
        Wrigley Building . . . Chicago." Vol. 77 (April
        1922), 437-439. illus (3 b&w).

G600.   ________. "American Ceramic Society Annual." Vol. 83
        (March 1925), 349-352.

G601.   ________. "American Ceramic Society Annual." Vol. 85
        (February 1926), 129-134. illus (7 b&w).

G602.   ________. "American Ceramic Society's Annual Meeting."
        Vol. 81 (February 1924), 147-148.

G603.   ________. "American Ceramic Society Elects Ross C.
        Purdy Full Time Secretary with Headquarters at
        Columbus, Ohio." Vol. 76 (July 1921), 35. illus
        (1 b&w).

G604.   CLAY-WORKER. "The American Ceramic Society: Fifth
        Annual Summer Meeting at Zanesville, O. . . . " Vol. 40
        (September 1903), 255-257.

G605.   ________ . "American Ceramic Society Holds Splendid
        Convention." Vol. 71 (February 1919), 125-130.
        illus (9 b&w).

G606.   ________ . "American Ceramic Society Holds Very Success-
        ful Convention." Vol. 91 (February 1929), 131-139.
        illus (12 b&w).

G607.   ________ . "American Ceramic Society Meeting." Vol. 75
        (March 12, 1921), 258-261, 286, 288, 290, 292. illus
        (8 b&w).

G608.   ________ . "American Ceramic Society Meeting." Vol. 77
        (February 28, 1922), 268.

G609.   ________ . "American Ceramic Society Meeting [Visits
        Crooksville China Co.; Ludowici-Celadon]" Vol. 70
        (July 1918), 21-31. illus (23 b&w).

G610.   ________ . "American Ceramic Society: Twenty-Second
        Annual Meeting at Philadelphia . . ." Vol. 73 (March
        12, 1920), 265-269.

G611.   ________ . "Ames Pottery [Iowa State]" Vol. 87 (Feb-
        ruary 1927), 219. illus (1 b&w).

G612.   ________ . "Annual Meeting of the National Brotherhood
        of Operative Potters." Vol. 36 (July 1901), 35-36.
        illus (1 b&w).

G613.   ________ . "Arbuckle & Son Tile Co." Vol. 47 (January
        1907), 78-79. illus (4 b&w).

G614.   ________ . "Art in Architecture: Beautifying Modern
        Buildings By the Use of Multicolored Terra Cotta and
        Art Tile [Indianapolis]" Vol. 85 (February 1926),
        111-112. illus (1 b&w).

G615.   ________ . "An Attractive Brick Structure for Panama-
        Pacific Exposition." Vol. 62 (November 1914), 528-
        529. illus (3 b&w).

G616.   ________ . "The Barnum Institute of Science and History,
        Bridgeport, Conn." Vol. 17 (February 1892), 231-232.
        illus (1 b&w).

G617.   ________ . "The Beauties of Terra Cotta and Faience as
        Shown by American Manufacturers at the World's Fair."
        Vol. 42 (October 1904), 341-342. illus (1 b&w).

G618.   ________ . "A Beautiful Terra Cotta Business Front
        [Mercantile Building, Indianapolis]" Vol. 83 (June
        1925), 612. illus (1 b&w).

G619.   CLAY-WORKER. "The Biggest Terra Cotta Job in the West
        [Conway Building, Chicago]" Vol. 60 (December 1913),
        625-628. illus (3 b&w).

G620.   ________ . "The Bradshaw China Co." Vol. 36 (October
        1901), 325. illus (1 b&w).

G621.   ________ . "Brazil, the Clay Center of Indiana." Vol.
        64 (August 1915), 141-146. illus (15 b&w).

G622.   ________ . "Brazil, the Clay Center of Indiana." Vol.
        64 (September 1915), 261-263. illus (7 b&w).

G623.   ________ . "Brazil, the Clay Center of Indiana." Vol.
        64 (October 1915), 392-393. illus (7 b&w).

G624.   ________ . "Brick and Art Tile in Architecture [Mueller
        Mosaic Co.]" Vol. 76 (July 1921), 21-24. illus
        (7 b&w).

G625.   ________ . "A Brick and Terra Cotta Office Building."
        Vol. 34 (December 1900), 431-432. illus (1 b&w).

G626.   ________ . "Brick and Tile Used to Brighten Ugly
        Cement Surfaces [San Jose State Normal School]"
        Vol. 54 (September 1910), 259-260. illus (2 b&w).

G627.   ________ . "Buffalo Pottery--Plant and Product Inspec-
        ted by those Attending the Mid-Summer Meeting of the
        American Ceramic Society." Vol. 72 (August 1919),
        125-130. illus (4 b&w).

G628.   ________ . "Burning Drain Tile in a Haigh Continuous
        Kiln [Lee Drain Tile Co.]" Vol. 54 (October 1910),
        392-394. illus (4 b&w).

G629.   ________ . "Ceramics Department of Iowa State College."
        Vol. 76 (October 1921), 358.

G630.   ________ . "Ceramics in Illinois [U. of Illinois]"
        Vol. 64 (October 1915), 381-387. illus (2 b&w).

G631.   ________ . "Chicago's Latest Architectural Achievement
        [Illinois Central Station]" Vol. 27 (April 1897),
        329-332. illus (4 b&w).

G632.   ________ . "Cincinnati's Greatest Art Enterprise
        [Rookwood]" Vol. 81 (January 1924), 24-26. illus
        (11 b&w).

G633.   ________ . "Clay Exhibits at the World's Fair." Vol.
        41 (January 1904), 90-92. illus (2 b&w).

G634.   ________ . "Clay Industries at Kushequa [Pa.]" Vol.
        58 (November 1912), 513-515. illus (9 b&w).

G635.   CLAY-WORKER. "Clay Milk Cooler [by D. Brown]" Vol.
         73 (May 1920), 611. illus (1 b&w).

G636.   ___________. "Clay Products in Armory Building [Indian-
         apolis]" Vol. 88 (August 1927), 101-103. illus
         (3 b&w).

G637.   ___________. "Clay Products in 1918." Vol. 72 (August
         1919), 138-140.

G638.   ___________. "Clay Products in 1920." Vol. 76 (August
         1921), 129-130.

G639.   ___________. "Clay Products Statistics [1926]" Vol. 88
         (September 1927), 181-183. illus (1 b&w).

G640.   ___________. "Clay Testing." Vol. 41 (January 1904),
         72-73. illus (8 b&w).

G641.   ___________. "Clay Tiles, the Roofing Material of the
         Future." Vol. 46 (October 1906), 365-367. illus
         (5 b&w).

G642.   ___________. "Clay Works of Zanesville, Ohio [South
         Zanesville Sewer Pipe and Brick Co.]" Vol. 36
         (December 1901), 532-533. illus (2 b&w).

G643.   ___________. "The Clayworkers' Art [Stephens, Cooper &
         Co.]" Vol. 32 (August 1899), 95-98. illus (4 b&w).

G644.   ___________. "Clayworkers' Tree of Knowledge." Vol. 73
         (February 1920), 150-151. illus (1 b&w).

G645.   ___________. "The Conkling-Armstrong Terra Cotta Company."
         Vol. 23 (February 1895), 137-138.

G646.   ___________. "The Convention City [Columbus]" Vol. 31
         (January 1899), 9-15. illus (15 b&w).

G647.   ___________. "Convention of the United States Potters'
         Association Held at Washington, D.C." Vol. 46
         (December 1906), 606. illus (1 b&w).

G648.   ___________. "The Corning Brick and Terra Cotta Company."
         Vol. 48 (September 1907), 256-258. illus (2 b&w).

G649.   ___________. "Craftsmanship and Tile Work [Mueller]"
         Vol. 85 (March 1926), 199-200.

G650.   ___________. "Cream Colored Brick--How They are Made in
         Milwaukee." Vol. 28 (September 1897), 183-185.
         illus (6 b&w).

G651.   ___________. "Crematory Vases." Vol. 39 (January 1903),
         44-45. illus (3 b&w).

G652.   CLAY-WORKER. "Death of Charles A. Bloomfield." Vol.
         92 (October 1929), 289. illus (1 b&w).

G653.   ________. "Death of Fritz Wagner." Vol. 73 (February
         1920), 161. illus (1 b&w).

G654.   ________. "The Death of William W. Taylor, President
         of the Rookwood Pottery Co., Cincinnati." Vol. 60
         (December 1913), 641-642. illus (1 b&w).

G655.   ________. "Dedication of the Ceramic Building, Univer-
         sity of Illinois." Vol. 66 (December 1916), 526-530.
         illus (3 b&w).
         Includes G1107.

G656.   ________. "Displays Made by Clay Product Manufacturers
         at St. Louis World's Fair." Vol. 55 (March 1911),
         486-487. illus (5 b&w).

G657.   ________. "Early American Clay Work and Clayworkers
         [Carlyle & McFadden]" Vol. 23 (April 1895), 489-490.
         illus (1 b&w).

G658.   ________. "English Ceramists Visit America." Vol. 91
         (May 1929), 477-479, 520. illus (5 b&w).

G659.   ________. "Examples of Beautiful Decorative and Sym-
         bolic Designs in the Entrance of the Y.M.C.A. and
         Other Public Buildings in the Ohio Metropolis
         Designed by Albert E. Skeel [Cleveland]" Vol. 73
         (April 1920), 473-475. illus (2 b&w).

G660.   ________. "An Exemplary Porcelain Insulator Factory
         [Westinghouse Electric]" Vol. 73 (February 1920),
         146-149. illus (4 b&w).

G661.   ________. "A Famous Brickmaker: Murrell Dobbins."
         Vol. 56 (December 1911), 624-625. illus (1 b&w).

G662.   ________. "Fine Examples of Architectural Terra Cotta."
         Vol. 76 (November 1921), 457. illus (1 b&w).

G663.   ________. "A Fine Roofing Tile Factory [Ludowici-
         Celadon, New Lexington]" Vol. 49 (January 1908),
         36-38. illus (9 b&w).

G664.   ________. "The Fire at the J. W. McCoy Pottery." Vol.
         39 (June 1903), 657. illus (2 b&w).

G665.   ________. "The Fire at the Roseville Pottery, Zanes-
         ville, Ohio." Vol. 39 (April 1903), 439. illus
         (1 b&w).

G666.   ________. "Fire at the Winkle Terra Cotta Plant, St.
         Louis." Vol. 43 (June 1905), 780. illus (3 b&w).

G667.   CLAY-WORKER. "Gates and His Pottery [American Terra
        Cotta and Ceramic Co.]" Vol. 57 (February 1912),
        245-251. illus (6 b&w, 1 col).

G668.   _________. "Gates Turns Editor [of Common Clay]" Vol.
        74 (September 1920), 232-233. illus (2 b&w).

G669.   _________. "General Edward Orton, Jr.--Our Tribute
        [Memorial]" Vol. 97 (February 1932), 74-75. illus
        (2 b&w).

G670.   _________. "General Orton Elected President [American
        Ceramic Society]" Vol. 93 (March 1930), 261-263.
        illus (2 b&w).

G671.   _________. "A Great Brick Structure Faced with Pavers
        [Home of the Friendless, Chicago]" Vol. 28 (Septem-
        ber 1897), 177-179. illus (3 b&w).

G672.   _________. "A Great Clayworking Establishment [Fords
        Porcelain Works]" Vol. 66 (October 1916), 341-343.
        illus (6 b&w).

G673.   _________. "The Great Question of Wages." Vol. 76
        (July 1921), 38-39.

G674.   _________. "A Great Sewer Pipe Manufactory [National]"
        Vol. 28 (December 1897), 438-439. illus (1 b&w).

G675.   _________. "Harrison Everett Ashley, Obituary." Vol.
        55 (February 1911), 345-346. illus (1 b&w).

G676.   _________. "High Tribute to Charles Fergus Binns."
        Vol. 83 (June 1925), 617-621. illus (3 b&w).

G677.   _________. "Hollow Tile Burned with Oil on Fine Plant
        at South River, N.J.: Used in World's Largest Sky-
        scraper [Empire State Building]" Vol. 94 (November
        1930), 299-305. illus (27 b&w).

G678.   _________. "Hollow Tile [Los Angeles Pressed Brick
        Co.]" Vol. 74 (December 1920), 497-501. illus
        (8 b&w).

G679.   _________. "Home of the New York School for Clay-
        workers." Vol. 36 (September 1901), 211. illus
        (1 b&w).

G680.   _________. "The Illinois Clayworkers Association's
        Annual Convention." Vol. 49 (January 1908), 72-75.
        illus (1 b&w).

G681.   _________. "Impetus Given to Clayworking in Northwest
        [U. of Washington]" Vol. 76 (November 1921), 454-
        455. illus (1 b&w).

G682.   CLAY-WORKER. "Important Changes at Illinois Ceramic
        School." Vol. 78 (July 1922), 44-45. illus (1 b&w).

G683.   ________. "An Improved Form of Hollow Building Block
        [Twin City Brick Co.]" Vol. 51 (June 1909), 817-819.

G684.   ________. "An Inspection Tour through Louisville's
        Clay Plants." Vol. 55 (January 1911), 44-51. illus
        (25 b&w).

G685.   ________. "Isaac W. Knowles of East Liverpool, O.,
        First White-Ware Potter in the West, Passes Away in
        California." Vol. 38 (August 1902), 140-141. illus
        (3 b&w).

G686.   ________. "James Taylor, a Pioneer Terra Cotta Manu-
        facturer and Writer [Obituary]" Vol. 31 (January
        1899), 15. illus (1 b&w).

G687.   ________. "Koch's Improved Interlocking Blocks."
        Vol. 53 (January 1910), 88-89. illus (3 b&w).

G688.   ________. "Lisbon's New Pottery: . . . Thomas China
        Co." Vol. 36 (November 1901), 423-424. illus
        (4 b&w).

G689.   ________. "The McAlpin Terra Cotta Grill." Vol. 67
        (February 1917), 141-143, 146-147.

G690.   ________. "Making High Potential Porcelain Insulators
        [New Lexington High Voltage Porcelain Co.]" Vol. 55
        (January 1911), 70-71. illus (4 b&w).

G691.   ________. "The Manufacture of Clay Pots: Pittsburgh
        Clay Pot Company's Plant." Vol. 53 (January 1910),
        42-44. illus (8 b&w).

G692.   ________. "The Manufacture of Dinner Ware [H. Laughlin
        China Co.]" Vol. 81 (April 1924), 451-466. illus
        (19 b&w).

G693.   ________. "The Manufacture of Sewer Pipe [Cannelton
        Sewer Pipe Co.]" Vol. 81 (April 1924), 472-476.
        illus (12 b&w).

G694.   ________. "The Manufacture of Sewer Pipe [Chicago
        Sewer Pipe Co.]" Vol. 53 (January 1910), 71-73.
        illus (5 b&w).

G695.   ________. "Manufacture of Spark Plugs." Vol. 74
        (October 1920), 324-327. illus (10 b&w).

G696.   ________. "The Maryland Terra Cotta Company." Vol.
        49 (January 1908), 64-66. illus (7 b&w).

G697.   CLAY-WORKER. "The Message of Brick [All-Clay House,
         Panama-Pacific Exh.]" Vol. 64 (July 1915), 42-43.
         illus (2 b&w).

G698.   ________. "Mid-Summer Meeting, American Ceramic
         Society." Vol. 66 (September 1916), 246-249. illus
         (5 b&w).

G699.   ________. "Mid-Summer Meeting of American Ceramic
         Society." Vol. 68 (July 1917), 46-48. illus (4 b&w).

G700.   ________. "Million-Dollar Pottery for Alliance, Ohio
         [Crescent China Co.]" Vol. 78 (July 1922), 43.

G701.   ________. "A Model Modern Structure [Chamber of Com-
         merce Building, Cleveland]" Vol. 32 (July 1899),
         11-16. illus (6 b&w).

G702.   ________. "A Modern Plant in the Badger State [White
         Water Brick and Tile Co.]" Vol. 67 (April 1917),
         486-487. illus (3 b&w).

G703.   ________. "The Modern Plant of the Louisville Pottery
         Company." Vol. 50 (July 1908), 22-24. illus (3 b&w).

G704.   ________. "Modern Uses of Colored Glazed Tile." Vol.
         64 (November 1915), 501-503.

G705.   ________. "A Monument in Brick [and Tile: McAlpin
         Hotel]" Vol. 60 (July 1913), 21-24. illus (4 b&w).

G706.   ________. "The New and the Old Bell Potteries." Vol.
         43 (June 1905), 770-771. illus (2 b&w).

G707.   ________. "New Brick and Tile Company at Cleveland,
         Ohio [Target]" Vol. 78 (November 1922), 458.

G708.   ________. "New Ceramics Building Dedicated at Rutgers."
         Vol. 78 (July 1922), 21-25. illus (5 b&w).

G709.   ________. "A New Continuous Kiln [Grath]" Vol. 34
         (December 1900), 447. illus (1 b&w).

G710.   ________. "The New Home of the C. W. Raymond Company
         [Dayton]" Vol. 54 (December 1910), 640-642. illus
         (7 b&w).

G711.   ________. "New Jersey Clayworkers." Vol. 74 (July
         1920), 33-35. illus (1 b&w).

G712   ________. "New Jersey Clayworkers." Vol. 76 (July
         1921), 37. illus (1 b&w).

G713.   ________. "New Jersey Clayworkers Discuss Tariff and
         Cost Accounting at Well Attended Summer Meeting."
         Vol. 88 (July 1927), 25-27.

G714.   CLAY-WORKER. "New Jersey Clayworkers Meet." Vol. 71
         (January 1919), 32-36. illus (1 b&w).

G715.   ________ . "A New Life of Lincoln, A Most Wonderful
         Story Told in Terra Cotta [University of Illinois]"
         Vol. 57 (April 1912), 605-610. illus (10 b&w).

G716.   ________ . "New York School of Ceramics." Vol. 47
         (May 1907), 773-776. illus (5 b&w).

G717.   ________ . "New York Subways [City Hall Station, N.Y.]"
         Vol. 41 (June 1904), 705-706. illus (2 b&w).

G718.   ________ . "The Norse Room of the Fort Pitt Hotel
         [Rookwood]" Vol. 53 (January 1910), 57-60. illus
         (7 b&w, 1 col).

G719.   ________ . "The North American Manufacturing Company
         [Purchases Tract in Newell, W.Va.]" Vol. 38
         (December 1902), 531. illus (1 b&w).

G720.   ________ . "The North State Pottery." Vol. 87 (Janu-
         ary 10, 1927), 50-51. illus (5 b&w).

G721.   ________ . "The Northwestern Terra Cotta Company's New
         Fireproof Factory." Vol. 57 (February 1912), 254-257.
         illus (5 b&w).

G722.   ________ . "The Northwestern Terra Cotta Co.'s Products
         in Chicago." Vol. 59 (February 1913), 224-225.
         illus (3 b&w).

G723.   ________ . "A Notable Clay Product." Vol. 38 (July
         1902), 17. illus (1 b&w).

G724.   ________ . "A Noted Terra Cotta Manufacturer Dies [K.
         Mathiasen]" Vol. 74 (August 1920), 129. illus
         (1 b&w).

G725.   ________ . "The O. W. Ketchum Terra Cotta Company."
         Vol. 48 (October 1907), 366-367. illus (3 b&w).

G726.   ________ . "Obituary [A. J. Gladding]" Vol. 92
         (September 1929), 219.

G727.   ________ . "Of Interest to Drain Tile Manufacturers."
         Vol.78 (July 1922), 27-28. illus (1 b&w).

G728.   ________ . "On the Trail of a Tile Idea [Hollow Tile]"
         Vol. 76 (August 1921), 139-141. illus (6 b&w).

G729.   ________ . "A $1,000,000 Clay Products Factory [Clay
         Products Co., Brazil, Ind.]" Vol. 64 (December 1915),
         616-618. illus (4 b&w).

G730.   ________ . "One Woman's Success [M. Duschek]" Vol. 54
         (July 1910), 20-21.

G731.   CLAY-WORKER. "An Outdoors 'Way of the Cross' Built of
        Clay Products Near Allegany, N.Y." Vol. 86 (July
        1926), 19-21. illus (5 b&w).

G732.   ________. "Output and Value of Clay Products in the
        United States in 1911." Vol. 58 (September 1912),
        294-296.

G733.   ________. "The Passing of L. R. H. Minton." Vol. 97
        (January 1932), 43. illus (1 b&w).

G734.   ________. "Perfection in Architecture [Farmer's
        National Bank, Owatonna, Minn.]" Vol. 51 (January
        1909), 29-31. illus (5 b&w).

G735.   ________. " . . . Pertinent Facts Concerning America's
        Oldest Ceramic School [Ohio State U.]" Vol. 73
        (February 1920), 125-131. illus (16 b&w).

G736.   ________. "Peter McBean Passes." Vol. 78 (October
        1922), 350.

G737.   ________. "Plant of Streator Drain Tile Co." Vol. 68
        (November 1917), 424-426. illus (7 b&w).

G738.   ________. "Potteries of the U.S. Shut Down Owing to a
        Strike of Operatives." Vol. 78 (October 1922), 359.

G739.   ________. "Pottery Industry in 1920." Vol. 76 (July
        1921), 22-23.

G740.   ________. "Pottery Industry [Trenton]" Vol. 51
        (January 1909), 53. illus (1 b&w).

G741.   ________. "Prof. Edward Orton [Sr., Obituary]" Vol.
        32 (October 1899), 282.

G742.   ________. "A Prosperous Whiteware Manufactory:
        Crooksville China Company." Vol. 50 (August 1908),
        144-147. illus (7 b&w).

G743.   ________. "The Railway Exchange Building." Vol. 42
        (July 1904), 17-18. illus (2 b&w).

G744.   ________. "A Remarkable Stein." Vol. 37 (January
        1902), 25. illus (1 b&w).

G745.   ________. "Review Mid-Summer Meeting American
        Ceramic Society [Visit to Akron and Barberton, Ohio
        Companies]" Vol. 54 (September 1910), 272-279.
        illus (13 b&w).

G746.   ________. "Review of Thirty-Ninth Annual Convention
        of the Illinois Clay Manufacturers' Association."
        Vol. 67 (January 1917), 46-47.

G747.   CLAY-WORKER. "Rookwood, America's Foremost Art
         Pottery--A Trip through the Great Plant." Vol. 41
         (January 1904), 25-29. illus (11 b&w).

G748.   ________. "Salt Glazing." Vol. 41 (June 1904), 704.

G749.   ________. "Sanitary Ware and Its Production [Fords
         Porcelain Works]" Vol. 84 (November 1925), 475-480.
         illus (10 b&w).

G750.   ________. "Seger Cones." Vol. 28 (August 1897),
         111-114. illus (9 b&w).

G751.   ________. "A Side Trip to Bucyrus [American Clay
         Machinery Co.]" Vol. 49 (February 1908), 293.
         illus (1 b&w).

G752.   ________. "Some Remarkable Pottery [Van Briggle Urns]"
         Vol. 54 (July 1910), 28-29. illus (2 b&w).

G753.   ________. "Something about Illinois Potteries." Vol.
         41 (April 1904). 480-481. illus (1 b&w).

G754.   ________. "A Structure of Combined Beauty and Strength
         in Clay [Van Briggle Factory]" Vol. 49 (June 1908),
         792-797. illus (8 b&w).

G755.   ________. "Summer Meeting A.C.S." Vol. 76 (August
         1921), 132-138. illus (5 b&w).

G756.   ________. "Summittville Factory of the National Drain
         Tile Company." Vol. 50 (September 1908), 262-263.
         illus (5 b&w).

G757.   ________. "The Teco Inn [Hotel Radison]" Vol. 59
         (February 1913), 220-222. illus (2 b&w).

G758.   ________. "Terra Cotta--Ancient and Modern [Brick
         Terra Cotta & Supply Co., Corning]" Vol. 32
         (September 1899), 190-193. illus (4 b&w).

G759.   ________. "Terra Cotta at the World's Fair." Vol. 42
         (August 1904), 140-141. illus (2 b&w).

G760.   ________. "Terra Cotta Book Ends of Distinction
         [Indianapolis Terra Cotta Co.]" Vol. 88 (September
         1927), 205. illus (1 b&w).

G761.   ________. "Terra Cotta Company Takes Advantage of
         Industrial Exposition for Displaying Ware [Indiana-
         polis]" Vol. 82 (November 1924), 397. illus
         (1 b&w).

G762.   ________. "Terra Cotta in Architecture [American
         Terra Cotta and Ceramic Co.]" Vol. 49 (January
         1908), 30-35. illus (6 b&w).

G763. CLAY-WORKER. "Terra Cotta in Landscape Architecture."
       Vol. 43 (April 1905), 531. illus (1 b&w).

G764. ________ . "Terra Cotta: Its Wonderful Architectural
       Possibilities Being Demonstrated in Indianapolis."
       Vol. 75 (May 1921), 553-556. illus (4 b&w).

G765. ________ . "A Terra Cotta Playhouse [Woods Theater,
       Chicago]" Vol. 70 (August 1918), 123-125. illus
       (3 b&w).

G766. ________ . "Terra Cotta--The Material Grows in Useful-
       ness in the Builder's Hands." Vol. 28 (July 1897),
       34. illus (1 b&w).

G767. ________ . "Terra Cotta Work in Philadelphia." Vol. 25
       (January 1896), 40-42. illus (3 b&w).

G768. ________ . "A Thriving Pottery Town [Sebring, Ohio]"
       Vol. 38 (November 1902), 433-434. illus (2 b&w).

G769. ________ . "Tile Roofs [Unitarian Church, Ithaca, N.Y.]"
       Vol. 28 (July 1897), 25. illus (1 b&w).

G770. ________ . "Traction Engine Used for Hauling Drain Tile
       [Lombard Brick and Tile Co.]" Vol. 49 (January 1908),
       68-69. illus (4 b&w).

G771. ________ . "Trenton School of Industrial Arts." Vol.
       53 (January 1910), 51. illus (1 b&w).

G772. ________ . "A Trip Through the Works of the Camden
       Pottery Co. . . . " Vol. 43 (January 1905), 35-38.
       illus (11 b&w).

G773. ________ . "Twentieth Annual Convention of the Wiscon-
       sin Clay Manufacturers' Association . . ." Vol. 73
       (February 1920), 140-142. illus (3 b&w).

G774. ________ . "Twentieth Annual Meeting, American Ceramic
       Society." Vol. 69 (February 1918), 138-140. illus
       (6 b&w).

G775. ________ . "The Value of Our Clay Products." Vol. 41
       (June 1904), 702-704. illus (1 b&w).

G776. ________ . "Van Briggle Pottery." Vol. 43 (May 1905),
       645-647. illus (3 b&w).

G777. ________ . "A Visit to a Modern Terra Cotta Plant."
       Vol. 76 (September 1921), 233-234.

G778. ________ . "Volkmar Kilns [C. Volkmar & Son, Metuchen]"
       Vol. 55 (January 1911), 63-65. illus (5 b&w).

G779. CLAY-WORKER. "W. E. Wells Passed Away Suddenly."
       Vol. 96 (September 1931), 165.

G780. _________. "W. Paul Gates Succumbs." Vol. 74
       (September 1920), 289.

G781. _________. "The Wellsville Pottery." Vol. 35
       (April 1901), 373-375. illus (7 b&w).

G782. _________. "Who's Who Among Clayworkers: Side Lights
       on Herman Mueller . . .." Vol. 76 (September 1921),
       234-235. illus (1 b&w).

G783. _________. "With New Jersey Clayworkers." Vol. 84
       (July 1925), 19-22. illus (2 b&w).

G784. _________. "A Woman Potter [C. Poillon]" Vol. 38
       (August 1902), 129-130.

G785. _________. "The World's Largest Olla [Pacific Clay
       Products Co.]" Vol. 86 (July 1926), 37. illus
       (1 b&w).

G786. CLEMENS, Laura Lee. "Early American Cake Forms and
       Pudding Molds." American Collector 11 (July 1942),
       8-9, 20. illus (9 b&w).

G787. CLEMENT, Arthur W. "The American Ceramic Collection
       1944-1950." Brooklyn Museum Bulletin 12 (Spring
       1951), 10-15. illus (5 b&w).

G788. _________. "Ceramics in the South." Antiques 59
       (February 1951), 136-138. illus (5 b&w); bibliog.

G789. _________. "New Jersey Pottery Rarities in a Special
       Exhibition." American Collector 16 (May 1947),
       14-15. illus (6 b&w).

G790. CLENDENNIN, W. W. "Clays of Louisiana." Engineering
       and Mining Journal 66 (October 15, 1898), 456-457.

G791. CLEVELAND, Dana. "Strongest Pottery Made [Greenwood
       Pottery Co.]" Glass and Pottery World 16 (May 1908),
       33.

G792. COBURN, Frederic W. "George De Forest Brush and the
       Brush Guild." Art Education 7 (February 1901),
       257-260. illus (6 b&w).

G793. COCHRAN, Jean. "An Investigation of the 19th Century
       'Pot Shops' of Ohio's Hocking and Vinton Counties."
       American Ceramic Society Bulletin 21 (September
       1942), 188-189. illus (2 b&w).

G794.   COLEMAN, Duke. "Henry Chapman Mercer: The Moravian
         Pottery and Tile Works . . . A Legacy in Concrete
         and Tile." American Art Pottery, Number 32
         (January 1979), 1, 4-6. illus (7 b&w); bibliog.

G795.   COLEMAN, Oliver. "The Brush Guild Pottery." House
         Beautiful 14 (September 1903), 240-241. illus
         (6 b&w).

G796.   ________. "The Mercer Tiles and Other Matters."
         House Beautiful 14 (July 1903), 79-82. illus
         (7 b&w).

G797.   COLLINS, R. Lee and ROBERTS, Joseph K. "Resources and
         Ceramic Industries of Tennessee." Ceramist 7
         (January 1926), 232-242. illus (8 b&w).

G798.   COMSTOCK, Helen. "A Painter Who Became a Potter [H.
         V. Poor]" International Studio 79 (May 1924),
         135-138. illus (5 b&w).

G799.   CONE, Constance A. "Women in American Ceramics."
         Ceramic Age 53 (January 1949), 27-29.

G800.   CONNOISSEUR. "American Ceramic Types and Their
         European Background." Vol. 114 (December 1944),
         115-119. illus (10 b&w).

G801.   CONWAY, Bob. "The Golden Era of Mountain Potters:
         Three Men Whose Talents Highlight a Remarkable Tar
         Heel Tradition [O. L. Bachelder, W. B. Stephen,
         E. A. Hilton]" State 43 (October 1975), 8-11.
         illus (13 b&w).

G802.   COOK, Charles D. "Early Rhode Island Pottery."
         Antiques 19 (January 1931), 37-38. illus (3 b&w).

G803.   ________. "Early Rhode Island Pottery." Rhode Island
         Historical Society Collections 18 (July 1925), 81-83.

G804.   ________. "Unusual Bennington Pitchers." Antiques
         14 (December 1928), 544-546. illus (4 b&w).

G805.   COOK, Ma[r]y Elizabeth. "Coördination of Art, Science
         and Practice." American Ceramic Society Bulletin 5
         (March 1926), 179-182.

G806.   ________. "The Making of a Good Ceramist [Ohio State
         U.]" Sketch Book 3 (November 1903), 89-91.

G807.   ________. "Rose Valley." Sketch Book 6 (October
         1906), 76-84. illus (7 b&w).

G808.   ________. "Our American Potteries--Weller Ware."
         Sketch Book 5 (May 1906), 340-346. illus (9 b&w).

G809.   COOLIDGE, Edwin H. "The Pottery Business in Sterling,
         Mass." Old-Time New England 23 (July 1932), 17-21.
         illus (2 b&w).

G810.   COOPER, Nancy. "Chats on Antiques: Early American
         Pottery Whistles." House Beautiful 65 (January
         1929), 72-73. illus (1 b&w).

G811.   CORNELIUS, Charles Over. "Early American Ceramics."
         Country Life 40 (June 1921), 61-62. illus (21 b&w).

G812.   COUNTRY LIFE. "Portrait Tiles with Designs by Ella
         Ström-Grainger." Vol. 59 (March 1931), 50. illus
         (6 b&w).

G813.   COUNTS, Charles, and COUNTS, Rubynelle. "A Potter's
         Journey through the Southern Highlands." Ceramics
         Monthly 13 (June 1965), 19-26. illus (15 b&w).

G814.   COUSLEY, Sam A. "Presidential Clay Pipes." Antiques
         Journal 27 (November 1972), 24-26. illus (10 b&w).

G815.   COWAN, R. Guy. "In Defence of American China
         [Letter]" New Republic 31 (July 26, 1922), 256.
         Reply to G1671.

G816.   ______. "Some Problems in Ceramic Education."
         American Ceramic Society Transactions 12 (1910),
         207-225.

G817.   ______. "What is Art?" American Ceramic Society
         Bulletin 5 (November 1926), 416-421. illus (3 b&w).

G818.   COX, Lucille T.   "Centenary Anniversary of Harker
         Pottery Company." American Ceramic Society Bulletin
         20 (January 1941), 25-27. illus (1 b&w).

G819.   ______. "Isaac Watts Knowles." American Ceramic
         Society Bulletin 21 (August 1942), 152-157. illus
         (4 b&w).

G820.   ______. "The Story of John Goodwin, Pioneer Potter."
         American Ceramic Society Bulletin 21 (November 1942),
         241-247. illus (4 b&w); bibliog.

G821.   COX, Paul E. "American Ceramics for Interior Decora-
         ting: the Silver Lining in the Cloud." American
         Ceramic Society Bulletin 4 (September 1925), 418-
         423.

G822.   ______. "A Better Design for a Jug Mold Clinch."
         American Ceramic Society Journal 6 (December 1923),
         1230-1231. illus (5 b&w).

G823.   ______. "Ceramics Industries in Iowa." Ceramic Age
         13 (June 1929), 213-216.

G824.   COX, Paul E. "Ceramic Industries in Iowa." Clay-
        Worker 91 (May 1929), 496-498.

G825.   ________. "Department of Ceramic Engineering of Iowa
        State College." American Ceramic Society Journal 6
        (January 1923), 104-107. illus (1 b&w).

G826.   ________. "Discussion Concerning the Needs of the
        Tile Manufacturers for School Trained Designers."
        American Ceramic Society Journal 13 (May 1930),
        37-39.

G827.   ________. "Frederick Hurten Rhead." American Ceramic
        Society Bulletin 23 (February 1944), 64-65.

G828.   ________. "Potteries of the Gulf Coast: An Individu-
        alistic Ceramic Art District." Ceramic Age 25
        (April 1935), 116-119, 140. illus (11 b&w).

G829.   ________. "Potteries of the Gulf Coast: An Individu-
        alistic Art District (Second Installment)" Ceramic
        Age 25 (May 1935), 152-156. illus (12 b&w).

G830.   ________. "Potteries of the Gulf Coast (Concluding
        Installment)" Ceramic Age 25 (June 1935), 196-198.
        illus (9 b&w).

G831.   ________. "Technical Practice at the Newcomb Pottery."
        American Ceramic Society Journal 1 (August 1918),
        521-528.

G832.   ________. "Two Human Interest Stories of a Ceramic
        Pioneer [K. Langenbeck]" Ceramic Age 48 (November
        1946), 213-214.

G833.   ________. "Vitrified Terra Cotta." American Ceramic
        Society Bulletin 10 (August 1931), 265-267.

G834.   COYNE, John. "The Meaderses of Mossy Creek: A
        Dynasty of Folk Potters." Americana 8 (March-April
        1980), 40-45. illus (2 b&w, 12 col).

G835.   CRAFTSMAN. "The Frackelton 'Blue and Gray'." Vol. 3
        (January 1903), 255-256.

G836.   ________. "Glen Tor Pottery: One Woman's Contribu-
        tion to Practical Beauty." Vol. 28 (July 1915),
        424-426. illus (5 b&w).

G837.   ________. "Picture Fireplaces: Illustrating Stories
        for Sitting Room, Library, and Nursery." Vol. 31
        (December 1916), 247-253, 287-288. illus (8 b&w).

G838.   ________. "The Potters of America: Examples of the
        Best Craftsmen's Work for Interior Decorations:
        Number One." Vol. 27 (December 1914), 295-303.
        illus (6 b&w).

G839.   CRAFTSMAN.   "The Rookwood Pottery: 'Dux Foemina Facti'."
         Vol. 3 (January 1903), 247-248. illus (6 b&w).

G840.   ________. "Some American Garden Pottery Inspired by
         Classic Designs." Vol. 22 (September 1912), 681-
         682. illus (2 b&w).

G841.   ________. "Some Pottery Bowls with Incised Decoration,
         the Work of Students in a Philadelphia School." Vol.
         17 (March 1910), 706-709. illus (6 b&w).

G842.   ________. "Stone Ware That Combines Utility with
         Loveliness: A Recently Revived Craft." Vol. 24
         (September 1913), 643-645. illus (5 b&w).

G843.   ________. "Terra Cotta Garden Furnishings in Simple
         and Elegant Design." Vol. 28 (May 1915), 190-191,
         235-236. illus (7 b&w).

G844.   ________. "Terra-Cotta Garden Furniture." Vol. 22
         (August 1912), 567-568. illus (6 b&w).

G845.   CRAMER, W. E. "The Harrop Tunnel Kiln." American
         Ceramic Society Journal 5 (August 1922), 492-499.
         illus (5 b&w).

G846.   CRANE, Anne Winslow. "The Middle Lane Pottery."
         Art Interchange 45 (August 1900), 32-33. illus
         (3 b&w).

G847.   CRANE, Charles Albert. "North Carolina Kaolin Mining."
         Clay-Worker 37 (April 1902), 427-428. illus
         (1 b&w).

G848.   CRAWFORD, Jean. "Jugtown Pottery." Western Collector
         6 (July 1968), 7-11. illus (12 b&w).

G849.   ________. "Jugtown Pottery . . . A Way of Life."
         Spinning Wheel 32 (May 1976), 8-11. illus (9 b&w).

G850.   CRAWFORD, Rachael B. "Ceramics at the 1876 Centennial."
         Antiques Journal 31 (May 1976), 16-18, 46. illus
         (8 b&w).

G851.   ________. "The Origins of American Art Ceramics."
         Antiques Journal 31 (July 1976), 18-21, 44. illus
         (8 b&w); bibliog.

G852.   CROCKERY AND GLASS JOURNAL. "Boston's Art Product--
         Grueby Ware." Vol. 54 (December 12, 1901), [131-132,
         135].

G853.   ________. "The Ethics of Pottery Decoration." Vol. 76,
         (December 19, 1912), 31-32, 35.

G854.   CROCKERY AND GLASS JOURNAL. "History of a Great
        Pottery [Knowles, Taylor & Knowles]" Vol. 60
        (December 15, 1904), [57-59]. illus (17 b&w).

G855.   ________. "Jervis and His Work." Vol. 76 (December
        19, 1912), 181-182. illus (1 b&w).

G856.   ________. "Pottery Making in England and America: A
        Comparison of Methods." Vol. 76 (December 19, 1912),
        41-42, 45.

G857.   ________. "Potting as a Comfortable, Restful Business
        [C. Poillon]" Vol. 56 (December 11, 1902), [2p.].

G858.   ________. "Prominent Trenton Potters [C. H. Cook;
        H. B. Moses]" Vol. 58 (December 17, 1903), [4p.].
        illus (6 b&w).

G859.   ________. "Reminiscences of Trenton." Vol. 54
        (December 12, 1901), [153-154].

G860.   ________. "Thirty-Fourth Annual Convention of the
        United States Potters' Association." Vol. 76
        (November 14, 1912), 9-15. illus (1 b&w).

G861.   ________. "A Visit to the Ceramic Art Works, Trenton."
        Vol. 58 (December 17, 1903), [5p]. illus (7 b&w).

G862.   ________. "Volkmar Art Pottery." Vol. 54 (December
        12, 1901), [147-149].

G863.   ________. "The World-Famous Rookwood Ware." Vol. 54
        (December 12, 1901), 113-114.

G864.   CROLY, Herbert D. "Glazed and Colored Terra-Cotta."
        Architectural Record 19 (April 1906), 313-323.
        illus (9 b&w).

G865.   ________. "The Proper Use of Terra Cotta, III."
        Architectural Record 19 (January 1906), 73-81.
        illus (9 b&w).

G866.   CROSBY, Charles. "The Work of American Potters.
        Article Four: How Teco Came to Be." Arts & Decora-
        tion 1 (March 1911) 214-215. illus (5 b&w).
            Articles 1, 2, 3, 5 are: G948, G2311, G1297, G1675.

G867.   CROSS, Nellie A. "National League of Mineral Painters."
        Keramic Studio 10 (August 1908), 79-80. illus
        (5 b&w).

G868.   CROWLEY, Lilian Hall. "It's Now the Potter's Turn."
        International Studio 75 (September 1922), 539-546.
        illus (23 b&w).

G869.   CUMMINS, A. L. "Commercial China Decoration: The
         Partnership of Artist and Manufacturer in Reaching
         a Higher Standard." Arts & Decoration 1 (September
         1911), 442. illus (1 b&w).

G870.   __________. "Some Recent Developments in Overglaze
         China Decoration." Arts & Decoration 2 (August
         1912), 369. illus (2 b&w).

G871.   CURRIE, C. W. Y. "Terra Cotta and Brick in Railroad
         Structures [Grand Central Terminal]" Clay-Worker
         93 (June 1930), 475-477. illus (3 b&w).

G872.   CURTIS, Edmund DeForest. "Ceramic Art and the Ceramic
         Artist." American Ceramic Society Bulletin 5
         (January 1926), 42-45.

G873.   __________. "The Course in Pottery at the Pennsylvania
         Museum School of Industrial Art." American Ceramic
         Society Journal 8 (March 1925), 138-142. illus
         (2 b&w).

G874.   __________. "Industrial Potter Craftsmen." American
         Ceramic Society Bulletin 5 (March 1926), 177-179.

G875.   __________. "The Relation of Art to the Business of
         Ceramics." Ceramic Age 16 (July 1930), 14-17.
         illus (1 b&w).

G876.   __________. "The Rôle of Art in Industrial Ceramics."
         American Ceramic Society Journal 13 (May 1930),
         7-11.

G877.   __________. "The Small Shop." American Ceramic Society
         Bulletin 6 (January 1927), 17-22. illus (4 b&w).

G878.   CUSHMAN, Paul. "Paul Cushman, the Potter, 1767-1833."
         Early American Industries Association Chronicle 2
         (December 1939), 89-90, 92. bibliog.

G879.   DANIELSON, Leon E. "The Hilton Potteries of the
         Catawba Valley, North Carolina." Ceramic Circle of
         Charlotte Journal of Studies 4 (1980), 21-32.
         illus (11 b&w); bibliog.
            Prefatory to C23.

G880.   DARLING, Sharon S. "Flower Pots to Skyscrapers:
         Chicago Ceramics & Glass." Hobbies 84 (January
         1980), 91-94. illus (3 b&w).

G881.   DARRAH, W. A. "The Vitreous Sanitary Ware Industry."
         American Ceramic Society Bulletin 4 (June 1925),
         261-283. illus (21 b&w).

G882.   DAVIDSON, Clair. "The Ridge Pottery of Evans Crowley."
         Antiques Journal 27 (August 1972), 17-18. illus
         (9 b&w).

G883.   DAVIDSON, Marshall. "Early New York Stoneware Jug [J.
        Crolius]" Design 37 (December 1935), 14. illus
        (1 b&w).

G884.   ________. "A New York Stoneware Jug [J. Crolius]"
        Metropolitan Museum of Art Bulletin 30 (July 1935),
        146. illus (1 b&w); bibliog.

G885.   DAVIS, Charles T.   "Architectural Terra-Cotta--I."
        American Architect and Building News 17 (June 6,
        1885), 267-268.

G886.   ________. "Architectural Terra-Cotta--II." American
        Architect and Building News 18 (July 4, 1885), 3-4.

G887.   ________. "Decorative Tiles--II." American Architect
        and Building News 17 (March 7, 1885), 111-113.

G888.   DAVIS, Chester. "The AETCO Tiles of Walter Crane."
        Spinning Wheel 29 (June 1973), 18-20. illus
        (11 b&w).

G889.   ________. "Bybee Pottery." Spinning Wheel 29 (July-
        August 1973), 16-18. illus (6 b&w).

G890.   ________. "The Later Years of Rookwood Pottery, 1920-
        1967." Spinning Wheel 25 (October 1969), 10-12.
        illus (9 b&w).

G891.   ________. "The Orchard Kilns of Paul St. Gaudens."
        Spinning Wheel 30 (March 1974), 54-56. illus
        (9 b&w).

G892.   DAVISON, Mary E. "William H. Farrar, Potter."
        Antiques 35 (March 1939), 122-123. illus (5 b&w).

G893.   DAWES, E. L. "Some Early Experiences in Enameling
        Cast Iron." American Ceramic Society Bulletin 19
        (May 1940), 177-178.

G894.   De BRIE, Sydney. "Faience Tiles in Interior Decoration
        [American Encaustic Tiling Co.]" Country Life 41
        (April 1922), 122, 124. illus (6 b&w).

G895.   De JONGE, Eric. "Tucker China: America's Porcelain."
        Early American Life 5 (December 1974), 50-53, 83.
        illus (9 b&w).

G896.   De KAY, Charles. "Art from the Kilns." Munsey's
        Magazine 26 (October 1901), 46-53. illus (19 b&w).

G897.   ________. "Keramic Society of Greater New York."
        Art World 2 (July 1917), 400-402. illus (9 b&w).

G898.   DeKAY, Charles. "Pottery from the Durant Kilns:
         Some Recent Work of Jean Durant Rice and Leon
         Volkmar." Arts & Decoration 3 (January 1913), 96-
         97. illus (4 b&w).

G899.   DENNIS, Lee. "Restoration of the Moravian Pottery and
         Tile Works, Doylestown, Pennsylvania." National
         Antiques Review 3 (July 1971), 29-31. illus
         (5 b&w).

G900.   DESIGN. "Adelaide Alsop Robineau." Vol. 39 (November
         1937), 36. illus (4 b&w).

G901.   _________. "Adelaide Alsop Robineau: A Significant
         American." Vol. 37 (December 1935), 20-22, 41.
         illus (1 b&w); bibliog.

G902.   _________. "Charles F. Binns." Vol. 39 (November
         1937), 35. illus (2 b&w).

G903.   _________. "Early Stoneware [Ohio]" Vol. 39 (November
         1937), 33-34. illus (5 b&w).

G904.   _________. "Exhibition of the Newark Keramic Society."
         Vol. 29 (September 1927), 74-77. illus (9 b&w).

G905.   _________. "Exhibition of the Newark, N.J. Ceramic
         Club." Vol. 28 (September 1926), 67-69. illus
         (6 b&w).

G906.   _________. "Exhibition of the Newark Society of Keramic
         Art." Vol. 26 (September 1924), 74-77. illus
         (7 b&w).

G907.   _________. "Tioughnioga Pottery." Vol. 37 (December
         1935), 15, 40. illus (1 b&w).
             Originally published in Ceramic Age. See G522.

G908.   _________. "Tulip Ware." Vol. 39 (February 1938),
         12-17. illus (7 b&w).

G909.   _________. "Two Fireplaces Made of Moravian Tile."
         Vol. 33 (November 1931), 136. illus (2 b&w).

G910.   DIBBLE, Mabel C. "The Atlan Ceramic Club of Chicago."
         Brush and Pencil 4 (April 1899), 33-39. illus
         (6 b&w).

G911.   _________. "Atlan Club Exhibit." Keramic Studio 2
         (January 1901), 193. illus (4 b&w).

G912.   DIXON, John Morris. "Recipes for Baked Earth: Terra
         Cotta Restoration." Progressive Architecture 58
         (November 1977), 98-101. illus (9 b&w, 2 col).

G913. DOAT, Taxile. "Grand Feu Ceramics, I: The Ceramic
       Movement in Europe in 1900." Keramic Studio 5
       (May 1903), 6-11. illus (14 b&w).

G914. ________. "Grand Feu Ceramics, II: Sèvres at the
       Paris Exposition of 1900." Keramic Studio 5 (June
       1903), 30-33. illus (6 b&w)...

G915. ________. "Grand Feu Ceramics, II: Sèvres at the
       Paris Exposition of 1900--(Concluded)." Keramic
       Studio 5 (July 1903), 57-60. illus (15 b&w).

G916. ________. "Grand Feu Ceramics, III: The Manufactory
       at Sèvres--Its Organization." Keramic Studio 5
       (August 1903), 80-82. illus (11 b&w).

G917. ________. "Grand Feu Ceramics, IV: Preparation of
       Ceramic Bodies--Grés and Porcelain." Keramic Studio
       5 (September 1903), 99-102. illus (1 b&w).

G918. ________. "Grand Feu Ceramics, V: The Making of
       Ceramic Shapes--Grés and Porcelain--Throwing and
       Pressing." Keramic Studio 5 (October 1903), 124-125.
       illus (5 b&w).

G919. ________. "Grand Feu Ceramics, VI: Casting." Keramic
       Studio 5 (November 1903), 146-149. illus (21 b&w).

G920. ________. "Grand Feu Ceramics, VII: Glazing."
       Keramic Studio 5 (December 1903), 172-174. illus
       (4 b&w).

G921. ________. "Grand Feu Ceramics, VIII: Kilns." Keramic
       Studio 5 (January 1904), 194-197. illus (13 b&w).

G922. ________. "Grand Feu Ceramics, VIII: Kilns (Contin-
       ued)" Keramic Studio 5 (February 1904), 228-229.
       illus (6 b&w).

G923. ________. "Grand Feu Ceramics, IX: Saggers, Placing
       and Setting." Keramic Studio 5 (March 1904), 242-
       245. illus (19 b&w).

G924. ________. "Grand Feu Ceramics, IX: Saggers, Placing
       and Setting, Continued." Keramic Studio 5 (April
       1904), 266-268. illus (15 b&w).

G925. ________. "Grand Feu Ceramics, X: Firing." Keramic
       Studio 6 (May 1904), 4-7. illus (6 b&w).

G926. ________. "Grand Feu Ceramics, X[1]: Firing."
       Keramic Studio 6 (June 1904), 30-32. illus (2 b&w).

G927. ________. "Grand Feu Ceramics, XII: Grand Feu Colors
       --Colored Pastes, Pâtes sur Pâtes." Keramic Studio
       6 (July 1904), 53-55. illus (1 b&w).

G928.   DOAT, Taxile. "Grand Feu Ceramics XIII: Grand Feu
        Colors--Colored Glazes--Flamme Glazes--Flowing
        Glazes." Keramic Studio 6 (August 1904), 78-81.
        illus (2 b&w).

G929.   _________. "Grand Feu Ceramics, XIV: Grand Feu Colors
        --Mat and Crystalline Glazes." Keramic Studio 6
        (September 1904), 100-101. illus (1 b&w).
          G913-929 also published as A80.

G930.   DOCKSTADER, Frederick. "Clay as Container: One
        Thousand Years of Pottery in America." Craft
        Horizons 22 (September-October 1962), 10-19. illus
        (28 b&w).

G931.   DOLE, Nathan Haskell. "The Best American Pottery
        [Dedham]" House Beautiful 2 (September 1897), 87-94.
        illus (5 b&w).

G932.   DOMMEL, Darlene. "Coors Porcelain Company." Spinning
        Wheel 30 (April 1974), 20-22. illus (10 b&w).

G933.   _________. "Fulper and Stangl Pottery." National
        Antiques Review 6 (April 1975), 33-34. illus (7 b&w).

G934.   _________. "A Guide to Collecting UND Pottery."
        Antiques Journal 34 (January 1979), 26-29, 48.
        illus (11 b&w); bibliog.

G935.   _________. "Red Wing and Rum Rill Pottery." Spinning
        Wheel 28 (December 1972), 22-24. illus (10 b&w).

G936.   _________. "University of North Dakota Pottery."
        Spinning Wheel 29 (June 1973), 30-31. illus (6 b&w).

G937.   DONLEY, Angeline Scott. "The Homely Pottery of Old
        New England." Country Life in America 19 (November
        1910), 46, 62. illus (4 b&w).

G938.   DOYLE, Dixie. "Pottery [Peoria Pottery Co., Etc.]"
        Clay Record 1 (October 28, 1892), 301-302.

G939.   DOYLE, Maude M. "Lotus Ware." American Antiques
        Journal 2 (November 1947), 4-5. illus (5 b&w).

G940.   DREPPERD, Carl W. "Sgraffito and Slip Decoration on
        American Redware Pottery." Spinning Wheel 11 (June
        1955), 16, 18. illus (2 b&w).

G941.   DRESSLER, Conrad. "The Artistic Needs of Modern
        Faience." American Ceramic Society Journal 6
        (February 1923), 398-404. illus (1 b&w).

G942.   _________. "Dressler Tunnel Kilns' Genesis." American
        Ceramic Society Bulletin 14 (June 1935), 216-217.
        bibliog.

G943.   DRESSLER, Constance W. "Rookwood." Spinning Wheel 11
         (September 1955), 18, 20, 22-23. illus (5 b&w).

G944.   DRESSLER, Philip. "Tunnel Kiln Development in the
         Ceramic Industries." Ceramic Age 10 (September
         1927), 81-91. illus (25 b&w).

G945.   ________. "Tunnel Kiln Development in the Ceramic
         Industries [Part 2]" Ceramic Age 10 (October 1927),
         122-130. illus (39 b&w).

G946.   DRINKWATER, Frank L. "Tile Manufacturing Company
         Establishes Attractive Headquarters [Pomona Tile
         Co.]" Ceramic Age 12 (October 1928), 142-143.
         illus (5 b&w).

G947.   DUBOIS, H. B. "Development and Growth of the Feldspar
         Industry." American Ceramic Society Bulletin 19
         (June 1940), 206-213.

G948.   DUDLEY, Pendleton. "The Work of American Potters.
         Article One: Examples of the Work of the Grueby
         Pottery." Arts & Decoration 1 (November 1910),
         20-21. illus (4 b&w).
              Articles 2, 3, 4, 5 are: G2311, G1297, G866, G1675.

G949.   DUKA, John. "Pots to Watch [Roseville Pottery]"
         New York 12 (January 29, 1979), 38-39. illus
         (3 col).

G950.   DUNBAR, Gary S. "Henry Chapman Mercer: Pennsylvania
         Folklife Pioneer." Pennsylvania Folklife 12 (Summer
         1961), 48-52. illus (4 b&w).

G951.   DUNNAGAN, M. R. "Brick, Tile, Pipe Making Important
         N.C. Industries." E.S.C. Quarterly 5 (Spring-Summer
         1947), 39-40, 65. illus (1 b&w).

G952.   ________. "Pottery Making, Ancient Art, Increasing in
         State [N.C.]" E.S.C.Quarterly 5 (Spring-Summer 1947),
         53-55.

G953.   DURRELL, Jane. "The Ladies, God Bless 'Em." American
         Antiques 4 (April 1976), 32-35. illus (10 b&w).

G954.   DYER, Walter A. "Early Art Industries of the Pennsyl-
         vania Dutch." Country Life in America 30 (May 1916),
         100, 102, 104, 106. illus (8 b&w).

G955.   ________. "Early Pottery of New England." Antiques 1
         (January 1922), 19-22. illus (13 b&w).

G956.   ________. "The First American Porcelain [Tucker]"
         Country Life in America 31 (January 1917), 58, 60.
         illus (4 b&w).

G957.   [DYER, Walter A.] "Tucker China." Hobbies 57
        (January 1953), 84-85.

G958.   E.S.C. QUARTERLY. "Ceramic Education and Research at
        State College [N.C. State U.]" Vol. 5 (Spring-Summer
        1947), 52, 65.

G959.   _________. "Number of Small Hand Potteries Operate in
        this State [N.C.]" Vol. 5 (Spring-Summer 1947),
        57-59.

G960.   EBERLEIN, Harold Donaldson. "The Decorated Pottery of
        the Pennsylvania Dutch." Arts & Decoration 4 (Janu-
        ary 1914), 109-112. illus (6 b&w).

G961.   _________. "Tucker, Craftsman in China." Country Life
        56 (September 1929), 69-70, 92, 94. illus (9 b&w).

G962.   EDGAR, William Harold. "Another American Pottery:
        Where Artists are in Close Communion with Nature and
        Mechanical Facilities Are Extraordinary [Gates Pot-
        teries]" Pottery & Glass 1 (December 1908), 14-16.
        illus (4 b&w).

G963.   _________. "The Teco Pottery." International Studio
        36 (November 1908), xxviii-xxix. illus (4 b&w).

G964.   EDSON, Mira Burr. "Ceramic Work of Mrs. Steward."
        Arts & Decoration 1 (May 1911), 308-309. illus
        (3 b&w).

G965.   _________. "Decorated China of Mrs. S. E. Price."
        Arts & Decoration 1 (June 1911), 354. illus (2 b&w).

G966.   _________. "Exhibition of Ceramics [N.Y. Society of
        Keramic Arts]" Arts & Decoration 1 (April 1911),
        260-261. illus (4 b&w).

G967.   _________. "The Keramic Society of Greater New York."
        International Studio 56 (June 1917), cxxviii-cxxix.
        illus (2 b&w).

G968.   _________. "Some Significant American Pottery [Marble-
        head]" Arts & Decoration 23 (June 1925), 58, 83.
        illus (6 b&w).

G969.   EDWARDS, Deborah. "Haydenville, A Town of Clay."
        Ceramics Monthly 28 (January 1980), 47-51. illus
        (14 b&w).

G970.   EDWARDS, O. K. "Firing 'Hogged Fuel' in a Continuous
        Chamber Brick Kiln." American Ceramic Society
        Bulletin 6 (July 1927), 195-197.

G971.   EHLERS, Jetta. "Exhibition of Newark, N.J., Keramic
        Society." Keramic Studio 16 (June 1914), 28-33.
        illus (8 b&w).

G972. EHRMANN, Eric. "The Lenox Heritage: A National Tra-
       dition in Fine China." Collector Editions 8 (Winter
       1980), 33-36. illus (2 b&w, 8 col).

G973. EIDELBERG, Martin. "American Ceramics and Internation-
       al Styles, 1876-1916." Princeton University Art
       Museum Record 34 (no. 2, 1975), 13-19. illus
       (16 b&w); bibliog.

G974. __________. "The Ceramic Art of William H. Grueby."
       Connoisseur 184 (September 1973), 47-54. illus
       (15 b&w); bibliog.

G975. __________. "Tiffany Favrile Pottery." Connoisseur 169
       (September 1968), 57-61. illus (7 b&w); bibliog.

G976. ELLETT, William H. "In Search of Vermont Stoneware."
       Yankee 43 (May 1979), 176-180, 183-184, 187. illus
       (8 col).

G977. ELLIS, Carey P. "Fuller's Earth." Clay-Worker 56
       (October 1911), 384-385.

G978. ELLSBERG, Helen. "Lenox China, Part 1." Western
       Collector 8 (September 1970), 4-8. illus (7 b&w).

G979. __________. "Lenox China, Part 2." Western Collector 8
       (November 1970), 12-15. illus (6 b&w).

G980. ELWOOD, P. H. "Ceramic Products in Landscape Archi-
       tecture." American Ceramic Society Bulletin 5
       (September 1926), 366-368.

G981. ELZNER, A. O. "Rookwood Pottery." Architectural
       Record 17 (April 1905), 294-304. illus (12 b&w).

G982. EMERSON, Gertrude. "Marblehead Pottery." Craftsman
       29 (March 1916), 671-673. illus (4 b&w).

G983. EMORY, Emma Vance. "The Overglaze Decoration of
       China." Arts & Decoration 1 (September 1911), 437-
       438. illus (4 b&w).

G984. ENLOE, Scroop W., Jr. "North Carolina China Clay."
       American Ceramic Society Bulletin 29 (June 1950),
       224-226.

G985. ESKESEN, Eckardt V. "Water-Tight Terra Cotta Construc-
       tion." American Ceramic Society Bulletin 13 (June
       1934), 154-162. illus (13 b&w); bibliog.

G986. ESTEY, J. A., ET AL. "Laura Anne Fry [Obituary]"
       American Ceramic Society Bulletin 22 (September
       1943), 322.

126   AMERICAN CERAMICS BEFORE 1930

G987.   EVANOFF, Betty. "North Carolina's Moravian Pottery."
         Antiques Journal 35 (February 1980), 22-24, 47.
         illus (6 b&w); bibliog.

G988.   _______. "Tucker China." Americana 4 (March 1976),
         34-35. illus (11 b&w).

G989.   EVANS, Mary. "Beautiful Bennington Ware." American
         Home 75 (February 1972), 64-67, 98, 100. illus
         (7 col).

G990.   EVANS, Paul F. "American Art Porcelain, Two--The
         Work of The University City Pottery." Spinning
         Wheel 27 (December 1971), 24-26. illus (6 b&w).
         Part 1 is G375.

G991.   _______. "America's Finest Pottery." Yankee 32
         (June 1968), 92-95, 168-170. illus (4 b&w).

G992.   _______. "Art Pottery Checklist: United States
         Producers." Spinning Wheel 31 (May 1975), 23-24.

G993.   _______. "Art Pottery Comes of Age." Spinning
         Wheel 30 (December 1974), 24-25. illus (5 b&w).

G994.   _______. "The Art Pottery Era in the United States,
         1870 to 1920, Part One." Spinning Wheel 26
         (October 1970), 52-53, 56. illus (4 b&w).

G995.   _______. "The Art Pottery Era in the United States,
         1870-1920, Part Two." Spinning Wheel 26 (November
         1970), 52-53. illus (5 b&w).

G996.   _______. "Art Pottery of William Dell." Spinning
         Wheel 30 (June 1974), 44-45. illus (3 b&w).

G997.   _______. "Art Tiles of the New York Subway, 1904."
         Spinning Wheel 35 (November 1979), 8-12. illus
         (11 b&w).

G998.   _______. "Artware of the Ohio Pottery." Spinning
         Wheel 32 (December 1976), 15-16. illus (2 b&w);
         bibliog.

G999.   _______. "Brouwer's Middle Lane Pottery." Spinning
         Wheel 29 (December 1973), 48-49, 54. illus (4 b&w).

G1000.   _______. "California's Mission Inn." Spinning Wheel
         32 (November 1976), 32-33. illus (4 b&w).

G1001.   _______. "Cincinnati Faience: An Overall Perspec-
         tive." Spinning Wheel 28 (September 1972), 16-18.
         illus (6 b&w).

G1002.   _______. "The Confusing McCoy Potteries." Spinning
         Wheel 29 (January-February 1973), 8-9. illus
         (5 b&w).

G1003.   EVANS, Paul F. "Hampshire Pottery." _Spinning Wheel_
          26 (September 1970), 22-24. illus (9 b&w).

G1004.   __________. "Jalan: Transitional Pottery of San Fran-
          cisco." _Spinning Wheel_ 29 (April 1973), 24-25, 48.
          illus (5 b&w).

G1005.   __________. "K.T.K. in California: The Homer Knowles
          Pottery." _Spinning Wheel_ 34 (January-February 1978),
          33-34. illus (2 b&w).

G1006.   __________. "Newcomb Pottery Decorators." _Spinning
          Wheel_ 30 (April 1974), 54-55. illus (1 b&w).

G1007.   __________. "The Niloak Pottery." _Spinning Wheel_ 26
          (October 1970), 18-20. illus (5 b&w).

G1008.   __________. "Ouachita Pottery." _Spinning Wheel_ 33
          (July-August 1977), 33-35. illus (8 b&w).

G1009.   __________. "Redlands Art Pottery." _Spinning Wheel_
          36 (January-February 1980), 38. illus (2 b&w).

G1010.   __________. "The Robertson Saga. I: The Creative
          Years, 1866-1889." _Western Collector_ 5 (April
          1967), 7-12. illus (10 b&w).

G1011.   __________. "The Robertson Saga. II: The Commercial
          Years, 1891-1943." _Western Collector_ 5 (May 1967),
          7-12. illus (7 b&w).

G1012.   __________. "The Roblin Art Pottery of San Francisco."
          Spinning Wheel 31 (July-August 1975), 42-44.
          illus (9 b&w).

G1013.   __________. "Salmagundi Club Mugs: Early Collector
          Annuals." _Spinning Wheel_ 34 (December 1978), 20-22.
          illus (8 b&w).

G1014.   __________. "The Sign of the Potter." _Spinning Wheel_
          31 (September 1975), 23. illus (3 b&w).

G1015.   __________. "Stockton Pottery--Early California Art-
          ware." _Spinning Wheel_ 27 (October 1971), 24-26, 67.
          illus (10 b&w).

G1016.   __________. "Stoneware and the Dorchester Pottery."
          Western Collector 6 (May 1968), 7-11. illus
          (10 b&w).

G1017.   __________. "Swastika Keramos." _Spinning Wheel_ 33
          (April 1977), 32-33. illus (4 b&w).

G1018.   __________. "Valentien Pottery: The Missing Shape
          Book." _Spinning Wheel_ 35 (September 1979), 37-39.
          illus (5 b&w).

G1019.   EVANS, PAUL F. "Vance & Avon Faience." Spinning
          Wheel 30 (January-February 1974), 20-21. illus
          (3 b&w).

G1020.   ________. "Victorian Art Tiles." Western Collector
          5 (November 1967), 18-22. illus (6 b&w); bibliog.

G1021.   FARRINGTON, Frank. "American Porcelain." Hobbies
          45 (November 1940), 53-55. illus (1 b&w).

G1022.   FARRINGTON, Mary H. "Chicago Ceramic Art Association."
          Keramic Studio 10 (August 1908), 84.

G1023.   FAWCETT, Waldon. "The Production of American Pottery
          [Rookwood]" Scientific American 83 (November 10,
          1900), 296-297. illus (6 b&w).

G1024.   FEDERAL REPORTER. "Case of Laura Fry vs. Rookwood
          Pottery Company, et al.," Vol. 90 (1899), 494-500.

G1025.   FEGLEY, H. Winslow. "An American Kaolin Industry
          [Pa.]" Pottery & Glass 14 (June 1915), 12-13, 27.
          illus (4 b&w).

G1026.   FELTS, James K., Sr. "The Anna Pottery." Chicago
          History n.s. 3 (Spring-Summer 1974), 36-44. illus
          (9 b&w).

G1027.   FEROLA, Janice. "Bennington Pottery: An Auction in
          Vermont." National Antiques Review 7 (October
          1975), 10-12. illus (5 b&w).

G1028.   FIELD, Zane. "Art Pottery of America." Western
          Collector 9 (July-August 1971), 12B-14. illus
          (11 b&w, 16 col).

G1029.   FINE ARTS JOURNAL. "The Potter's Art: Teco Ware."
          Vol. 14 (January 1903), 8-11. illus (9 b&w).

G1030.   ________. "Prize Winners of the Ceramic Exhibition."
          Vol. 31 (November 1914), 542-545. illus (4 b&w).

G1031.   FITZGERALD, Francis A. J. "The Harper Electric Kiln."
          American Ceramic Society Journal 9 (November 1926),
          766-772. illus (5 b&w).

G1032.   FITZ-GIBBON, Costen. "Tiles--Their Use in Architec-
          ture and Decoration." Arts & Decoration 23 (Octo-
          ber 1925), 58-59, 78, 90. illus (6 b&w).

G1033.   FITZPATRICK, Nancy. "America's First Art Pottery:
          Rookwood." Spinning Wheel 16 (October 1960), 16-17.
          illus (1 b&w).

G1034.   ________. "The Chesapeake Pottery Company." Mary-
          land Historical Magazine 52 (March 1957), 65-71.
          illus (2 b&w); bibliog.

G1035. FITZPATRICK, Nancy. "The Chesapeake Pottery Company,
        Baltimore, Md., 1882-1914." Spinning Wheel 13
        (September 1957), 14, 16, 18. illus (5 b&w).
        Abridged from G1034.

G1036. __________. "Rookwood Decoration and Decorators."
        Spinning Wheel 16 (November 1960), 14, 16. illus
        (2 b&w).

G1037. FITZPATRICK, Paul J. "Chesapeake Pottery." Antiques
        Journal 33 (December 1978), 16-19, 48. illus
        (5 b&w); bibliog.

G1038. __________. "Maria L. Nichols and the Rookwood Pottery."
        Antiques Journal 35 (October 1980), 24-29, 50-51.
        illus (17 b&w); bibliog.

G1039. FLINT, William W. "The Millville Pottery, Concord,
        N.H." Old-Time New England 17 (January 1927), 98-
        106. illus (8 b&w).

G1040. FLU, E. B. "The Pewabic Pottery at Detroit--A Unique
        Institution." Ceramic Age 9 (January 1927), 13-16.
        illus (9 b&w).

G1041. FORAKER, David. "Hull Pottery, Crooksville, Ohio."
        Western Collector 9 (January-February 1971), 4-8.
        illus (5 b&w).

G1042. FOREMAN, Grant. "Settlement of English Potters in
        Wisconsin." Wisconsin Magazine of History 21
        (June 1938), 375-396. bibliog.

G1043. FORTUNE. "Lonely Lenox: An Idyl in Fine China."
        Vol. 19 (April 1939), 60-65, 120, 122, 124, 126.
        illus (7 b&w, 4 col).

G1044. FORYST, Carole A. "Lenox China 'Turns-On' Dynamic
        Tableware Market." Ceramic Industry 93 (August
        1969), 29-38. illus (19 b&w).

G1045. FOSDICK, Marion L. "The Problem of Printed Table-
        ware." American Ceramic Society Bulletin 7 (July
        1928), 171-173.

G1046. FOSTER, Edith Dunham. "Dedham Pottery." House
        Beautiful 36 (August 1914), xii.

G1047. __________. "Dedham Pottery, II." House Beautiful 36
        (September 1914), 117. illus (5 b&w).

G1048. __________. "William A. Robertson, Master Potter."
        International Studio 51 (November 1913), xcv-xcvi.
        illus (2 b&w).

G1049.   FOSTER, Kate McCrea. "The Purposes and Aims of Clay
          Modeling in the Schools." Art Education 3 (Decem-
          ber 1896), 51-52.

G1050.   FOX, Charles James. "Mosaic Pictures in the Library
          of Congress [E. Vedder]" Clay-Worker 49 (March
          1908), 411-413. illus (3 b&w).

G1051.   FOX, Claire Gilbride. "Henry Chapman Mercer:
          Tilemaker, Collector and Builder Extraordinary."
          Antiques 104 (October 1973), 678-685. illus (9 b&w,
          3 col); bibliog.

G1052.   FRACKELTON, S[usan] S[tuart]. "Organized Effort."
          Keramic Studio 3 (September 1901), 100-101.

G1053.   __________. "Our American Potteries: Maratta's and
          Albert's Work at the Gates Potteries." Sketch Book
          5 (October 1905), 73-80. illus (9 b&w).

G1054.   __________. "Our American Potteries--Newcomb College."
          Sketch Book 5 (July 1906), 430-433. illus (8 b&w).

G1055.   __________. "Our American Potteries: Teco Ware."
          Sketch Book 5 (September 1905), 13-19. illus
          (5 b&w).

G1056.   __________. "Rookwood Pottery." Sketch Book 5 (Febru-
          ary 1906), 272-277. illus (11 b&w).

G1057.   FRANCHET, Louis. "The Decoration of Artistic Grand
          Feu Grès." Keramic Studio 10 (January 1909), 192,
          194. illus (4 b&w).

G1058.   __________. "The Decoration of Artistic Grand Feu
          Grès [II]" Keramic Studio 10 (February 1909), 214-
          216. illus (3 b&w).

G1059.   __________. "The Decoration of Grand Feu Grès, III."
          Keramic Studio 10 (March 1909), 236, 238. illus
          (1 b&w).

G1060.   __________. "The Decoration of Grand Feu Grès, Con-
          tinued." Keramic Studio 10 (April 1909), 258, 260,
          262. illus (1 b&w).

G1061.   __________. "The Decoration of Grand Feu Grès, Con-
          tinued: Reds of Copper." Keramic Studio 11 (May
          1909), 2, 4.

G1062.   __________. "The Decoration of Hard Porcelain." Ker-
          amic Studio 11 (November 1910), 142, 144, 146, 148.

G1063.   __________. "The Decoration of Hard Porcelain (Cont'd)"
          Keramic Studio 11 (December 1910), 164, 166.

G1064.   FRANCHET, Louis. "The Decoration of Hard Porcelain
         (Cont'd): Vitrifying Colors." Keramic Studio 11
         (January 1910), 188-190, 192.

G1065.   ________. "Metallic Deposits on Glazes." Keramic
         Studio 9 (March 1908), 248, 250, 252. illus
         (1 b&w).

G1066.   ________. "Metallic Deposits on Glazes, Continued."
         Keramic Studio 9 (April 1908), 274-276, 278. illus
         (2 b&w).

G1067.   ________. "Metallic Deposits on Glazes, Continued."
         Keramic Studio 10 (May 1908), 10-12.

G1068.   ________. "Metallic Deposits on Glazes, Continued."
         Keramic Studio 10 (August 1908), 74, 76-77. illus
         (2 b&w).

G1069.   FRANCO, Barbara. "Stoneware Made by the White Family
         in Utica, N.Y." Antiques 99 (June 1971), 872-876.
         illus (10 b&w).

G1070.   FRANKLIN, (Mrs.) Chester L. "The Newark Society of
         Keramic Arts, Annual Exhibition." Keramic Studio
         25 (June 1923), 24-32. (18 b&w).

G1071.   FRANKLIN INSTITUTE JOURNAL. "American Ceramic Clays."
         Vol. 108 (October 1879), 271-272.

G1072.   ________. "Secrets in Pottery [Glazes]" Vol. 12
         (July 1833), 59-60.

G1073.   ________. "Secrets in Pottery, Concluded." Vol. 12
         (August 1833), 128-132.

G1074.   FRANKLIN, Robert. "Mountains of Kaolin for America's
         Kilns." Technical World Magazine 20 (December
         1913), 614,616. illus (2 b&w).

         FREAS, Adelaide L., see also FRIES, Adelaide L.

G1075.   FREAS, Adelaide L. "Moravian Tile Stoves of Salem,
         North Carolina." Bucks County Historical Society
         Collections 4 (1917), 477-479.

G1076.   FREDGANT, Don. "The York Pottery of Lake Butler,
         Florida." Antiques Journal 35 (November 1980),
         28-30, 49. illus (9 b&w); bibliog.

G1077.   FREEMAN, Helen. "The Rookwood Pottery in Cincinnati,
         Ohio." House Beautiful 47 (June 1920), 499-501,
         530. illus (16 b&w).

G1078.   FRENCH, Myrtle Meritt. "Art Pottery." American Cer-
         amic Society Journal 13 (May 1930), 33-37.

G1079.   FRENCH, Myrtle Meritt. "Freeing the Creative Power
          of the Individual through the Making of Pottery."
          Design 28 (April 1927), 201-203. illus (5 b&w).

G1080.   __________. "Pottery as Taught at the School of the
          Art Institute [of Chicago]" Design 26 (May 1924),
          21. illus (4 b&w).

G1081.   __________. "Uses of Ceramics in Interior Decoration:
          An Interview with Lionel Robertson of Tobey Furni-
          ture Co." American Ceramic Society Bulletin 4
          (September 1925), 415-418.

          FRIES, Adelaide L., see also FREAS, Adelaide L.

G1082.   FRIES, Adelaide L. "Early Moravians in Old Salem
          Made Household Pottery." E.S.C. Quarterly 5
          (Spring-Summer 1947), 62.

G1083.   FRIES, George M. "Interesting Historical Facts on
          Drain Tile." Clay-Worker 86 (December 1926), 490-
          491. (1 b&w).

G1084.   FROEHLICH, Hugo. "Decorations for a Cup and Saucer
          from a Cicada Motif." Keramic Studio 6 (March
          1905), 240-250. illus (56 b&w).

G1085.   __________. "Principles of Design--Color." Keramic
          Studio 6 (July 1904), 48-50. illus (6 col).

G1086.   FRONCEK, Thomas. "The Moravian Pottery and Tile
          Works." Americana 4 (July 1976), 29-33. illus
          (30 b&w).

G1087.   [FRY, Laura] "High Art Pottery." Clay-Worker 28
          (November 1897), 386-387.

G1088.   FRY, Marshal. "Alfred Summer School of Ceramic Art."
          Keramic Studio 3 (December 1901), 165-166.

G1089.   __________. "The Art of Table Decoration." Keramic
          Studio 17 (March 1916), 156-160. illus (6 b&w).

G1090.   [FRYATT, F. E.] "Pottery in the United States."
          Crockery and Glass Journal 52 (December 13, 1900),
          [7p.] illus (9 b&w).
              Originally published in Harper's New Monthly
          Magazine. See G1091.

G1091.   __________. "Pottery in the United States." Harper's
          New Monthly Magazine 62 (February 1881), 357-369.
          illus (14 b&w).

G1092.   [__________]. "Pottery in the United States." Hobbies
          53 (February 1949), 104-105, 109, 119-120.
              Originally published in Harper's New Monthly
          Magazine. See G1091.

G1093.   GAINES, Edith. "Collectors' Notes: K.T.& K. Belleek
         and Lotus Ware." Antiques 91 (June 1967), 777-778.
         illus (2 b&w).

G1094.   __________. "Collectors' Notes: Rebekah from East
         Liverpool." Antiques 91 (June 1967), 777. illus
         (1 b&w).

G1095.   GALLOWAY, George D. "The Van Briggle Pottery."
         Brush and Pencil 9 (October 1901), 1-11. illus
         (9 b&w).

G1096.   GARDY, Elizabeth W. "Pennsylvania Dutch Pottery."
         Spinning Wheel 6 (July 1950), 36-37. illus (2 b&w).

G1097.   GARRETT, Brice. "American Art Pottery in 1904."
         Spinning Wheel 19 (July-August 1963), 33.

G1098.   __________. "Buffalo Pottery and the Larkin Company."
         Spinning Wheel 19 (January-February 1963), 18-19.
         illus (13 b&w).

G1099.   __________. "Lamberton China on the B&O." Spinning
         Wheel 18 (September 1962), 35. illus (1 b&w).

G1100.   __________. "Ohio's Lotus Ware." Spinning Wheel 22
         (January-February 1966), 16-17. illus (5 b&w).

G1101.   __________. "Weller Ware." Spinning Wheel 21 (May
         1965), 8-10. illus (6 b&w).

G1102.   GATES, Burton Noble. "Boston Earthenware: Frederick
         Mear, Potter." Antiques 5 (June 1924), 310-311.
         illus (4 b&w).

G1103.   GATES, William D. "Brick and Terra Cotta [Yerkes
         Observatory]" Clay-Worker 32 (December 1899),
         431-433. illus (4 b&w).

G1104.   __________. "A Clean Front [Inter Ocean Building,
         Chicago]" Clay-Worker 35 (May 1901), 467-469.
         illus (2 b&w).

G1105.   __________. "A Fitting Use for Terra Cotta [Commemora-
         tive Panels]" Clay-Worker 30 (August 1898), 93-94.
         illus (1 b&w).

G1106.   __________. "The Influence of the American Ceramic
         Society in the Terra Cotta Industry." American
         Ceramic Society Journal 6 (January 1923), 231-232.

G1107.   __________. "The Manufacturers' Dependence on Ceramic
         Research." Potter 1 (February 1917), 109-115.
         Also published as part of G655.

G1108.   GATES, William D. "The Revival of the Potter's Art."
          Clay-Worker 28 (October 1897), 275-276.

G1109.   ________. "A Terra Cotta Residence: Method of Con-
          struction." Clay-Worker 21 (January 1894), 20-21.
          illus (2 b&w).

G1110.   ________. "'There's Music in the Air' at Terra Cotta
          [Teco Band]" Clay-Worker 40 (November 1903), 441.
          illus (1 b&w).

G1111.   ________. "A Tribute to George H. Lacey." Clay-
          Worker 75 (May 1921), 557. illus (1 b&w).
          Originally published in Common Clay.

G1112.   GEARE, Randolph I. "The Early Production of Pottery
          in West Virginia." Glass and Pottery World 16
          (October 1908), 18.

G1113.   GEIJSBEEK, S. "The Ceramics of the Louisiana Purchase
          Exposition." American Ceramic Society Transactions
          7, Pt. 3 (1905), 289-355.

G1114.   ________. "The Clay Deposits of Washington." Ameri-
          can Ceramic Society Transactions 13 (1911), 751-764.
          illus (1 b&w).

G1115.   GERNERT, Dee Albert. "Buffalo Pottery's Deldare
          Ware." Spinning Wheel 19 (March 1963), 14-15.
          illus (11 b&w).

G1116.   GIBSON, Gerald G. "Marked American Porcelain."
          Antiques Journal 15 (February 1960), 8-10. illus
          (8 b&w).

G1117.   GIBSON, Louis H. "Buffalo's Great Commercial Struc-
          tures: Ellicott Square Building." Clay-Worker
          27 (January 1897), 13-15. illus (2 b&w).

G1118.   ________. "A House Built of Terra Cotta [J. R. True
          residence]" Clay-Worker 36 (November 1901), 411-
          413. illus (2 b&w).

G1119.   ________. "The Indiana Soldiers' Monument." Clay-
          Worker 25 (June 1896), 535-536. illus (1 b&w).

G1120.   GILBERT, Alfred Holley. "The Dorset Fenton Potteries."
          Vermont History n.s. 34 (October 1966), 268-274.
          bibliog.

G1121.   GILLINGHAM, Harrold E. "Pottery, China, and Glass
          Making in Philadelphia [Before 1800]" Pennsylvania
          Magazine of History and Biography 54 (April 1930),
          97-129. illus (1 b&w); bibliog.

G1122.   GILMER, Ruth Monroe. "Andrew Duché." Apollo 48
         (September 1948), 63-65. illus (2 b&w).

G1123.   ________. "Andrew Duché and His China, 1738-1743."
         Apollo 45 (May 1947), 128-130. illus (1 b&w).

G1124.   GITTER, Josephine. "Pottery Industry in Muskingum
         County, Ohio." American Ceramic Society Bulletin
         15 (October 1936), 371-372.

G1125.   GLASS AND POTTERY WORLD. "Dedham Pottery Distinctly
         Different." Vol. 16 (October 1908), 15-16. illus
         (1 b&w).

G1126.   ________. "Good Green Ware Gave Fame to Grueby Name."
         Vol. 16 (June 1908), 13-14. illus (5 b&w).

G1127.   ________. "Hugh C. Robertson." Vol. 16 (November
         1908), 16. illus (1 b&w).

G1128.   ________. "Marblehead Pottery." Vol. 16 (July 1908),
         20-21. illus (5 b&w).

G1129.   ________. "Newcomb Pottery of Old New Orleans." Vol.
         16 (September 1908), 13-14. illus (4 b&w).

G1130.   ________. "Tariff Discussion in Washington." Vol.
         16 (December 1908), 28-30.

G1131.   ________. "Tariff Talk." Vol. 16 (November 1908),
         17.

G1132.   ________. "Teco Ware Made with Care by Gates and
         Mates." Vol. 16 (May 1908), 24-26. illus (3 b&w).

G1133.   ________. "United States Potters' Association." Vol.
         16 (December 1908), 17-25. illus (10 b&w).

G1134.   ________. "Van Briggle Name Adds to Colorado's Fame."
         Vol. 16 (April 1908), 15-16. illus (8 b&w).

G1135.   ________. "Wheeling Potteries Company Permanently
         Close Their General Ware Plants." Vol. 16 (July
         1908), 13.

G1136.   GOLDMAN, Judith. "Word is Out: Buy American Art
         Pottery." Vogue 170 (March 1980), 52. illus
         (2 b&w).

G1137.   GOLDNER, Steven. "The Moravian Pottery and Tile
         Works." Ceramics Monthly 26 (December 1978), 45-55.
         illus (20 b&w, 12 col).

G1138.   GOLDSMITH, M. O. "An Ancient Art in Modern Dress."
         Scientific American 125 (August 13, 1921), 120, 124.
         illus (4 b&w).

G1139.   GOLDSMITH, Margaret O. "Jugtown Pottery: Descendants
          of the Potters of Staffordshire Carry on the Tradi-
          tions in North Carolina." House Beautiful 52 (Octo-
          ber 1922), 311, 358, 360. illus (2 b&w).

G1140.   GOLDSTEIN, FANNY. "Editorial." S.E.G. News 4 (Novem-
          ber 13, 1915), 2-3.

G1141.   GOOD FURNITURE. "Our Native Stoneware [North Caroli-
          na]" Vol. 23 (October 1924), 178-179. illus (1 b&w).

G1142.   ________. "What Talent and Skill Can Do in the Pot-
          tery Industry." Vol. 8 (June 1917), 313-323.
          illus (12 b&w).

G1143.   GOODMAN, Guy. "Two Phases of American Pottery [Rook-
          wood; Dedham]" Arts for America 7 ([May]-June
          1898), 542-544, 546.

G1144.   GORDON, Eleanor and NERENBERG, Jean. "Chicago's Color-
          ful Terra Cotta Facades." Chicago History n.s.8
          (Winter 1979-1980), 224-233. illus (8 b&w); bibliog.

G1145.   GORDY, William J. "A Part of My Experience in the
          Pottery Business and My Father's Experience." Amer-
          ican Ceramic Society Bulletin 17 (September 1938),
          373-374. illus (3 b&w).

G1146.   GORTON, E. E. "A Pacific Coast Clayworking Plant:
          Gladding, McBean & Co." Clay-Worker 36 (October
          1901), 311-313. illus (2 b&w).

G1147.   GOULD, Charles N. "Clays and Shales of Oklahoma."
          Ceramist 7 (January 1926), 267-272. illus (4 b&w).

G1148.   GRAHAM, John Meredith, II. "A Bonnin and Morris Sweet-
          meat Dish." Antiques 50 (September 1946), 166.
          illus (1 b&w).

G1149.   ________. "The Earthenware of Bonnin and Morris."
          Antiques 45 (January 1944), 14-16. illus (8 b&w).

G1150.   GRAY, Walter Ellsworth. "Latter-Day Developments in
          American Pottery." Brush and Pencil 9 (January
          1902), 236-243. illus (8 b&w, 1 col).

G1151.   ________. "Latter-Day Developments in American Pot-
          tery--II." Brush and Pencil 9 (February 1902), 289-
          296. illus (10 b&w).

G1152.   ________. "Latter-Day Developments in American Pot-
          tery--[II]" Clay-Worker 38 (July 1902), 25-27.
          illus (6 b&w).
              Originally published in Brush and Pencil. See
          G1151.

G1153.   GRAY, Walter Ellsworth. "Latter-Day Developments in
         American Pottery--III." Brush and Pencil 9 (March
         1902), 353-360. illus (7 b&w).

G1154.   ________. "Latter-Day Developments in American Pot-
         tery--IV." Brush and Pencil 10 (April 1902), 31-38.
         illus (8 b&w).

G1155.   GREAVES-WALKER, A. F. "Ceramic Resources of the South."
         Ceramic Age 9 (February 1927), 37-39.

G1156.   ________. "The Development of the Ceramic Industries
         in North Carolina." Ceramist 7 (January 1926), 207-
         214. illus (5 b&w).

G1157.   ________. "The Laying of Drainage Tile." Claycrafter
         1 (March 1911), 87-89. illus (6 b&w).

G1158.   GREEMAN, Tamara. "Spongeware." Americana 5 (March
         1977), 32-33. illus (12 b&w).

G1159.   GREEN, Charles W. "Bennington Hid Royal Profiles:
         Victoria and Albert's Portraits Eliminated from
         Early Parian Vase." American Collector 2 (November
         29, 1934), 1, 11. illus (2 b&w).

G1160.   ________. "Color as Used on Bennington Parian." Amer-
         ican Collector 7 (April 1938), 10-11. illus (6 b&w).

G1161.   ________. "The Identification of Bennington Cameo Par-
         ian." Antiques 16 (September 1929), 197-199. illus
         (4 b&w).

G1162.   ________. "Old New England Porcelain [Bennington Par-
         ian]" Old-Time New England 22 (January 1932), 114-
         120. illus (5 b&w).

G1163.   ________. "Old New England Porcelain: The Fenton
         Potteries at Bennington, Vermont." Vermonter 37
         (August 1932), 169-173. illus (5 b&w).
         Reprint of G1162.

G1164.   ________. "Pond Lily Pitchers of Bennington." An-
         tiques 21 (January 1932), 26-27. illus (3 b&w).

G1165.   ________. "Some Bennington Pitchers." Antiques 17
         (May 1930), 431-433. illus (7 b&w).

G1166.   GREEN, Doris M. "Bennington Parian." Antiques
         Journal 17 (June 1962), 11-13. illus (10 b&w).

G1167.   GREEN, (Mrs.) H. G. "Cooking Utensils from Benning-
         ton, Vermont." Antiques Journal 21 (November 1966),
         20-22. illus (5 b&w).

G1168.   ________. "Household Items from Bennington, Vt." An-
         tiques Journal 17 (February 1962), 8-9. illus (6
         b&w).

G1169. GREER, Georgeanna H. "Alkaline Glazes and Groundhog
        Kilns: Southern Pottery Traditions." _Antiques_ 111
        (April 1977), 768-773. illus (7 b&w, 6 col); bibliog.

G1170. _________. "Southern Alkaline Glazed Stoneware: A
        Unique American Tradition." _Ceramic Circle of
        Charlotte Journal of Studies_ 4 (1980), 7-9. illus
        (2 b&w); bibliog.
           Prefatory to C23.

G1171. GRUNEWALD, Frederick L. "Gold in China Painting."
        Ceramic Monthly 2 (October 1895), 14-15.

G1172. GUIDOS, Harold R. "Chemical Stoneware Dipping Bas-
        kets." _Spinning Wheel_ 32 (March 1976), 32-33.
        illus (7 b&w).

G1173. GUILD, Lurelle Van Arsdale. "[Bell Potteries, Stras-
        burg, Va.]" _Country Life_ 60 (September 1931), 72.
        illus (1 b&w).

G1174. GUNTER, Herman. "The Clay Working Industries of
        Florida." _Ceramist_ 7 (January 1926), 273-276.

G1175. GUTHRIE, Hugh. "Man in a Hurry [H. C. Mercer]"
        American Life 5 (1965), 74-79. illus (28 b&w).

G1176. GUTMAN, Walter. "Four Potters [H. V. Poor, C. Walters,
        L. G. Volkmar, Soini]" _Arts_ 14 (September 1928),
        154-158. illus (5 b&w).

G1177. HADDON, Rawson W. "Early Slip Decorated Canister [J.
        Smith, Wrightstown, Pa.]" _Antiques_ 9 (March 1926),
        166. illus (1 b&w).

G1178. HALL, Alice C. "Cincinnati Faience." _Potter's Ameri-
        can Monthly_ 15 (November 1880), 357-365. illus
        (7 b&w).

G1179. HALL, Herbert J. "Marblehead Pottery." _Keramic
        Studio_ 10 (June 1908), 30-31. illus (7 b&w).

G1180. HALL, Horatio,F. "Tile Roofing in California." _Clay-
        Worker_ 74 (November 1920), 407-409. illus (3 b&w).

G1181. HAMBLETT, Theora. "Some Uses of Pottery [Ussery's
        Pottery, Water Valley-Banner, Miss.]" _Mississippi
        Folklore Register_ 3 (Spring 1969), 5-6.

G1182. HAMELL, George R. "Sewer-Pipe Pottery in Rochester,
        New York." _Antiques_ 106 (August 1974), 274-277.
        illus (6 b&w); bibliog.

G1183.   HAMILTON, Alice. "Hazards in American Potteries
         [Letter to Editor]" New Republic 31 (July 12, 1922),
         187.

G1184.   ______ . "Leadless Glaze: What It Means to Pottery
         and Tile Workers." Survey 31 (October 4, 1913),
         22-26. illus (2 b&w).

G1185.   HAMILTON, Byrde. "Ceramic Raw Materials in Texas."
         Ceramic Age 10 (December 1927), 220-221. illus
         (5 b&w).

G1186.   HAMILTON, Henry W. and HAMILTON, Jean Tyree. "Clay
         Pipes from Pamplin." Missouri Archaeologist 34
         (December 1972), 1-47. illus (23 b&w); bibliog.

G1187.   HAMPTON-COLUMBIAN MAGAZINE. "Personalities [M. L.
         McLaughlin]" Vol. 27 (January 1912), 835-836.
         illus (1 b&w).

G1188.   HANDICRAFT. "Enfield Pottery and Tile." Vol. 5
         (May 1912), 21-22.

G1189.   ______ . "Modern Maiolica [Marblehead Pottery]"
         Vol. 5 (June 1912), 42-43.

G1190.   ______ . "A Social and Business Experiment in the
         Making of Pottery [Paul Revere]" Vol. 3 (February
         1911), 411-416. illus (4 col).

G1191.   HANSON, E. S. "Development of a Sanitary Ware Plant:
         Woodbridge Ceramic Corporation." Ceramist 8 (Octo-
         ber 1926), 466-468, 472-477. illus (10 b&w).

G1192.   HARBY, J. M. "Clay Washing." American Ceramic
         Society Bulletin 6 (July 1927), 197-199.

G1193.   HARDCASTLE, Mildred Veley. "The Ack Potters of
         Mooresburg, Pa." Spinning Wheel 27 (October 1971),
         54. illus (2 b&w).

G1194.   ______ . "Cassville's Norman Greenland Pottery."
         Spinning Wheel 27 (June 1971), 58. illus (4 b&w).

G1195.   ______ . "The Cowden & Wilcox Pottery Story."
         Antiques Journal 23 (January-February 1968), 38-39.
         illus (2 b&w).

G1196.   ______ . "The Hyssong Potters." Spinning Wheel 26
         (June 1970), 30-31, 63. illus (5 b&w).

G1197.   ______ . "The Pfaltzgraff Pottery of York, Pa."
         Spinning Wheel 24 (December 1968), 24-25. illus
         (6 b&w).

G1198.   HARDCASTLE, Mildred Veley. "Potteries of Exeter Town-
          ship, Berks County, Pennsylvania." Spinning Wheel
          26 (January-February 1970), 14-15, 63. illus
          (6 b&w).

G1199.   __________. "Pottery: Patterson--Brookville--Brock-
          ville, near Pottsville, Pa." National Antiques
          Review 5 (July 1973), 35-36. illus (3 b&w).

G1200.   __________. "The Sipe Pottery of Williamsport, Penna."
          Antiques Journal 23 (April 1968), 23-24. illus
          (3 b&w).

G1201.   HARPER'S NEW MONTHLY MAGAZINE. "Porcelain-Painting."
          Vol. 61 (November 1880), 903-907.

G1202.   HARPER'S WEEKLY. "Cincinnati Art Pottery." Vol. 24
          (May 29, 1880), 341-342. illus (1 b&w).

G1203.   HARRINGTON, Mildred. "The Master Potter of Jugtown
          [J. Busbee]" American Magazine 103 (June 1927),
          72-74. illus (6 b&w).

G1204.   HARRIS, Cora. "The Virginian China [Lenox]" Arts &
          Decoration 1 (September 1911), 443. illus (2 b&w).

G1205.   HARRIS, Thomas C. "How Jugs are Made [N.C.]" Scien-
          tific American 86 (May 10, 1902), 331.

G1206.   HARRIS, W. S. "Curiosities of American Potting."
          Pottery, Glass & Brass Salesman 3 (February 16,
          1911), 43-44.

G1207.   HARRISON, James M. "The Case of the Disappearing
          Potters [E. Birmingham, Pa.]" Antiques Journal 34
          (March 1979), 32-33, 49. illus (2 b&w); bibliog.

G1208.   __________. "Some Early Buffalo Stoneware." Antiques
          Journal 32 (February 1977), 32, 50. illus (4 b&w).

G1209.   HARROP, C. B. "Continuous Tunnel Kilns at the Plant
          of Mount Clemens Pottery Company." American Ceramic
          Society Journal 4 (August 1921), 673-680. illus
          (5 b&w).

G1210.   HARTZELL, Cleve. "How Clay Products Can Win the War."
          Clay-Worker 69 (June 1918), 737-739. illus (3 b&w).

G1211.   HASKIN, Leslie L. "Three Early Oregon Potteries of
          Barnet Ramsay." Oregon Historical Quarterly 43
          (September 1942), 174-193. illus (5 b&w); bibliog.

G1212.   HASSELLE, Bob. "Rookwood: An American Art Pottery."
          Ceramics Monthly 26 (June 1978), 27-37. illus
          (20 b&w).

G1213.   HASWELL, Ernest Bruce. "American Pottery: A Recent
         Development of Faience in the Middle West [Rookwood]"
         Art World 3 (October 1917), 78-80. illus (5 b&w).

G1214.   HAWES, Lloyd E. "Hugh Cornwall Robertson and the
         Chelsea Period." Antiques 89 (March 1966), 409-413.
         illus (14 b&w).

G1215.   HAYWOOD, Maude. "Founded by a Woman [Rookwood]"
         Ladies' Home Journal 9 (October 1892), 3. illus
         (21 b&w).

G1216.   HEATH, Roger. "Bennington Pottery." Americana 7
         (January-February 1980), 28-32. illus (3 b&w,
         6 col).

G1217.   HECKMAN, Albert W. "Birds as Motifs in Design."
         Keramic Studio 21 (October 1919), 80-82. illus
         (9 b&w).

G1218.   __________. "A Design of To-Day--Mrs. Nina Hatfield."
         Design 26 (June 1924), 31-32. illus (4 b&w).

G1219.   __________. "The Rose as a Motif." Keramic Studio 21
         (September 1919), 61-64. illus (6 b&w).

G1220.   __________. "The Twenty-Fourth Annual Exhibition
         of the New York Society of Ceramic Art." Keramic
         Studio 24 (June 1922), 20-31. illus (49 b&w).

G1221.   HEGARTY, Marjorie. "Pewabic Pottery." Detroit Insti-
         tute of Arts Bulletin 26 (no. 3, 1947), 69-70.
         illus (1 b&w).

G1222.   HEIMLICH, Jane. "Pipes of Clay." Americana 7 (July-
         August 1979), 68-70. illus (2 b&w, 1 col).

G1223.   HEISEY, M. Luther. "The Makers of Pottery in Lancas-
         ter County." Lancaster County Historical Society
         Papers 50 (nos. 4/5, 1946), 117-128. illus (9 b&w);
         bibliog.

G1224.   __________. "Were Imported Bricks Used in Colonial
         America?" Lancaster County Historical Society
         Papers 50 (no. 3, 1946), 80-93. illus (3 b&w);
         bibliog.

G1225.   HELME, J. Burn. "Recent Developments in Architectural
         Ceramics." American Ceramic Society Bulletin 12
         (August 1933), 281-283.

G1226.   HENDERSON, (Mrs.) Palmer. "Henrietta Barclay Wright."
         Ceramic Monthly 4 (September 1896), 34-36. illus
         (2 b&w).

G1227.   HENRY, A. V. "The Ceramic Resources of Georgia."
          Ceramist 7 (January 1926), 195-198. illus
          (2 b&w).

G1228.   HENZKE, Lucile. "Art Pottery." Western Collector 9
          (July-August 1971), 36B-40. illus (12 b&w, 12 col).

G1229.   ________. "Newcomb Art Pottery." Spinning Wheel 24
          (September 1968), 12-13. illus (9 b&w).

G1230.   ________. "Roseville Pottery, Part One." Spinning
          Wheel 25 (November 1969), 16-17, 56. illus (10 b&w).

G1231.   ________. "Roseville Pottery, Part Two." Spinning
          Wheel 25 (December 1969), 22-24, 40. illus (10 b&w).

G1232.   ________. "Weller's Dickens Ware." Spinning Wheel
          24 (October 1968), 16-18. illus (9 b&w).

G1233.   ________. "Weller's Sicardo." Spinning Wheel 25
          (September 1969), 26-28, 67. illus (10 b&w).

G1234.   HERSH, J. Joseph. "Steins Americana." Antiques
          Journal 35 (May 1980), 30-33, 51 illus (12 b&w);
          bibliog.

G1235.   HETTINGER, Edwin L. "Early Pennsylvania Potters."
          American-German Review 9 (December 1942), 23-26.
          illus (6 b&w).

G1236.   ________. "The Importance of Pottery to the Early
          Settlers." Ceramic Industry 39 (July 1942), 48, 50.
          illus (3 b&w).

G1237.   HICE, Richard R. "The White Clay Possibilities of
          Pennsylvania." American Ceramic Society Journal 2
          (September 1919), 685-694. illus (3 b&w).

G1238.   HIGHTOWER, John M., Jr. "Clay Smoking Pipes."
          Antiques Journal 31 (April 1976), 30-33, 46. illus
          (33 b&w).

G1239.   HILL, Charles W. "Opinions of a Factory Man on Ceramic
          Education." Ceramist 7 (November 1925), 94-102, 107-
          111.

G1240.   ________. "Terra Cotta." Ceramist 4 (September 1924),
          363-370. illus (6 b&w).

G1241.   HINMAN, (Mrs.) Teanna McLennan. "The Annual Exhibition
          of the Chicago Ceramic Art Association." Keramic
          Studio 4 (December 1902), 166-167. illus (5 b&w).

G1242.   HOAGLAND, Jane. "Jugtown Pottery." Art Center New
          York Bulletin 1 (April 1923), 167-168. illus
          (1 b&w).

G1243.   HOBBIES. "Ceramic Studio Attracts Wide Notice [De Dou
          Studio]" Vol. 38 (March 1933), 82.

G1244.   _________. "Historical Bennington Pitcher." Vol. 42
          (October 1937), 72-74. illus (1 b&w).

G1245.   _________. "Old Motor Cars Shown as Old Shaving Mugs."
          Vol. 59 (March 1954), 99. illus (1 b&w).

G1246.   _________. "Presidential Plates [Lenox]" Vol. 57
          (June 1952), 82-83. illus (1 b&w).

G1247.   HOCKER, Edward W. "How an Archaeologist Became a
          Craftsman and Developed a New Art-Industry [H. C.
          Mercer]" Craftsman (August 1907), 549-551.

G1248.   HOFMAN, Caroline. "Design for the Decoration of
          China." Keramic Studio 9 (January 1908), 210-212.
          illus (3 b&w).

G1249.   _________. "Design for the Decoration of China, First
          Paper, Continued." Keramic Studio 9 (February 1908),
          226-227. illus (6 b&w).

G1250.   _________. "Design for the Decoration of China, Second
          Paper." Keramic Studio 9 (March 1908), 254-255.
          illus (5 b&w).

G1251.   _________. "Design for the Decoration of China, Second
          Paper, Continued." Keramic Studio 9 (April 1908),
          282-284. illus (4 b&w).

G1252.   _________. "Design for the Decoration of China, Third
          Paper." Keramic Studio 10 (May 1908), 15-17. illus
          (5 b&w).

G1253.   _________. "Design for the Decoration of China, Fourth
          Paper." Keramic Studio 10 (July 1908), 50-53.
          illus (9 b&w).

G1254.   _________. "Design for the Decoration of China, Fifth
          Paper." Keramic Studio 10 (August 1908), 86-87.
          illus (3 b&w).

G1255.   _________. "Design for the Decoration of China, Sixth
          Paper." Keramic Studio 10 (September 1908), 104-105.
          illus (3 b&w).

G1256.   _________. "Design for the Decoration of China,
          Seventh Paper." Keramic Studio 10 (October 1908),
          133-134. illus (5 b&w).

G1257.   HOLDEN, Marion L. "The Pewabic Pottery." American
          Magazine of Art 17 (January 1926), 22-27. illus
          (6 b&w).

G1258.   HOLMBERG, Millicent B. "Fascinating Figurals [Bottles]"
          Western Collector 9 (July-August 1971), 35. illus
          (2 b&w).

G1259.   HOLMES, George Sanford. "A Master Craftsman--Walter
          Scott Lenox." American Magazine of Art 16 (January
          1925), 21-25.

G1260.   ________. "Walter Scott Lenox." American Ceramic
          Society Bulletin 16 (April 1937), 177-180. illus
          (1 b&w).
              Excerpted from A114.

G1261.   HOMER, William I. "Carl Walters, Ceramic Sculptor."
          Art in America 44 (Fall 1956), 42-47, 64-65. illus
          (9 b&w, 1 col).

G1262.   HOMMEL, Martha Hill. "Some More about Lithophanes."
          Hobbies 55 (July 1950), 76-77. illus (4 b&w).

G1263.   HOMMEL, Rudolf. "The Duché Family, Colonial Master
          Potters." Hobbies 54 (May 1949), 80-81.

G1264.   [________] (Pseud.: Goyle, G. A. R.) "First Porcelain
          Making in America." Early American Industries Asso-
          ciation Chronicle 1 (November 1934), 1, 3-4.

G1265.   ________. "First Porcelain Making In America [Part
          2]" Early American Industries Association Chronicle
          1 (January 1935), 3, 7.

G1266.   ________. "First Porcelain Making In America [Part
          3]" Early American Industries Association Chronicle
          1 (March 1935), 3.

G1267.   ________. "First Porcelain Making In America [Part
          4]" Early American Industries Association Chronicle
          1 (May 1935), 6.

G1268.   HOOD, Graham. "Bonnin and Morris of Philadelphia:
          The First American Porcelain Factory, 1770-1772."
          Antiques 102 (December 1972), 1088-1090. illus
          (6 b&w).

G1269.   ________. "The Career of Andrew Duché." Art Quarterly
          31 (Summer 1968), 168-184. bibliog.

G1270.   ________. "New Light on Bonnin and Morris." Antiques
          95 (June 1969), 812-817. illus (13 b&w).

G1271.   HOPF, Carroll. "Oddities in Early American Pottery."
          Spinning Wheel 25 (July-August 1969), 10-12. illus
          (18 b&w).

G1272.   ________. "Redware Pottery." Spinning Wheel 27 (July-
          August 1971), 14-15, 58. illus (10 b&w).

G1273.   HORNEY, Wayne B. "Pottery of the Galena Area."
         Spinning Wheel 22 (July-August 1966), 20-21. illus
         (5 b&w).

G1274.   HORNOR, W. M., Jr. "Tucker and Hemphill Porcelain
         Works." Antiques 13 (June 1928), 480-484. illus
         (7 b&w).

G1275.   HOTTINGER, A. F. "Looking Backward in the Terra Cotta
         Field." American Ceramic Society Journal 6 (January
         1923), 306-308.

G1276.   HOUGH, Walter. "An Early American Pottery [at Morgan-
         town, W.Va.]" House Beautiful 11 (January 1902),
         85-92. illus (9 b&w).

G1277.   HOUSE & GARDEN. "An American Potter [H. C. Mercer]"
         Vol. 1 (August 1901), 12-19. illus (12 b&w).

G1278.   __________. "A Colorado Industry [Van Briggle]" Vol.
         4 (October 1903), 165-168. illus (6 b&w).

G1279.   __________. "The Ornamentation of the New Subway Sta-
         tions in New York." Vol. 5 (February 1904), 96-99.
         illus (8 b&w).

G1280.   __________. "The Ornamentation of the New Subway Sta-
         tions in New York (Second Article)" Vol. 5 (June
         1904), 287-292.

G1281.   HOUSE BEAUTIFUL. "American Slip Ware." Vol. 25 (Feb-
         ruary 1909), xvi. illus (1 b&w).

G1282.   __________. "The Art-Craft Movement in a College Art
         Department [Newcomb]" Vol. 15 (March 1904), 204-
         207. illus (7 b&w).

G1283.   __________. "Charming Pieces of Pottery for Your Garden
         Which Are Reproductions of Masterpieces of Ceramic
         Art, Designed by E. E. Soderholtz." Vol. 45 (March
         1919), 132-133. illus (15 b&w).

G1284.   __________. "Decorative Tiles." Vol. 40 (July 1916),
         76-77. illus (13 b&w).

G1285.   __________. "The Paul Revere Pottery: An American
         Craft Industry." Vol. 51 (January 1922), 50, 70.
         illus (3 b&w).

G1286.   HOVEY, H. C. "How Crucibles Are Made." Scientific
         American Supplement 50 (November 24, 1900), 20828-
         20829.

G1287.   HOWE, Ruth Wood. "Memories of the Fentons." Antiques
         8 (September 1925), 150-154. illus (11 b&w).

G1288.   HUDSON, Charles J. "A Study of the Operation of a
          Dressler Tunnel Kiln." American Ceramic Society
          Journal 4 (September 1921), 738-754. illus (8 b&w).

G1289.   HUDSON, J. Paul. "Earliest Yorktown Pottery."
          Antiques 73 (May 1958), 472-473.

G1290.   HUDSON, J. Paul, and WATKINS, C. Malcolm. "The
          Earliest Known English Colonial Pottery in America."
          Antiques 71 (January 1957), 51-54. illus (11 b&w).

G1291.   HULL, A. E., Jr. "One Fire Whiteware and Art Ware
          through Direct Fired Car Tunnel Kiln [Hull Pottery
          Co.]" American Ceramic Society Journal 7 (April
          1924), 285-287. illus (3 b&w).

G1292.   HULL, Mary L. "Training Required for the Work of an
          Architectural Colorist." American Ceramic Society
          Journal 13 (May 1930), 40-44.

G1293.   HULL, Walter A. "Hollow Tile as a Factor in Fire
          Prevention." Clay-Worker 69 (June 1918), 740-743.
          illus (3 b&w).

G1294.   HULL, William. "Some Notes on Early Robineau Porce-
          lains." Everson Museum of Art Bulletin 22 (no. 2,
          1960), [1-6]. illus (7 b&w).

G1295.   HUMPHREYS, Mary Gay. "Volkmar Faïence." Art Amateur
          8 (January 1883), 42-43. illus (1 b&w).

G1296.   HUNGERFORD, Nicholas. "The Aid of Architectural Pot-
          tery to Garden Design: The Emphasis of Well-Placed
          Water Jars of Terra Cotta in the Semi-Formal
          Garden." Arts & Decoration 3 (July 1913), 309-311.
          illus (5 b&w).

G1297.   __________. "The Work of American Potters. Article
          Three: The Story of Rookwood." Arts & Decoration 1
          (February 1911), 160-162. illus (5 b&w).
              Articles 1, 2, 4, 5 are: G948, G2311, G866, G1675.

G1298.   HUNT, W. D. "Porcelains [A. A. Robineau]" Keramic
          Studio 9 (December 1907), 178-180. illus (9 b&w).

G1299.   HUNT, W. F. "Midget Sample Jugs." Spinning Wheel 25
          (June 1969), 28. illus (1 b&w).

G1300.   HUTCHINSON, Elmer T. "Keen Pruden's Earthenware Pot-
          tery in Elizabethtown." New Jersey Historical
          Society Proceedings 73 (January 1955), 24-27.
          bibliog.

G1301.   HUTSON, Ethel. "Encaustic and Mosaic Tiles . . .
          United States Encaustic Tile Works, Indianapolis."
          Clay-Worker 45 (January 1906), 49-53. illus (9 b&w).

G1302. HUTSON, Ethel. "The McDade Pottery, Where Charcoal
        Furnaces Are Made." Clay-Worker 45 (June 1906),
        848-849. illus (4 b&w).

G1303. ________. "Newcomb Pottery, a Successful Experiment
        in Applied Art." Clay-Worker 45 (May 1906), 732-
        734. illus (5 b&w).

G1304. ________. "Quaint Biloxi Pottery [G. Ohr]" Clay-
        Worker 44 (September 1905), 225-227. illus (6 b&w).

G1305. IGLEHART, Margaret Ellen. "National League of Mineral
        Painters: Study Courses for 1908-1909." Keramic
        Studio 10 (September 1908), 97.

G1306. INDEPENDENT. "Rookwood Pottery: A Woman's Contribu-
        tion to American Craftsmanship." Vol. 77 (March 16,
        1914), 377. illus (3 b&w).

G1307. INGHAM, John H. "Moravian Tiles [Moravian Pottery and
        Tile Works]" Handicraft 5 (May 1912), 22-23.

G1308. INGRAM, Sara. "Characteristic Tucker Porcelain at the
        DAR Museum." American Antiques 6 (January 1978),
        18-19. illus (3 b&w).

G1309. INLAND ARCHITECT AND BUILDER. "Some Recent Terra-
        Cotta Work." Vol. 7 (July 1886), 97-98.

G1310. INTERIOR ARCHITECTURE AND DECORATION. "From the Native
        Potter's Wheel [Sloane Exh.]" Vol. 37 (December
        1931), 280-281. illus (4 b&w).

G1311. INTERNATIONAL STUDIO. "Clay Industries at the Newark
        Museum." Vol. 55 (March 1915), xviii.

G1312. ________. "An Interesting Ceramic Exhibition [Burley
        & Tyrrell]" Vol. 45 (January 1912), lxxx. illus
        (2 b&w).

G1313. ________. "New York Society of Keramic Arts." Vol.
        38 (September 1909), lxix-lxxii. illus (10 b&w).

G1314. JACK, Phil R. and MICHAEL, Ronald L. "Stoneware from
        New Geneva and Greensboro, Pennsylvania." Pennsyl-
        vania Folklife 22 (Summer 1973), 34-42. illus
        (14 b&w).

G1315. JACOBY, H. S. "Modern Trend of Design for Pottery
        Plants." American Ceramic Society Bulletin 7
        (July 1928), 184-190. illus (6 b&w).

G1316. JAMES, Arthur E. "'Tucker and Hemphill China'."
        American Antiques Journal 2 (August 1947), 14-15.
        illus (3 b&w).

G1317.   JAMISON, M. "A Queen of Egypt ['Cleopatra' by I.
          Broome]" Ceramic Monthly 2 (August 1895), 12-14.
          illus (1 b&w).

G1318.   JANS, John T. "Operation Data on Continuous Decorating
          Kiln at Mt. Clemens Pottery Co." American Ceramic
          Society Journal 7 (August 1924), 626-629. illus
          (4 b&w).

G1319.   JAQUES, Bertha. "The American Potteries--The Pauline
          Pottery." Sketch Book 5 (June 1906), 377-381.
          illus (8 b&w).

G1320.   JARVIE, Lillian Gray. "Our American Potteries: The
          Markham Pottery." Sketch Book 5 (November 1905),
          123-129. illus (4 b&w).

G1321.   JAYNE, Horace H. F. "A Note on Thomas Tucker."
          Philadelphia Museum of Art Bulletin 52 (Spring 1957),
          55-58. illus (1 b&w).

G1322.   ________. "Tucker Porcelain: Thomas Tucker's Share."
          Antiques 72 (September 1957), 237-239. illus
          (5 b&w).

G1323.   JENKINS, Marguerite. "Is the Potter's Wheel Passing?"
          Ceramic Age 16 (October 1930), 219-220. illus
          (1 b&w).

G1324.   JENNEY & MUNDRIE, Architects. "A New Departure in
          Terra Cotta Work: Will D. Gates's Beautiful Home."
          Clay-Worker 21 (January 1894), 19-20. illus
          (1 b&w).

G1325.   JERVIS, W. P. "American Pottery--Jervis Mat Glazes."
          Sketch Book 6 (November 1907), 307-310. illus
          (4 b&w).

G1326.   ________. "Greatback's [sic] Hound Handle Pitcher [D.
          Greatbach]" Old China 2 (February 1903), 95-97.
          illus (3 b&w).

G1327.   ________. "Pottery at Home." Handicraft 4 (December
          1911), 315-318.

G1328.   ________. "Pottery Flower Vases." House & Garden 9
          (May 1906), 223-227. illus (12 b&w).

G1329.   ________. "A Pottery Primer: United States [Part 1]."
          Pottery, Glass & Brass Salesman 2 (December 29,
          1910), 11-12, 24. illus (1 b&w).

G1330.   ________. "A Pottery Primer: United States [Part 2]."
          Pottery, Glass & Brass Salesman 2 (January 5, 1911),
          17-19, 28. illus (2 b&w).
              G1329 and 1330 also appear as a chapter in Jervis'
          Pottery Primer. See B46.

G1331.   JERVIS, William Percival. "Rose Valley Pottery."
         Artsman 2 (November 1904), 47-50.

G1332.   ________. "Rose Valley Pottery." Crockery and Glass
         Journal 60 (December 15, 1904), [185-186]. illus
         (3 b&w).

G1333.   ________. "Taxile Doat." Keramic Studio 4 (July
         1902), 54-55. illus (5 b&w).

G1334.   JEWELL, Margaret H. "The Corliss Pottery at Woolwich,
         Maine." Old-Time New England 22 (April 1932), 180-
         183. illus (3 b&w).

G1335.   ________. "Notes on Maine Potteries." Old-Time New
         England 22 (April 1932), 184-187. illus (3 b&w).

G1336.   JILLSON, Herbert L. "George DeForest Brush." Art
         Interchange 46 (April 1901), 75-76. illus (1 b&w).

G1337.   JILLSON, Willard Rouse. "The Clays of Kentucky."
         Ceramist 7 (February 1926), 280-285. illus (3 b&w).

G1338.   JOHNS, H. W. "Making Terra Cotta Columns." Clay-
         Worker 58 (September 1912), 274-276. illus (4 b&w).

G1339.   ________. "Making Terra Cotta Columns. Part II:
         Form and Working Methods." Clay-Worker 58 (October
         1912), 390-392. illus (4 b&w).

G1340.   JOHNSON, Deb, and JOHNSON, Gini. "Peters and Reed and
         Zane Pottery." Antiques Journal 30 (April 1975),
         10-13, 44. illus (12 b&w).

G1341.   ________. "A Roseville Sleeper." Antiques Journal 29
         (July 1974), 31-33. illus (9 b&w).

G1342.   JOHNSON, Henry Lewis. "Merrimac Pottery." House
         Beautiful 13 (February 1903), 177-180. illus
         (5 b&w).

G1343.   JOHNSON, Jane Stannard. "Domestic Art Pottery and
         Its Manufacture." Scientific American Supplement 63
         (May 25, 1907), 26237-26238. illus (8 b&w).

G1344.   JOHNSON, Virginia Coleman. "Niloak Pottery." Antiques
         Journal 28 (July 1973), 28-30, 45. illus (4 b&w).

G1345.   JOHNSTON, Pat H.   "Omar Khayyam Pottery." Antiques
         Journal 29 (September 1974), 10-13, 48. illus
         (10 b&w).

G1346.   ________. "Pisgah Forest and Nonconnah Pottery."
         Antiques Journal 32 (May 1977), 12-15, 46-47, 49.
         illus (11 b&w).

G1347.   JONES, Annie M. "The Grueby Pottery." Scrip 1 (March
          1906), 197-199.

G1348.   JONES, Robert W. "Albany Slip Clay." American Ceramic
          Society Transactions 18 (1916), 242-262. illus
          (9 b&w).

G1349.   JOOR, Harriet. "Pottery-Making Without a Wheel."
          Craftsman 19 (November 1910), 204-206. illus
          (7 b&w).

G1350.   JUDGE, F. P., Jr. "Need for Research and Education
          in the Dinnerware Branch of the Ceramic Industry."
          American Ceramic Society Bulletin 6 (January 1927),
          34-36.

         KAHLE, Katharine Morrison, see also McCLINTON,
         Katharine Morrison.

G1351.   KAHLE, Katharine Morrison. "American Shaving Mugs."
          Antiques 33 (May 1938), 268-270. illus (5 b&w).

G1352.   KAMERLING, Bruce. "Anna and Albert Valentien: the
          Arts and Crafts Movement in San Diego." Journal of
          San Diego History 24 (Summer 1978), 343-366. illus
          (21 b&w); bibliog.

G1353.   KANE, Bill. "Names and Dates on Pottery." Hobbies 52
          (October 1947), 72-73.

G1354.   KANE, Thomas F. "A Lifetime of Work in Ceramics:
          Dean Earle J. Babcock, University of North Dakota
          [Obituary]" American Ceramic Society Bulletin 4
          (October 1925), 554-555.

G1355.   KAYE, Myrna. "Art Noveau Ceramics." American Home 72
          (November 1969), 22, 24. illus (3 b&w).

G1356.   KECHIJIAN, (Mrs.) Harry M. "Belleek." Antiques
          Journal 22 (October 1967), 8-20. illus (29 b&w);
          bibliog.

G1357.   KEELER, R. B. "The Use of Clay Products in Modern
          Homes." American Ceramic Society Bulletin 4 (July
          1925), 310-320. illus (16 b&w).

G1358.   KEEN, Kirsten H. "American Art Pottery, 1875-1930."
          American Art Review 4 (May 1978), 100-103, 123-125.
          illus (2 b&w, 10 col); bibliog.

G1359.   KEENER, William G. "Ohio Potters and Potteries."
          Spinning Wheel 19 (July-August 1963), 47. illus
          (2 b&w).

G1360.   KELSEY, V. V. "Cincinnati and Ceramics." Ceramic Age
          23 (February 1934), 36, 55.

G1361.   KELSO, William M., and CHAPPELL, Edward A. "Excavation
          of a Seventeenth Century Pottery Kiln at Glebe Harbor,
          Westmoreland County, Virginia." Historical Archaeol-
          ogy 8 (1974), 53-63. illus (8 b&w); bibliog.

G1362.   KEMPF, William C. "A Day in the Raritan River District
          of New Jersey." Ceramic Age 10 (October 1927), 136-
          138. illus (6 b&w).

G1363.   KENNEDY, Donald. "Industrial Relations in the Pottery
          Industry." Journal of Political Economy 35 (August
          1927), 522-542. bibliog.

G1364.   KENO, Leigh. "Odell & Booth Brothers: Art Potters of
          Tarrytown." Arts & Antiques 3 (March-April 1980),
          96-101. illus (6 b&w, 1 col).

G1365.   KERAMIC STUDIO. "The Alhambra Ceramic Works." Vol. 8
          (April 1907), 272. illus (1 b&w).

G1366.   _______. "Atlan Club Exhibit." Vol. 3 (January
          1902), 203. illus (3 b&w).

G1367.   _______. "The Atlan Club of Chicago." Vol. 1
          (August 1899), 75-76. illus (6 b&w).

G1368.   _______. "Beautiful China for White House." Vol. 4
          (November 1902), 154-155.

G1369.   _______. "Burley & Co.'s Exhibition." Vol. 15
          (December 1913), 124-216. illus (8 b&w).

G1370.   _______. "Burley & Tyrrell Company's Exhibit." Vol.
          17 (May 1915), 6-10. illus (10 b&w).

G1371.   _______. "Burley Exhibit." Vol. 13 (January 1912),
          200-203. illus (6 b&w).

G1372.   _______. "Burley Exhibition." Vol. 14 (December
          1912), 166.

G1373.   _______. "The Burley Exhibition." Vol. 17 (January
          1916), 121-129. illus (7 b&w).

G1374.   _______. "Ceramics at the Art Institute, Chicago."
          Vol. 10 (March 1909), 251-254. illus (17 b&w).

G1375.   _______. "Chautauqua Studio of Mrs. Vance Phillips."
          Vol. 5 (October 1903), 135. illus (2 b&w).

G1376.   _______. "The Chicago Art Association." Vol. 18
          (January 1917), 133-135. illus (9 b&w).

G1377.   _______. "Chicago Ceramic Art Association." Vol. 17
          (February 1916), 136-138. illus (6 b&w).

G1378.   KERAMIC STUDIO.   "Chicago Ceramic Art Association."
         Vol. 19 (April 1918), 186-189.   illus (13 b&w).

G1379.   _________.   "Chicago Ceramic Art Association."   Vol. 21
         (December 1919), 125-128.   illus (8 b&w).

G1380.   _________.   "Chicago Exhibition [Chicago Ceramic Art
         Assoc.]"   Vol. 2 (February 1901), 206.

G1381.   _________.   "Chicago Exhibition [Chicago Ceramic Art
         Assoc.]"   Vol. 8 (July 1906), 50-51.   illus (6 b&w).

G1382.   _________.   "A Class in Design--Mr. Arthur Dow, Instruc-
         tor."   Vol. 3 (August 1901), 75-80.   illus (21 b&w).

G1383.   _________.   "Duquesne Ceramic Club."   Vol. 18 (May
         1916), 2-6.   illus (7 b&w).

G1384.   _________.   "Eighth Annual Exhibition--National Society
         of Craftsmen."   Vol. 17 (July 1915), 33-35.   illus
         (12 b&w).

G1385.   _________.   "Enameling by Dorothea Warren O'Hara."
         Vol. 14 (February 1913), 204-208.   illus (14 b&w).

G1386.   _________.   "Exhibit of Hartford Keramic Art Club,
         Hartford, Conn."   Vol. 21 (September 1919), 66-67.
         illus (2 b&w).

G1387.   _________.   "Exhibit of the Buffalo Society of Mineral
         Painters."   Vol. 14 (June 1912), 31-33.   illus
         (5 b&w).

G1388.   _________.   "Exhibit of the Keramic Society of Greater
         New York."   Vol. 16 (March 1915), 198-208.   illus
         (38 b&w).

G1389.   _________.   "Exhibition: National League of Mineral
         Painters."   Vol. 1 (July 1899), 44-45.

G1390.   _________.   "Exhibition of the Chicago Ceramic Art
         Association.   Vol. 9 (August 1907), 88-89.   illus
         (4 b&w).

G1391.   _________.   "Exhibition of the National Society of
         Craftsmen, New York [Ceramic Guild]"   Vol. 15
         (March 1914), 180-187.   illus (24 b&w).

G1392.   _________.   "Exhibition of the New York Society."   Vol.
         7 (June 1905), 25-28.   illus (11 b&w).

G1393.   _________.   "Exhibition of the New York Society of
         Ceramic Arts."   Vol. 9 (June 1907), 37-42.   illus
         (23 b&w).

G1394.   KERAMIC STUDIO. "Exhibition of the New York Society
          of Keramic Arts." Vol. 2 (January 1901), 184-186.
          illus (9 b&w).

G1395.   _______. "Exhibition of the N[ew] Y[ork] S[ociety of]
          K[eramic] A[rts]" Vol. 4 (February 1903), 216-218.
          illus (9 b&w).

G1396.   _______. "Exhibition of the N[ew] Y[ork] S[ociety of]
          K[eramic] A[rts], Continued." Vol. 4 (March 1903),
          237-240. illus (13 b&w).

G1397.   _______. "Exhibition of the New York Society of
          Keramic Arts." Vol. 5 (February 1904), 222-224.
          illus (10 b&w).

G1398.   _______. "Exhibition of the New York Society of
          Keramic Arts." Vol. 11 (June 1909), 33-41. illus
          (29 b&w).

G1399.   _______. "Exhibition of the Newark Society of Keramic
          Arts." Vol. 10 (May 1908), 4-7. illus (6 b&w).

G1400.   _______. "Four Winds Pottery Summer School." Vol. 14
          (October 1912), 115-122. illus (14 b&w).

G1401.   _______. "Frackelton Blue and Grey." Vol. 3 (Decem-
          ber 1901), 166. illus (2 b&w).

G1402.   _______. "[Gold Work]" Vol. 7 (December 1905), 167-
          168, 170, 172-173.

G1403.   _______. "Gold Work, Continued." Vol. 7 (January
          1906), 191-192, 194, 196, 198.

G1404.   _______. "An Historical Collection of the Rookwood
          Pottery [Cincinnati Art Museum]" Vol. 8 (April
          1907), 274. illus (4 b&w).

G1405.   _______. "Individual Exhibits at the Paris Exhibi-
          tion." Vol. 2 (September 1900), 95.

G1406.   _______. "Louisiana Purchase Exposition Ceramics:
          Rookwood Pottery." Vol. 6 (January 1905), 193-194.
          illus (6 b&w).

G1407.   _______. "Louisiana Purchase Exposition Ceramics,
          Continued." Vol. 6 (February 1905), 216-219. illus
          (14 b&w).

G1408.   _______. "Louisiana Purchase Exposition Ceramics,
          Continued." Vol. 6 (March 1905), 251-252. illus
          (6 b&w).

G1409.   KERAMIC STUDIO. "Louisiana Purchase Exposition Ceram-
          ics, Continued." Vol. 6 (April 1905), 268-269.
          illus (8 b&w).

G1410.   _________. "Louisiana Purchase Exposition Ceramics,
          Continued." Vol. 7 (May 1905), 7-8. illus (9 b&w).

G1411.   _________. "Minneapolis Keramic Club Exhibit." Vol.
          21 (July-August 1919), 43. illus (4 b&w).

G1412.   _________. "Moravian Pottery [and Tile Works]" Vol.
          11 (August 1909), 79-80. illus (7 b&w).

G1413.   _________. "The National Arts Club Exhibit of Porce-
          lain and Pottery at the Pan-American." Vol. 3
          (November 1901), 144-145.

G1414.   _________. "National Arts Club [Exhibition of Pottery]"
          Vol. 1 (February 1900), 212-213. illus (3 b&w).

G1415.   _________. "National League Exhibit at the Pan-Ameri-
          can." Vol. 3 (December 1901), 173-174.

G1416.   _________. "New York Society of Keramic Arts." Vol.
          3 (February 1902), 219-222. illus (24 b&w).

G1417.   _________. "New York Society of Keramic Arts: List
          of Members." Vol. 10 (June 1908), 45.

G1418.   _________. "Newark Society of Keramic Arts." Vol. 14
          (September 1912), 104-108. illus (6 b&w).

G1419.   _________. "Newcomb Pottery." Vol. 3 (February 1902),
          214-215. illus (5 b&w).

G1420.   _________. "Philadelphia Exhibit." Vol. 17 (February
          1916), 142-143. illus (5 b&w).

G1421.   _________. "Pottery at the Arts and Crafts Exhibit,
          Craftsman Building, Syracuse." Vol. 5 (June 1903),
          36-38. illus (7 b&w).

G1422.   _________. "Pottery at University City." Vol. 11
          (January 1910), 185.

G1423.   _________. "Roblin Ware of Mrs. Linna Irelan." Vol. 3
          (January 1902), 190-191. illus (7 b&w).

G1424.   _________. "Rookwood Architectural Faience." Vol. 5
          (September 1903), 110-111. illus (5 b&w).

G1425.   _________. "Rookwood Pottery for Paris Exhibit."
          Vol. 1 (March 1900), 221, 228, 231. illus (8 b&w).

G1426.   _________. "Shawsheen Ware." Vol. 13 (September 1911),
          104-105. illus (7 b&w).

G1427.   KERAMIC STUDIO. "Steins of the Salmagundi Club."
         Vol. 2 (May 1900), 7. illus (5 b&w).

G1428.   _________. "Steins of the Salmagundi Club." Vol. 3
         (May 1901), 7. illus (7 b&w).

G1429.   _________. "A Summer Pottery School [Alfred]" Vol. 2
         (January 1901), 183.

G1430.   _________. "The Summer School of Clay Working at Alfred,
         N.Y." Vol. 5 (October 1903), 125-126. illus (3 b&w).

G1431.   _________. "Twin City Keramic Club." Vol. 17 (Septem-
         ber 1915), 59-61. illus (8 b&w).

G1432.   _________. "Work of the Summer School at Alfred." Vol.
         4 (October 1902), 119-121. illus (10 b&w).

G1433.   KERAMIC TILE JOURNAL. "Announcing the Formation of
         the Pardee Matawan Tile Company." Vol. 2 (September
         1930), 27-29. illus (6 b&w).

G1434.   _________. "Art Finds Expression in World's Largest
         Doll's House [Flint Faience]" Vol. 2 (October 1930),
         12-13. illus (3 b&w).

G1435.   _________. "The Faience Facadi of the Stewart Building,
         Fifth Avenue and Fifty-Sixth Street, New York." Vol.
         2 (January 1930), 15-17. illus (5 b&w).

G1436.   _________. "The History of Rodgers Tile Company." Vol.
         2 (November 1930), 34-36. illus (6 b&w).

G1437.   _________. "Increasing the Lure of the Swimming Pool."
         Vol. 2 (December 1930), 31-35, 55-56. illus (8 b&w).

G1438.   _________. "A Modern Showroom [Star Tiling Co.]" Vol.
         2 (January 1930), 34-35. illus (2 b&w).

G1439.   _________. "More Convention Exhibits Seen at the Recent
         Detroit Convention." Vol. 1 (June 1929), 38-40.
         illus (9 b&w).

G1440.   _________. "The New Showrooms of Pardee Tiles." Vol.
         1 (November 1929), 36-37, 40. illus (5 b&w).

G1441.   KETCHUM, William C., Jr. "Advertising Stoneware."
         Antiques Journal 29 (May 1974), 25-26, 54. illus
         (6 b&w).

G1442.   _________. "American Stoneware: The Product of a
         Single Century." Antique Collecting 1 (August 1977),
         6-7. illus (10 b&w).

G1443.   _________. "Decorative Techniques in American Stone-
         ware." Antiques Journal 34 (April 1979), 22-24, 51.
         illus (5 b&w).

G1444.   KETCHUM, William C., Jr. "Early American Porcelain
          & Pottery." Western Collector 9 (July-August 1971),
          4-8. illus (10 b&w).

G1445.   ________. "Mid 19th Century New York City Stoneware."
          Spinning Wheel 30 (July-August 1974), 40-41. illus
          (5 b&w).

G1446.   ________. "Miniature Pottery." Antiques Journal 31
          (October 1976), 21-23. illus (3 b&w).

G1447.   ________. "The Pottery of the South." Antiques Jour-
          nal 28 (September 1973), 13-15, 54. illus (6 b&w).

G1448.   ________. "Yellowware." Americana 6 (March-April
          1978), 42-44. illus (2 col).

G1449.   KEYES, Homer Eaton. "The 'Cupid and Psyche' Pattern."
          Antiques 24 (October 1933), 132-133. illus (3 b&w).

G1450.   ________. "Perplexities in Pottery." Antiques 23
          (February 1933), 54-55. illus (7 b&w).

G1451.   KIM, George. "Shaving Mugs." Antiques Journal 22
          (January 1967), 15-17, 21. illus (20 b&w).

G1452.   KINDIG, Joe, Jr. "A Note on Early North Carolina
          Pottery." Antiques 27 (January 1935), 14-15. illus
          (4 b&w).

G1453.   KING, Martha Feller. "'Spotting' as Motif in China
          Decoration." Keramic Studio 10 (September 1908),
          110-111. illus (4 b&w).

G1454.   KING, Pauline. "Decorated Mugs at the New York Sal-
          magundi Club." House Beautiful 6 (November 1899),
          276-281. illus (7 b&w).

G1455.   KING, William A. "Ceramic Art at the Pan-American
          Exposition." Crockery & Glass Journal 53 (May 30,
          1901), 15-18. illus (5 b&w).

G1456.   KINGSLEY, Rose G. "Rookwood Pottery." Art Journal
          (London) 49 (November 1897), 341-346. illus
          (11 b&w).

G1457.   KIRK, Charles J. "The Dressler Tunnel Kiln's Early
          History." American Ceramic Society Bulletin 13
          (November 1934), 325-326.

G1458.   KIRKPATRICK, Frank A. "Manufacture of Stoneware and
          Flower Pots in a Small Plant." American Ceramic
          Society Journal 11 (December 1928), 896-903.

G1459.   KISSINGER, Isabelle C. "Chicago Ceramic Art Associa-
          tion." Keramic Studio 13 (January 1912), 186-187.
          illus (4 b&w).

G1460.   KNIGHT, (Mrs.) Harold G. "Old Shaving Mugs." Mont-
         gomery County Historical Society Bulletin 7 (Octo-
         ber 1949), 63-65. illus (2 b&w).

G1461.   KNITTLE, Rhea Mansfield. "Beginnings of Pottery Indus-
         try in East Liverpool." Ceramic Age 12 (September
         1928), 120-121.

G1462.   __________. "Henry McQuate, Pennsylvania Potter."
         Antiques 8 (November 1925), 286-287. illus (2 b&w).

G1463.   __________. "Muskingum County, Ohio, Pottery." Antiques
         6 (July 1924), 15-18. illus (7 b&w).

G1464.   __________. "Ohio Pottery Jars and Jugs." Antiques 24
         (October 1933), 144-145. illus (11 b&w).

G1465.   KOCH, Robert. "The Pottery of Artus Van Briggle."
         Art in America 52 (June 1964), 120-121. illus
         (5 b&w).

G1466.   __________. "Rookwood Pottery." Antiques 77 (March
         1960), 288-289. illus (3 b&w).

G1467.   KOEHLER, W. A. "Some Data on the Whiteware Industry
         of West Virginia." American Ceramic Society Bulletin
         9 (March 1930), 57-60.

G1468.   KOENIG, F. J. M. "Art and the Manufacturer." American
         Ceramic Society Bulletin 5 (September 1926), 363-365.

G1469.   KOHLENBERGER, Lois H. "Ceramics at The People's Uni-
         versity." Ceramics Monthly 24 (November 1976), 33-
         37. illus (10 b&w).

G1470.   KOVEL, Ralph, and KOVEL, Terry. "The Mad Potter of
         Biloxi." Western Collector 10 (May 1972), 18-20.
         illus (4 b&w).

G1471.   LACEY, Betty. "Pewabic Pottery in Detroit." National
         Antiques Review 2 (March 1971), 22-23. illus (3 b&w).

G1472.   LAFFAN, W. McKay, and STRAHAN, Edward. "The Tile Club
         Afloat." Scribner's Monthly 19 (March 1880), 641-
         671. illus (39 b&w).

G1473.   LA FORGE, Zoe. "Health Hazards of Pottery Workers
         [East Liverpool, Ohio]" Public Health Nurse 12
         (January 1920), 26-31.

G1474.   LaGRANGE, Marie J., and GOLDMAN, J. D. "More About
         Makers of American Majolica." Hobbies 44 (June
         1939), 54-55.

G1475.   LAMSON, Everett C., Jr. "Lamson Pottery Works of
         Exeter, N.H." Spinning Wheel 33 (June 1977), 32-33.
         illus (5 b&w).

G1476. LANDER, DAVID. "Stoneware: Our Enduring Fascination
        with Kitchen Pots." Americana 2 (January 1975),
        23-26. illus (10 b&w).

G1477. LANGENBECK, Karl. "Chemical Considerations on the
        Pottery Industries of the United States, Part I."
        American Chemical Society Journal 15 (November 1893),
        651-655.

G1478. ________. "Chemical Considerations on the Pottery
        Industries of the United States, Part II." American
        Chemical Society Journal 15 (December 1893), 695-703.

G1479. ________. "The Chemistry of the Pottery Industry."
        Franklin Institute Journal 143 (May 1897), 321-337.

G1480. ________. "The Early Stages of the Science of Ceram-
        ics in America." American Ceramic Society Bulletin
        4 (July 1925), 306-309.

G1481. ________. "An Ideal Endeavor in Science and Art."
        American Ceramic Society Bulletin 4 (September 1925),
        423-425.

G1482. LANGWORTHY, C. F. "Pottery Glazes and Their Solubil-
        ity." Journal of Home Economics 7 (April 1915),
        191-193.

G1483. LAURENCE, F. S. "Terra Cotta in Architectural Design:
        The Part of the Ceramic Chemist." American Ceramic
        Society Journal 8 (February 1925), 79-83.

G1484. LAURENCE, Sturgis. "Architectural Faience." Archi-
        tectural Record 21 (January 1907), 63-72. illus
        (9 b&w).

G1485. LAWLESS, Dorothy. "Those Sportsman Shaving Mugs."
        Western Collector 9 (July-August 1971), 22. illus
        (4 b&w).

G1486. LAWTON, Lewis H. "The Making of Crucibles [Bartley
        Crucible Co.]" Trenton 1 (May 1925), 8-11. illus
        (11 b&w).

G1487. LEACH, Mary James. "Louisville Potters and Potteries.
        Before 1850." Antiques 52 (November 1947), 320,
        322. illus (3 b&w).

G1488. LEAMING, Susan F. "Normal Department Pottery [Art
        Institute, Chicago]" Sketch Book 2 (February 1903),
        19-21. illus (3 b&w).

G1489. LEE, Anne. "Indian Life in Tile Panels [Nebraska
        State Capitol]" Mentor 16 (September 1928), 15.
        illus (1 b&w).

G1490. LEHMAN, F. "Clay Washing." Engineering and Mining
        Journal 67 (May 20, 1899), 592.

G1491. LEIBY, Joyce M. "George Ohr--The Potter's Potter."
        Antique Collecting 1 (August 1977), 10. illus
        (7 b&w).

G1492. LEIGHTON, Henry. "The Fire Clays of Pennsylvania."
        American Ceramic Society Bulletin 9 (February 1930),
        22-26.

G1493. LE PRINCE, Marie, and BARRINGER, L. E. "History of
        New York Society of Ceramic Arts." American Ceramic
        Society Bulletin 19 (January 1940), 45-46.

G1494. LEVIN, Elaine. "Pioneers of Contemporary American
        Ceramics: Charles Binns, Adelaide Robineau." Cer-
        amics Monthly 23 (November 1975), 22-27. illus
        (6 b&w).

G1495. LIEBERMAN, Frank. "Up Attic: Bennington Stoneware."
        Vermont Life 32 (Autumn 1977), 19. illus (1 b&w).

G1496. LINCOLN, George B. "The Tariff: A Summary of Condi-
        tions and Some of the Problems that Will Confront
        the Ways and Means Committee." Pottery & Glass 2
        (March 1909), 116-119.

G1497. LINTON, Robert. "Tertiary Clays of Southern Califor-
        nia." American Ceramic Society Journal (October
        1928), 771-781. illus (4 b&w); bibliog.

G1498. LITTLE, Flora Townsend. "A Short Sketch of American
        Pottery." Art and Archaeology 15 (May 1923), 219-
        227. illus (10 b&w).

G1499. LOCH, Marilyn. "American Parian Wares." Spinning
        Wheel 35 (December 1979), 9-12. illus (7 b&w).

G1500. LOCKINGTON, M. E. "The Manufacture of Architectural
        Terra Cotta in America." Clay-Worker 43 (June
        1905), 753-755. illus (5 b&w).

G1501. __________. "Maryland Terra Cotta Plant, Baltimore."
        Clay-Worker 53 (June 1910), 838. illus (1 b&w).

G1502. LOCKINGTON, W. P. "Architectural Decorations in
        Terra Cotta." Clay-Worker 40 (July 1903), 34-35.
        illus (2 b&w).

G1503. __________. "Brick and Terra Cotta in Philadelphia."
        Clay-Worker 37 (June 1902), 629-631. illus (3 b&w).

G1504. __________. "Brick and Terra Cotta in Philadelphia."
        Clay-Worker 41 (January 1904), 94-95. illus
        (1 b&w).

G1505.   LOCKINGTON, W. P. "The Drexel Institute of Philadel-
          phia; American Baptist Publication Society Building."
          Clay-Worker 38 (September 1902), 234-237. illus
          (3 b&w).

G1506.   _______. "Murrel Dobbins' Sanitary Vitreous Ware
          Plant." Clay-Worker 33 (June 1900), 525-527. illus
          (6 b&w).

G1507.   _______. "Pennsylvania Academy of Fine Arts--Clay-
          Working Department." Clay-Worker 27 (June 1897),
          529-531. illus (4 b&w).

G1508.   _______. "Philadelphia Brick, Terra Cotta." Clay-
          Worker 34 (November 1900), 349-351. illus (3 b&w).

G1509.   _______. "Philadelphia's Oldest Clayworking Estab-
          lishment--Thought to be the Oldest in the United
          States [R. C. Remmey & Son]" Clay-Worker 29 (May
          1898), 406. illus (2 b&w).

G1510.   _______. "Terra Cotta in Brick Construction [Phila-
          delphia]" Clay-Worker 33 (May 1900), 427-429.
          illus (2 b&w).

G1511.   _______. "Terra Cotta in Philadelphia." Clay-Worker
          25 (June 1896), 539-541. illus (3 b&w).

G1512.   _______. "Terra Cotta in Philadelphia Architecture."
          Clay-Worker 27 (March 1897), 237-240. illus
          (5 b&w).

G1513.   _______. "Terra Cotta Ornaments and Statuary [Gallo-
          way]" Clay-Worker 31 (April 1899), 342-343. illus
          (2 b&w).

G1514.   _______. "University of Pennsylvania and Its Many
          Brick and Terra Cotta Buildings." Clay-Worker 42
          (July 1904), 24-25. illus (2 b&w).

G1515.   LOEB, Sophie Irene. "Americans Need Not Copy Foreign
          Shapes." Pottery, Glass & Brass Salesman 1 (Febru-
          ary 9, 1910), 17.

G1516.   _______. "Best Sellers and Why." Pottery, Glass &
          Brass Salesman 1 (March 9, 1910), 15.

G1517.   _______. "Decalcomania, Its Use and Abuse." Pottery,
          Glass & Brass Salesman 1 (March 23, 1910), 13.

G1518.   _______. "The Greenwood Potteries at Trenton."
          Pottery, Glass & Brass Salesman 3 (February 9, 1911),
          11.

G1519.   _______. "Imitations of Hand-Painted China." Pot-
          tery, Glass & Brass Salesman 1 (March 2, 1910), 17.

G1520.   LOEB, Sophie Irene. "The Need of Pottery Schools."
         Pottery, Glass & Brass Salesman 1 (April 21, 1910),
         15. illus (1 b&w).

G1521.   ________. "The Potter and His Clay." Pottery, Glass
         and Brass Salesman 1 (March 16, 1910), 15.

G1522.   ________. "The Pottery That Points Nearest to Perfec-
         tion [Lenox]" Pottery, Glass & Brass Salesman 3
         (February 16, 1911), 47-48.

G1523.   ________. "Talks with Men Alive: Mr. Charles H.
         Cook." Pottery, Glass & Brass Salesman 5 (March 28,
         1912), 15, 27.

G1524.   ________. "The Value of Simple Decoration." Pottery,
         Glass & Brass Salesman 1 (February 16, 1910), 17.

G1525.   ________. "A Visit to the Buffalo Pottery." Pottery,
         Glass & Brass Salesman 2 (August 18, 1910), 13, 28.

G1526.   ________. "A Visit to the Largest Producing Pottery
         [H. Laughlin Co.]" Pottery, Glass & Brass Salesman 1
         (March 30, 1910), 13.

G1527.   ________. "What American Decorators Are Striving For."
         Pottery, Glass & Brass Salesman 1 (February 23, 1910),
         17.

G1528.   LONGCOPE, Henry. "Reviving the Art of Old Dutch Pot-
         tery [Pennsylvania Museum School of Industrial Art]"
         Arts & Decoration 12 (February 20, 1920), 252.
         illus (3 b&w).

G1529.   LORING, John. "American Art Pottery." Connoisseur
         200 (April 1979), 279-285. illus (30 col).

G1530.   LOUD, Marian V. "The Tile Floors in St. Pauls Cathe-
         dral, Detroit [Pewabic]" Handicraft 4 (May 1911),
         41-49. illus (4 b&w).

G1531.   LOVEJOY, Ellis. "A Discussion of Terra Cotta Dryers."
         American Ceramic Society Journal 1 (October 1918),
         667-674.

G1532.   LOVETT, Eva. "Colored Terra Cotta on Recent Build-
         ings." International Studio 35 (October 1908),
         cxi-cxiv. illus (7 b&w).

G1533.   ________. "Fifteenth Annual Exhibition of the New
         York Society of Keramic Arts." International Studio
         31 (June 1907), cxiv-cxx. illus (11 b&w).

G1534.   LUTHER, Louise R. "Tribute to a Remarkable Woman--
         Another Dimension of Grueby Pottery." Spinning
         Wheel 28 (March 1972), 40-41. illus (2 b&w).

G1535.   LYCETT, Lydia. "China Painting by the Lycetts."
          Atlanta Historical Bulletin 6 (July 1941), 201-214.

G1536.   LYMAN, Lila Parrish. "The Tile Club and Its Members."
          American Collector 14 (April 1945), 10-11, 19.
          illus (4 b&w).

G1537.   McAFEE, W. Keith. "Ceramic Education." Clay-Worker
          84 (November 1925), 482-483. illus (1 b&w).

G1538.   McCABE, Lida Rose. "Rise of American China Painting
          [D. W. O'Hara]" Art World 2 (April 1917), 92-93.
          illus (2 b&w).

G1539.   ________. "A Story-Telling Bird Bath [A. J. Saint-
          Gaudens]" Art World 1 (March 1917), 452-453. illus
          (1 b&w).

G1540.   McCALLIE, S. W. "Clay and Clay Products in Georgia."
          Ceramic Age 9 (February 1927), 40-41. illus (4 b&w).

G1541.   McCAMPBELL, Sara W. "An Appreciation of the Newark
          Society of Keramic Arts." Keramic Studio 19 (August
          1917), 59-60. illus (5 b&w).

G1542.   ________. "Newark Society of Keramic Arts." Keramic
          Studio 13 (July 1911), 58-63. illus (10 b&w).

          McCLINTON, Katharine Morrison, see also KAHLE,
          Katharine Morrison.

G1543.   McCLINTON, Katharine Morrison. "American Hand-Painted
          China." Spinning Wheel 23 (April 1967), 10-12, 43.
          illus (17 b&w).

G1544.   McDONALD, W. P. "Rookwood at the Pan-American."
          Keramic Studio 3 (November 1901), 146-147. illus
          (9 b&w).

G1545.   McDOWELL, C. "Grueby: American Art Pottery." Ameri-
          can Life: A Collectors Annual 5 (1965), 102-103.
          illus (3 b&w).

G1546.   MACFARLANE, Janet R. "Nathan Clark, Potter." Antiques
          60 (July 1954), 42-44. illus (7 b&w).

G1547.   MACHT, Carol M. "Rookwood Pottery." Antiques Journal
          21 (February 1966), 16-18, 25. illus (13 b&w).

G1548.   ________. "Rookwood Pottery." Ceramics Monthly 14
          (January 1966), 29. illus (1 b&w).

G1549.   McKEARIN, Helen. "According to the Papers: The
          Launching of Henderson's Flint Stoneware." Antiques
          55 (June 1949), 432-433.

G1550. McLAUGHLIN, M[ary] Louise. [Letter to Editor]"
        Keramic Studio 1 (August 1899), 65.

G1551. ________. "Losanti Ware." Craftsman 3 (December
        1902), 186-187. illus (1 b&w).

G1552. ________. "Losanti Ware." Keramic Studio 3 (December
        1901), 178-179. illus (3 b&w).

G1553. McLAUGHLIN, Rita. "The 'Washington-Wakefield' Pattern
        by Lenox of Trenton." Spinning Wheel 11 (January
        1955), 36. illus (1 b&w).

G1554. McLENNON, T. "The Art Industries of America. IV:
        China-Decorating." Brush and Pencil 15 (June 1905),
        131-140. illus (12 b&w).

G1555. McMAHON, J. F. "Charles Fergus Binns." American
        Ceramic Society Bulletin 17 (April 1938), 174-176.

G1556. MacSWIGGAN, Amelia E. "Dedham Pottery." Antiques
        Journal 8 (March 1953), 14-15. illus (4 b&w).

G1557. ________. "The Hews Pottery." Antiques Journal 8
        (November 1953), 36-37. illus (3 b&w).

G1558. ________. "The Marblehead Pottery." Spinning Wheel
        28 (March 1972), 20-21. illus (6 b&w).

G1559. ________. "Pioneer Potteries of Danvers and Peabody,
        Massachusetts." Antiques Journal 12 (February 1957),
        36-37. illus (1 b&w).

G1560. MADDEN, Betty I. "Jug Towns [Illinois potteries]"
        Spinning Wheel 27 (April 1971), 22-23, 64. illus
        (3 b&w).

G1561. MAGONIGLE, H. Van Buren. "A Potter and His Work--Leon
        V. Solon." Architectural Record 45 (April 1919),
        303-310. illus (8 b&w).

G1562. MANTLE, H. L. "Cost of Producing General White Ware
        Pottery." Glass & Pottery World 16 (January 1908),
        40-42. illus (3 b&w).

G1563. MARKHAM, Kenneth H. "Coxon and Morgan Belleek China."
        Antiques Journal 17 (September 1962), 8-9, 27.
        illus (6 b&w).

G1564. ________. "Weller Sicardo Art Pottery." Antiques
        Journal 19 (September 1964), 18. illus (1 b&w).

G1565. MARKS, Alfred T. "Uncle Sam's Dormitories [Hollow
        Tile Buildings for War Workers]" Clay-Worker 70
        (October 1918), 315-316. illus (2 b&w).

G1566.   MARSH, L. L. "Firing with a Wilke Gasoline Kiln."
         Keramic Studio 8 (June 1906), 29-30.

G1567.   MARTIN, E. A. "Enameled Brick in the United States."
         Clay Record 1 (August 27, 1892), 132-134.

G1568.   MASON, Elizabeth. "Mr. Arthur W. Dow's Summer School
         at Ipswich, Mass." Keramic Studio 4 (October 1902),
         123.

G1569.   MASON, Maud M. "The Design Class." Keramic Studio 12
         (October 1910), 114-121. illus (23 b&w).

G1570.   ________. "Exhibition of the New York Society of Ker-
         amic Arts." Keramic Studio 13 (May 1911), 8-15.
         illus (23 b&w).

G1571.   ________. "Museum Study for Ceramic Students."
         Keramic Studio 19 (February 1918), 157-158.

G1572.   ________. "Suggestions for Use of Plate Borders."
         Keramic Studio 12 (August 1910), 79-81. illus
         (12 b&w).

G1573.   MASON, William A. "The Value of Clay Modeling in
         Elementary Art Education." Art Education 1 (April
         1895), 90-92. illus (1 b&w).

G1574.   MATHEWS, Jessie Hughes. "Rozane Pottery [Roseville]"
         Fine Arts Journal 16 (January 1905), 33-35. illus
         (7 b&w).

G1575.   MEBANE, John. "Collecting Belleek China." Early
         American Life 7 (February 1976), 66-68.

G1576.   MELINE, Elva. "Art Tile in California--The Work of
         E. A. Batchelder." Spinning Wheel 27 (November
         1971), 8-10, 65. illus (11 b&w).

G1577.   MELLOR, E. A. B. "Old Times in the Pottery Trade of
         Trenton." Crockery and Glass Journal 60 (December
         15, 1904), [75-76].

G1578.   MENDENHALL, Lawrence. "Cincinnati's Contribution to
         American Ceramic Art." Brush and Pencil 17 (Febru-
         ary 1906), 47-58, 61. illus (9 b&w).

G1579.   MERCER, Henry C. "The Building of 'Fonthill' at
         Doylestown, Pennsylvania, in 1908, 1909 and 1910."
         Bucks County Historical Society Collections 6
         (1932), 321-330. illus (2 b&w).

G1580.   ________. "Notes on the Moravian Pottery of Doyles-
         town." Bucks County Historical Society Collections
         4 (1917), 482-487.

G1581.   MERCER, Henry C. "Pottery of the Pennsylvania
         Germans." Bucks County Historical Society Collec-
         tions 4 (1917), 187-191.

G1582.   __________. "The Pottery of the Pennsylvania-Germans."
         Pennsylvania-German 2 (April 1901), 86-88. illus
         (4 b&w).

G1583.   __________. "Two Stoveplates Described." Bucks County
         Historical Society Collections 4 (1917), 540.

G1584.   MERRILL, Frederick J. H. "Mineral Resources of New
         York State." New York State Museum Bulletin 3
         (September 1895), 361-595.
            Directory of clay manufacturers, pp. 502-518.

G1585.   MERRILL, Madeline Osborne. "The Osborn Family Potters
         in New Hampshire." Daughters of the American Revo-
         lution Magazine 101 (May 1967), 516-520. illus
         (4 b&w); bibliog.

G1586.   __________. "The Osborns and Their Redware--From South
         Danvers, Massachusetts to Loudon, New Hampshire."
         Old-Time New England 56 (October-December 1965),
         49-58. illus (5 b&w).

G1587.   METROPOLITAN MUSEUM OF ART BULLETIN. "Pennsylvania
         Slip-Ware." Vol. 7 (November 1912), 208-211.
         illus (6 b&w).

G1588.   [MICHAEL, George?] "Griffen, Smith and Hill Company,
         Phoenixville, Pa." National Antiques Review 3
         (October 1971), 16-19. illus (19 b&w).

G1589.   MICHAEL, Glenn William. "An International Show and
         Sale--Joplin, Missouri/A New Find in Pottery:
         Niloak." National Antiques Review 3 (December
         1971), 42. illus (1 b&w).

G1590.   MICHAEL, Ronald L., and JACK, Phil R. "Non-Ordinary
         Stoneware Pieces from New Geneva and Greensboro,
         Pennsylvania." Pennsylvania Folklife 25 (Autumn
         1975), 24-30. illus (22 b&w).

G1591.   __________. "The Stoneware Potteries of New Geneva and
         Greensboro, Pennsylvania." Western Pennsylvania
         Historical Magazine 56 (October 1973), 365-382.
         illus (2 b&w); bibliog.

G1592.   MILLER, David Kent. "The Pottery Patriarch [C. F.
         Decker]" Tennessee Conservationist 37 (November
         1971), 8-11. illus (10 b&w).

G1593.   MILLER, Leslie W. "The Necessity of Improving Our
         Pottery." American 19 (February 1, 1890), 315-317.

G1594.   [MILLER, Leslie W.?] "The Struggles of American
          Pottery." American 7 (January 12, 1884), 216-217.

G1595.   MILLER, Robert W. "The Tucker Family: Porcelain
          Pioneers." Antiques Journal 27 (September 1972),
          28. illus (1 b&w).

G1596.   MILLET, Frank D. "Some American Tiles [Low]" The
          Century Magazine 23 (April 1882), 896-904. illus
          (7 b&w).

G1597.   MILLIKEN, William M. "Ohio Ceramics." Design 38
          (November 1936), 17, 41.

G1598.   MILLS, R. G. "Ceramics as a Profession." Ceramic
          Age 13 (April 1929), 122, 162.

G1599.   MINTON, LeRoy H. "Dedication of the Ceramics Building
          at Rutgers College." Clay-Worker 78 (July 1922),
          25-26.

G1600.   _______. "New Jersey's Part in the Ceramic History
          of America." Ceramist 2 (Winter 1922-1923), 270-
          289. illus (10 b&w).

G1601.   _______. "The Sanitary Ware Industry in America."
          Ceramist 4 (September 1924), 336-350. illus
          (6 b&w).

G1602.   _______. "Sanitary Ware Manufacture in America."
          American Ceramic Society Journal 6 (January 1923),
          319-321.

G1603.   MITCHELL, Elmer C. "The Art Industries of America.
          II: The Making of Pottery [Teco]" Brush and
          Pencil 15 (April 1905), 67-76. illus (13 b&w).

G1604.   MITCHELL, James R. "The American Porcelain Tradition."
          Connoisseur 179 (February 1972), 123-131. illus
          (16 b&w).

G1605.   _______. "Ott & Brewer: Etruria in America." Winter-
          thur Portfolio 7 (1972), 217-228. illus (22 b&w);
          bibliog.

G1606.   _______. "Pottery and Porcelain from East Liverpool,
          Ohio." Early American Life 11 (June 1980), 32-35.
          illus (15 col).

G1607.   _______. "The Shape of Stoneware." Early American
          Life 9 (October 1978), 38-43. illus (21 b&w).

G1608.   MOCK, Esther. "An American Craft with a Pedigree
          [Jugtown Pottery]" Early American Life 4 (June
          1973), 42-43, 86. illus (6 b&w).

G1609.   MOLINIER, Émile. "Un decorateur américain: J. G.
          Low." L'Art 49 (1890), 138-140. illus (6 b&w)..

G1610.   MONACHESI, (Mrs.) [Nicola di Rienzi] "Miss M. Louise
          McLaughlin and Her New 'Losanti' Ware." Art Inter-
          change 48 (January 1902), 11. illus (3 b&w).

G1611.   __________. "Painting Under the Glaze." Art Inter-
          change 38 (June 1897), 144.

G1612.   __________. "Painting Under the Glaze, Second Paper."
          Art Interchange 39 (September 1897), 63. illus
          (1 b&w).

G1613.   __________. "Underglaze Painting, Third Paper." Art
          Interchange 39 (October 1897), 83.

G1614.   MONTAGUE, William E. "Early Pennsylvania Pottery."
          Bucks County Historical Society Collections 5 (1926),
          197-202.

G1615.   MONTFORT, M. Helen E. "The National League of Mineral
          Painters at the Pan-American Exposition." Keramic
          Studio 3 (September 1901), 97-98.

G1616.   MONTGOMERY, Marguerite. "Penmanship in Pottery:
          Pennsylvania Dutch Style." Ceramics Monthly 4
          (January 1956), 13, 30. illus (4 b&w).

G1617.   __________. "Pottery of the Pennsylvania Dutch."
          Ceramics Monthly 4 (April 1956), 18-21, 32. illus
          (13 b&w).

G1618.   __________. "Pottery of the Pennsylvania Dutch, Part 2:
          Early Works and Modern Adaptations." Ceramics
          Monthly 4 (June 1956), 18-20. illus (9 b&w).

G1619.   MONTGOMERY, Rosetta Schuyler. "Tucker China." Now
          and Then 7 (January 1942), 10-11.

G1620.   MONTHLY LABOR REVIEW. "Labor Relations in the Pottery
          Industry." Vol. 18 (February 1924), 240-242.

G1621.   __________. "Stability of Employment in the Pottery
          Industry." Vol. 29 (July 1929), 180-181.

G1622.   __________. "Wages and Conditions in the Pottery Indus-
          try." Vol. 24 (February 1927), 264-265.

G1623.   __________. "Wages and Hours of Labor in the Pottery
          Industry in 1925." Vol. 21 (December 1925), 1221-
          1243.

G1624.   __________. "Wages and Hours of Labor in the Pottery
          Industry, 1925 and 1932." Vol. 36 (April 1933),
          853-862.

G1625.   MOORE, George M. "Bennington Ware." Old China 2
          (November 1902), 22-26. illus (5 b&w).

G1626.   ________. "Bennington Ware (Continued)." Old China
          2 (January 1903), 73-75. illus (1 b&w).

G1627.   MOORE, R. Carl. "Mountain Pottery of North Carolina."
          Ceramic Age 14 (November 1929), 178-179. illus
          (1 b&w).

G1628.   MORRIS, Alfred. "The Robineau Porcelains." Sketch
          Book 5 (January 1906), 228-233. illus (7 b&w).

G1629.   MORSE, Barbara White. "Art Tiles." American Antiques
          5 (November 1977), 24-29. illus (11 b&w).

G1630.   ________. "The Art Tiles and Plastic Sketches of
          Arthur Osborne. Part One: Art Tiles." Spinning
          Wheel 35 (April 1979), 28-30, 32-33. illus
          (10 b&w).

G1631.   ________. "The Art Tiles and Plastic Sketches of
          Arthur Osborne. Part Two: Plastic Sketches."
          Spinning Wheel 35 (May 1979), 27-32. illus (9 b&w).

G1632.   ________. "Buying a Low Art Tile Stove, Part One."
          Spinning Wheel 26 (November 1970), 28-31. illus (b&w).

G1633.   ________. "Buying A Low Art Tile Stove, Part Two."
          Spinning Wheel 26 (December 1970), 12-15. illus
          (12 b&w); bibliog.

G1634.   ________. "The Framing of Art Tiles." Spinning
          Wheel 31 (July-August 1975), 45-47. illus (7 b&w).

G1635.   ________. "I Collect Low Art Tiles." Yankee 34
          (November 1970), 132-135, 142-144, 147. illus
          (8 col).

G1636.   ________. "John G. Low and Elihu Vedder as Artist
          Dreamers." Spinning Wheel 32 (May 1976), 24-27.
          illus (4 b&w).

G1637.   ________. "John Gardner Low and His Original Art
          Tile Soda Fountain, Part One." Spinning Wheel 27
          (July-August 1971), 26-28. illus (6 b&w).

G1638.   ________. "John Gardner Low and His Original Art
          Tile Soda Fountain, Part Two." Spinning Wheel 27
          (September 1971), 16-19. illus (9 b&w); bibliog.

G1639.   ________. "Low Art Tiles Illustrating the Victorian
          Japanese Vogue." Antiques Journal (November 1973),
          20-22, 49. illus (6 b&w); bibliog.

G1640. MORSE, Barbara White. "Low 'Art Tiles' Today: A
        Primer for the Novice Collector." National Antiques
        Review 5 (October 1973), 26-29. illus (13 b&w).

G1641. ________. "The Low Family of Chelsea, Massachusetts,
        and Their Pottery." Spinning Wheel 33 (September
        1977), 28-33. illus (12 b&w).

G1642. ________. "The Moravian Tiles of Dr. Mercer."
        Antiques Journal 32 (July 1977), 16-19, 45. illus
        (8 b&w).

G1643. ________. "The Sunflower Motif on Low Tiles."
        Spinning Wheel 30 (November 1974), 40-41. illus
        (4 b&w).

G1644. ________. "Tiles Made by Isaac Broome, Sculptor and
        Genius." Spinning Wheel 29 (January-February 1973),
        18-22. illus (11 b&w); bibliog.

G1645. ________. "Tiles to Treasure: Low Art Tiles."
        Spinning Wheel 25 (March 1969), 18-22. illus
        (8 b&w); bibliog.

G1646. MORTON, Julie. "Sewer Tile Art." Antiques Journal 35
        (December 1980), 18-20, 46-47. illus (11 b&w).

G1647. MUELLER, Herman C. "The Artistic Education of the
        Potter." Clay-Worker 29 (May 1898), 411-413.
        illus (1 b&w).

G1648. ________. "Ceramic Mosaic [Mosaic Tile Co.] Clay-
        Worker 39 (January 1903), 30-31. illus (2 b&w).

G1649. ________. "Industrial Co-operation." Clay-Worker 67
        (January 1917), 44-45. illus (1 b&w).

G1650. ________. "Industry and Market." Keramic Tile
        Journal 1 (December 1929), 48. illus (1 b&w).

G1651. ________. "Progress." Keramic Tile Journal 2
        (October 1930), 30. illus (1 b&w).

G1652. ________. "Promoting the Tile Business." Keramic
        Tile Journal 3 (July 1931), 13. illus (1 b&w).

G1653. ________. "Substitutions." Keramic Tile Journal 2
        (December 1930), 14, 52. illus (1 b&w).

G1654. ________. "The Tile Industry as I See It." Keramic
        Tile Journal 2 (April 1930), 26, 56. illus (1 b&w).

G1655. MUNSEY, Cecil. "Patent Medicine Ceramics." Antiques
        Journal 27 (March 1972), 25-28, 62. illus (14 b&w).

G1656.   MURPHY, James L. "Shaker Reed Stem Tobacco Pipes."
          Pennsylvania Archaeologist 48 (April 1978), 48-52.
          illus (2 b&w); bibliog.

G1657.   MUSEUMS JOURNAL. "Exhibition of the Clay Industries
          of New Jersey, U.S.A., to be Held by the Newark
          Museum." Vol. 14 (January 1915), 233-234.

G1658.   NASH, John. "Daniel Seagle and James F. Seagle."
          Ceramic Circle of Charlotte Journal of Studies 4
          (1980), 16. illus (2 b&w).
             Prefatory to C23.

G1659.   NAWROT, Emma L. "Early New Jersey Pottery [To 1870]"
          Ceramic Age 46 (November 1945), 178-180, 201, 203.
          illus (1 b&w).

G1660.   ________. "George Herbert Brown." _American Ceramic
          Society Bulletin_ 22 (July 1943), 212-214.

G1661.   NEALEY, J. B. "Buffalo Pottery and How It is Made."
          Ceramic Age 12 (August 1928), 52-54. illus (6 b&w).

G1662.   ________. "Gas-Fired Continuous Kilns in the China-
          ware Industry [H. Laughlin Co.]" _Ceramic Age_ 14
          (September 1929), 83-88. illus (8 b&w).

G1663.   ________. "Modern Tile Plant Uses Continuous Gas
          Fired Kilns [Cambridge Tile Mfg. Co.]" _Ceramic Age_
          16 (August 1930), 83-86. illus (7 b&w).

G1664.   NELSON, Edna Deu Pree. "Pennsylvania Pin-Decorated
          Slipware." _American Collector_ 9 (December 1940),
          6-7. illus (7 b&w).

G1665.   NELSON, Helen C. "Portrait of a Potter-Musician [J.
          Norton]" _Antiques_ 40 (July 1941), 33. illus
          (1 b&w).

G1666.   NELSON, Marion John. "Art Nouveau in American Ceram-
          ics." _Art Quarterly_ 26 (No. 4, 1963), 441-459.
          illus (15 b&w); bibliog.

G1667.   ________. "Indigenous Characteristics in American Art
          Pottery." _Antiques_ 89 (June 1966), 846-850. illus.

G1668.   [NELSON, W. H. de B.] "Some Recent Work of Dorothea
          Warren O'Hara." _International Studio_ 50 (October
          1913), lxxvii-lxxviii. illus (4 b&w)

G1669.   NEW JERSEY CERAMIST. "The New Ceramic Station at
          Rutgers College, State University of New Jersey."
          Vol. 1 (June 1921), 109-112. illus (1 b&w).

G1670.   ________. "New Jersey Clay Workers' Association Holds
          Annual Meeting." Vol. 1 (December 1921), 234-250.
          illus (2 b&w).

G1671. NEW REPUBLIC. "[Proposed Tariff on Potteries]" Vol.
        31 (June 21, 1922), 87.

G1672. NEWMAN, Bim, and NEWMAN, Doris. "Antique Pottery for
        Inspiration." Ceramics Monthly 5 (April 1957),
        13-14. illus (7 b&w).

G1673. NEWTON, Clara Chipman. "The Cincinnati Pottery Club."
        American Ceramic Society Bulletin 19 (September
        1940), 345-351. illus (5 b&w).

G1674. __________. "The Porcelain League of Cincinnati."
        American Ceramic Society Bulletin 18 (November
        1939), 445-446.

G1675. NOEL, Margaret. "Work of American Potters. Article
        Five: Poillon Pottery Indoors and Out." Arts &
        Decoration 1 (August 1911), 412. illus (2 b&w).
        Articles 1, 2, 3, 4: G948, G2311, G1297, G866.

G1676. NOEL HUME, Ivor. "A Late Seventeenth-Century Pottery
        Kiln Site Near Jamestown." Antiques 83 (May 1963),
        550-552. illus (3 b&w); bibliog.

G1677. NORMAN-WILCOX, Gregor. "Perhaps Bennington." Antiques
        Journal 5 (April 1950), 10-11. illus (3 b&w).

G1678. NORTHEND, Mary Harrod. "Paul Revere Pottery." House
        Beautiful 36 (August 1914), 82-83. illus (6 b&w).

G1679. NORTON, F. H. "A Check List of Early New England
        Potteries." American Ceramic Society Bulletin 18
        (May 1939), 181-185. illus (1 b&w); bibliog.

G1680. __________. "Clays of New England." Ceramic Age 15
        (May 1930), 271, 274-279. illus (8 b&w); bibliog.

G1681. __________. "The Crafts Pottery in Nashua, New Hamp-
        shire." Antiques 19 (April 1931), 304-305. illus
        (3 b&w).

G1682. __________. "The Exeter Pottery Works." Antiques 22
        (July 1932), 22-25. illus (7 b&w).

G1683. NORTON, F. H., and DUPLIN, V. J. Jr. "The Osbourne
        Pottery at Gonic, New Hampshire." Antiques 19
        (February 1931), 123-124. illus (4 b&w).

G1684. NOYCE, Dorothy. "The Pottery of Jugtown." Ford Times
        51 (March 1959), 25-27. illus (3 col).

G1685. NOYES, Henriette T. "Occupational Shaving Mugs."
        American Antiques Journal 2 (August 1947), 19.
        illus (1 b&w).

G1686. OAK, Sophie Knight. "Repairing Broken China." _Art Interchange_ 40 (April 1898), 100.

G1687. OAKEY, A. F. "The Possibilities of a Revived Industry [Architectural Terra Cotta]" _Harpers' New Monthly Magazine_ 68 (February 1884), 347-351. illus (6 b&w).

G1688. O'CONNELL, Annette. "Bennington's Ceramic Arts." _Antiques Journal_ 27 (March 1972), 18-20. illus (10 b&w).

G1689. OERTER, Albert L. "Tile Stoves of the Moravians at Bethlehem, Pa." _Bucks County Historical Society Collections_ 4 (1917), 479-481.

G1690. O'HARA, Dorothea Warren. "American Pottery." _Ladies' Home Journal_ 39 (May 1922), 31, 124. illus (10 b&w).

G1691. ________. "Exhibition of the Keramic Society of Greater New York." _Keramic Studio_ 15 (May 1913), 7-10. illus (12 b&w).

G1692. OHR, George E. "Some Facts in the History of a Unique Personality [Ohr]" _Crockery and Glass Journal_ 54 (December 12, 1901), [123-125]. illus (3 b&w).

G1693. OLD CHINA. "Crolius Stoneware Jug." Vol. 3 (July 1904), 201-202. illus (1 b&w).

G1694. OLMSTEAD, Anna W. "The Memorial Collection of Robineau Porcelains." _Design_ 33 (December 1931), 153. illus (1 b&w).

G1695. OLSEN, Peter C. "Eckardt V. Eskesen." _American Ceramic Society Bulletin_ 16 (October 1937), 412-413.

G1696. ORMSBEE, Thomas Hamilton. "An American Fire House Pitcher." _American Collector_ 14 (October 1945), 5 illus (4 b&w).

G1697. ________. "Poughkeepsie Was Also a Jugtown." _American Collector_ 5 (February 1936), 4-15, 13. illus (4 b&w).

G1698. ORTMAN, Fred B. "Ceramic Industry of Southern California." _American Ceramic Society Bulletin_ 23 (September 1944), 309-310.

G1699. ORTON, Edward, Jr. "The Beginnings of Ceramic Education in the United States." _American Ceramic Society Bulletin_ 4 (March 1925), 89-96.

G1700. ________. "Clayworking in Ohio, First Paper." _Clay-Worker_ 21 (January 1894), 27-29.

G1701.   ORTON, Edward, Jr.   "Clayworking in Ohio, Second
         Paper." Clay-Worker 21 (February 1894), 233-236.

G1702.   ________. "The Clayworking Industries of Ohio, Third
         Paper." Clay-Worker 21 (March 1894), 341-343.

G1703.   ________. "The Clayworking Industries of Ohio, Fourth
         Paper." Clay-Worker 21 (April 1894), 446-448.

G1704.   ________. "The Clayworking Industries of Ohio, Fifth
         Paper." Clay-Worker 21 (May 1894), 544-547.

G1705.   ________. "The Clayworking Industries of Ohio, Sixth
         Paper." Clay-Worker 21 (June 1894), 642-645.

G1706.   ________. "The Clayworking Industries of Ohio,
         Seventh Paper: The Tempering of Paving Brick Clays."
         Clay-Worker 22 (July 1894), 42-44.

G1707.   ________. "The Future of Ceramic Education in
         America." Clay-Worker 66 (July 1916), 28-30,
         78-79. illus (1 b&w).

G1708.   ________. "The Future of Ceramic Education in
         America." New Jersey Ceramist 1 (March 1921),
         8-16.

G1709.   ________. "Historical Statement of the Origin of the
         American Ceramic Society." American Ceramic Society
         Journal 6 (January 1923), 2-10.

G1710.   ________. "An Idyll(er) in Terra Cotta [American
         Terra Cotta and Ceramic Co.]" Clay-Worker 28
         (October 1897), 270-273. illus (11 b&w).

G1711.   ________. "Notes from the Ceramics Department, Ohio
         State University." Clay-Worker 49 (January 1908),
         27-29. illus (12 b&w).

G1712.   ________. "Ohio's School for Clayworkers: Its
         Equipment and Prospects." Clay-Worker 22 (September
         1894), 254-255.

G1713.   ________. "Ohio State University: Technical Educa-
         tion at Last." Clay-Worker 22 (July 1894), 25-28.
         illus (5 b&w).

G1714.   OSBORNE, Mildred R.   "Collecting Calendar Plates."
         Spinning Wheel 25 (January-February 1969), 10-11.
         illus (14 b&w).

G1715.   OSBORNE, W. R.   "A Great Jersey Clayworking Establish-
         ment [C. Pardee]" Clay-Worker 24 (October 1895),
         337-338. illus (2 b&w).

G1716.   OSBORNE, W. R. "A Terra Cotta Monument [G. Washington, Perth Amboy, N.J.]" Clay-Worker 25 (April 1896), 335-336. illus (1 b&w).

G1717.   OSGOOD, (Mrs.) Worth. "National League of Mineral Painters." Keramic Studio 1 (May 1899), 17.

G1718.   OTIS, Margaret. "Opalescent and Metal Lustre [H. H. Goodman]" Fine Arts Journal 17 (March 1906), 199-201. illus (2 b&w).

G1719.   OVERBECK, Hannah B. "Violet Designs." Keramic Studio 12 (June 1910), 34. illus (1 b&w).

G1720.   PAGE, Harvey L. "Missoula Brick and Sewer Pipe Works." Clay-Record 1 (September 27, 1892), 214-215.

G1721.   PALMER, C. Carroll. "Roach Traps." Early American Industries Association Chronicle 2 (April 1942), 169-170. illus (1 b&w).

G1722.   PARMELEE, Cullen W. "History of Ceramic Education at the University of Illinois." American Ceramic Society Journal 6 (January 1923), 97-104. illus (3 b&w).

G1723.   __________. "The New Department of Clay-Working and Ceramics at Rutgers College." American Ceramic Society Transactions 5 (1903), 122-129. illus (4 b&w).

G1724.   PARSHALL, Margaret T. "Majolica, Useful and Decorative." Antiques Journal 5 (May 1950), 17. illus (4 b&w).

G1725.   PASS, R. H. "Vocational and Apprenticeship School at Onondago Pottery." American Ceramic Society Bulletin 4 (October 1925), 560-561.

G1726.   PASS, Richard. "James Pass." American Ceramic Society Bulletin 15 (June 1936), 220-223.

G1727.   PATTISON, James William. "Exhibition of Decorated Porcelain [Burley & Co.]" Fine Arts Journal 29 (October 1913), 631-638. illus (8 b&w).

G1728.   PAYANT, Felix. "The Art of the North Carolina Potters." Design 29 (December 1927), 124-125, 129. illus (6 b&w).

G1729.   __________. "A Lesson in Design from the Sandhill Potters of North Carolina." American Ceramic Society Bulletin 7 (September 1928), 256-259.

G1730.   __________. "North Carolina Pottery--An Early American Survival." Design 29 (October 1927), 91-92. illus (7 b&w).

G1731. PAYNE, Elizabeth H. "A Group of Early American
        Ceramics." Detroit Institute of Arts Bulletin 30
        (no. 1, 1950-1951), 14-16. illus (1 b&w).

G1732. PEAR, Lilian Myers. "Pewabic Pottery." Spinning
        Wheel 31 (October 1975), 11-14. illus (17 b&w).

G1733. PEARL, Mignon W. "From Clay to Art [Pewabic Pottery]"
        Earth Science 32 (Summer 1979), 114-120. illus
        (6 b&w).

G1734. PECK, Herbert. "The Amateur Antecedents of Rookwood
        Pottery." Cincinnati Historical Society Bulletin 26
        (October 1968), 317-337. illus (5 b&w).

G1735. __________. "Rookwood Pottery and Foreign Museum Col-
        lections." Connoisseur 172 (September 1969), 43-49.
        illus (12 b&w, 3 col).

G1736. __________. "Some Early Collections of Rookwood Pottery."
        Auction 3 (September 1969), 20-23. illus (4 b&w).

G1737. PENCE, F. K. "Technical Development in the Whiteware
        Industries." American Ceramic Society Journal 6
        (January 1923), 308-311.

G1738. PENDLETON, Margaret. "Paul Revere Pottery." House
        Beautiful 32 (August 1912), 74. illus (3 b&w).

G1739. PENNSYLVANIA MUSEUM BULLETIN. "The Collection of
        American Pottery." Vol. 2 (April 1, 1904), 6.
        illus (1 b&w).

G1740. __________. "Edwin AtLee Barber, A.M., Ph.D. [Obituary]"
        Vol. 15 (January 1917), 1-4. illus (1 b&w).

G1741. __________. "Harrison Pitcher Wanted." Vol. 1 (January
        1903), 4. illus (1 b&w).

G1742. __________. "Old Philadelphia Porcelain [Kurlbaum &
        Schwartz]" Vol. 2 (January 1, 1904), 4. illus
        (1 b&w).

G1743. __________. "Some Rarities in the Museum [S. Girard
        Vase, by R. B. Beech]" Vol. 1 (July 1903), 4-5.
        illus (1 b&w).

G1744. PERRY, Margaret. "American Stoneware on Madison
        Avenue." Early American Life 5 (August 1974), 40-41.
        illus (6 b&w).

G1745. PERRY, (Mrs.) Aaron F. "Decorative Pottery of Cincin-
        nati." Harper's New Monthly Magazine 62 (May 1881),
        834-845. illus (19 b&w).

PERRY, Mary Chase, see also STRATTON, Mary Chase (Perry).

G1746. PERRY, Mary Chase. "American Ceramic Association Congress." Keramic Studio 2 (May 1900), 23-24.

G1747. ________. "A Few Ideas about Values." Keramic Studio 1 (December 1899), 154-155.

G1748. ________. "A Great Artist [G. Leykauf]" Ceramic Monthly 4 (January 1897), 99-102. illus (2 b&w).

G1749. ________. "Grueby Potteries." Keramic Studio 2 (April 1901), 250-252. illus (3 b&w).

G1750. ________. "National League Study Course." Keramic Studio 4 (September 1902), 106.

G1751 ________. "National League Study Course for 1904-1905." Keramic Studio 6 (March 1905), 254.

G1752. ________. "Notes on the Recent Exhibition of Mineral League." Keramic Studio 1 (August 1899), 84.

G1753. ________. "Review of the League Exhibition." Keramic Studio 5 (August 1903), 75-76.

G1754. ________. "Treatment for Corn-Flowers." Keramic Studio 1 (September 1899), 104-105. illus (2 b&w).

G1755. PETERSON, Arthur G. "Oyster Plates." Antiques Journal 24 (November 1969), 5, 18. illus (4 b&w).

G1756. PHILADELPHIA MUSEUM OF ART BULLETIN. "Ceramics: Pennsylvania Makes Major Contribution in Handcraft Era [Pennsylvania German]" Vol. 54 (Autumn 1958), 25-27. illus (9 b&w).

G1757. ________. "Two Tucker Beakers." Vol. 54 (Spring 1959), 67-70. illus (2 b&w).

G1758. PHILLIPS, Lois L. "Majolica Ware." American Home 15 (May 1936), 94-96. illus (2 b&w).

G1759. PILLING, Ronald W. "Henry Chapman Mercer and the Moravian Tile Works." American Art & Antiques 2 (November-December 1979), 78-83. illus (11 b&w, 6 col).

G1760. PLANK, Ross D. "Origin and Manufacture of California's Clay Roofing Tile." American Ceramic Society Bulletin 13 (July 1934), 180-183.

G1761. PLUMB, Helen. "The Pewabic Pottery." Art & Progress 2 (January 1911), 63-67. illus (4 b&w).

G1762. PLUSCH, Herman A. "The Development of Polychromatic
        Exterior Glaze Decoration." Keramic Studio 10
        (June 1908), 46-47.

G1763. POCHMANN, Ruth Fouts. "The Paul Revere Pottery, 1912-
        1942." Spinning Wheel 19 (November 1963), 24-25.
        illus (3 b&w).

G1764. PODMORE, Harry J. "Old Pottery Landmark Passes at
        Trenton [Etruria Works, Ott & Brewer]" Ceramic Age
        19 (June 1932), 271. illus (1 b&w).

G1765. ________. "Trenton--Its Place in the History of the
        Pottery Industry of the United States. I: Early
        Background." Ceramic Age 51 (March 1948), 125-126.

G1766. ________. "Trenton--Its Place in the History of the
        Pottery Industry of the United States. II:
        Richards' Stoneware Pottery." Ceramic Age 51
        (April 1948), 213.

G1767. ________. "Trenton--Its Place in the Development of
        the Pottery Industry of the United States. III:
        Hanlon's 'Potting Manufactory'." Ceramic Age 51
        (April 1948), 213-214.

G1768. ________. "Trenton--Its Place in the Development of
        the Pottery Industry of the United States. IV:
        Lamb Tavern Pottery." Ceramic Age 51 (May 1948),
        246-247. illus (2 b&w).

G1769. ________. "Trenton--Its Place in the Development of
        the Pottery Industry of the United States. V:
        Wimer-McCully Pottery." Ceramic Age 51 (June 1948),
        322, 332. illus (1 b&w).

G1770. ________. "Trenton--Its Place in the Development of
        the Pottery Industry of the United States. VI:
        Hester Pottery-Morton Pottery." Ceramic Age 52
        (July 1948),19.

G1771. ________. "Trenton--Its Place in the Development of
        the Pottery Industry of the United States. VII:
        Three Nottingham Potteries." Ceramic Age 52
        (August 1948), 76.

G1772. ________. "Trenton--Its Place in the Development of
        the Pottery Industry of the United States. VIII:
        Some Pioneer Potters." Ceramic Age 52 (September
        1948), 131, 157. bibliog.

G1773. ________. "Trenton--Its Place in the Development of
        the Pottery Industry of the United States. IX:
        Trends in Early Ware Development." Ceramic Age 52
        (October 1948), 206.

G1774.   POESE, Bill. "Love Affair with a Miniature Necessary."
         Antiques Journal 32 (March 1977), 38-39, 46, 63.
         illus (10 b&w).

G1775.   __________. "Majolica Wares." Antiques Journal 27
         (May 1972), 19-20. illus (9 b&w).

G1776.   __________. "Stoneware." Antiques Journal 30 (June
         1975), 24-25, 46. illus (12 b&w).

G1777.   POLYTECHNIC REVIEW. "The Condition of the Pottery
         Art in the United States." Vol. 4 (December 22,
         1877), 285.

G1778.   POOR, H. Varnum. "Modern Pottery." Design 32 (Febru-
         ary 1931), 214. illus (4 b&w).

G1779.   POPULAR SCIENCE MONTHLY. "Industry's Magic Wand
         Creates Pottery from the Air [Catalina, Calif.]"
         Vol. 120 (May 1932), 28. illus (6 b&w).

G1780.   POSTLE, Kathleen R. "Overbeck Pottery." Spinning
         Wheel 28 (May 1972), 10-12. illus (8 b&w).

G1781.   THE POTTER. "Developing a New Process in a Commercial
         Art Pottery: An Experiment with Unskilled Help
         [Roseville]" Vol. 1 (January 1917), 55-59. illus
         (4 b&w).

G1782.   __________. "Planning and Operating a Studio Pottery."
         Vol. 1 (December 1916), 25-28. illus (2 b&w).

G1783.   __________. "Planning and Operating a Studio Pottery
         (Second Article)" Vol. 1 (January 1917), 59-63.
         illus (4 b&w).

G1784.   __________. "Planning and Operating a Studio Pottery
         (Third Article)" Vol. 1 (February 1917), 94-97.
         illus (3 b&w).

G1785.   POTTER, Jeanne O. "The Uptons: Potters at East
         Greenwich." American Collector 8 (November 1939),
         8-9. illus (4 b&w).

G1786.   POTTERY AND GLASS. "Advance in American Pottery:
         . . . American Pottery Products Compete with High
         Class Imports." Vol. 2 (June 1909), 301-302.
         illus (3 b&w).

G1787.   __________. "American Art Pottery." Vol. 4 (April
         1910), 39-40. illus (6 b&w).

G1788.   __________. "The American Invasion: China Stores and
         Departments Show More Domestic Pottery on Display
         than in any Previous Year." Vol. 2 (May 1909),
         231-237. illus (14 b&w).

G1789. POTTERY AND GLASS. "Art Displayed on Semi-Porcelains
        [Steubenville Pottery]" Vol. 3 (October 1909), 174.
        illus (1 b&w).

G1790. __________. "Art Pottery Put to Practical Use [Fulper]"
        Vol. 6 (April 1911), 16-18. illus (3 b&w).

G1791. __________. "Changes in Wage Scale of Trenton Potters."
        Vol. 5 (September 1910), 17.

G1792. __________. "Charles Volkmar [Obituary]" Vol. 12
        (February 1914), 25.

G1793. __________. "China and Glassware Market: Trade is
        Booming . . . . " Vol. 3 (December 1909), 293-294.
        illus (2 b&w).

G1794. __________. "Col. John Nessly Taylor [Obituary]" Vol.
        13 (December 1914), 29. illus (1 b&w).

G1795. __________. "Death of David F. Haynes." Vol. 1 (Sep-
        tember 1908), 27.

G1796. __________. "The Decorative Value of Terra Cotta."
        Vol. 11 (July 1913), 11-12. illus (2 b&w).

G1797. __________. "Design Piracy in the Pottery Trade."
        Vol. 11 (November 1913), 9.

G1798. __________, "Domestic Pottery Improving." Vol. 5
        (September 1910), 15-16. illus (2 b&w).

G1799. __________. "The Domestic Pottery Industry." Vol. 4
        (April 1910), 9-11. illus (4 b&w).

G1800. __________. "Domestic Pottery Market." Vol. 4 (March
        1910), 33-34. illus (2 b&w).

G1801. __________. "Domestic Tableware and Cooking Utensils."
        Vol. 4 (May 1910), 30-31. illus (2 b&w).

G1802. __________. "Fine American Table Porcelain: America
        Possesses All the Requirements for Production and
        Is Making Notable Progress in Manufactures of Merit."
        Vol. 1 (July 1908), 11-12. (2 b&w).

G1803. __________. "How Modern Pottery Is Made." Vol. 12
        (June 1914), 7-8, 28-29.

G1804. __________. "James Pass [Obituary]" Vol. 11 (November
        1913), 26. illus (1 b&w).

G1805. __________. "Jersey Made Pottery Shown in Newark
        Exhibit." Vol. 14 (March 1915), 9-10. illus
        (4 b&w).

G1806.   POTTERY AND GLASS. "Jersey Pottery Wins Honors at
          International Fair." Vol. 15 (July 1915), 9-10.
          illus (2 b&w).

G1807.   _________. "Lamps, Lighting Fixtures, Shades and Art
          Metal [Fulper]" Vol. 7 (September 1911), 17-18.
          illus (4 b&w).

G1808.   _________. "Making Pottery at the Fulper Vase Kraft
          Shop." Vol. 9 (December 1912), 41-42. illus (1 b&w).

G1809.   _________. "Metropolitan Museum Gets Quaint Pitcher
          [by D. Greatbach]" Vol. 12 (February 1914), 18.
          illus (1 b&w).

G1810.   _________. "New American Introductions: Specialities
          Now Coming Out . . . " Vol. 3 (July 1909), 15-18.
          illus (6 b&w).

G1811.   _________. "New Jardinieres, Flower Pots, Etc." Vol.
          3 (August 1909), 65-67. illus (6 b&w).

G1812.   _________. "New York Society of Keramic Arts Exhibi-
          tion." Vol. 6 (March 1911), 14. illus (1 b&w).

G1813.   _________. "Novel Pottery that Comes From California
          [Arequipa]" Vol. 14 (January 1915), 9-10, 27.
          illus (5 b&w).

G1814.   _________. "Ohio Potteries Damaged by Flood." Vol. 10
          April 1913), 25-26.

G1815.   _________. "Porcelain Firing." Vol. 3 (December 1909),
          279-280.

G1816.   _________. "Possibilities of St. Louis Clay [R. P.
          Bringhurst]" Vol. 4 (March 1910), 23-24.

G1817.   _________. "Potters' Annual Convention [U.S. Potters'
          Association]" Vol. 3 (December 1909), 276-278.
          illus (1 b&w).

G1818.   _________. "The Potters' Annual Convention [U.S.
          Potters' Association]" Vol. 5 (October 1910),
          15-16.

G1819.   _________. "Potters' Convention [U.S. Potters' Asso-
          ciation]" Vol. 7 (December 1911), 45-46.

G1820.   _________. "Potters Hold Annual Convention [U.S.
          Potters' Association]" Vol. 9 (November 1912), 28.

G1821.   _________. "Potters Hold Annual Convention [U.S.
          Potters' Association]" Vol. 11 (December 1913),
          24-25. illus (1 b&w).

G1822.   POTTERY AND GLASS. "The Pottery Transfer Tariff."
          Vol. 1 (July 1908), 23.

G1823.   __________. "Slip Decorated Ware at Metropolitan
          Museum." Vol. 9 (December 1912), 28-29. illus
          (4 b&w).

G1824.   __________. "Tea Set for Children [Vodrey Pottery]"
          Vol. 3 (September 1909), 127. illus (1 b&w).

G1825.   __________. "Terra Cotta in the China Department."
          Vol. 6 (April 1911), 11-13. illus (13 b&w).

G1826.   __________. "The Wanamaker Jubilee . . . China Sale."
          Vol. 6 (April 1911), 22-24. illus (5 b&w).

G1827.   __________. "Young Women Potters: . . . The New York
          Y.W.C.A. is Moulding Young Women into First Rate
          Potters." Vol. 8 (June 1912), 17. illus (1 b&w).

G1828.   POTTERY, GLASS & BRASS SALESMAN. "American Ceramic
          Society: Thirteenth Annual Meeting Held in
          Trenton . . . ." Vol. 3 (February 16, 1911), 21.

G1829.   __________. "Archibald M. Maddock [Obituary]" Vol. 1
          (March 30, 1910), 26. illus (1 b&w).

G1830.   __________. "Big Fire at Crooksville [Star Stoneware
          Co.]" Vol. 5 (February 29, 1912), 23.

G1831.   __________. "Domestic Potters in Session: Thirty-
          Second Annual Convention [U.S. Potters' Association]"
          Vol. 2 (October 13, 1910), 7, 9-12.

G1832.   __________. "The Famous Old Union Porcelain Works of
          Brooklyn Takes New Life Under Pitcairn Management."
          Vol. 15 (February 15, 1917), 41, 43.

G1833.   __________. "James Tams, Dean Among Potters." Vol. 1
          (March 2, 1910), 11, 15. illus (1 b&w).
          Reprinted in G62.

G1834.   __________. "James Tams [Obituary]" Vol. 2 (November
          17, 1910), 9. illus (1 b&w).

G1835.   __________. "Jonathan Coxon, Jr. [Obituary]" Vol. 3
          (March 9, 1911), 20. illus (1 b&w).

G1836.   __________. "The Old Bell Pottery." Vol. 2 (January
          26, 1911), 7.

G1837.   __________. "Proposed Permanent Pottery Exhibit . . .
          Views of Frank Forrest Frederick, Director of the
          Trenton School of Industrial Arts." Vol. 1 (Febru-
          ary 2, 1910), 19. illus (1 b&w).

G1838.   POTTERY, GLASS & BRASS SALESMAN. "Receiver for Haynes."
          Vol. 5 (February 22, 1912), 7.

G1839.   ________. "A Rookwood Triumph in Tile: . . . Norse
          Room, Fort Pitt Hotel, Pittsburg[h]" Vol. 1 (March
          16, 1910), 17. illus (2 b&w).

G1840.   ________. "Trenton in the Early Eighties." Vol. 1
          (April 14, 1910), 19. illus (4 b&w).

G1841.   POUCHER, J. Wilson. "The Caire Pottery at Poughkeep-
          sie." Dutchess County Historical Society Year Book
          26 (1941), 73-77. illus (1 b&w).

G1842.   POWELL, Elizabeth. "Pennsylvania German Pottery . . .
          Tools and Processes." Ceramics Monthly 19 (Novem-
          ber 1971), 18-22. illus (9 b&w).

G1843.   POWELL, Robert Blake. "American Shaving Mug Art and
          Artists: The Koken Barber Supply Company, St. Louis,
          Missouri." Spinning Wheel 36 (March-April 1980),
          32-36. illus (10 b&w).

G1844.   PRESTON, Thomas B. "Potters and Their Craft."
          Chautauquan 14 (November 1891), 171-175.

G1845.   [PRIESTMAN, Fanny Rowell]   "Early Experience of a
          Noted Keramist [C. Volkmar]" Ceramic Monthly 6
          (September 1897), 128-129. illus (1 b&w).

G1846.   ________. "Early Experience of Noted Keramists [S. E.
          LePrince; A. B. Leonard]" Ceramic Monthly 6 (August
          1897), 106-108. illus (2 b&w).

G1847.   ________. "Experiences of Noted Keramists [M. M.
          Mason; E. Mason]" Ceramic Monthly 6 (October 1897),
          145-146. illus (2 b&w).

G1848.   ________. "Noted Keramic Artists [Mrs. W. Osgood;
          C. B. Doremus]" Ceramic Monthly 6 (November 1897),
          164-165. illus (2 b&w).

G1849.   PURDY, Ross C. "American Ceramics." American Ceramic
          Society Bulletin 4 (September 1925), 425-427.

G1850.   ________. "Ceramic Education in Illinois." American
          Ceramic Society Transactions 8 (1906), 312-326.

G1851.   ________. "Co-operation in the Clay Industries."
          Clay-Worker 93 (April 1930), 352-353.

G1852.   ________. "Why American Pottery is Not the Vogue in
          America." Ceramic Age 18 (October 1931), 220-222.

G1853.   QUAINTANCE, Paul A.   "Silicosis: A Study of 106
         Pottery Workers." American Journal of Public
         Health 24 (December 1934), 1244-1251.

G1854.   RAMSAY, John. "American Art Pottery." American
         Collector 16 (April 1947), 12-14, 18. illus
         (8 b&w).

G1855.   ________. "American Majolica." Hobbies 50 (May 1945),
         45, 48.

G1856.   ________. "American Pottery." Hobbies 45 (December
         1940), 57-60. illus (2 b&w).

G1857.   ________. "American Rockingham Tableware." American
         Antiques Journal 2 (October 1947), 4-5. illus
         (2 b&w).

G1858.   ________. "Early American Pottery: A Résumé."
         Antiques 20 (October 1931), 224-229. illus (19 b&w).

G1859.   ________. "East Liverpool, Ohio, Pottery in the
         Museum of the East Liverpool Historical Society,
         Part I." American Collector 17 (April 1948), 17-19.
         illus (9 b&w)

G1860.   ________. "East Liverpool, Ohio, Pottery in the
         Museum of the East Liverpool Historical Society,
         Part II." American Collector 17 (May 1948), 9-11.
         illus (8 b&w).

G1861.   ________. "East Liverpool vs. Bennington: Notes on
         Some Distinctive Ohio Pottery." Antiques 49 (Janu-
         ary 1946), 42-44. illus (6 b&w).

G1862.   ________. "Lotus Ware." Hobbies 47 (October 1942),
         55-56. illus (3 b&w).

G1863.   ________. "'Made in America' Dogs." Hobbies 48
         (December 1943), 48-49. illus (1 b&w).

G1864.   ________. "Redware Pottery." American Antiques
         Journal 2 (July 1947), 19-20. illus (3 b&w).

G1865.   RANDALL, J. E. "'The Clay-Worker,' A Potential Factor
         in the Up-Building of the Ceramic Industries."
         American Ceramic Society Journal 6 (January 1923),
         120-228. illus (1 b&w); bibliog.

G1866.   RANDALL, James E., et al. "Our Tribute to Theodore
         A. Randall [Memorial]" Clay-Worker 86 (August
         1926), 107-117. illus (1 b&w).

G1867.   RANEY, E. Marvin. "Edgerton Potters I: The Samson
         Brothers." Rock County Chronicle 8 (Spring 1962),
         3-9.

G1868. RAUSCHENBERG, Bradford L. "American Tin-Glaze:
        The John Bell Inkstand." Journal of Early Southern
        Decorative Arts 3 (May 1977), 27-35. illus (2 b&w);
        bibliog.

G1869. ________. "'B. DuVal & Co/Richmond': A Newly Dis-
        covered Pottery." Journal of Early Southern Decora-
        tive Arts 4 (May 1978), 45-75. illus (6 b&w);
        bibliog.

G1870. RAWSON, Jonathan A., Jr. "Garden Pottery and Its
        Various Uses." House Beautiful 33 (March 1913),
        105-107. illus (9 b&w).

G1871. ________. "Recent American Pottery." House Beautiful
        31 (April 1912), 148-150. illus (8 b&w).

G1872. ________. "Teco and Robineau Pottery." House
        Beautiful 33 (April 1913), 151-152. illus (5 b&w).

G1873. RAY, Marcia. "Pisgah Forest Pottery." Spinning Wheel
        27 (January-February 1971), 16-17, 58. illus
        (6 b&w).

G1874. RAYMOND, W. Oakley. "Colonial and Early American
        Earthenware." Antiquarian 9 (January 1928),
        38-41, 46. illus (4 b&w).

G1875. ________. "Remmey Family: American Potters."
        Antiques 31 (June 1937), 296-297. illus (7 b&w).

G1876. ________. "Remmey Family: American Potters, Part
        II." Antiques 32 (September 1937), 132-133. illus
        (5 b&w).

G1877. ________. "Remmey Family: American Potters, Part
        III." Antiques 33 (March 1938), 142-143. illus
        (5 b&w).

G1878. ________. "Remmey Family: American Potters, Part
        IV." Antiques 34 (July 1938), 30-31. illus
        (6 b&w).

G1879. ________. "Unmarked New York Pottery: Crolius and
        Remmey." Antiquarian 14 (January 1930), 54-55, 88.
        illus (11 b&w).

G1880. REDDALL, Amy C. "Clay Modeling in Elementary Art
        Education." Art Education 1 (April 1895), 98.

G1881. REHMANN, Elsa. "Pottery in the Garden." House &
        Garden 49 (June 1926), 70-71, 150, 186. illus
        (9 b&w).

G1882. REILLY, Anna D. "American Belleek." Spinning Wheel
        8 (June 1952), 6, 8, 10, 24. illus (4 b&w).

G1883.   REINERT, Guy F. "History of the Pennsylvania German
         Potteries of Berks County." American Ceramic
         Society Bulletin 19 (January 1940), 24-28. illus
         (1 b&w).
            Originally published in Historical Review of Berks
            County. See G1887.

G1884.   ________. "Johann Georg Bühler, Master Potter."
         American-German Review 5 (June 1939), 14-15. illus
         (4 b&w).

G1885.   ________. "Johann Georg Bühler, Master Potter."
         Historical Review of Berks County 4 (July 1939),
         98-99. illus (4 b&w).
            Reprint of G1884.

G1886.   ________. "Medinger, Last Pennsylvania Folk Potter."
         American Collector 3 (May 2, 1935), 3, 9. illus
         (7 b&w).

G1887.   ________. "Pennsylvania German Potteries of Berks
         County." The Historical Review of Berks County 2
         (January 1937), 42-49, 56. illus (7 b&w).

G1888.   ________. "Pennsylvania-German Potters of Bucks
         County, Pennsylvania." Bucks County Historical
         Society Collections 7 (1937), 580-585. illus
         (1 b&w).

G1889.   ________. "Slip Decorated Pottery of the Pennsylvania-
         Germans." The American-German Review 2 (March 1936),
         12-14, 49.

G1890.   REMENSNYDER, John P. "The Potters of Poughkeepsie."
         Antiques 90 (July 1966), 90-95. illus (17 b&w).

G1891.   REYNOLDS, S. Adelaide. "Concerning the Dedham Plates."
         House Beautiful 18 (November 1905), 25. illus
         (3 b&w).

G1892.   RHEAD, Frederick Alfred. "The Decoration of Pottery
         in the Clay State: Pâte-sur-Pâte." Keramic Studio
         14 (May 1912), 13-16. illus (12 b&w).

G1893.   ________. "The Decoration of Pottery in the Clay
         State: Pâte-sur-Pâte (Continued)." Keramic Studio
         14 (June 1912), 42.

G1894.   ________. "The Decoration of Pottery in the Clay
         State: Pâte-sur-Pâte (Concluded)." Keramic Studio
         14 (July 1912), 47-48.

G1895.   ________. "Etched Gold on Porcelain." Keramic Studio
         13 (July 1911), 48-50, 52. illus (8 b&w).

G1896.   ________. "Underglaze Decoration." Keramic Studio 9
         (October 1907), 128, 130-131.

G1897.   RHEAD, Frederick Alfred. "Underglaze Painting."
         Keramic Studio 9 (January 1908), 202-203, 206.
         illus (2 b&w).

G1898.   __________. "Underglaze Painting, Concluded." Keramic
         Studio 9 (February 1908), 222-224. illus (2 b&w).

G1899.   RHEAD, Frederick Hurten. "Adelaide Alsop Robineau,
         Maker of Porcelains." Potter 1 (February 1917),
         81-88. illus (7 b&w).

G1900.   __________. "America as a Ceramic Art Center. Chapter
         I." Fine Arts Journal 22 (April 1910), 183-193.
         illus (13 b&w).
            Chapter II is G2109.

G1901.   __________. "American Ceramic Society Exhibition: The
         First American Ceramic Society Ceramic Display."
         American Ceramic Society Bulletin 1 (May 1922),
         10-17. illus (4 b&w).

G1902.   __________. "The Art Division of the American Ceramic
         Society." American Ceramic Society Journal 5
         (February 1922), 57-65.

G1903.   __________. "Discussion on 'The American Interest in
         Chinese Art'." American Ceramic Society Bulletin 2
         (May 1923). 117-119.

G1904.   __________. "An Experiment in Glaze Decoration on Fire
         Tile." Potter 1 (December 1916), 19-22. illus
         (1 b&w).

G1905.   __________. "The Italian Majolica Process and Painting
         over Tin Enamels." American Ceramic Society Bulletin
         1 (September 1922), 177-180.

G1906.   __________. "Kiln Manipulation in Relation to School
         and Studio Pottery." American Ceramic Society Bul-
         letin 1 (August 1922), 131-133. illus (1 b&w).

G1907.   __________. "May Elizabeth Cook, Architectural Potter."
         Potter 1 (December 1916), 1-6. illus (5 b&w).

G1908.   __________. "Notes on Shape Construction." American
         Ceramic Society Journal 10 (June 1927), 389-401.
         illus (12 b&w).

G1909.   __________. "The Organization of a Decorative Ceramic
         Research Department." American Ceramic Society
         Journal 5 (November 1922), 758-787. illus (3 b&w).

G1910.   __________. "Shape, Construction and Design." Potter
         1 (December 1916), 29-35. illus (7 b&w).

G1911.   RHEAD, Frederick Hurten. "Shape, Construction and
         Design (Second Article)." Potter 1 (January 1917),
         66-70. illus (7 b&w).

G1912.   ________. "Shape, Construction and Design (Third
         Article)." Potter 1 (February 1917), 98-101.

G1913.   ________. "Suggestions on Ceramic Art Education."
         American Ceramic Society Bulletin 5 (November 1926),
         410-416.

G1914.   ________. "Tariff Situation in the Whiteware Indus-
         try." Ceramic Age 12 (July 1928), 11-15.

G1915.   ________. "Technical Description, Black 'Hawthorne
         Beaker'." Potter 1 (December 1916), 23-24.

G1916.   ________. "Theophilus A. Brouwer, Jr.: Maker of
         Iridescent Glazed Faience." Potter 1 (January
         1917), 43-49. illus (7 b&w).

G1917.   ________. "What the Industries Want From the Ceramic
         Artist." American Ceramic Society Bulletin 4
         (April 1925), 158-164.

G1918.   RHEAD, Geo. F. "China Rivetting for Amateurs."
         Keramic Studio 11 (September 1909), 114-115. illus
         (2 b&w).

G1919.   RICHARDS, Agnes Gertrude. "An Exhibition of Ceramics
         [Atlan Club]" Fine Arts Journal 34 (January 1916),
         40-43. illus (5 b&w).

G1920.   ________. "Important Exhibition of American Ceramics
         [Burley & Co.]" Fine Arts Journal 33 (October 1915),
         438-443. illus (4 b&w).

G1921.   RICHARDSON, W. D. "Choice of a Kiln." Clay-Worker 57
         (February 1912), 253-254.

G1922.   ________. "The Possibilities of the Tunnel Kiln for
         Sewer Pipe." American Ceramic Society Journal 10
         (September 1927), 693-698. illus (3 b&w).

G1923.   RICKER, Ruth. "The Fulper Doll Head." Spinning
         Wheel 12 (July 1956), 28, 33. illus (2 b&w).

G1924.   RIDDLE, F. H. "The American Ceramic Industries."
         American Ceramic Society Journal 6 (January 1923),
         67-86.

G1925.   ________. "The New Pottery and Art Terra Cotta Plant
         of the Van Briggle Pottery Company at Colorado
         Springs, Colo." American Ceramic Society Trans-
         actions 10 (1908), 65-75. illus (7 b&w).

G1926.   RIDDLE, L. E., Jr. "A Visit to a Few Potteries [Ohio,
          Ky., Tenn., Va.]" New Jersey Ceramist 1 (December
          1921), 295-296.

G1927.   RIEFSTAHL, R. Meyer. "Tucker China." Country Life
          41 (February 1922), 68-69. illus (17 b&w).

G1928.   RIES, Estelle H. "The Decorative Use of Tiles
          Outdoors." Garden Magazine & Home Builder 41
          (July 1925), 391-393. illus (9 b&w).

G1929.   RIES, Heinrich. "Bibliography of Clay Deposits."
          American Ceramic Society Bulletin 4 (September 1925),
          428-471.

G1930.   __________. "Clay Industries of New York." New York
          State Museum Bulletin 3 (March 1895), 97-262.

G1931.   __________. "Effect of the War on the Development of
          the Clays of the United States." Clay-Worker 68
          (October 1917), 338-339.

G1932.   __________. "Fire Clays of the Eastern Coalfield of
          Kentucky." American Ceramic Society Journal 5
          (July 1922), 397-408. illus (6 b&w).

G1933.   __________. "The Occurrence of High Grade American
          Clays, and the Possibility of Their Further Develop-
          ment." American Ceramic Society Journal 1 (July
          1908), 446-467. illus (16 b&w).

G1934.   RIGHTER, Miriam. "Belleek in America." Antiques
          Journal 11 (October 1956), 34-35. illus (4 b&w).

G1935.   RIGHTS, T. M. "Remarks on Tile Stoves." Bucks
          County Historical Society Collections 4 (1917),
          481-482.

G1936.   ROBACKER, Earl F. "Pennsylvania Redware." Pennsylva-
          nia Dutchman 8 (Fall-Winter 1956-1957), 2-7. illus
          (14 b&w).

G1937.   __________. "Redware for Pretty." Antique Collecting 1
          (August 1977), 4-5. illus (9 b&w).

G1938.   __________. "Stoneware--Stepchild of Early Pottery."
          Pennsylvania Folklife 13 (July 1964), 2-7. illus
          (12 b&w); bibliog.

G1939.   ROBERTS, Janet. "Family Pottery [Boggs]" Ceramics
          Monthly 17 (June 1969), 28-29. illus (3 b&w).

G1940.   ROBERTSON, J. Milton. "The Background of Dedham
          Pottery." American Ceramic Society Bulletin 20
          (November 1941), 411-413. illus (2 b&w).

G1941. ROBERTSON, J. Milton. "Cracqule Ware." Compleat Col-
        lector 1 (April 1941), 6.

G1942. ROBINEAU, Adelaide Alsop. "American Pottery:
        Artistic Porcelain-Making." Art World 3 (November
        1917), 153-155. illus (8 b&w).

G1943. __________. "Ceramics at Syracuse University." Keramic
        Studio 25 (April 1924), 232-235. illus (23 b&w).

G1944. __________. "Hand Made Lunch Sets." Keramic Studio 24
        (September 1922), 63. illus (3 b&w).

G1945. __________. "Miss Maud M. Mason." Keramic Studio 18
        (February 1917), 160. illus (1 b&w).

G1946. __________. "Mrs. Dorothea Warren O'Hara." Keramic
        Studio 18 (January 1917), 143. illus (2 b&w).

G1947. __________. "Mrs. Kathryn E. Cherry." Keramic Studio
        18 (March 1917), 178-179. illus (2 b&w).

G1948. __________. "Poppies." Keramic Studio 3 (October 1901),
        122-126. illus (12 b&w).

G1949. __________. "Pottery Problems [Making Bowls]" Keramic
        Studio 24 (December 1922), 129-134. illus (23 b&w).

G1950. __________. "Report of the Ceramics of the International
        Exposition of Paris, 1925." American Ceramic Society
        Bulletin 5 (March 1926), 185-190.

G1951. __________. "Tiles in School Work [Syracuse U.]"
        Keramic Studio 24 (October 1922), 85-87. illus
        (10 b&w).

G1952. __________. "Tulips." Keramic Studio 3 (July 1901),
        52-57. illus (14 b&w).

G1953. ROBINEAU, S. E. "Adelaide Alsop-Robineau." Design 30
        (April 1929), 201-209. illus (35 b&w).

G1954. __________. "Can We Improve American Made Porcelain?"
        Brick and Clay Record 45 (October 6, 1914), 689-690.
        illus (3 b&w).

G1955. __________. "The Robineau Porcelains." Keramic Studio
        13 (August 1911), 80-84. illus (9 b&w).

G1956. ROBINSON, Ednah. "Newcomb Pottery: Its Makers and
        the Lesson They Are Teaching Southern Women."
        Sunset 11 (June 1903), 131-135. illus (4 b&w).

G1957. ROGERS, Jane Grey. "Lines to a Newcomb Vase [Poem]"
        House Beautiful 11 (February 1902), 174. illus
        (1 b&w).

G1958.   ROMAINE. Lawrence B.   "American Porcelain Clay [Ver-
          mont]" Early American Industries Association
          Chronicle 2 (April 1939), 68.

G1959.   ROORBACH, Eloise.   "Art as a Tonic [Arequipa]" Crafts-
          man 24 (June 1913), 343-346. illus (5 b&w).

G1960.   ROSE, Arthur V.   "Porcelain Made in America [Lenox]"
          International Studio 37 (April 1909), xlix-lii.
          illus (5 b&w)

G1961.   _________. "Sicardo Ware." China, Glass and Pottery
          Review 13 (October 5, 1903), 19-21. illus (2 b&w).

G1962.   ROSENOW, Jane. "Peoria Pottery and How It Grew."
          Antiques Journal 24 (December 1969), 30-31. illus
          (3 b&w).

G1963.   ROUECHÉ, Berton. "A Reporter at Large: The Last Lap
          [Dorcester Pottery Works]" New Yorker 30 (March 13,
          1954), 37-38, 40, 42, 44, 46, 48, 50, 53-54, 56-57,
          59.

G1964.   RUCKER, Kathryn. "The Present Popularity of Ceramic
          Art, With Particular Reference to the Work of
          Dorothea Warren O'Hara." Arts & Decoration 3 (Septem-
          ber 1913), 382. illus (3 b&w).

G1965.   RUGE, Clara. "American Ceramics--A Brief Review of
          Progress." International Studio 28 (March 1906),
          xxi-xxviii. illus (19 b&w).

G1966.   _________. "American Pottery: Great Advancement
          Noticed in this Season's Introductions . . . . "
          Pottery & Glass 2 (January 1909), 27-36. illus
          (17 b&w).

G1967.   _________. "Amerikanische Keramik." Dekorative Kunst
          14 (January 1906), 167-176. illus (29 b&w).

G1968.   _________. "Development of American Ceramics: Ameri-
          can Materials Fashioned by American Artists and
          Artisans are Taking Their Place Beside the World's
          Best Potteries." Pottery & Glass 1 (August 1908),
          2-8. illus (11 b&w).

G1969.   _________. "Grand Feu Porcelain in America." Pottery
          & Glass 1 (September 1908), 17-19. illus (3 b&w).

G1970.   RUSSELL, Arthur. "Grueby Pottery." House Beautiful
          5 (December 1898), 3-9. illus (8 b&w).

G1971.   RUSSELL, (Mrs.) E. E. "Kokomo Keramic Club." Keramic
          Studio 13 (February 1912), 208-210. illus (5 b&w).

G1972. RUSSELL, Elizabeth H. "The Pottery of Marblehead."
        House Beautiful 59 (March 1926), 362, 364, 366.
        Illus (5 b&w).

G1973. RUSSELL, J. Almus. "American Pottery of Yesterday."
        Antiques Journal 19 (December 1964), 16-21. illus
        (19 b&w).

G1974. S.E.G. NEWS. "The Paul Revere Pottery." Vol. 4
        (December 11, 1915), 3.

G1975. ________. "The Potter." Vol. 5 (December 9, 1916),
        8-9.

G1976. SAMMIS, Romanah. "The Pottery at Huntington." Long
        Island Forum 2 (March 1939), 7-8, 19. illus (1 b&w).

G1977. ________. "The Pottery at Huntington, Long Island."
        Antiques 3 (April 1923), 161-165. illus (14 b&w).

G1978. SARGENT, Irene. "An Art Industry of the Bayous: The
        Pottery of Newcomb College." Craftsman 5 (October
        1903), 70-76. illus (6 b&w).

G1979. ________. "Chinese Pots and Modern Faïence." Crafts-
        man 4 (September 1903), 415-425. illus (4 b&w).

G1980. ________. "Clay in the Hands of the Potter [A. A.
        Robineau]" Keystone 57 (September 1929), 131-133,
        135, 137, 139, 141. illus (14 b&w).

G1981. ________. "Potters and Their Products." Clay-Worker
        40 (September 1903), 240-244. illus (4 b&w).
        Originally published in Craftsman. See G1982.

G1982. ________. "Potters and Their Products." Craftsman 4
        (June 1903), 148-160. illus (3 b&w).

G1983. ________. "Some Potters and Their Products [Part II]"
        Craftsman 4 (July 1903), 248-257. illus (7 b&w).

G1984. ________. "Some Potters and Their Products [Part III]"
        Craftsman 4 (August 1903), 328-337. illus (2 b&w).

G1985. ________. "Taxile Doat." Keramic Studio 8 (December
        1906), 171-173, 193. illus (6 b&w).

G1986. SAUER, Jim. "Rare and Beautiful American Belleek
        Steins." Prosit no. 47 (March 1977), 385-387.
        illus (8 b&w).

G1987. SAUNIER, Charles. "Poteries de la Cie Grueby (Boston)"
        L'Art décoratif (August 1901), 203-206, 208. illus
        (7 b&w).

G1988. SCAMMELL, D. William. "The Development of Vitreous
        China and Porcelain in the United States." Ceramic
        Age 15 (June 1930), 332-333.

G1989. SCHALTENBRAND, Phil. "Hamilton and Jones, Pioneer
        Pottery of Pennsylvania." Antiques Journal 33
        (November 1978), 20-23, 50. illus (8 b&w).

G1990. _________. "New Geneva and Its Stoneware Production."
        Antiques Journal (December 1978), 38-41, 53. illus
        (7 b&w).

G1991. _________. "The Stoneware of Greensboro-New Geneva."
        Ceramics Monthly 28 (September 1980), 30-36. illus
        (5 b&w).

G1992. _________. "The Stoneware Pottery of Isaac Hewitt, Jr."
        Spinning Wheel 33 (October 1977), 8-13. illus
        (12 b&w).

G1993. SCHANTZ, E. F. "Mug Hunting." Hobbies 39 (April
        1934), 72. illus (1 b&w).

G1994. SCHEETZ, Grier, "Bucks County Potters." Bucks County
        Historical Society Collections 4 (1917), 192-197.

G1995. SCHNEIDER, Norris F. "Roseville Pottery." Western
        Collector 7 (July 1969), 302-307. illus (13 b&w).

G1996. SCHOOL SCIENCE AND MATHEMATICS. "Beginnings of Ameri-
        can Porcelain [Chemical Porcelain]" Vol. 15 (Octo-
        ber 1915), 624-625.

G1997. SCHURECHT, H. G. "The Properties of Some Ohio and
        Pennsylvania Stoneware Clays." American Ceramic
        Society Journal 1 (April 1918), 267-272.

G1998. SCHWARTZ, Jeri. "Let's Talk about American Pottery--
        Redware." National Antiques Review 6 (January
        1975), 36-37. illus (5 b&w).

G1999. _________. "Let's Talk about American Stoneware--Ben-
        nington--Rockingham. National Antiques Review 6
        (March 1975), 34-35. illus (5 b&w).

G2000. SCHWARTZ, Marvin D. "Art Pottery: Its Time Has Come."
        Antique Monthly 2 (September 1978), 13C. illus
        (3 b&w).

G2001. _________. "Fine American Ceramics of the Victorian
        Period." Antiques 77 (April 1960), 386-389. illus
        (9 b&w).

G2002. _________. "A Gift of Early American Ceramics [to
        Brooklyn Museum]" Brooklyn Museum Bulletin 17
        (Winter 1956), 1-2. illus (1 b&w).

G2003.   SCHWARTZ, Stuart C. "The Reinhardt Potteries."
         Ceramic Circle of Charlotte Journal of Studies 4
         1980, 33-38. illus (6 b&w); bibliog.
            Prefatory to C23.

G2004.   SCIENCE. "The Annual Meeting of the American Ceramic
            Society." Vol. n.s. 55 (June 2, 1922), 588-589.

G2005.   _________. "Pottery Products." Vol. n.s. 48 (December
            6, 1918), 568.

G2006.   SCIENTIFIC AMERICAN. "Industrial Preparedness for
            Peace: What the Bureau of Standards Has Done for
            the Clay Industries." Vol. 115 (October 7, 1916),
            328-329. illus (5 b&w).

G2007.   SCIENTIFIC AMERICAN SUPPLEMENT. "Artistic Pottery
            Made in America." Vol. 82 (November 4, 1916), 296-
            297. illus (4 b&w).

G2008.   _________. "Engobes or Slips."   Vol. 63 (June 22,
            1907), 26302-26303.

G2009.   _________. "The Pottery Industry of the United States."
            Vol. 79 (April 24, 1915), 263.

G2010.   _________. "Pottery Products of the United States."
            Vol. 66 (November 28, 1908), 354-355.

G2011.   SCOON, Carolyn. "New York State Stoneware in the New-
            York Historical Society." New-York Historical
            Society Quarterly Bulletin 29 (April 1945), 83-91.
            Illus (9 b&w).

G2012.   SEARES, Mabel Urmy. "Ernest Batchelder and His Tiles."
            International Studio 58 (April 1916), liii-lvi.
            illus (10 b&w).

G2013.   SEARLE, Alfred B. "Some Industrial Uses of Stoneware."
            Ceramic Age 12 (December 1928), 211-212.

G2014.   SELLARDS, E. H. "The Clays of Florida." American
            Ceramic Society Journal 1 (May 1918), 313-321.
            illus (1 b&w).

G2015.   SHARKEY, Samuel M. "The Clays of Mercer County."
            New Jersey Ceramist 1 (June 1921), 131-136.

G2016.   SHEERER, Mary G. "Death of Elizabeth Bennett Mills--
            An Appreciation." Keramic Studio 12 (July 1910),
            45.

G2017.   _________. "The Development of Decorative Processes
            at Newcomb." American Ceramic Society Journal 7
            (August 1924), 645-649. illus (3 b&w).

G2018.   SHEERER, Mary G. "History of Newcomb Pottery." American Ceramic Society Journal 1 (August 1918), 518-521. illus (3 b&w).

G2019.   ________. "Newcomb Pottery." Keramic Studio 1 (November 1899), 151-152. illus (3 b&w).

G2020.   ________. "A 'Reaction' to a Visit to the Ceramic Sections of the International Exposition at Paris, 1925." American Ceramic Society Bulletin 5 (March 1926), 182-185.

G2021.   ________. "The Training Necessary for the Pottery Craftsman." American Ceramic Society Bulletin 6 (January 1927), 5-8.

G2022.   SHEFFIELD, Albert H. "To a Teco Vase [Poem]" Clay-Worker 61 (January 1914), 43.

G2023.   SHEPHERD, Tryon Mason. "Campaign Plates." Hobbies 61 (August 1956), 72-74. illus (1 b&w).

G2024.   SHERIDAN, Millicent M. "Rookwood--A Good Field to Explore." Hobbies 57 (July 1952), 84, 96, 99. illus (4 b&w).

G2025.   SHERWOOD, Robert F. "A Method for Determining the Life of a Sagger." American Ceramic Society Bulletin 4 (July 1925), 323-326.

G2026.   SHIRAYAMADANI, K. "Suggestions for Our Study [Daisy Design]" Ceramic Monthly 5 (February 1897), 4-5.

G2027.   SHIRLEY, Bernice Cook. "Rookwood Pottery." American Antiques Journal 3 (November 1948), 10-12. illus (5 b&w).

G2028.   ________. "Rookwood Pottery." Spinning Wheel 5 (April 1949), 33, 46. illus (1 b&w).

G2029.   SHORT, Elizabeth M. "A Clarkson Crolius Jug." Craftsman 6 (May 1904), 180-182. illus (1 b&w).

G2030.   SHOTLIFF, Don A. "The 1894 Tariff and the Pottery Strike: The Rebirth of the National Brotherhood of Operative Potters." Western Pennsylvania Historical Magazine 58 (July 1975), 307-325. illus (4 b&w); bibliog.

G2031.   ________. "The Ohio Pottery Industry: The Influences on Its Development and the Struggle for a Stabilized Wage, 1877-1900." Northwest Ohio Quarterly 45 (Summer 1973), 87-107. bibliog.

G2032.   SHRIMPTON, Louise. "An Art Potter and Her Home [A. A. Robineau]" Good Housekeeping 50 (January 1910), 57-63. illus (8 b&w).

G2033. SHULL, Thelma. "Pottery Jugs, Mugs, and Shoes."
        Hobbies 48 (December 1943), 58-59. illus (1 b&w).
        Republished as B76.

G2034. __________. "The Robertson Family and Dedham Pottery."
        Hobbies 47 (December 1942), 58-60. illus (1 b&w).
        Republished as B77.

G2035. __________. "Rookwood Pottery." Hobbies 47 (October
        1942), 66-67.
        Republished as B78.

G2036. SHUMAN, Susan W., and SHUMAN, John A. III. "George E.
        Ohr: Eccentric and Genius." Antiques Journal 32
        (June 1977), 12-14, 47. illus (9 b&w).

G2037. SHUMWAY, Harry Irving. "To Watch a Potter Thumping
        His Wet Clay [Dedham Pottery]" American Cookery
        37 (May 1933), 642-650. illus (10 b&w).

G2038. SILVA, William P. "Newcomb Pottery." Art and Progress
        2 (June 1911), 230-233. illus (3 b&w)

G2039. SILVERMAN, Alexander. "Albert Victor Bleininger, Man
        and Scientist." American Ceramic Society Bulletin
        27 (May 15, 1948), 204-209. bibliog.

G2040. SIM, Robert J., and CLEMENT, Arthur W. "The Cheese-
        quake Potteries." Antiques 45 (March 1944), 122-125.
        illus (8 b&w).

G2041. SLIVKA, Rose. "A Panorama of American Ceramics:
        Exhibition Review [Everson Museum]" Museum News 58
        (July-August 1980), 58-64. illus (18 b&w).

G2042. SMALL, Eleanor C. "Firing with A Fitch Charcoal Kiln."
        Keramic Studio 8 (June 1906), 30.

G2043. SMITH, Clarissa. "Etruscan Majolica." Antiques Jour-
        nal 12 (June 1957), 8-11. illus (7 b&w).

G2044. SMITH, Dolores. "Echoes from the Past: George Ohr's
        Pottery." Popular Ceramics 17 (September 1965),
        8-11. illus (4 b&w).

G2045. SMITH, Eugene A. "The Clay Resources of Alabama and
        the Industries Dependent Upon Them." Engineering
        and Mining Journal 66 (September 24, 1898), 369.

G2046. SMITH, G. Hubert. "Minnesota Potteries: From
        Pioneer Craft to Modern Factory." Minnesota History
        33 (Summer 1953), 229-235. illus (6 b&w); bibliog.

G2047.   SMITH, Howard A. "The History of the Hartsoe Family
          in Lincoln County, North Carolina." Ceramic Circle
          of Charlotte Journal of Studies 4 (1980), 17-20.
          illus (3 b&w).
             Prefatory to G23.

G2048.   SMITH, Katherine Louise. "Architectural Terra Cotta."
          House Beautiful 9 (February 1901), 153-157. illus
          (6 b&w).

G2049.   SMITH, Kenneth E. "Laura Anne Fry: Originator of the
          Atomizing Process for Application of Underglaze
          Colors." American Ceramic Society Bulletin 17 (Sep-
          tember 1938), 368-372. illus (7 b&w); bibliog.

G2050.   ________. "The Origin, Development, and Present
          Status of Newcomb Pottery." American Ceramic Society
          Bulletin 17 (June 1938), 257-259.

G2051.   SMITH, Kenneth L. "High Efficiency Developed in Tile
          Production [Standard Floor and Wall Tile Co.]"
          Ceramic Age 13 (January 1929), 8-12. illus (15 b&w).

G2052.   SMITH, Leonora M. "Pickard China." Spinning Wheel
          22 (March 1966), 30. illus (2 b&w).

G2053.   SMITH, Richard W. "Sedimentary Kaolins of Georgia."
          Ceramic Age 14 (August 1929), 39-45. illus (12 b&w).

G2054.   ________. "A Visit to Jugtown." Forestry-Geological
          Review (March 1934), 7. illus (1 b&w).

G2055.   SMITH, Robert E. "The Ceramics Factory at Oklahoma
          State University." Chronicles of Oklahoma 50
          (Summer 1972), 205-218. illus (4 b&w); bibliog.

G2056.   SNOW, Richard F. "Collecting Shaving Mugs." Ameri-
          cana 1 (May 1973), 8-9. illus (9 b&w).

G2057.   ________. "Occupational Shaving Mugs: Symbols of
          American Pride in Profession." American Art &
          Antiques 1 (September-October 1978), 100-107. illus
          (6 b&w, 7 col).

G2058.   SOLON, Leon V. "Color in the Tile Industry." Keramic
          Tile Journal 2 (June 1930), 35-37.

G2059.   ________. "The Display Rooms of a Tile Manufactory
          [American Encaustic Tiling Co.]" Architectural
          Record 52 (November 1922), 362-370. illus (18 b&w,
          2 col).

G2060.   ________. "The Increasing Importance of Ornamental
          Design in Architectural Practice." Architectural
          Record 56 (December 1924), 583-584.

G2061. SOLON, Leon V. "The Mutual Relations between Art and
        Technology." American Ceramic Society Journal 4
        (April 1921), 263-270.

G2062. ________. "The Philadelphia Museum of Art, Fairmount
        Park, Philadelphia: A Revival of Polychrome Archi-
        tecture and Sculpture." Architectural Record 60
        (August 1926), 96-111. illus (19 b&w, 1 col).

G2063. ________. "The Problem of Display." Keramic Tile
        Journal 2 (April 1930), 19-21. illus (4 b&w).

G2064. SOPER, E. K. "Fire Clays in Northern Idaho." Ameri-
        can Ceramic Society Journal 1 (February 1918), 94-98.

G2065. SOUTH, Stanley. "Alkaline Glazed Pottery from South
        Carolina to Texas." University of South Carolina
        Institute of Archaeology and Anthropology Notebook 2
        (September-December 1970), 3-5. illus (2 b&w).

G2066. ________. "Anthropomorphic Pipes from the Kiln Waster
        Dump of Gottfried Aust--1755 to 1771." Florida
        Anthropologist 18 (September 1965), 49-60. illus
        (4 b&w).

G2067. SPANGLER, Meredith Riggs. "In Prayse of Pots."
        Ceramic Circle of Charlotte Journal of Studies 2
        (1973), 5-26. illus (10 b&w); bibliog.

G2068. SPARGO, John. "Burlington Pottery; An Informal Jot-
        ting." Antiques 6 (November 1924), 254.

G2069. ________. "The Facts About Bennington Pottery. Part
        I: The Stoneware of the Norton Potteries." Antiques
        5 (January 1924), 21-25. illus (8 b&w).

G2070. ________. "The Facts About Bennington Pottery. Part
        II: The Work of Christopher Webber Fenton."
        Antiques 5 (May 1924), 230-237. illus (7 b&w).

G2071. ________. "The Fentons--Pioneer American Potters."
        Antiques 4 (October 1923), 166-169. illus (6 b&w).

G2072. SPECTOR, Stephen. "American Art Pottery Revived."
        Architectural Digest 33 (July-August 1976), 68-71,
        132-133. illus (11 col).

G2073. SPILLER, Burton. "One Pottery Bottle Fully Identified
        [Carter's Ink]" Western Collector 9 (July-August
        1971), 30. illus (3 b&w).

G2074. SPINNEY, Frank O. "The Collections: Pottery [Old
        Sturbridge Village]" Antiques 68 (September 1955),
        250-251. illus (7 b&w).

G2075.   SPINNEY, Frank O. "A New Hampshire Potter [D. D.
         Webster]" New-England Galaxy 3 (Fall 1961), 41-44.
         illus (4 b&w).

G2076.   SPINNING WHEEL. "Antiques for Investment [Art Pottery]"
         Vol. 25 (September 1969), 54-57. illus (1 b&w).

G2077.   ________. "Baltimore, Maryland's Bennett Pottery."
         Vol. 14 (November 1958), 22. illus (4 b&w).

G2078.   ________. "Dedham Pottery Exhibition, Dedham Histori-
         cal Society." Vol. 24 (September 1968), 52. illus
         (2 b&w).

G2079.   ________. "John Bell--Master Potter." Vol. 21 (Sep-
         tember 1965), 16, 38. illus (3 b&w).

G2080.   ________. "Lenox China from 1894." Vol. 18 (January
         1962), 16-17. illus (3 b&w).

G2081.   ________. "More About . . . Buffalo Pottery's Art
         Ware: Lunaware--Ivory--Cafe Au Lait." Vol. 19
         (May 1963), 20. illus (5 b&w).

G2082.   ________. "Pennsylvania Pioneer Pottery." Vol. 9
         (October 1953), 10. illus (1 b&w).

G2083.   SPRACKLING, Helen. "Some Contemporary American Pot-
         ters." House Beautiful 72 (November 1932), 311-314,
         346. illus (12 b&w).

G2084.   SPRAGUE, P. E. "Chronic Lead Poisoning Banished in
         New Jersey Potteries." Ceramic Age 10 (October 1927),
         131-132, 139. bibliog.

G2085.   SPRAGUE, William B. "Clay Tobacco Pipes." Early
         American Industries Association Chronicle 1 (March
         1937), 1-2. illus (1 b&w); bibliog.

G2086.   ________. "Dr. Henry C. Mercer." Early American In-
         dustries Association Chronicle 1 (July 1936), 7.

G2087.   SPRINGER-PAPA, Joan. "The Legacy of Stoneware in
         America." Antiques Journal 24 (March 1969), 16-17,
         29. illus (6 b&w).

G2088.   STAHL, I. S. "Pennsylvania German Pottery." Ceramic
         Age 38 (September 1941), 69-71. illus (5 b&w).

G2089.   STEFANO, Frank, Jr. "James Clews, Nineteenth-Century
         Potter: The American Experience." Antiques 105
         (March 1974), 553-555. illus (4 b&w); bibliog.

G2090.   STEINHOFF, F. L. "'Brick and Clay Record': Its
         History." American Ceramic Society Journal 6 (Janu-
         ary 1923), 128-132.

G2091. STERN, Anna M. P. "Phoenixville Majolica." American
         Antiques Journal 2 (August 1947), 10-12. illus
         (4 b&w).

G2092. STIEF, W. C. and HEMSTEGER, S. E. "A Modern Frit
         Furnace." American Ceramic Society Bulletin (Decem-
         ber 1926), 473-476. illus (3 b&w).

G2093. STILL, John S. "Ohio Ceramics." Museum Echoes 31
         (July 1958), 51-54.

G2094. STILLWELL, John E. "Crolius Ware and Its Makers."
         New-York Historical Society Quarterly 10 (July 1926),
         52-66. illus (4 b&w); bibliog.

G2095. STONE AND WEBSTER JOURNAL. "An Interesting Boston
         Handicraft [Paul Revere]" Vol. 43 (October 1928),
         499-506. illus (8 b&w).

G2096. STORM, Nicholas. "The Art of Decorating Underglaze."
         Pottery, Glass & Brass Salesman 1 (February 2, 1910),
         21. illus (1 b&w).

G2097. STOUDT, John Baer. "Inscriptions on the Pottery of the
         Pennsylvania Germans." Bucks County Historical
         Society Collections 4 (1917), 587-599.

G2098. STOUT, Wilber. "Refractory Clays of Ohio." American
         Ceramic Society Bulletin 9 (February 1930), 29-37.

G2099. STOVER, Frances. "Susan Goodrich Frackelton and the
         China Painters." Milwaukee County Historical Society
         Historical Messenger 10 (March 1954), 8-11. illus
         (2 b&w).

G2100. STOVER, J. Homer. "Trenton, the Staffordshire of
         America: Its Potteries, Old and New." Clay-Worker
         45 (January 1906), 92-97. illus (12 b&w).

G2101. STOW, Charles Messer. "The 'Deacon Potter' of Green-
         wich [A. Mead]" Antiquarian 14 (March 1930), 46-47,
         92, 94. illus (5 b&w).

G2102. _________. "Pennsylvania Slip Ware." Antiquarian 13
         (November 1929), 46-47, 82. illus (13 b&w).

G2103. STRADLING, J. G. "American Ceramics and the Philadel-
         phia Centennial." Antiques 110 (July 1976), 146-158.
         illus (17 b&w); bibliog.

G2104. STRATTON, Howard Fremont. "Sgraffito Pottery Made in
         America." Good Furniture 5 (August 1915), 98-103.
         illus (5 b&w).

G2105.   STRATTON, H. J. "Technological Development of the
          American Pottery Industry." Journal of Political
          Economy 40 (October 1932), 661-676. bibliog.

          STRATTON, Mary Chase (Perry), see also PERRY, Mary
          Chase.

G2106.   STRATTON, Mary Chase. "Pewabic Records." American
          Ceramic Society Bulletin 25 (November 15, 1936),
          363-365. illus (2 b&w).

G2107.   STRONG, Janet. "A Flower Painter and Ceramic Decorator
          [E. Rorabeck]" Fine Arts Journal 17 (March 1906),
          201-202. illus (1 b&w).

G2108.   STUART, Evelyn Marie. "About Teco Art Pottery." Fine
          Arts Journal 20 (June 1909), 338, 340-345. illus
          (5 b&w).

G2109.   ________.   "America as a Ceramic Art Center. Chapter
          II." Fine Arts Journal 22 (May 1910), 254-267.
          illus (17 b&w).
            Chapter I is G1900.

G2110.   ________.   "Art Tiling--Its Place in Architecture and
          Decoration [American Encaustic Tiling Co.]" Fine
          Arts Journal 29 (December 1913), 736-750. illus (b&w).

G2111.   ________.   "Pottery Art at the Panama-Pacific Exposi-
          tion." Fine Arts Journal 32 (January 1915), 32-36.
          illus (5 b&w).

G2112.   ________.   "Teco Pottery and Faience Tile." Fine Arts
          Journal 25 (August 1911), 98-111. illus (20 b&w).

G2113.   ________.   "VaseKraft--An American Art Pottery." Fine
          Arts Journal 29 (October 1913), 607-616. illus
          (14 b&w).

G2114.   STUCKEY, Jasper L. "Kaolin, Feldspar and Pyrophyllite
          in North Carolina." Ceramist 7 (January 1926), 215-
          222.

G2115.   ________.   "The Kaolins and Kaolin Production of North
          Carolina." Ceramic Age 12 (September 1928), 85-89.
          illus (10 b&w).

G2116.   STULL, R. T. "The Advantages of Thorough Clay Prepar-
          ation." Claycrafter 1 (July 1910), 39-41, 44.

G2117.   ________.   "Georgia Kaolins: Wilkinson County the
          Center of Production." Ceramist 7 (January 1926),
          200-202, 204, 206.

G2118.   ________.   "Notes on the Manufacture of Enamel Brick."
          Clay-Worker 54 (November 1910), 515-517. illus
          (3 b&w).

G2119. STURGIS, Russell. "American Pottery." Scribner's
        Magazine 32 (November 1902), 637-640. illus (7 b&w).

G2120. ________. "American Pottery--Second Paper." Scrib-
        ner's Magazine 33 (March 1903), 381-384. illus
        (9 b&w).

G2121. SUDLOW, E. W. "Florida Home is Tile Conscious [Miami
        Tile & Marble Co.]" Tiles and Tile Work 4 (July
        1931), 13-14. illus (3 b&w).

G2122. SUNSET. "Catalina's Colorful Old Tile . . . Where to
        See It." Vol. 161 (November 1978), 30. illus
        (4 b&w).

G2123. SUTHERLAND, Frances Livingston. "The New Lustre Ware
        Made by Anne Taylor Brown." American Magazine of
        Art 16 (January 1925), 32-35. illus (3 b&w).

G2124. SUYDAM, Richard M. "Bennington Plus: Auction at
        Berlin Center, Mass." National Antiques Review 5
        (September 1973), 31-33.

G2125. ________. "Shaving Mugs--Collectible Americana."
        National Antiques Review 6 (November 1974), 31-33.
        illus (6 b&w).

G2126. SWAN, Mabel M. "The Dedham Pottery." Antiques 10
        (August 1926), 116-121. illus (7 b&w).

G2127. SWIFT, Samuel. "American Garden Pottery." House &
        Garden 4 (July 1903), 28-40. illus (35 b&w).

G2128. TACHAU, Hanna. "America Re-Discovers Tiles." Inter-
        national Studio 75 (March 1922), 74-78. illus
        (5 b&w).

G2129. ________. "American-Made Pottery Exemplified in Lenox
        China." International Studio 67 (May 1919), xcii-
        xcvi. illus (4 b&w).

G2130. TANENHAUS, Ruth Amdur. "Rookwood: A Cincinnati Art
        Pottery." Art & Antiques 3 (July-August 1980), 74-
        81. illus (6 b&w, 7 col).

G2131. ________. "Salt-Glazed Stoneware of North America."
        American Art & Antiques 2 (November-December 1979),
        108-115. illus (9 b&w, 5 col).

G2132. TARTER, Jabe. "The Art of Clewell Pottery." Antiques
        Journal 25 (February 1970), 22-23. illus (3 b&w).

G2133. TAURANAC, John. "Art and the I.R.T.: The First Sub-
        way Art." Historic Preservation 25 (October-Decem-
        ber 1973), 26-31. illus (1 b&w, 14 col).

G2134.   TAYLOR, James. "A Great Newspaper Building [New York Herald]" Clay-Worker 29 (March 1898), 217-220. illus (6 b&w).

G2135.   ________. "The History of Terra Cotta in New York City." Architectural Record 2 (October-December 1892), 136-148. illus (9 b&w).

G2136.   ________. "Joseph Joiner, Architectural Clayworker [Obituary]" Clay-Worker 30 (November 1898), 356. illus (1 b&w).

G2137.   ________. "Modern Terra Cotta Construction--How Good Work is Marred Sometimes [Yale Gymnasium]" Clay-Worker 28 (October 1897), 264-265. illus (2 b&w).

G2138.   ________. "Terra Cotta--Some of Its Characteristics." Architectural Record 1 (July-September 1891), 63-68. illus (3 b&w).

G2139.   ________. "Terra Cotta Work in New York City." Clay-Worker 21 (January 1894), 23-25.

G2140.   TAYLOR, Marjorie. "Stoneware of Ripley, Illinois." Antiques 56 (November 1949), 370-371. illus (4 b&w).

G2141.   TAYLOR, William Watts. "The Rookwood Pottery." Faenza 3 (January-March 1915), 10-15.

G2142.   ________. "The Rookwood Pottery (Continuazione e fine)" Faenza 3 (July-September 1915), 81-88.

G2143.   ________. "The Rookwood Pottery." Forensic Quarterly 1 (September 1910), 203-218. illus (5 b&w).

G2144.   TEALL, Gardner. "Parian Ware." House & Garden 44 (November 1923), 162, 164, 166, 168. illus (6 b&w).

G2145.   TEETOR, Paul. "The Clays of Eastern Kansas." American Ceramic Society Transactions 16 (1914), 120-126.

G2146.   THISTLETHWAITE, F. "The Atlantic Migration of the Pottery Industry." Economic History Review 2.ser. 11 (December 1958), 264-278. bibliog.

G2147.   THOMAS, B. B. (Ted), Jr. "Clay Smoking Pipes Produced at Point Pleasant, Ohio." Spinning Wheel 33 (April 1977), 13-16. illus (13 b&w).

G2148.   THOMAS, C. H. "Delaware Kaolin Asset to Potters." Hobbies 39 (June 1934), 73-74.

G2149.   TIFFANY, G. S. "The Renaissance of Roofing Tile." Clay-Worker 25 (May 1896), 438-439. illus (2 b&w).

G2150.   TILES AND TILE WORK. "Tile in the Chicago Public
          Library." Vol. 1 (October 1928), 6-9. illus
          (5 b&w).

G2151.   TILLOTSON, E. W. "The Future of Ceramic Education."
          American Ceramic Society Bulletin 4 (March 1925),
          100-103.

G2152.   TIMMERMAN, Walter. "Polychrome Terra Cotta." Ameri-
          can Ceramic Society Bulletin 12 (August 1933), 276-
          280.

G2153.   TJOSSEM, Morla W. "Picard China: Art for the Carriage
          Trade." Antiques Journal 35 (August 1980), 12-17,
          43-44. illus (12 b&w).

G2154.   TOWER, Lilian Leslie. "The Quaint Old Ware of Ben-
          nington." Country Life in America 19 (January 1911),
          226-228. illus (13 b&w).

G2155.   TOWNSEND, Everett. "Development of the Tile Industry
          in the United States." American Ceramic Society
          Bulletin 22 (May 15, 1943), 126-152. illus (7 b&w).

G2156.   TRAPP, Kenneth R. "Japanese Influence in Early Rook-
          wood Pottery." Antiques 103 (January 1973), 193-
          197. illus (10 b&w).

G2157.   __________. "Rookwood's Printed-Ware." Spinning Wheel
          29 (January-February 1973), 26-28. illus (5 b&w).

G2158.   TREISCHEL, C. C. "1927 in the White Wares Industry."
          Ceramic Age 11 (January 1928), 9-10.

G2159.   TRENTON. "Adding Color to Our Architecture: Mueller
          Mosaic Company Manufactures Colorful Tile and
          Faience for Beautiful Structures . . . " Vol. 2
          (March 1926), 1-3. illus (4 b&w).

G2160.   __________. "An Ancient Art Applied to Modern Sanita-
          tion: Trent Tile Company's Products Help Keep
          Nation Clean." Vol. 3 (February 1928), 4, 21, 24.
          illus (1 b&w).

G2161.   __________. "The Mercer Pottery Company, Trenton, New
          Jersey." Vol. 1 (March 1925), 1, 12-14. illus
          (9 b&w).

G2162.   __________. "Robertson Mfg. Co.: National Leader in
          the Tile Industry for 70 Years." Vol. 35 (November
          1959), 8-9, 21-27. illus (10 b&w).

G2163.   __________. "Robertson-American Corporation." Vol. 52
          (June 1976), 31-32.

G2164.   TRENTON. "The Story of Lenox China." Vol. 1 (September 1924), 1-2, 18-21. illus (3 b&w).

G2165.   ________. "Thomas Maddock's Sons Company Building Large Plant." Vol. 1 (September 1924), 14-15. illus (2 b&w).

G2166.   TRUAX, William J. "Early Pottery Lighting Devices of Pennsylvania." Antiques 37 (May 1940), 246-247. illus (8 b&w).

G2167.   TUCKER, Thomas. "American Porcelain." Franklin Institute Journal 3.ser.25 (January 1853), 43-44.

G2168.   TWITCHELL, M. W. "The Clay, Clay Products and Kindred Mineral Industry of New Jersey." Ceramist 6 (June 1925), 505-511.

G2169.   UNIVERSITY OF NORTH DAKOTA QUARTERLY JOURNAL. "Dean Earle Jay Babcock." Vol. 16 (November 1925), 3-18. illus (1 b&w); bibliog.

G2170.   URQUHART, L. K. "Automatic Handling [H. Laughlin Co.]" Factory and Industrial Management 79 (January 1930), 80-81. illus (2 b&w).

G2171.   VALENTINE, John. "Rookwood Pottery." House Beautiful 4 (September 1898), 120-129. illus (16 b&w).

G2172.   VAN BRIGGLE, Anne Gregory. "The Potter's Art." Scrip 1 (February 1906), 157-161.

G2173.   VANCE-PHILLIPS, L. "Newark Keramic Society." Keramic Studio 17 (December 1915), 108-113. illus (10 b&w).

G2174.   ________. "Studies in Flesh Painting: Decorative and Pictorial." Keramic Studio 10 (September 1908), 98, 100.

G2175.   VANCE-PHILLIPS, (Mrs.) L. "Ceramics at Chautauqua." Keramic Studio 17 (June 1915), 26-29. illus (11 b&w).

G2176.   VAN RAVENSWAAY, Charles. "Missouri Potters and Their Wares, 1780-1924." Missouri Historical Society Bulletin 7 (July 1951), 453-472. illus (8 b&w); bibliog.

G2177.   VAN VLISSENGEN, Arthur Jr. "Art Pays a Profit [Rookwood]" Factory and Industrial Management 79 (February 1930), 301-303. illus (5 b&w).

G2178.   VARICK, Vernon. "The First and Second Potteries at Norwich, Conn." Hobbies 40 (May 1935), 73-74.

G2179.   VARICK, Vernon. "Notes on Early New Jersey Pottery."
         Hobbies 49 (July 1944), 64.

G2180.   VAUGHAN, Malcolm. "Crolius and Early American Stone-
         ware." International Studio 87 (August 1927), 56-60.
         illus (6 b&w).

G2181.   ________. "Earliest Piece of American Porcelain."
         American Collector 15 (August 1946), 5. illus
         (1 b&w).

G2182.   VEATCH, Otto. "The Clay Mines of the Georgia Kaolin
         Company." Clay-Worker 48 (August 1907), 148-149.
         illus (2 b&w).

G2183.   VERNEUIL, M. P. "Taxile Doat, céramiste." Art et
         décoration 16 (September 1904), 76-86. illus
         (13 b&w, 1 col).

G2184.   VODREY, William H., Jr. "Record of Pottery Industry
         in East Liverpool District." American Ceramic
         Society Bulletin 24 (August 1945), 282-288.

G2185.   VOLKMAR, Charles. "Hints on Underglaze." Keramic
         Studio 1 (May 1899), 5.

G2186.   ________. "The Potter's Wheel." Keramic Studio 2
         (December 1900), 168-169. illus (2 b&w).

G2187.   ________. "Underglaze Gold." Keramic Studio 10
         (June 1908), 46. illus (2 b&w).

G2188.   VOLKMAR, Leon. "The Making of Pottery." House Beau-
         tiful 17 (December 1904), 32-35. illus (4 b&w).

G2189.   ________. "The Pottery Department [School of Indus-
         trial Art]" Pennsylvania Museum Bulletin 3 (April 1,
         1905), 23-26. illus (4 b&w).

G2190.   VOLPE, Todd M. "Rookwood Landscape Vases and Placques."
         Antiques 117 (April 1980), 838-846. illus (4 b&w,
         15 col); bibliog.

G2191.   VOLPE, Todd M., and BLASBERG, Robert W. "Fulper Art
         Pottery: Amazing Glazes." American Art & Antiques
         1 (July-August 1978), 76-83. illus (6 b&w, 7 col).

G2192.   VOZAR, Linda. "Early Bennington Potteries." Ceramics
         Monthly 25 (October 1977), 54-57. illus (8 b&w).

G2193.   WALKER, C. Howard. "The Grueby Pottery." Keramic
         Studio 1 (March 1900), 237.

G2194.   WALKER, Raymond J. "The Potteries of Maine." Hobbies
         39 (September 1934), 71-72.

G2195.   WALKER, Sophia Antoinette. "The Art School of the
          Y.W.C.A. of New York." Keramic Studio 4 (August
          1902), 71. illus (2 b&w).

G2196.   __________. "Modeling at the Y.W.C.A. Art School."
          Keramic Studio 10 (June 1908), 34. illus (4 b&w).

G2197.   __________. "Pottery for Educational Purposes [Y.W.C.A.
          Art School]" Pottery & Glass 7 (December 1911),
          28-29, 48. illus (3 b&w).

G2198.   WALLACE, Addie M. "Brick and Terra Cotta [Seattle,
          Wash. and Portland, Ore.]" Clay-Worker 78 (November
          1922), 437-440. illus (5 b&w).

G2199.   WALLACH, Amei. "The Flamboyant Pottery of George E.
          Ohr." Antiques World 1 (November 1978), 64-70.
          illus (8 b&w, 12 col.).

G2200.   WALTON, William. "Charles Volkmar, Potter." Inter-
          national Studio 36 (January 1909), lxxv-lxxx.
          illus (6 b&w).

G2201.   __________. "Charles Volkmar, the Potter." Pottery &
          Glass 3 (December 1909), 271-275. illus (4 b&w).

G2202.   WARE, W. Porter. "Occupational and Other Barbershop
          Shaving Mugs." American Antiques Journal 3 (March
          1948), 12-14. illus (17 b&w).

G2203.   __________. "Occupational Shaving Mugs." Hobbies 46
          (August 1941), 55-57.

G2204.   __________. "Old Shaving Mugs." Hobbies 44 (January
          1940), 55-56. illus (3 b&w).

G2205.   WARMAN, Edwin G. "The Classic Era of the Shaving
          Mug." Antiques Journal 17 (August 1962), 18-20.
          illus (4 b&w).

G2206.   WARRINGDON, Anne. "Something New in Pottery [S.
          Frackelton]" Sketch Book 3 (September 1903), 5-6,
          23.

G2207.   WASHBURN, Edward W. "The Organization of Our Ceramic
          Resources for National Service." Clay-Worker 69
          (April 1918), 542-543.

G2208.   WATERBURY, Ivan C. "Great Industries of the United
          States, IX: Pottery." Cosmospolitan 38 (March
          1905), 593-602. illus (16 b&w).

G2209.   __________. "Pottery Making In America." China, Glass
          and Pottery Review 16 (April 1905), 13-14, 17-20.
          illus (10 b&w).
              Originally published in Cosmopolitan. See G2208.

G2210. WATKINS, Lura Woodside. "The ABC's of American Pot-
        tery." Antiques 42 (September 1942), 134.

G2211. ______. "The ABC's of American Pottery, II."
        Antiques 42 (October 1942), 196.

G2212. ______. "American Pottery Lamps." Antiques 64
        (August 1953), 108-110. illus (9 b&w).

G2213. ______. "The Bayleys: Essex County Potters.
        Part I: Chiefly Biographical." Antiques 34 (Novem-
        ber 1938), 253-255. illus (3 b&w).

G2214. ______. "The Bayleys: Essex County Potters.
        Part II: Their Products." Antiques 35 (January
        1939), 22-27. illus (17 b&w).

G2215. ______. "Beans and Bean Pots." Antiques 46 (Novem-
        ber 1944), 276-277. illus (1 b&w).

G2216. ______. "The Brooks Pottery in Goshen, Connecticut."
        Antiques 37 (January 1940), 29-31. illus (10 b&w).

G2217. ______. "A Check List of New England Stoneware
        Potters." Antiques 42 (August 1942), 80-83. illus
        (9 b&w).

G2218. ______. "Early New England Redware Potters." Early
        American Industries Association Chronicle 3 (April
        1945), 21, 30, 32-33, 36. illus (2 b&w).

G2219. ______. "Henderson of Jersey City and His Pitchers."
        Antiques 50 (December 1946), 388-392. illus (17
        b&w).

G2220. ______. "Low's Art Tiles." Antiques 45 (May 1944),
        250-252. illus (7 b&w).

G2221. ______. "New England Pottery in the Smithsonian
        Institution." Antiques 72 (September 1957), 232-
        236. illus (10 b&w).

G2222. ______. "New Light on Boston Stoneware and Frederick
        Carpenter." Antiques 101 (June 1972), 1052-1057.
        illus (12 b&w).

G2223. ______. "Pioneer Potters of New Hampshire." New
        Hampshire Troubadour 20 (December 1950), 7-13.
        illus (1 b&w).

G2224. ______. "The Potters of Whately, Massachusetts
        [Part I]" American Collector 7 (July 1938), 6-7,
        20. illus (5 b&w).

G2225. ______. "The Potters of Whately, Massachusetts
        [Part II]" American Collector 7 (August 1938), 10-
        11. illus (6 b&w).

G2226.   WATKINS, Lura Woodside. "Some Unrecorded Pottery:
          American Molded Pitchers." _Antiques_ 74 (August
          1958), 135-137. illus (6 b&w).

G2227.   __________. "The Stoneware of South Ashfield, Massa-
          chusetts." _Antiques_ 26 (September 1934), 94-97.
          illus (8 b&w).

G2228.   WATTS, Arthur S. "Classification of Ceramic Dinner-
          ware." _American Ceramic Society Bulletin_ 18
          (August 1939), 314-315.

G2229.   __________. "The Construction and Equipment of a White
          Ware Pottery." _China, Glass and Pottery Review_ 14
          (February 5, 1904), 24-28. illus (1 b&w).

G2230.   __________. "The Development of Definitions for Ceramic
          Terms." _American Ceramic Society Bulletin_ 5 (July
          1926), 305-308.

G2231.   __________. "Early History of the Electrical Porcelain
          Industry in the United States." _American Ceramic
          Society Bulletin_ 18 (October 1939), 404-408.

G2232.   __________. "History of the Ceramic Industry in Ohio."
          Ceramic Age 40 (July 1942), 24-26.

G2233.   __________. "A Survey of the Whiteware Industry of
          Ohio." _Ceramic Age_ 12 (July 1928), 9-11.

G2234.   WEAVER, Edward. "Architectural Tiles [Columbian Exh.]"
          Clay-Worker 20 (November 1893), 437-440. illus
          (27 b&w).

G2235.   WEBB, Thomas G. "The Pottery Industry of DeKalb,
          White, and Putnam Counties." _Tennessee Historical
          Quarterly_ 30 (Spring 1971), 110-112.

G2236.   WEBB, Warfield. "American Pottery--Its Development."
          Brick and Clay Record 44 (January 6, 1914), 81-82.
          illus (5 b&w).

G2237.   WEIDMAN, S. "The Clays and Clay Products of Wiscon-
          sin." _Claycrafter_ 2 (June 1911), 7-8.

G2238.   WEIDNER, Ruth Irwin. "The Majolica Wares of Griffen,
          Smith & Company. Part I: History and Manufacture."
          Spinning Wheel 36 (January-February 1980), 13-17.
          illus (8 b&w).

G2239.   __________. "The Majolica Wares of Griffen, Smith &
          Company. Part II: The Designs and Their Sources."
          Spinning Wheel 36 (March-April 1980), 14-19. illus
          (11 b&w).

G2240. WEIGEL, W. M. "High Grade Clays of the Southeastern
        States." Ceramist 8 (May 1926), 86-100. illus
        (3 b&w).

G2241. ________. "White Clay Industry in the Vicinity of
        Langley, South Carolina." Ceramist 2 (Winter 1922-
        1923), 290-297.

G2242. WELLS, E. D. "Duché, the Potter." Georgia Historical
        Quarterly 41 (December 1957), 383-390. bibliog.

G2243. WELLS, Helen E. "Pottery in the Early American Home."
        American Home 16 (November 1936), 44, 56, 58, 60.
        illus (5 b&w).

G2244. WELLS, J. M. "W. E. Wells, a Pioneer Potter." Ameri-
        can Ceramic Society Bulletin 16 (December 1937), 490.

G2245. WELLS, W. E., [with] URQUHART, Lewis K. "Acres of
        Dishes [H. Laughlin Co.]" Factory and Industrial
        Management 77 (April 1929), 697-700. illus (6 b&w).

G2246. WENHAM, Edward. "Early Hard-Paste China of Carolina."
        Fine Arts 20 (August 1933), 30-31, 47-48. illus
        (5 b&w).

G2247. WERTIME, Marcia. "Henry Chapman Mercer: Nineteenth-
        Century Renaissance Man." Archaeology 31 (July-
        August 1978), 44-51. illus (4 b&w, 3 col).

G2248. WEST, Mildred Veitch. "A Wedding Gift Started My
        Hobby [Lenox]" Hobbies 45 (April 1940), 50-53.
        illus (5 b&w).

G2249. WEST VIRGINIA REVIEW. "The D. E. McNicol Pottery
        Company in West Virginia." Vol. 9 (October 1931),
        50-51.

G2250. ________. "A Factory That Has a Commanding Position
        in the Pottery Industry [Bowers Co.]" Vol. 5 (May
        1928), 302-305. illus (b&w).

G2251. ________. "The Potter and His Wheel [H. R. Wyllie
        Co.]" Vol. 6 (March 1929), 180-181.

G2252. ________. "A Pottery of a Commanding Position in the
        Industry [Bowers Co.]" Vol. 7 (September 1930),
        410-412, 477. illus (b&w).

G2253. ________. "Second Largest Dinner-Ware Factory in the
        U.S. [E. M. Knowles Co.]" Vol. 7 (September 1930),
        438-439. illus (b&w).

G2254. ________. "Warwick China Company is a Pioneer." Vol.
        9 (October 1931), 15.

G2255. WEYGANDT, Cornelius. "The Last of the 'Dutch' Potters
        [J. Medinger]" General Magazine and Historical
        Chronicle 35 (October 1932), 12-20.

G2256. ________. "A Maker of Pennsylvania Redware [J.
        Medinger]" Antiques 49 (June 1946), 369-370.
        illus (6 b&w).

G2257. WHATLEY, L. McKay. "The Mount Shepherd Pottery: Cor-
        relating Archaeology and History." Journal of
        Early Southern Decorative Arts 6 (May 1980), 21-57.
        illus (22 b&w); bibliog.

G2258. WHEELER, H. A. "The Birth of the American Ceramic
        Society." American Ceramic Society Bulletin 13
        (April 1934), 82-84.

G2259. WHEELER, Ione L. "Chicago Ceramic Art Exhibit."
        Keramic Studio 14 (January 1913), 188-190. illus
        (6 b&w).

G2260. ________. "Exhibit of Chicago Ceramic Association."
        Keramic Studio 15 (January 1914), 150-151. illus
        (7 b&w).

G2261. ________. "Exhibit of Chicago Ceramic Society."
        Keramic Studio 16 (January 1915), 177-179. illus
        (9 b&w).

G2262. WHEELER, Robert G. "A Checklist of Potters of Albany
        and the Upper Hudson Area." New York History 25
        (October 1944), 540-543. bibliog.

G2263. ________. "The Potters of Albany." Antiques 46
        (December 1944), 345-347. illus (4 b&w).

G2264. WHERRITT, Edith Cornelia. "Firing with Gasoline."
        Keramic Studio 8 (June 1906), 28-29.

G2265. WHITAKER, Fred A. "Chemical Stoneware." Ceramist 4
        (May 1924), 70-81. illus (8 b&w).

G2266. WHITE, I. C. "Clay Resources of West Virginia."
        Ceramist 7 (January 1926), 254-260.

G2267. WHITE, Jessie Mae. "Majolica." American Antiques
        Journal 1 (October 1946), 6-8. illus (5 b&w).

G2268. WHITE, Lela Phelps. "A Clever Ceramic Artist of
        Colorado [Mrs. E. Schofield Wright]" Fine Arts
        Journal 25 (February 1911), 101-103. illus (4 b&w).

G2269. WHITING, Margaret C. "Charles Volkmar's Crown Point
        Pottery." House Beautiful 8 (October 1900), 613-
        617. illus (4 b&w).

G2270. WHITLATCH, Geo. I. "The Ceramic Industries of West
         and Middle Tennessee." Ceramic Age 23 (January
         1934), 5-8. illus (6 b&w).

G2271.   ________. "The Ceramic Industries of West and Middle
         Tennessee." Ceramic Age 23 (February 1934), 39-42.
         illus (6 b&w).

G2272.   ________. "Ceramics in East Tennessee." Ceramic Age
         21 (February 1933), 39-41. illus (3 b&w).

G2273.   ________. "Ceramics in East Tennessee." Ceramic Age
         21 (March 1933), 76-77, 93. illus (2 b&w).

G2274. WHITTEMORE, Edwin C. "A Rare Early Food 'Package'."
         Spinning Wheel 25 (April 1969), 41. illus (1 b&w).

G2275. WHITTLE, Charles L. "The Clays and Clay Industry of
         Massachusetts." Engineering and Mining Journal 66
         (August 27, 1898), 245-246.

G2276. WHYTE, Bertha Kitchell. "Pauline Pottery of Edgerton,
         Wisconsin." Spinning Wheel 14 (April 1958), 24, 26,
         38. illus (9 b&w).

G2277. WILDER, Katherine A. "The Wachusett Pottery Company,
         an Old-Time Industry of West Sterling, Massachusetts."
         New-England Galaxy 12 (Spring 1971), 50-54. illus
         (2 b&w).

G2278. WILLIAMS, Lena. "Majolica, Like Gold, Is Where You
         Find It." Hobbies 44 (March 1939), 70-71.

G2279.   ________. "Majolica, Like Gold, Is Where You Find
         It." Hobbies 56 (January 1952), 96-97. illus
         (2 b&w).
           Reprint of G2278.

G2280. WILLIAMSON, J. "Continuous Kiln for Firing Pottery
         and Other Clay Products." Ceramic Age 11 (May 1928),
         182-185. illus (5 b&w).

G2281. WILLIS, Katharine. "Early New York Pottery [N.Y.
         City]" Country Life 54 (September 1928), 72, 77-78.
         illus (15 b&w).

G2282.   ________. "Founders of Early American Pottery."
         Antiquarian 11 (August 1928), 33-35. illus (7 b&w).

G2283. WILSON, Hewitt. "The Ceramic Engineering Department
         of the University of Washington, Seattle." American
         Ceramic Society Journal 6 (January 1923), 110-114.
         illus (2 b&w).

G2284.   WILSON, Hewitt. "Monograph and Bibliography on Terra
          Cotta." American Ceramic Society Bulletin 5 (Febru-
          ary 1926), 94-145. bibliog.

G2285.   __________. "Our Ceramic Family." Clay-Worker 79 (May
          1923), 552-553.

G2286.   __________. "Polychrome Decoration of Terra Cotta with
          Soluble Metallic Salts." American Ceramic Society
          Journal 1 (May 1918), 353-366.

G2287.   WILSON, Hewitt, BENNETT, A. Lee, and HEATH, Fred T.
          "Preliminary Report on the Residual Kaolin and
          Feldspar in the Pacific Northwest." American Cer-
          amic Society Journal 6 (March 1923), 475-490.
          illus (8 b&w); bibliog.

G2288.   WILSON, Joan S. "Parian Ware and the Bennington
          Potteries." Metropolitan Museum of Art Bulletin
          n.s. 7 (February 1949), 169-172. illus (4 b&w).

G2289.   WINCHESTER, Alice. "Footnote to Tucker History."
          Antiques 30 (October 1936), 164-167. illus (8 b&w).

G2290.   WINSLOW, Henry W. "Bennington Pottery." Vermonter 25
          (no. 7, 1920), 94-95.

G2291.   WINTERMUTE, H. Ogden. "More about Majolica." Ameri-
          can Antiques Journal 1 (October 1946), 9-11. illus
          (5 b&w).

G2292.   WINTON, Andrew L., and WINTON, Kate Barber. "Norwalk
          Potteries." Old-Time New England 24 (January 1934),
          75-92. illus (27 b&w).

G2293.   __________. "Norwalk Potteries [Part II]" Old-Time
          New England 24 (April 1934), 110-128. illus
          (25 b&w).

G2294.   WIRES, E. Stanley. "How Tiles Have Interpreted Aesop's
          Great Fables." Antiques Journal 25 (May 1970),
          10-12, 31. illus (3 b&w).

G2295.   WISE, Ethel Brand. "Adelaide Alsop Robineau--American
          Ceramist." American Magazine of Art 20 (December
          1929), 687-691. illus (5 b&w).

G2296.   WISEMAN, Edith Phillips. "Decorative Work on China."
          Brush and Pencil 9 (February 1902), 270-273. illus
          (3 b&w).

G2297.   __________. "Plea for More Originality in China Decor-
          ation." Brush and Pencil 11 (November 1902), 114-
          121. illus (8 b&w).

G2298.   WOLFE, Julia W. "The History of Pottery in America
          [Morgantown Pottery]" School Arts Magazine 28
          (December 1928), 201-204. illus (2 b&w).

G2299.   WOOD, Marie Stevens Walker. "One Hundred One Years
          in Ceramics: Stevens-Bone Family Manufactures
          Georgia Clay for Six Generations." Georgia Maga-
          zine 3 (August-September 1959), 16-22. illus
          (16 b&w).

G2300.   WOOD, Ruth Howe. "Memories of the Fentons." Antiques
          8 (September 1925), 150-154. illus (11 b&w).

G2301.   WOOD, Ruth Kedzie. "Jugtown, Where They Make Jugs."
          Mentor 16 (April 1928), 32-36. illus (6 b&w).

G2302.   WOODHOUSE, Samuel H. "Old Pennsylvania Dutch Pottery."
          Brick and Clay Record 62, (June 26, 1923), 1142, 1146.

G2303.   WOODHOUSE, Samuel W. "The First Philadelphia Porcelain
          [Tucker, Smith, Fife]" Antiques 24 (October 1933),
          134-135. illus (4 b&w).

G2304.   WOODS, Virginia. "Clay Products Play an Important
          Part in the Color Scheme of Los Angeles New City
          Hall." Clay-Worker 90 (August 1928), 109-111.
          illus (3 b&w).

G2305.   WOOD-SAFFORD, Sara. "Suggestions in Shapes and
          Decorations." American Pottery Gazette 7 (April-
          May 1908), 16-17, 20. illus (4 b&w)
            Reprint of 2306.

G2306.   ________. "Valuable Suggestions for the American Pot-
          ter." American Pottery Gazette 1 (May 5, 1905),
          45-47. illus (4 b&w).

G2307.   ________. "Valuable Suggestions for the American Pot-
          ter." American Pottery Gazette 1 (June 5, 1905),
          51-53. illus (4 b&w).

G2308.   ________. "Valuable Suggestions for the American Pot-
          ter." American Pottery Gazette 1 (July 5, 1905),
          41-43. illus (3 b&w).

G2309.   WOODWARD, Ellsworth. "Newcomb Pottery." Art Educa-
          tion.7 (September 1900), 9-12. illus (5 b&w).

G2310.   ________. "Reflections upon Art and Manufacture."
          American Ceramic Society Bulletin 4 (May 1925), 218-
          220.

G2311.   WOODWORD [sic], E. [Ellsworth Woodward?] "The Work
          of American Potters. Article Two: Newcomb Pottery
          Typical of the South." Arts & Decoration 1 (January
          1911), 124-125. illus (3 b&w).
            Articles 1, 3, 4, 5 are: G948, G1297, G866, G1675.

G2312.   WOOLF, Doris S. "Pennsylvania Redware." Antiques
          Journal 16 (October 1961), 9, 29. illus (3 b&w).

G2313.   WORLD'S WORK. "The Craft of Rookwood Potters." Vol.
          8 (August 1904), unpaged. illus (2 b&w).

G2314.   ________. "A New Uplift to American Pottery [Teco]"
          Vol. 8 (August 1904), unpaged. illus (2 b&w).

G2315.   WRIGHT, Frank Lloyd. "In the Cause of Architecture.
          V: The Meaning of Materials--The Kiln." Architec-
          tural Record 63 (June 1928), 555-561. illus (4 b&w).

G2316.   WRIGHT, Grace Radcliff. "Potters of the Shenandoah
          Valley." Hobbies 42 (September 1937), 71,74.

G2317.   WRIGHT, Livingston. "Boston's Five-Million-Dollar
          Brick and Terra Cotta Hotel [Copley-Plaza]" Clay-
          Worker 58 (October 1912), 379-380. illus (1 b&w).

G2318.   ________. "Girls' Club Establishes Pottery and Ulti-
          mately Makes It a Financial Success [Paul Revere
          Pottery]" Art World 2 (September 1917), 578-579.
          illus (4 b&w).

G2319.   YAEGER, Dorothea. "Rookwood, Pioneer American Art
          Pottery." American Collector 12 (July 1943), 8-9,
          19. illus (6 b&w).

G2320.   YANCEY, Mary Lanier. "Conventional Versus Natural-
          istic Design." American Ceramic Society Bulletin 4
          (July 1925), 321-323.

G2321.   YOUNG, Jennie J. "The Ceramic Art in America."
          Atlantic Monthly 44 (November 1879), 588-598.
          bibliog.

G2322.   YOUNG, Mahonri Sharp. "The Tile Club Revisited."
          American Art Journal 2 (Fall 1970), 81-91. illus
          (12 b&w); bibliog.

G2323.   YOUTZ, L. A. "Clays of the Indianola Brick, Tile and
          Pottery Works." Iowa Academy of Sciences Proceed-
          ings 3 (1895), 40-44.

G2324.   ZIMMERMANN, H. Russell. "Milwaukee's Cream City
          Brick." Milwaukee County Historical Society Histor-
          ical Messenger 26 (March 1970), 2-13. illus (3 b&w).

G2325.   ZUG, Charles G. "The Alkaline Glazed Stoneware of
          Catawba Valley." Ceramic Circle of Charlotte Jour-
          nal of Studies 4 (1980), 11-15. illus (2 b&w).
          Prefatory to C23.

G2326.   ZWERMANN, Carl H. "The Zwermann Tunnel Kiln and Its
          Operation." American Ceramic Society Journal 1
          (April 1918), 262-266. illus (1 b&w).

GUIDE TO SELECTED AMERICAN CLAYWORKING, CERAMICS, CHINA PAINTING, AND CROCKERY JOURNALS BEFORE 1930

TITLE	PLACE OF PUBLICATION	FREQUENCY	DATE & BEGAN	DATE CEASED (IF BEFORE 1930)	COMMENTS
American Ceramic Society Bulletin	Easton, Pa.	monthly	v.1,no.1 (May 1922)	-------	
American Ceramic Society Journal	Easton, Pa.	monthly	v.1,no.1 (Jan. 1918)	-------	Supersedes American Ceramic Society Transactions.
American Ceramic Society Transactions	Columbus, Ohio	annual	v.1 (1899)	v.19 (1917)	Superseded by American Ceramic Society Journal
American Potters' Journal	Trenton, N.J.	weekly	v.1,no.1 (Sept. 1, 1888)	Aug. 1912?	"Published in the interests of organized labor." Last extant issue: vol. 19, no. 2 (September 8, 1905)?
American Pottery and Glassware Reporter	Pittsburgh, Pa.	weekly	v.1,no.1 (May 1, 1879)	v.6 (Apr. 20, 1882)	Became Pottery and Glassware Reporter.

216

Title	Place	Frequency	First issue	Last issue	Notes
American Pottery Gazette	New York	monthly	v.1,no.1 (Mar. 1905)	v.11,no.3 (June 1910)	"Devoted to the requirements of the china, earthenware, glass and kindred trades of America."
Atlantic Terra Cotta	New York	monthly	v.1,no.1 (Nov. 1913)	-------	Atlantic Terra Cotta Co. "For architects." Suspended 1918-1921.
Brick	Chicago	monthly	v.1,no.1 (July 1894)	v.33,no.6 (Dec. 1910)	United with Clay Record to form Brick and Clay Record.
Brick and Clay Record	Chicago	semi-monthly	v.38,no.1 (Jan. 1, 1911)	-------	Formerly Brick; absorbed Clay Record in January 1911 and adopted its volume numbering.
Brickbuilder	Boston	monthly	v.1,no.1 (Jan. 1892)	v.25,no.12 (Dec. 1916)	Continued as Architectural Forum.
Brickmaker	Chicago	semi-monthly	v.1,no.1 (Sept. 16, 1889)	v.22 (Feb. 15, 1895)	"Devoted exclusively to the interests of brick manufacturers."
Ceramic Age	New Brunswick, N.J.	monthly	v.9,no.1 (Jan. 1927)	-------	New Jersey Clayworkers' Association; supersedes Ceramist.

TITLE	PLACE OF PUBLICATION	FREQUENCY	DATE BEGAN	DATE CEASED (IF BEFORE 1930)	COMMENTS
Ceramic Industry	Chicago	monthly	v.1,no.1 (June 1923)	-------	"Devoted to the manufacture of glass, enamel, whiteware, refractory, and allied products."
Ceramic Monthly	Chicago	monthly	v.1,no.1 (Aug.? 1895)	v.10,no.4 (Jan. 1900)	
Ceramist	East Orange, N.J. Trenton, N.J.	quarterly through v.3; monthly there-after	v.2,no.1 (Mar. 1922)	v.8,no.9 (Dec. 1926)	New Jersey Clayworkers' Association; formerly New Jersey Ceramist; superseded by Ceramic Age.
China Decorator	New York	monthly	v.1,no.1 (June 1887)	v.27, nos.5-6 (May-June 1901)	"Devoted exclusively to the art of decorating china with mineral colors, and the firing of same."
China, Glass and Pottery Review	New York	monthly	v.1 1897	v.4,no.6 July 1899	Became House-Furnisher: China, Glass & Pottery Review.
China, Glass & Lamps	Pittsburgh New York	weekly	v.1,no.1 (Dec. 17, 1890)	-------	Continued as China and Glass

Title	Place	Frequency	First issue	Last issue	Notes
Clay Record	Chicago	semi-monthly	v.1,no.1 (July 11, 1892)	v.37,no.12 (Dec. 30, 1910)	In January 1911 united with Brick to form Brick and Clay Record. (Kept Clay Record volume numbers.)
Claycrafter	Dayton, Ohio	bi-monthly in 1910; irregular, 1911-1915	v.1,no.1 (Mar. 1910)	v.3,no.6 (Feb. 1915)	"Dedicated to arts and science of claycrafting."
Clay-Worker	Indian-apolis, Ind.	monthly	v.1,no.1 (Jan. 1884)	-------	National Brick Manufacturers' Association.
Crockery and Glass Journal	New York	weekly	v.1,no.1 (Nov. 28, 1874)	-------	
Design and Keramic Studio	Syracuse, N.Y.	monthly	v.26,no.1 (May 1924)	v.31,no.11 (Apr. 1930)	Formerly Keramic Studio; became Design.
Glass and Pottery World	Chicago	monthly	v.1 1893	v.17,no.3 (Mar. 1909)	Merged into Pottery and Glass
House Furnisher: China, Glass and Pottery Review	New York	monthly	v.5,no.1 (Aug. 1899)	v.16,no.2 (Apr. 1905)	Formerly China, Glass and Pottery Review; merged into Glass & Pottery World.

TITLE	PLACE OF PUBLICATION	FREQUENCY	DATE BEGAN	DATE CEASED (IF BEFORE 1930)	COMMENTS
Keramic Studio	Syracuse, N.Y.	monthly	v.1,no.1 (May 1899)	v.25,no.12 (Apr. 1924)	Editor: A. A. Robineau "A monthly magazine for the china painter and potter." Became Design and Keramic Studio.
Keramic Tile Journal	Milwaukee, Wisc., Wilmington, Del., Washington, D.C.	monthly	v.1,no.1 (Dec. 1928?)	-------	Tile and Mantel Contractors' Association of America. October 1929 not published.
Mantel Tile & Grate Monthly	Utica, N.Y.	monthly	v.1,no.1 (July 1906?)	v.13,no.7 (Feb. 1919)	Interstate Mantel and Tile Dealers' Association.
New Jersey Ceramist	New Brunswick, N.J.	quarterly	v.1,no.1 (Mar. 1921)	v.1,no.4 (Dec. 1921)	New Jersey Clayworkers' Association. "In the interest of the ceramic industries of New Jersey." Continued as Ceramist.
Old China	Syracuse, N.Y.	monthly	v.1,no.1 (Oct. 1901)	v.3,no.12 (Sept. 1904	
Potter	Santa Barbara, Calif.	monthly	v.1,no.1 (Dec. 1916)	v.1,no.3 (Feb. 1917)	Editor: F. H. Rhead

Pottery and Glass	New York	monthly	v.1,no.1 (July 1908)	v.15,no.4 (Oct. 1915)	Absorbed Glass and Pottery World; merged into Pottery Glass and Brass Salesman.
Pottery and Glassware Reporter	Pittsburgh, Pa.	weekly	v.7?,no.1? (Apr. 27, 1882)	v.31,no.4 (Oct. 26, 1893)	Formerly American Pottery and Glassware Reporter.
Pottery, Glass and Brass Salesman	New York	weekly	v.1,no.1 (Feb. 2, 1910)	-------	Pottery, Glass and Brass Salesmen's Association of America. Absorbed Pottery and Glass.
Tile Talk	New York	bi-monthly	v.1,no.1 (Jan. 1926)	v.4,no.3 (July 1929?) (all published?)	"Devoted to the interests of sanitary, decorative and lasting building construction."
Tiles and Tile Work	Milwaukee, Wisc., Chicago	monthly	v.1,no.1 (Oct. 1928)	v.4,no.12 (Dec. 1931)	Published in Milwaukee from October 1929 to July 1930.
Tilecraft	Beaver Falls, Pa.	monthly	v.1,no.1 (Dec. 1917)	v.5,no.1 (Jan. 1922)	Associated Tile Manufacturers. Not published in 1918.

AUTHOR INDEX

Abraham, Evelyn, G1
Adams, Ella L., G2-3
Adams, John, G4
Adamson, Jack E., A1
Adler, Hazel H., G5-6
Agranoff, Barbara, A141
Agranoff, Joseph, A141
Albery, Duane F., G7-8
Albright, Frank P., G9
Alexander, Donald E., A2
Alexander, Julia S., G10
Alexander, Letitia H., G11
Alfred University, E1
Allen, Frederick W., G12
Allison, Grace, G13
Allison, LeRoy W., G14
Alsop-Robineau, Adelaide. See
   Robineau, Adelaide Alsop
Altman, Seymour, A3
Altman, Violet, A3
American Ceramic Society, A4
American Clay Machinery Co.,
   F1
American Encaustic Tiling Co.,
   F2-4
American Life Foundation, C1
Anderson, Alexandra, G136-137
Anderson, Mary F., A5, G138
Anthony, Ronald W., B1
Armstrong, Henry R., G151
Armstrong, Irene, G152-153
Arnest, Barbara M., C7
Arts Resources of Connecticut,
   C2
Ashbery, John, G171
Ashby, Geo. J. M., G172-173
Ashley, Harrison Everett,
   G174
Associated Tile Manufacturers,
   F5-12

Atherton, Carlton, G175
Atlantic Terra Cotta Co.,
   F13-15
Auman, Dorothy Cole, G176
Avery, C. Louise, G177
Aye, James H., G178

Bach, Richard F., G179-180
Back, Robert, G181
Backlund, Herman, G182-183
Baggs, Arthur E., G184-187
Bailey, Worth, G188
Baker, A. C., G189
Baker, Gordon C., G190-199
Baker, Mary F., G200
Ball, Berenice M., G201-207
Ball, F. Carlton, G208-209
Ballard, Margaret, G210
Balluff, George Erhart, A6
Bane, Reynolds, G211
Barber, Edwin AtLee, A7-22,
   B2-3, C44, G212-265
Barber, Daniel M., G266
Bargloff, Elva Zesiger, A23
Barka, Norman F., B4-5
Barker, Eva M., G267
Barker, M. E., G268-269
Barnard, Charles, G271
Barnard, Julian, A24
Barnes, Benjamin H., A25
Barons, Richard I., C52
Barr, Margaret Libby, A26
Barr, Robert, A26
Barrett, Richard Carter, A27-
   29, G272-275
Barringer, L. E., G1493

Bartley, Jonathan, Crucible
  Co., F16
Batchelder-Wilson Co., F17
Bayer, Ralph E., G276
Beard, James C., A30
Beasley, Ellen, C54
Beck, William O., G277
Beckwith, Arthur, A31
Beecher, M. F., G278
Behrendt, L., G279
Belknap, Henry W., G280
Bellmark Pottery Co., F18
Benjamin, Marcus, A32
Benner, Russell L., G281
Bennett, A. Lee, G2287
Bennett, B., G282
Bennett, Charles A., G283
Bennett, J. A. W., G284
Bensel, L. M., G285
Bergengren, Ralph, G286
Bergmans, Carl, G287
Berky, Andrew S., A33
Bernstein, Melvin, B6
Berrill, Jacquelyn, G288
Beyer, Nancy, G289
Biddle, Dorothy, G290-291
Billinger, R. D., G292
Binns, Charles F., A34-36,
  A80, G293-373
Bishop, Robert, B7-8
Bivins, John F., Jr., A37,
  B9, G374
Black, Harding, A101
Blair, C. Dean, A38
Blasberg, Robert W., A39, C17,
  G375-384, G2191
Blatchley, W. S., G385-386
Bleicher, Fred, A40
Bleininger, A. V., G387-394
Bognar, E. J., G395
Bogue, Dorothy McGraw, A41
Bohdan, Carol L., C17
Boicourt, Jane, G396
Bole, G. A., E36
Bond, Harold Lewis, G397
Bopp, H. F., G398
Boston Architectural Terra
  Cotta Works, F19
Bott, Leo P., Jr., G399
Boulden, Jane Long, G400
Bowdoin, W. G., G401-402
Bowles, Elsie Shannon, G403
Boyers, C. J., G404
Brace, Ernest, G405
Bradford, Emma F., G406
Brandenburg, Marie, G407

Branin, Manlif Lelyn, A42-43,
  G408-414
Branner, George C., G415-416
Brasier de la Vauguyon, (Mme.)
  L. H., A44
Breck, Joseph, C21
Breese, Jessie Martin, G417
Breininger, Lester P., Jr.,
  A45, G418
Brewer, Harriet E., G419
Bridges, Daisy Wade, C23, G423
Brodbeck, John, G424
Brooklyn Institute of Arts and
  Sciences. See Brooklyn
  Museum
Brooklyn Museum, C3-4
Brown, E. H., G425
Brown, George H., G426
Brown, Joshua, B10
Brown, Nell, G427
Bruhn, Thomas P., C55
Brunk, Thomas W., A46, B11
Brunsman, Sue, D1
Bucher, Robert C., G430
Buck, Kenneth E., E11
Buckley, Ernest Robertson, E2
Bucks County Historical Society,
  A47-48
Buehler, H. A., G432-433
Bullen, Ripley P., B12
Burbage, Beverly S., G434
Burbank, Leonard F., G435
Burgeon, Adelbert Joseph, A49
Burley & Tyrrell Co., F20
Burnett, Richard M., B91
Burrison, John A., B13, C12,
  D2, G436-438
Burslem, Alexander Young, G439
Burt, Stanley G., A50, G440
Burton., G441
Burton, William, G442
Busbee, Jacques, G443
Busbee, Juliana Royster, G444-
  445
Buskey, Leo Albert, G446-447
Butler, Joseph T., B14
Butler, Lorine Letcher, G448
Butterworth, Elsie Walker, G449
Buxton, Bessie W., G450
Buxton, Virginia Hillway, A51,
  G451-452

Cable, Margaret Kelly, G453-455
Calhoun, F. H. H. G456

Calkins, S. Homer, G457
Camehl, Ada Walker, G458
Camp, Helen B., G459
Campana, Domenic Mathews, A52-53, G460
Canaday, John, A185
Canfield, Ruth, G461
Cardwell, Kenneth C., G462
Carr, James, G463-468
Carrick, Alice Van Leer, G469-470
Carroon, Robert G., G471
Carruthers, John L., G472-473
Carson, Courtenay, G474
Case, Richard G., C10, G475
Chadwick, J. H., G572-573
Chamberlain, Georgia S., G574
Chamberlain, Jacqueline, G575
Chambers Brothers Co., F21
Chandler, Reginald, G576
Chappell, Edward A., G577, G1361
Chard, Louise C., G578
Chase, Paul G., G569-571
Cherry, Kathryn E., G579
Chiolino, Barbara B., G581
Christensen, Erwin O., A55
Cincinnati Art Museum, C5
Clark, Edna Maria, B15
Clark, Garth, A56-57, B6, B11, B16, B31, B33, B47, B70-71, B73, B92, C25, G583-585
Clark, Robert Judson, C46
Clark, William H., G586
Clarke, D. S., G587
Clarke, J. F. Gates, G588-591
Clarke, John M., A58
Clauser, John W., D3
Clemens, Laura Lee, G786
Clement, Arthur W., A60-64, C4, G787-789, G2040
Clendennin, W. W., G790
Cleveland, Dana, G791
Cleveland Museum of Art, C6
Coates, Pamela, A65-66
Coblentz, Patricia, B8
Coburn, Frederic W., G792
Cochran, Jean, G793
Coleman, Duke, G794
Coleman, Oliver, G795-796
Collins, R. Lee, G797
Colorado Springs Fine Arts Center, C7
Comstock, Helen, G798
Cone, Constance A., G799
Conkling-Armstrong Terra Cotta Co., F22

Connelly, John, A67
Conway, Bob, A68, G801
Cook, Charles D., G802-804
Cook, Ma[r]y Elizabeth, G805-808
Coolidge, Edwin H., G809
Cooper, Nancy, G810
Coors Porcelain Co., F23
Corlette, Suzanne, C36
Cornelius, Charles Over, G811
Cosentino, Geraldine, A243
Cotz, JoAnn, B13, B21, B41, B54, B104
Counts, Charles, A69, G813
Counts, Rubynelle, G813
Cousley, Sam A., G814
Cowan, R. Guy, A244, G815-817
Cox, George James, A70
Cox, Lucille T., G818-820
Cox, Paul E., E3, G821-833
Cox, Warren E., B17
Coyne, John, G834
Craig, James H., B18
Cramer, W. E., G845
Crane, Anne Winslow, G846
Crane, Charles Albert, G847
Crawford, Jean, A71, G848-849
Crawford, Rachael B., G850-851
Croly, Herbert D., G864-865
Crosby, Charles, G866
Cross, Nellie A., G867
Crossley Machine (Manufacturing) Co., F24-25
Crouch, Lois K., C7
Crowley, Lilian Hall, G868
Cummings, John, A78
Cummins, A. L., G869-870
Cummins, Virginia Raymond, A72
Cunningham, John T., B19
Currie, C. W. Y., G871
Curtis, Edmund DeForest, G872-877
Curtis, Philip H., B20, D4
Cushman, Paul, G878

Danielson, Leon E., G879
Darling, Sharon S., A73, G880
Darrah, W. A., G881
Davenport, S. W., A74
Davidson, Clair, G882
Davidson, Marshall, G883-884
Davis, Charles Thomas, A75-77, G885-887
Davis, Chester, G888-891
Davis, Theodore R., F44

Davison, Mary E., G892
Dawes, E. L., G893
De Brie, Sydney, G894
Dedham Pottery, F26-28
De Jonge, Eric, G895
De Kay, Charles, G896-898
Delaware Art Museum, C8
Demmin, Euphemia B., C7
Demorest, D. J., E35
Denker, Ellen Paul, B21, D5
Dennis, Lee, G899
Denver Fire Clay Co., F29
Depew, Chauncey M., B61
Dewhurst, C. Kurt, B54
Dibble, Mabel C., G910-911
Dickey, W. S., Clay Manufac-
    turing Co., F30
Dieter, Gerald W., A78
Dixon, John Morris, G912
Doat, Taxile, A80, G913-929
Dockstader, Frederick, G930
Dole, Nathan Haskell, G931
Dommel, Darlene, G932-936
Donhauser, Paul Stefan, A81,
    D6
Donley, Angeline Scott, G937
Dow, George Francis, B22
Doyle, Dixie, G938
Doyle, Maude M., G939
Drepperd, Carl W., G940
Dressler, Conrad, G941-942
Dressler, Constance W., G943
Dressler, Philip, G944-945
Drinkwater, Frank L., G946
Dubois, H. B., G947
Dudley, Pendleton, G948
Duemler, Ginger, A168
Duffy, Thomas J., A82
Duka, John, G949
Duke, Harvey, A83
Dümmler, Karl, A84
Dunbar, Gary S., G950
Dunnagan, M. R., G951-952
Duplin, V. J., Jr., G1683
Durrell, Jane, G953
Dyer, Walter A., B23-24, G954-
    957

Earle, Alice Morse, B25
Earthenware Association of
    Boston, A85
Earthenware Trade of New York
    City, A86

East Liverpool School of China
    Painting, A87
Eastern Mennonite College, C9
Eaton, Allen H., B26-27
Eberlein, Harold Donaldson,
    B28-30, G960-961
Edgar, William Harold, G962-
    963
Edson, Mira Burr, G964-968
Edwards, Deborah, G969
Edwards, O. K., G970
Ehlers, Jetta, G971
Ehrmann, Eric, G972
Eidelberg, Martin, B31, C46,
    G973-975
Ellett, William H., G976
Elliott, Charles Wyllys, B32
Ellis, Carey P., G977
Ellsberg, Helen, G978-979
Elwood, P. H., G980
Elzner, A. O., G981
Emerson, Gertrude, G982
Emory, Emma Vance, G983
Enfield Pottery and Tile Works,
    F31
Enloe, Scroop W., Jr., G984
Eskesen, Eckardt V., G985
Estey, J. A., G986
Evanoff, Betty, G987-988
Evans, Mary, G989
Evans, Paul, A88, B33, G990-
    1020
Everson Museum of Art, C10
Ewan, N. R., A89

Fair Hill Terra Cotta & Lava
    Works. See Steavenson &
    Cassel
Farrington, Frank, G1021
Farrington, Mary H., G1022
Fawcett, Waldon, G1023
Feeny, Bill, A215
Fegley, H. Winslow, G1025
Felts, James K., Sr., G1026
Ferola, Janice, G1027
Ferrell, Stephen T., C13
Ferrell, T. M., C13
Feustel, Walz & Co., F32
Field, Zane, G1028
Filkins, (Mrs.) Clarable
    (Childs), A90
Finke, Hans-Joachim, A91
Fitzgerald, Francis A. J.,
    G1031

Fitz-Gibbon, Costen, G1032
Fitzpatrick, Nancy, G1033-1036
Fitzpatrick, Paul J., G1037-
  1038
Flint, William W., G1039
Flu, E. B., G1040
Foraker, David, G1041
Foreman, Grant, G1042
Foryst, Carole A., G1044
Fosdick, Marion L., G185-187,
  G1045
Foster, Edith Dunham, G1046-
  1048
Foster, Kate McCrea, G1049
Fox, Charles James, G1050
Fox, Claire Gilbride, G1051
Frackelton, Susan Stuart,
  A92-94, G1052-1056
Francet, Louis, G1057-1068
Franco, Barbara, C29, G1069
Franklin, (Mrs.) Chester L.,
  G1070-1073
Franklin, Robert, G1074
Freas, Adelaide L., G1075.
  See also Fries, Adelaide L.
Fredgant, Don, G1076
Freeman, Helen, G1077
French, Myrtle Meritt, G1078-
  1081
Fries, Adelaide L., G1082.
  See also Freas, Adelaide L.
Fries, George M., G1083
Froehlich, Hugo, G1084-1085
Froncek, Thomas, G1086
Fry, Laura, G1087
Fry, Marshal, G1088-1089
Fryatt, F. E., G1090-1092
Fulper Pottery Co., F33

Gaines, Edith, G1093-1094
Gall, Irma M., A95
Galloway, George D., G1095
Galloway & Graff Co., F34-35.
  See also Galloway Terra
  Cotta Co.
Galloway Terra Cotta Co.,
  F36-39. See also Galloway
  & Graff Co.
Gardy, Elizabeth W., G1096
Garrett, Brice, G1097-1101
Garrison, W. C., E4
Garve, T. W., A96
Gates, Burton Noble, G1102

Gates, William D., G1103-1111
Geare, Randolph I., G1112
Geer, Walter, A97
Geijsbeek, S., G1113-1114
Georgia Council for the Arts
  and Humanities, C11
Georgia State University Art
  Gallery, C12
Gernert, Dee Albert, G1115
Gibson, Gerald G., G1116
Gibson, Louis H., G1117-1119
Gilbert, Alfred Holley, G1120
Gilfillen, Statler, A98
Gillingham, Harrold E., G1121
Gilmer, Ruth Monroe, G1122-
  1123
Gitter, Josephine, G1124
Gladding, McBean & Co., F40-41
Goldman, J. D., G1474
Goldman, Judith, G1136
Goldner, Steven, G1137
Goldsmith, M. O., G1138
Goldsmith, Margaret O., G1139
Goldstein, Fanny, G1140
Goodman, Guy, G1143
Goodyear, Clarissa, A99
Gordon, Eleanor, G1144
Gordy, William J., G1145
Gorton, E. E., G1146
Gottesman, Rita Susswein,
  B34-36
Gould, Charles N., G1147
Goyle, C. A. R., pseud.,
  G1264-1267
Graham, John Meredith, II,
  G1148-1149
Graley, Helen F., A100
Grave, Alexandra, C2
Gray, Walter Ellsworth, G1150-
  1154
Greaves-Walker, A. F., G1155-
  1157
Greeman, Tamara, G1158
Green, Charles W., G1159-1165
Green, Doris M., G1166
Green, (Mrs.) H. G., G1167-
  1168
Greenville County Museum of
  Art, C13
Greer, Georgeanna H., A101,
  B37-39, C26, E14, G1169-1170
Griffen, Smith & Co., F42-43
Grunewald & Busher. See
  Western Decorating Works
Grunewald, Frederick L., G1171
Grusheski, Ed, C36

228 AUTHOR INDEX

Guappone, Carmen A., A102-104
Guidos, Harold R., G1172
Guild, Lurelle Van Arsdale,
    B40, G1173
Guilland, Harold F., A105
Gunter, Herman, G1174
Guthrie, Hugh, G1175
Gutman, Walter, G1176

Haddon, Rawson W., G1177
Hall, Alice C., G1178
Hall, Fanny E., A106
Hall, Herbert J., G1179
Hall, Horatio F., G1180
Hamblett, Theora, G1181
Hamell, George R., B41, G266,
    G1182
Hamilton, Alice, E5, G1183-
    1184
Hamilton, Byrde, G1185
Hamilton, Henry W., G1186
Hamilton, Jean Tyree, G1186
Hanson, E. S., G1191
Harbin, Edith, A107
Harby, J. M., G1192
Hardcastle, Mildred Veley,
    G1193-1200
Hark, Ann, B42
Harper, George, A108
Harrington, Mildred, G1203
Harris, Cora, G1204
Harris, Thomas C., G1205
Harris, W. S., A109, G1206
Harrison, James M., G1207-
    1208
Harrop, C. B., G1209
Hartzell, Cleve, G1210
Haskin, Leslie L., G1211
Haslam, Malcolm, B43
Hasselle, Bob, G1212
Haswell, Ernest Bruce, G1213
Haviland & Co., F44
Hawes, Lloyd E., A110, G1214
Haywood, Maude, G1215
Hazen, Edward, B44
Heath, Fred T., G2287
Heath, Roger, G1216
Heckman, Albert W., G1217-
    1220
Hegarty, Marjorie, G1221
Heimlich, Jane, G1222
Heisey, M. Luther, G1223-1224
Helme, J. Burn, G1225

Helms, Charles Douglas, D7
Hemsteger, S. E., G2092
Henderson, (Mrs.) Palmer,
    G1226
Henry, A. V., G1227
Henzke, Lucile, A111, G1228-
    1233
Hersh, J. Joseph, G1234
Hettinger, Edwin L., G1235-1236
Hice, Richard R., G1237
Hightower, John M., Jr., G1238
Hill, Charles W., G1239-1240
Hill, F. Stanhope, A113
Hinman, (Mrs.) Teanna McLennan,
    G1241
Historical Society of York
    County, C14
Hoagland, Jane, G1242
Hocker, Edward W., G1247
Hofman, Caroline, G1248-1256
Holden, Marion L., G1257
Holmberg, Millicent B., G1258
Holmes, George Sanford, A114-
    115, G1259-1260
Homer, William I., C31, G1261
Hommel, Martha Hill, G1262
Hommel, Rudolf P., G1263-1267
Hood, Graham, A116, G1268-
    1270
Hopf, Carroll, G1271-1272
Hopkins, Thomas C., E6-8
Horney, Wayne B., A117, G1273
Hornor, W. M., Jr., G1274
Hottinger, A. F., G1275
Hough, Walter, E9, G1276
Hovey, H. C., G1286
Howe, Ruth Wood, G1287
Hu, William C., A40
Hudgeons, Thomas F., III, A215
Hudson, Charles J., G1288
Hudson, J. Paul, G1289-1290
Hughto, Margie, A57
Hull, A. E., Jr., G1291
Hull, Mary L., G1292
Hull, Walter A., G1293
Hull, William, G1294
Humphreys, Mary Gay, G1295
Humphries, Sherry B., C51
Hungerford, Nicholas, G1296-
    1297
Hunt, W. D., G1298
Hunt, W. F., G1299
Hutchinson, Elmer T., G1300
Hutson, Ethel, G1301-1304
Huxford, Bob, A118-122
Huxford, Sharon, A118-122

Iglehart, Margaret Ellen,
  G1305
Indianapolis Museum of Art,
  C15
Ingham, John H., G1307
Ingram, Sara, G1308
International Antiques Exposi-
  tion, C16
Irelan, Linna, E10
Irvine, Mary E., A185
Irwin, Ruth Frances. See
  Weidner, Ruth Irwin

Jack, Phil R., E16, G1314,
  G1590-1591
Jacoby, H. S., G1315
James, Arthur E., A123-124,
  G1316
Jamison, M., G1317
Jans, John T., G1318
Jaques, Bertha, G1319
Jarvie, Lillian Gray, G1320
Jayne, Horace F., C45, G1321-
  1322
Jeffords, J. E., & Co., F45
Jenkins, Marguerite, G1323
Jenney & Mundrie, Architects,
  G1324
Jervis, William Percival, B45-
  46, G1325-1333
Jewell, Margaret H., G1334-
  1335
Jillson, Herbert L., G1336
Jillson, Willard Rouse, G1337
Johns, H. W., G1338-1339
Johnson, Deb, A125-126, G1340-
  1341
Johnson, Gini. See Johnson,
  Virginia
Johnson, Henry Lewis, G1342
Johnson, Jane Stannard, G1343
Johnson, Virginia, A125-126,
  G1340-1341, G1344
Johnston, Pat H., G1345-1346
Jones, Annie M., G1347
Jones, Robert W., G1348
Joor, Harriet, G1349
Jordan-Volpe Gallery, C17-18
Judge, F. P., Jr., G1350

Kahle, Katharine Morrison,
  G1351. See also McClinton,
  Katharine Morrison
Kamerling, Bruce, G1352
Kane, Bill, G1353
Kane, Thomas F., G1354
Kauffman, Henry J., A21
Kaufman, Stanley A., C9
Kaye, Myrna, G1355
Kechijian, (Mrs.) Harry M.,
  G1356
Keeler, R. B., G1357
Keen, Kirsten Hoving, B47,
  C8, G1358
Keener, William G., G1359
Kelsey, V. V., G1360
Kelso, William M., G1361
Kempf, William C., G1362
Kendall, A. Harold, A127, A189
Kennedy, Donald, G1363
Keno, Leigh, G1364
Keramic Studio Publishing Co.,
  A128-136
Kersey, Jesse, A137
Ketchum, William C., Jr., A138-
  139, B48, C14, C30, G1441-
  1448
Keyes, Homer Eaton, G1449-1450
Kim, George, G1451
Kindig, Joe, Jr., G1452
King, Martha Feller, G1453
King, Pauline, G1454
King, William A., G1455
Kingsley, Rose G., G1456
Kircher, Edwin J., A140-141
Kirk, Charles J., G1457
Kirkpatrick, Frank A., G1458
Kissinger, Isabelle C., G1459
Klamkin, Marian, B49
Knight, (Mrs.) Harold G., G1460
Knittle, Rhea Mansfield, G1461-
  1464
Koch, Robert, G1465-1466
Koehler, W. A., E11, G1467
Koenig, F. J. M., G1468
Kohlenberger, Lois H., G1469
Koos, E. K., E11
Kovel, Ralph, A142, G1470
Kovel, Terry, A142, G1470
Kümmel, Henry B., E27

Lacey, Betty, G1471
Ladd, George E., E12
Laffan, W. McKay, G1472
La Forge, Zoe, G1473
La Grange, Marie J., G1474
Lamson, Everett C., Jr., A143,
  G1475
Lancaster Iron Works, F46
Lander, David, G1476
Langenbeck, Karl, A144, G1477-
  1481
Langworthy, C. F., G1482
Lasansky, Jeanette, A145-147
Lau, William, D8
Laughlin, Homer, China Co.,
  F47
Laurence, Frederick Sturgis,
  A148, G1483-1484
Lawless, Dorothy, G1485
Lawton, Lewis H., G1486
Leach, Mary James, G1487
Leaming, Susan F., G1488
Lee, Anne, G1489
Lehman, F., G1490
Lehner, Lois, A149-150
Leiby, Joyce M., G1491
Leighton, Henry, A212, G1492
Lenox, Inc., A5, A114-115,
  F48
Le Prince, Marie, G1493
Levin, Elaine, G1494
Lewis, Florence, A151
Lewis, H. A., See Boston
  Architectural Terra Cotta
  Works
Lichten, Frances, B50
Lieberman, Frank, G1495
Lincoln, George B., G1496
Linton, Robert, G1497
Little, Flora Townsend, G1498
Loar, Peggy A., C15
Loch, Marilyn, G1499
Lockington, M. E., G1500-1501
Lockington, W. P., G1502-1514
Loeb, Sophie Irene, G1515-
  1527
Longcope, Henry, G1528
Loring, John, G1529
Loud, Marian V., G1530
Loughlin, Gerald Francis, E13
Lovejoy, Ellis, A152-153,
  G1531
Lovett, Eva, G1532-1533
Low, J. and J. G., F49
Low, J. G. and J. F., F50-51

Lucas, Dorothy F., B51
Luther, Louise R., G1534
Lycett, Lydia, G1535
Lyman, Lila Parrish, G1536

McAfee, W. Keith, G1537
McBeath, Stuart H., D9
McCabe, David A., A154
McCabe, Lida Rose, G1538-1539
McCallie, S. W., G1540
McCampbell, Sara W., G1541-
  1542
McCaughey, William J., E35
McClinton, Katharine Morrison,
  B52-53, G1543. See also
  Kahle, Katharine Morrison
McClure, Abbot, B28-29
McCollam, C. Harold, A155
McDanel, W. W., G394
McDonald, W. P., G1544
McDowell, C., G1545
MacDowell, Marsha, B54
Macfarlane, Janet R., G1546
Macht, Carol, C5, G1547-1548
McKearin, George S., C16
McKearin, Helen, G1549
McKee, Floyd W., A156
McKnight, David, Jr., E22
McLaughlin, Mary Louise, A157-
  164, G1550-1552
McLaughlin, Rita, G1553
McLennon, T., G1554
McMahon, J. F., G1555
MacSwiggan, Amelia E., G1556-
  1559
Madden, Betty I., B55, G1560
Maddock, Archibald M., II.,
  A165
Maddock's, Thomas, Sons Co.,
  A166
Magonigle, H. Van Buren, G1561
Malone, James M., E14
Mantle, H. L., G1562
Markham, Kenneth H., G1563-
  1564
Marks, Alfred T., G1565
Marsh, L. L., G1566
Martin, E. A., G1567
Maryland Historical Society,
  C19-20
Mason, Elizabeth, G1568
Mason, Maud M., G1569-1572
Mason, William A., G1573

Mathews, Jessie Hughes, G1574
Maynard, Thomas Poole, E15
Mebane, John, G1575
Meline, Elva, G1576
Mellor, E. A. B., G1577
Mendenhall, Lawrence, G1578
Ment, David, B10
Mercer, Henry Chapman, A167-
    168, G1579-1583
Mercer Pottery Co., F52
Merrill, Frederick J. H.,
    G1584
Merrill, Madeline Osborne,
    G1585-1586
Mesre, Moses, A265
Metropolitan Museum of Art,
    C21
Michael, George, B56, G1588
Michael, Glenn William, G1589
Michael, Ronald L., B5, B38,
    B57-58, B62, B88, E16,
    G1314, G1590-1591
Middleton, Jefferson, E17
Miller, David Kent, G1592
Miller, Donald, A26
Miller, Leslie William, A169,
    A249, G1593-1594
Miller, Noda May Senter, (Mrs.
    W. H. Miller, Jr.), A170
Miller, Robert W., G1595
Millet, Frank D., G1596
Milliken, William M., G1597
Mills, R. G., G1598
Milwaukee Art Center, C22
Mint Museum, C23-24
Minton, LeRoy H., G1599-1602
Mississippi State Historical
    Museum, C25-26
Mitchell, Elmer C., G1603
Mitchell, James R., B58-59
    G1604-1607
Mitchell, Jerry J., D10
Mock, Esther, G1608
Molinier, Émile, G1609
Monachesi, (Mrs.) Nicola di
    Rienzi, A171, G1610-1613
Monmouth County Historical
    Association, C27
Montague, William E., G1614
Montfort, M. Helen E., G1615
Montgomery, Marguerite, G1616-
    1618
Montgomery, Rosetta Schuyler,
    G1619
Moore, Don D., C15
Moore, George M., G1625-1626
Moore, R. Carl, G1627

Moravian Pottery and Tile
    Works, F53-57
Morgan, A. R., Co., F58
Morris, Alfred, G1628
Morris, Robert E., C7
Morrow, Frank C., B60
Morse, Barbara White, G1629-
    1645
Morton, Julie, G1646
Mosaic Tile Company, F59
Moses, John, B61
Mueller, Herman C., G1647-1654
Mueller Mosaic Co., F60
Munsey, Cecil, G1655
Munson-Williams-Proctor Insti-
    tute, C28-29
Murphy, James L., G1656
Museum of American Folk Art,
    C30
Museum of Art of Ogunquit, C31
Museum of Contemporary Crafts,
    C32
Myers, Susan H., B62, C33,
    D11, E18
Myers, William Starr, B51

Nash, John, G1658
National Mercantile Publishing
    Co., A172
National Museum of History and
    Technology, C33
National Terra Cotta Society,
    A173-176
Nawrot, Emma L., G1659-1660
Nealey, J. B., G1661-1663
Nelson, Edna Deu Pree, G1664
Nelson, Helen C., G1665
Nelson, Marion John, G1666-
    1667
Nelson, W. H. de B., G1668
Nerenberg, Jean, G1144
New Jersey Clayworkers' Associ-
    ation, A177
New Jersey State Museum, C34-
    37
New York Blower Co., F61
Newark Museum, A178, C38-42
Newcomb, Rexford, A179
Newkirk, David A., A180
Newman, Bim, G1672
Newman, Doris, G1672
Newton, Clara Chipman, G1673-
    1674
Newton, Robert Wyman, C7
Nichols, George Ward, A181

232 AUTHOR INDEX

Niloak Pottery, F62-63
Noel, Margaret, G1675
Noel Hume, Ivor, B63, E40,
  G1676
Norman-Wilcox, Gregor, G1677
North State Pottery Co., F64-
  68
Northend, Mary Harrod, G1678
Northwestern Terra Cotta Works
  (True, Brunkhorst & Co.),
  F69
Norton, F. H., G1679-1683
Norwood, John Nelson, A182
Noyce, Dorothy, G1684
Noyes, Henriette T., G1685

Oak, Sophie Knight, G1686
Oakey, A. F., G1687
O'Connell, Annette, G1688
Oerter, Albert L., G1689
O'Hara, Dorothea Warren,
  A183, G1690-1691
Ohio State University, E19
Ohr, George E., G1692
Olin, Jacqueline S., B64
Olmstead, Anna W., G1694
Olsen, Peter C., G1695
"One Who Has Succeeded", A184
Onondaga Pottery Co., B65
Ormond, Suzanne, A185
Ormsbee, Thomas Hamilton,
  G1696-1697
Ortman, Fred B., G1698
Orton, Edward, Jr., E20, E45,
  G1699-1713
Osborne, Mildred R., G1714
Osborne, W. R., G1715-1716
Osgood, Adelaide Harriet,
  A186
Osgood Art School, F70
Osgood, Cornelius, A187
Osgood, (Mrs.) Worth, G1717
Otis, Margaret, G1718
Overbeck, Hannah B., G1719

Page, Harvey L., G1720
Paist, Henrietta Barclay,
  A188
Palestine Pottery. See
  Feustel, Walz & Co.

Palmer, C. Carroll, G1721
Panama-Pacific International
  Exposition, C43
Pappas, Joan, A189
Parmelee, Cullen W., E21,
  G1722-1723
Parshall, Margaret T., G1724
Pass, R. H., G1725
Pass, Richard, G1726
Pattison, James William, G1727
Payant, Felix, G1728-1730
Payne, Elizabeth H., G1731
Pear, Lillian Myers, A190,
  G1732
Pearce, John N., D12
Pearl, Mignon W., G1733
Peck, Herbert, A50, A191,
  G1734-1736
Pelichet, Edgar, B66
Pence, F. K., G1737
Pendleton, Margaret, G1738
Pennsylvania Museum and School
  of Industrial Art, C44. See
  also Philadelphia Museum
Perkins, Dorothy Wilson, D13
Perry, Margaret, G1744
Perry, Mary Chase, G1746-1754.
  See also Stratton, Mary
  Chase (Perry)
Perry, (Mrs.) Aaron F., G1745
Persick, Roberta Stokes, D14
Persick, William Thomas, D15
Perth Amboy Terra-Cotta Co.,
  A247, F71
Peterson, Arthur G., G1755
Philadelphia China and Tile
  Works, F72
Philadelphia City Pottery.
  See Jeffords, J. E. & Co.
Philadelphia Museum of Art,
  C45. See also Pennsylvania
  Museum and School of Indus-
  trial Art
Phillips, Lois L., G1758
Pilling, Ronald W., G1759
Pitkin, Albert Hastings, A193
Piton, Camile, A194
Plank, Ross D., G1760
Platt, Dorothy Pickard, A195
Plumb, Helen, G1761
Plusch, Herman A., A1762
Pochmann, Ruth Fouts, G1763
Pockrandt, Florence Delores,
  D16
Podmore, Harry J., G1764-1773
Poese, Bill, G1774-1776

Poor, H. Varnum, G1778
Porter, George Richardson, A196
Postle, Kathleen R., A197, G1780
Potter, A. D., E22
Potter, Jeanne O., G1785
Poucher, J. Wilson, G1841
Powell, Elizabeth A., A198, G1842
Powell, Robert Blake, A199-200, G1843
Priestman, Fanny Rowell, G1845-1848
Prime, Alfred Coxe, B67-68
Princeton University Art Museum, C46
Purdy, Ross C., G1849-1852
Purviance, Evan, A201-204
Purviance, Louise, A201-204

Quaintance, Paul A., G1853
Quimby, Ian M. G., B4, B9, B20, B59, B94

R. W. Norton Art Gallery, C47
Radford, Fred W., A205
Ramsay, John, A206-208, G1854-1864
Ramsdell, Roger Wearne, B30
Randall, James E., G1865-1866
Raney, E. Marvin, G1867
Rauchenberg, Bradford L., B69, G1868-1869
Rawson, Jonathan A., Jr., G1870-1872
Ray, Marcia, G1873
Raycraft, Carol, A209
Raycraft, Don, A209
Raymond, W. Oakley, G1874-1879
Reddall, Amy C., G1880
Reed, Cleota, B70
Rehl, Norma, A210
Rehmann, Elsa, G1881
Reilly, Anna D., G1882
Reinert, Guy F., G1883-1889
Remensnyder, John P., G1890
Reynolds, S. Adelaide, G1891
Rhead, Frederick Alfred, G1892-1898

Rhead, Frederick Hurten, A211, G1899-1917
Rhead, Geo. F., G1918
Rhodes, Lynette I., C6
Rice, A. H., C48
Rice, A. H., Collection, C48
Richards, Agnes Gertrude, G1919-1920
Richardson, W. D., G1921-1922
Ricker, Ruth, G1923
Riddle, F. H., G1924
Riddle, Frank H., G1925
Riddle, L. E., Jr., G1926
Riefstahl, R. Meyer, G1927
Ries, Estelle H., G1928
Ries, Heinrich, A212, E23-27, G1929-1933
Righter, Miriam, G1934
Rights, T. M., G1935
Ringo, Fredonia Jane, A213
Robacker, Earl F., G1936-1938
Roberts, Clarence Nelson, D17
Roberts, Janet, G1939
Roberts, Joseph K., G797
Robertson, J. Milton, G1940-1941
Robertson, Sarah, A214
Robineau, Adelaide Alsop, G1942-1952
Robineau, Samuel E., A80, G1953-1955
Robinson Clay Product Co., F73
Robinson, Dorothy, A215
Robinson, Ednah, G1956
Rochester Museum and Science Center, C49
Rocky River Public Library, A216
Rogers, Jane Grey, G1957
Rogers, Stephen T., E32
Romaine, Lawrence B., G1958
Rookwood Pottery Co., F74-81
Roorbach, Eloise, G1959
Rose, Arthur Veel, A217, G1960-1961
Rosenow, Jane, G1962
Roseville Pottery Co., F82-83
Roueché, Berton, G1963
Rucker, Kathryn, G1964
Ruge, Clara, G1965-1969
Russell, Arthur, G1970
Russell, Elizabeth H., G1972
Russell, J. Almus, G1973
Russell, (Mrs.) E. E., G1971

St. Gaudens, Paul, A218
St. John, Richard W., D18
Sammis, Romanah, A219, G1976-
   1977
Sargent, Irene, G1978-1985
Saturday Evening Girls, A220
Sauer, Jim, G1986
Saunier, Charles, G1987
Scammell, D. William, G1988
Schaaf, Downs, E36
Schaltenbrand, Phil, A221,
   G1989-1992
Schantz, E. F., G1993
Scheetz, Grier, G1994
Scherma, George W., B71
Schiffer, Margaret, B72
Schmidt, Johnell L., C51
Schneider, Norris F., A202-
   204, A222, A265, G1995
Schurecht, H. G., E28, G1997
Schwartz, Jeri, G1998-1999
Schwartz, Marvin D., A223-224,
   G2000-2002
Schwartz, Stuart C., A225-226,
   G2003
Scoon, Carolyn, G2011
Seares, Mabel Urmy, G2012
Searle, Alfred B., A227,
   G2013
Sellards, E. H., G2014
Selvage, Nancy, B73
Sharkey, Samuel M., G2015
Shaw, Joseph B., E29
Shaw, Myril C., E36
Sheerer, Mary G., G2016-2021
Sheffield, Albert H., G2022
Shepherd, Tryon Mason, G2023
Sheridan, Chris, B5
Sheridan, Millicent M., G2024
Sherman, Frederic Fairchild,
   B74
Sherwood, Robert F., G2025
Shirayamadani, K., G2026
Shirley, Bernice Cook, G2027-
   2028
Shoemaker, Henry Wharton, A228
Short, Elizabeth M., G2029
Shotliff, Don Anthony, D19,
   G2030-2031
Shrimpton, Louise, G2032
Shull, Thelma, B75-79, G2033-
   2035
Shuman, John A., III, G2036

Shuman, Susan W., G2036
Shumway, Harry Irving, G2037
Silva, William P., G2038
Silverman, Alexander, G2039
Sim, Robert J., B80-83, E30-
   31, G2040
Simons, Helen, E14
Slivka, Rose, G2041
Small, Eleanor C., G2042
Smith, Clarissa, G2043
Smith, Dolores, G2044
Smith, Elmer L., A229
Smith, Eugene A., G2045
Smith, G. Hubert, G2046
Smith, Howard A., G2047
Smith, Katherine Louise, G2048
Smith, Kenneth E., G2049-2050
Smith, Kenneth L., G2051
Smith, Leonora M., G2052
Smith, Richard W., G2053-2054
Smith, Robert E., G2055
Smith, Samuel D., E32
Snider, Luther C., E33
Snook, Anna, A230
Snook, Josh, A230
Snow, Richard F., G2056-2057
Solon, Leon V., G2058-2063
Soper, E. K., G2064
Sotheby Parke Bernet, Inc., C50
South, Stanley, B1, B12, B37,
   B39, B64, B69, B84-87, B91,
   B93, E34, G2065-2066
Spangler, Meredith Riggs,
   G2067
Spargo, John, A231-238, G2068-
   2071
Sparkes, John C. L., A239
Spector, Stephen, G2072
Spiller, Burton, G2073
Spinney, Frank O., G2074-2075
Sprackling, Helen, G2083
Sprague, P. E., G2084
Sprague, William B., G2085-2086
Springer-Papa, Joan, G2087
Springsted, Brenda Lockhart,
   B88
Squires, Frederick, A240
Stahl, I. S., G2088
Standard Sanitary Manufactur-
   ing Co., F84-85
Stangl Pottery, F86
Star of the Republic Museum,
   C51
State University College at
   New Paltz, C52
Steavenson & Cassel, F87
Stefano, Frank, Jr., G2089

Steinhoff, F. L., G2090
Stern, Anna M. P., G2091
Stevens, A., A241
Steward, Florence Pratt, (Mrs.
  LeRoy T.), A242
Stewart, Regina, A243
Stief, W. C., G2092
Stiles, Helen E., A244
Still, John S., G2093
Stillwell, John E., G2094
Storm, Nicholas, G2096
Stoudt, John Baer, C48, G2097
Stoudt, John Joseph, B89
Stout, Wilber, E35-36, G2098
Stover, Frances, G2099
Stover, J. Homer, G2100
Stow, Charles Messer, G2101-
  2102
Stradling, Diana, A245
Stradling, J. Garrison, A245,
  G2103
Strahan, Edward, G1472
Stratton, Herman John, D20,
  G2105
Stratton Howard Fremont, G2104
Stratton, Mary Chase (Perry),
  A246, G2106. See also
  Perry, Mary Chase
Strong, Janet, G2107
Stuart, Evelyn Marie, G2108-
  2113
Stuckey, Jasper L., G2114-2115
Stull, R. T., G2116-2118
Stull, William, E35
Sturgis, Russell, G2119-2120
Sudbury, Byron, B90
Sudlow, E. W., G2121
Sutherland, Frances Living-
  ston, G2123
Suydam, Richard M., G2124-2125
Swan, Mabel M., G2126
Swift, Samuel, G2127
Syracuse Museum of Fine Arts,
  C53

Tachau, Hanna, G2128-2129
Taft, Lisa Factor, C36
Talbot, James J., A247
Talbot, Mary White. See
  White, Mary
Tanenhaus, Ruth Amdur, G2130-
  2131
Tarter, Jabe, G2132

Tauranac, John, G2133
Taylor, James, G2134-2139
Taylor, Marjorie, G2140
Taylor, William Watts, G2141-
  2143
Teall, Gardner, G2144
Teetor, Paul, G2145
Tennessee Fine Arts Center,
  C54
Thistlethwaite, F., G2146
Thomas, B. B. (Ted), Jr., B91,
  G2147
Thomas, C. H., G2148
Thompson, Erwin N., E37
Tiffany & Co., F88
Tiffany, G. S., G2149
Tillotson, E. W., G2151
Tilton, Stephen Willis, A248
Timmerman, Walter, G2152
Tjossem, Morla W., G2153
Tower, Lilian Leslie, G2154
Townsend, Everett, G2155
Tracy, Berry B., C39
Trapp, Kenneth R., B92, C18,
  G2156-2157
Treischel, C. C., G2158
Trent Tile Co., F89-91
Trenton Potteries Co., F92
Truax, William J., G2166
True, Brunkhorst & Co. See
  Northwestern Terra Cotta
  Works
Tucker, Thomas, G2167
Twitchell, M. W., G2168
Tyrrell, George V., Jr., D21

U.S. Department of Commerce,
  Bureau of Standards, E38-39
U.S. Potters' Association,
  A249-250
Uren, Marjorie E., A40
Urquhart, Lewis K., G2170,
  G2245

Valentine, John, G2171
Van Briggle, Anne Gregory,
  G2172
Van Briggle Tile and Pottery
  Co., F93
Van Etta, Vivian M., A95

Van Winkle, William Mitchell, A252
Vance-Phillips, L., A251, G2173-2174
Vance-Phillips, (Mrs.)L., G2175
Van Ravenswaay, Charles, G2176
Van Vlissengen, Arthur, Jr., G2177
Varick, Vernon, G2178-2181
Veatch, Otto, G2182
Verneuil, M. P., G2183
Viel, Lyndon C., A253-254
Vodrey, William H., Jr., G2184
Volkmar, Charles, A251, G2185-2187
Volkmar, Leon, G2188-2189
Volpe, Todd M., G384, G2190-2191
Vozar, Linda, G2192

Wadsworth, Anna, C11
Waitt, Madalaine, A255
Walker, C. Howard, G2193
Walker, Iain C., B93
Walker, Raymond J., G2194
Walker, Sophia Antoinette, G2195-2197
Wallace, Addie M., G2198
Wallach, Amei, G2199
Walton, William, G2200-2201
Ware, W. Porter, A256, G2202-2204
Warman, Edwin G., G2205
Warringdon, Anne, G2206
Washburn, Edward W., G2207
Waterbury, Ivan C., G2208-2209
Watkins, C. Malcolm, B94, E40, G1290
Watkins, Lura Woodside, A257-259, G2210-2227
Watts, Arthur S., E41-42, G2228-2233
Weaver, Edward, G2234
Webb, Judson Thomas, A260
Webb, Thomas G., G2235
Webb, Warfield, G2236
Webster, Donald Blake, A261
Weedon, George, C22
Weidman, S., G2237
Weidner, Ruth Irwin, D22, G2238-2239
Weigel, W. M., G2240-2241

Weinhardt, Carl J., Jr., C15
Wells, E. D., G2242
Wells, Helen E., G2243
Wells, J. M., G2244
Wells, W. E., G2245
Wellsville China Co., F94
Wenham, Edward, G2246
Wertime, Marcia, G2247
West, Mildred Veitch, G2248
Western Decorating Works (Grunewald & Busher), F95
Weygandt, Cornelius, B95-97, G2255-2256
Whatley, L. McKay, G2257
Wheatley Pottery Co., F96
Wheeler, H. A., G2258
Wheeler, Ione L., G2259-2261
Wheeler, Robert G., G2262-2263
Wherritt, Edith Cornelia, G2264
Williamson, Scott Graham, B99
Whitaker, Fred A., G2265
White, Charles E., Jr., A262
White, I. C., G2266
White, Jessie Mae, G2267
White, Lela Phelps, G2268
White, Margaret F., B98
White, Mary, A263
Whitford, W. G., E43
Whiting, Margaret C., G2269
Whitlatch, George I., D23, E44, G2270-2273
Whitman, J. Franklin, Co., F97
Whittemore, Edwin C., G2274
Whittemore, O. J., E43
Whittle, Charles L., G2275
Whyte, Bertha Kitchell, G2276
Wilder, Katherine A., G2277
Willets Manufacturing Co., F98
William Benton Museum of Art, C55
Williams, Lena, G2278-2279
Williamson, J., G2280
Willis, Katharine, G2281-2282
Wilson, Hewitt, F29, G2283-2287
Wilson, Joan S., G2288
Wiltshire, William E., A264
Winchester, Alice, G2289
Winslow, Henry W., G2290
Wintermute, H. Ogden, G2291
Winton, Andrew L., G2292-2293
Winton, Kate Barber, G2292-2293
Wires, E. Stanley, A265, G2294

Wise, Ethel Brand, G2295
Wiseman, Edith Phillips,
  G2296-2297
Wolfe, Julia W., G2298
Wolfe, Richard, A224
Wood, Marie Stevens Walker,
  G2299
Wood, Ruth Howe, G2300
Wood, Ruth Kedzie, G2301
Woodhouse, Charles Platten,
  B100-101
Woodhouse, Samuel H., G2302
Woodhouse, Samuel W., G2303
Woods, Virginia, G2304
Wood-Safford, Sara, G2305-
  2308
Woodward, Ellsworth, G2309-
  2311
Woodword, E., G2311
Woolf, Doris S., G2312
Worcester Historical Museum,
  C56
Worcester, Wolsey Garnet,
  E45
Work Projects Administration,
  New Hampshire, B102
Wright, Frank Lloyd, G2315
Wright, Grace Radcliff,
  G2316
Wright, Livingston, G2317-
  2318
Wright, Tyndale & Van Roden,
  F99

Young, Jennie J., B103, G2321

Zane Pottery Co., F100-101
Zaug, Dawson D., D24
Zimmermann, H. Russell, G2324
Zserdin, (Sister) Mary
  Carmelle, D25
Zug, Charles G., III, B104,
  G176, G2325
Zwermann, Carl H., G2326

SUBJECT INDEX

Dates of birth and death for potters and other personnel
have been supplied wherever possible. Although every effort
has been made to verify these dates in other sources, they
are intended primarily as a guide for the user of this bibliography and should not be considered authoritative information.

Ack family potters, Moores-
    burg, Pa., G1193
Aesop's fables, G888, G2294
Afro-American wares, B1
Air Panel (Low), G1981
Albany (N.Y.) potteries,
    G2262-2263
Albert, Fritz, G1053, G1603
Albino Ware (Buffalo
    Pottery), A3
Albion (E. Bennett), G2077
Alexandria (Va.) potteries,
    G140
Alfred University School of
    Ceramics. See New York
    State School of Clay-
    working and Ceramics
Alhambra Ceramic Works,
    Chicago, Ill., G407,
    G1365
Ali Baba Vase (M. L. McLaugh-
    lin), G1984
Alkaline-glazed stoneware
    and pottery, B39, B86-87,
    B104, C13, D2, E14, G436,
    G438, G1170, G2065,
    G2325. See also Glazes
    and glazing, alkaline
    glazes
Allentown Barber Supply Com-
    pany, Allentown, Pa.,
    G404

Allison, LeRoy W., G552
    portrait, G552
Alsop-Robineau, Adelaide.
    See Robineau, Adelaide
    Alsop
American Art China Works,
    Trenton, N.J., F95
American Ceramic Society,
    B6, G23, G60, G70, G78,
    G95-97, G99, G103, G373,
    G550, G600-610, G627,
    G670, G698-699, G755,
    G774, G1106, G1709, G1746,
    G1828, G2004, G2258,
  Art Division, A4, G100,
    G185, G476-477, G529,
    G815, G826, G875-876,
    G1078, G1292, G1902,
    G1909
  exhibitions, G1901
American Clay Machinery Co.,
    Bucyrus, Ohio, F1, G640,
    G751
American Encaustic Tiling Co.,
    Zanesville, Ohio, A265,
    C36, F2-4, G491, G888,
    G894, G2059, G2110
American Indian influences.
    See under Influences
American Pottery Co., Jersey
    City, N.J., G2219

American Pottery Co., Peoria,
    Ill., G1962
American Sewer Pipe Co.,
    Barberton, Ohio, G745
American Terra Cotta and Cer-
    amic Co., Chicago, Ill.,
    G631, G651, G667-668,
    G671, G715, G734, G744,
    G757, G761, G764-765,
    G1103-1105, G1110, G1119,
    G1151-1152, G1324, G1710,
    G1967. See also Gates
    Potteries; Gates, William
    Day; Indianapolis Terra
    Cotta Co.
"American Vernacular," FAR
    Gallery, New York City,
    N.Y., G1744
Ames Pottery (Iowa State Col-
    lege), G611
Anderson Keramic Club, G1971
Animal figures, C50. See
    also Dogs
Anna Pottery, Anna, Ill.,
    B21, D5, G144-146, G148,
    G1026. See also Kirk-
    patrick, Cornwall; Kirk-
    patrick, Wallace V.
Apotheosis of the Toiler.
    See Scarab Vase
Arbuckle & Son Tile Co.,
    Homer, Ind., G613
Architectural terra cotta,
    A73, A75-77, A84, A97-98,
    A173-176, A244, A247,
    A262, F19, F22, F69, F71,
    G493, G759, G864-865,
    G885-886, G985, G1109,
    G1225, G1240, G1292,
    G1309, G1483-1484, G1502,
    G1532, G1687, G2048,
    G2138. See also Terra
    cotta
  Connecticut--Bridgeport
    Barnum Institute of Sci-
      ence and History, G616
  Connecticut--New Haven
    Yale Gymnasium, G2137
  Illinois--Chicago, G722,
      G1144
    Central Music Hall, G18
    Conway Building, G619
    Home of the Friendless,
      G671
    Illinois Central Station,
      G631
    Inter-Ocean Building,
      G1104

Architectural terra cotta
    (Cont'd)
  Illinois--Chicago (Cont'd)
    Railway Exchange Building,
      G743
    Schlesinger & Mayer, G598
    True, John R., residence,
      G1118
    Woods Theater, G765
    Wrigley Building, G599
  Indiana--Indianapolis
    Hampton Court Apartments,
      G764
    Indiana National Guard
      Armory, G636
    Indianapolis Gospel
      Tabernacle, G614
    Indianapolis Public Li-
      brary, Branch No. 3,
      G764
    Maryden Apartments, G764
    Mercantile Building, G618
    Soldiers Monument, G1119
    Transmission and Service
      Station, 38th and Ken-
      wood, G614
  Massachusetts--Boston
    Copley Plaza Hotel, G2317
  Minnesota--Owatonna
    Farmer's National Bank,
      G734
  Missouri--St. Louis, G172
  New Jersey--New Brunswick
    Rutgers, State University,
      Ceramics Building, G555
  New Jersey--Perth Amboy
    George Washington Monu-
      ment, G1716
  New York--Brooklyn
    Academy of Music, G1532
    Long Island Cold Storage
      Warehouse, G441
  New York--Buffalo, F13
    Ellicott Square Building,
      G1117
  New York--Corning
    Brick, Terra Cotta, and
      Supply Co., G625
  New York--Long Branch
    McCall, John A., residence
      fountain, G763
  New York--New York City,
      G2135, G2139
    Empire State Building,
      G677
    Grand Central Terminal
      G871

Architectural terra cotta
    (Cont'd)
  New York--New York City,
    (Cont'd)
    McAlpin Hotel, G689, G705
    Metropolis Theatre, 132nd
      St. & 3rd Ave., G766
    New York Herald Building,
      G2134
    Steward Building, 5th
      Ave. & 46th St., G1435
    Vanderbilt, Cornelius,
      stable, G22
    Woolworth Building, F14
  Ohio--Cleveland
    Chamber of Commerce
      Building, G701
    City Hospital for Conta-
      gious Diseases, G659
    Ott Memorial Building,
      G659
    Y.M.C.A., G659
  Pennsylvania--Philadelphia
      G767, G1503-1504, G1508,
      G1511-1512
    American Baptist Publica-
      tion Society, G1505
    Drexel Institute, G1505
    Medico-Chirurgical Hos-
      pital, 17th & Cherry
      Sts., G1510
    Rittenhouse Building,
      G1510
    University of Pennsylva-
      nia, G1514
  polychrome, A148, G1762
  restoration, G912
  Washington--Seattle
    University of Washington,
      Philosophy Hall, G2198
  Wisconsin--Lake Geneva
    Yerkes Observatory (U. of
      Chicago), G1103
Architectural Tile Co., Key-
    port, N.J., G499, G526,
    G532
Arequipa Pottery. Fairfax,
    Calif., G376, G1813,
    G1959
Arkansas potteries. See Pot-
    tery industry, Arkansas
Art Institute of Chicago,
    G1374
  exhibition of art crafts,
    G282
  Normal Class, G1079-1080,
    G1374, G1488

Art Nouveau in ceramics, A185,
    B66, G1355, G1666
Art pottery, A32, A81, A88,
    A111, A125-126, A142, A244,
    A263, B31, B33, B47, B53,
    C8, C46, E35, G109-112,
    G136, G381, G384, G402,
    G851, G868, G953, G973,
    G992-995, G1028, G1087,
    G1097, G1150-1151, G1153-
    1154, G1228, G1358, G1414,
    G1498, G1529, G1570,
    G1871, G1900, G1965,
    G1967, G2000, G2072,
    G2119-2120, G2209. See
    also under names of indi-
    vidual potteries
  theories and philosophies,
    B73, G340
Art tiles. See Tiles, orna-
    mental
Ashfield (Mass.) potteries,
    G141. See also South
    Ashfield (Mass.) potteries
Ashley, Harrison Everett (1876-
    1911), G675
  portrait, G675
Associated Tile Manufacturers,
    Beaver Falls, Pa., F5,
    F7-12, G44
Atchison, Henry K. (1820-1893),
    New Jersey and Greensboro/
    New Geneva, Pa., G192
Athens (N.Y.) potteries,
    G569, G1546
Atlan Club, G178, G910-911,
    G1365-1367, G1405, G1919
Atlantic Terra Cotta Co., New
    York, N.Y., F13-16, G530,
    G689, G705, G840, G871,
    G1279-1280, G1532, G2062
Aust, Gottfried (1722-1788),
    Bethabara and Salem, N.C.,
    B9, B84, B93, E34, G2066
Austin, Harry W., Old Lyme,
    Conn., G510
  portrait, G510
Avalon Ware (Chesapeake Pot-
    tery Co.), G1034-1035,
    G1037
Avon Faience Co., Tiltonville,
    Ohio, G1019
Ayars, Alice Annie (1895-1946),
    G27
  portrait, G27

Babcock, Earle Jay (1865-
    1925), G277, G1354, G2169
  portraits, G277, G2169
Bachelder, Oscar Lewis (1852-
    1935), G38, G459, G498,
    G801, G1345
  portraits, G38, G459, G498,
    G801, G1345
Baggs, Arthur E. (1886-1947),
    D14-15, G23, G184, G513,
    G1179, G1558
  portrait, G23
Baily, Charles, G1015
Baking pans, G1590
Ballard and Brothers, Bur-
    lington, Vt., G2068
Baltimore (Md.) Potteries,
    D12
Bannerman, R., Tobacco Pipe
    Manufactory, Rouses Point,
    N.Y., B90
Barber, Edwin AtLee (1851-
    1916), G1740
  collection, Philadelphia
      Museum, C44
  portraits, G264, G1740
Barnum, Fayette, Louisville,
    Ky., G11
Bartley, Jonathan, Crucible
    Co., Trenton, N.J., F16,
    G1486
Baseball Vase (I. Broome, Ott
    & Brewer), G850, G1499,
    G1605, G1644
Batchelder, Ernest A. (1875-
    1957), G1576, G2012
Batchelder-Wilson Co., Los
    Angeles, Calif., F17
Bathroom fixtures. See Sani-
    tary wares
Baur, Theodore, G1596
Bay View Pottery, South
    Amboy, N.J., G412
Bayley, Daniel (1729-1792),
    Newbury, Mass., G2213
Bayley family potters, Essex
    County, Mass., G2213-
    2214
Bayley, Joseph (1701-1761),
    Newbury, Mass., G2213
Bean pots, G2215
Beatty, Richard L., Blooms-
    bury, Trenton, N.J.,
    G1771
Beaver Falls Art Tile Co.,
    Beaver Falls, Pa., G253,
    G363

Bedtime Madonna (St. Gaudens),
    G470
Beech, Ralph Bagnall, Kensing-
    ton, Philadelphia, Pa.,
    (1810-ca.1857), G251,
    G1743
Beehives, G1271
Bell, Charles F. (d.1911),
    G1836
Bell, John (1775-1847),
    Waynesboro, Pa. and Win-
    chester, Va., G1836,
    G1868, G2079
Bell Potteries, Columbus,
    Ohio, G706
Bell potteries, Strasburg,
    Va., G1173
Bell Pottery, Waynesboro, Pa.,
    G1836
Belleek, B53, F98, G156, G419,
    G851, G1093, G1356, G1563,
    G1575, G1882, G1934,
    G2001
Bellmark Pottery Co., Trenton,
    N.J., F18
Bennett, Edwin, Baltimore,
    Md., C19
Bennett, Edwin, Pottery Co.,
    Baltimore, Md., C19, G221,
    G508, G588-589, G2077
Bennett, James (1812-1862),
    East Liverpool, Ohio,
    G562
Bennington Museum, Bennington,
    Vt., G989
Bennington (Vt.) potteries,
    A27-29, A187, A193, A231-
    232, A236-238, B24, C50,
    G272-275, G448, G469,
    G581, G804, G989, G1027,
    G1159-1168, G1216, G1495,
    G1625-1626, G1688, G1999,
    G2069-2070, G2154, G2192,
    G2288, G2290
Benson, Grace Bohne, G574
Berge, Benjamin, Montgomery
    County, Pa., G244
Bethabara (N.C.) potteries,
    D3
Bethlehem (Pa.) potteries,
    A91. See also Moravian
    potteries, at Bethlehem,
    Pa.
Bethune (S.C.) potteries, G474
Betrothal Candlestick (St.
    Gaudens), G470

Bibliographies
  clays, G1929
  North Carolina potteries,
    A225
  terra cotta, G2284
Biloxi Art Pottery, Biloxi,
    Miss., A39, C25, G137,
    G285, G1304, G2036, G2044,
    G2199. See also Ohr,
    George E.
Binns, Charles Fergus (1857-
    1934), D15, E1, G32-33,
    G95, G177, G478, G540,
    G676, G902, G1429, G1494,
    G1555, G1812
  "E Concremation Confirma-
    tio," E1, G327
  portraits, E1, G32-33, G333
    G336, G540, G676, G1494
Binns Medal, G67
Bird baths, G1539. See also
    Garden pottery
Bird motifs. See under
    Motifs
Birdhouses, G1272
Bissett family potters, Old
    Bridge, N.J., B81
Black-glazed teapots, G2225
Blakey, John W., G1015
Blakey, Thomas W., G1015
Blanchard, Adelaide M., G303
Bleininger, Albert Victor
    (1873-1946), G24, G26,
    G95, G2039
  portraits, G26, G87, G630
Bloomfield, Charles A. (1849-
    1929), G31, G482, G563,
    G652
  portraits, G31, G482, G563,
    G652
Bloomsburg (Pa.) potteries,
    G1196, G1973
Bloomsbury, Trenton (N.J.)
    potteries, G1771
Bloor, Ott & Brewer, Trenton,
    N.J., G1605
Bloor, William H. (1821-1877),
    G90
"Blue and Gray" (S. Frackel-
    ton), G835, G1401
Blue and white wares, A107
Blue Willow Ware (Buffalo
    Pottery), G627
Boggs family potters, Ran-
    dolph County, Ala.,
    G1939

Boggs Pottery, near Montgom-
    ery, Ala., G1939
Bone family potters, Georgia,
    G2299
Bone, Jesse Stevens (1861-
    1939), G2299
  portrait, G2299
Bonnin and Morris, Philadel-
    phia, Pa., A116, B30,
    G143, G245, G1148-1149,
    G1268, G1270
Book ends, F76, G760, G2111
Book flasks, C50, G1688,
    G2192
Boston Architectural Terra
    Cotta Works, South Boston,
    Mass., F19
Boston Earthenware Manufactur-
    ing Co., East Boston,
    Mass., G1102
Boston Terra Cotta Co.,
    Boston, Mass., G20, G616
Bottles (pottery), G2073
  figural, G1258
Bowers Pottery Co., Manning-
    ton, W. Va., G2250, G2252
Bowie residence, San Mateo,
    Calif. (roof tiles),
    G1180
Bowls, F77, G1949
Bowman, Oliver Otis (1838-?),
    G57
Bowman, Robert K. (1868-?),
    G57
Bowman, William J. J. (1866-
    ?), G57
Boy and Girl Candlesticks
    (St. Gaudens), G470
Bradshaw China Co., Niles,
    Ohio, G620
Bradwell, (Mrs.) Thomas,
    portrait, G189
Brewer, John Hart (1844-ca.
    1900?), G419
Brick, A75-77
  enameled, A75-77, G1567,
    G2118
Brick and Clay Record, G2090
Brick industry, A89
  Milwaukee, Wisc., G650,
    G2324
  Missouri, D17
  Ohio, A155
Brick, Terra Cotta and Tile
    Co., Corning, N.Y., G625,
    G648, G723, G758

Bridgeport Crucible Works,
    Bridgeport, Conn., G1286
Bringhurst, R. P., St. Louis,
    Mo., G128, G1816
British influences. See
    under Influences
Brockville Works, Pottsville,
    Pa., G1199
Brooklyn Museum, Brooklyn,
    N.Y., A61, G787, G2001-
    2002
Brooklyn (N.Y.) potteries,
    B10
Brooks, Hervey (1779-1873),
    Goshen, Conn., A252
Brooks, Hervey, Pottery,
    Goshen, Conn., A252,
    G2216
Broome, Isaac (1835-1922),
    G253, G850, G1317, G1499,
    G1644
Broome, "Jug Jim," Union
    County, N.C., D7
Brotherhood Bowl (St.
    Gaudens), G470
Brouwer, Theophilus Anthony,
    Jr. (1864-1932), G846,
    G896, G999, G1916
  portraits, G846, G999,
    G1916
Brown, Anne Taylor, Oak Park,
    Ill., G2123
Brown, Davis, G635
Brown, Edith, G548
Brown, George Herbert (1884-
    1943), G552, G1660
  portrait, G552
Brown, Otto, family potters,
    G474
Brown, Philip King, M.D.,
    G1813. See also Arequipa
    Pottery
Brush, George DeForest (1855-
    1941), G170, G792, G1336
  portraits, G792, G1336
Brush Guild, New York City,
    N.Y., G792, G795
Brush Pottery Co., Zanes-
    ville, Ohio, A118
Brushes, A92
Brush-McCoy Pottery Co.,
    Zanesville, Ohio, A65-66,
    A118-119, G1002
Bühler, Johann Georg, Lees-
    port, Pa., G1884-1885

Buffalo (New York) potteries,
    G1208
Buffalo Pottery Co., Buffalo,
    N.Y., A3, G627, G1031,
    G1098, G1115, G1525,
    G1661, G2081
Buffalo Society of Mineral
    Painters, G1387
Burial urns. See Crematory
    vases
Burley & Co., Chicago, Ill.,
    G1369, G1372-1373, G1727,
    G1920
Burley & Tyrrell Co., Chicago,
    Ill., F20, G869, G1312,
    G1370-1371
Burlington (Vt.) potteries,
    G2068
Burning. See Firing
Burroughs & Mountford Co.,
    Trenton, N.J., A109, G223
Burt, Stanley G. (1870-1950),
    G95
  portrait, G95
Busbee, Jacques (d.1947), G38,
    G417, G444, G1139, G1203,
    G1242
  portrait, G1203
Busbee, Juliana (d.1962),
    G38, G1203, G1242
  portrait, G1203
Busher, George R. (1864-?),
    G536
  portraits, G536
Bybee Pottery, Bybee, Ky.,
    G889

Cable, Margaret Kelly (1884-
    1960), A26
Cadmus, Abraham, Congress
    Pottery, S. Amboy, N.J.,
    G1696
Cafe Au Lait (Buffalo Pot-
    tery), G2081
Caire Pottery, Poughkeepsie,
    N.Y., G1841
Cake molds. See Molds, cake
Calendar plates, G1714
California Art Pottery and
    Tile Association, San
    Francisco, Calif., G1012
California China Products,
    National City, Calif.,
    G704

California potteries, B33.
    See also Catalina Island
    (Calif.) potteries
Cambridge Tile Manufacturing
    Co., Cincinnati, Ohio,
    G1663
Campaign plates. See Presi-
    dential campaign souve-
    nirs
Campana, Dominic Mathews,
    G2296
Candlesticks, F78, G2166
Cannelton Sewer Pipe Co.,
    Cannelton, Ind., G693
Carlyle & McFadden, Freeman's
    Landing, W. Va., G657
Carlyle, George (1821-?)
    portrait, G657
Carpenter, Frederick (1771-
    1827), Boston, Mass.,
    G2222
Carr, James (1820-?), G463-
    G468
    portrait, G463
Carter's Ink Co. pottery
    bottles, G2073
Cartlidge, Charles (1800-
    1860), G227
    portraits, A9, G227
Cartlidge, Charles & Co.,
    Greenpoint, Brooklyn,
    N.Y., A9, B10, G227-231
Casa Bonita (House of Tiles),
    F6
Casting, G919
Catalina Island (Calif.)
    potteries, G1784
Celadon Roofing Tile Co. See
    Ludowici-Celadon Roofing
    Tile Co.
Centennial Exhibition. See
    under Exhibitions and
    expositions
Centennial Vase. See Century
    Vase
"A Century of Ceramics in the
    United States, 1878-1978,"
    G2041
Century Vase (K. Müller),
    G114, G850, G2001
The Ceramic Age, G551
Ceramic Art Co., Trenton,
    N.J., F95, G117, G119,
    G861, G1986. See also
    Lenox, Inc.

Ceramic League of Philadel-
    phia, G1420
Ceramics in interior decora-
    tion, G821, G1081, G2243
The Ceramist, G552
Challis, Edward, Jamestown,
    Va., G1676
Chamber pots, miniature,
    G1774
Chambers Brothers Co., Phila-
    delphia, Pa., F21
Chandeliers, G458
The Chapel (A Robineau),
    G1942
Charcoal furnaces, G1302
Charles Cartlidge & Co. See
    Cartlidge, Charles & Co.
Chautauqua Institute, Arts
    and Crafts School, Ceram-
    ic Dept., G2175
Cheesequake (N.J.) potteries,
    B59, G2040
Chelsea Keramic Art Works,
    Chelsea, Mass., A110,
    G254, G397, G1010, G1214,
    G1556, G1940, G2126. See
    also Dedham Pottery
Chelsea Pottery, U.S.,
    Chelsea, Mass., G1214,
    G2078
Chemical stoneware and por-
    celain, F23, G1172,
    G1996, G2013, G2265
Chemistry of pottery, A144,
    G1477-1479
Cherokee Brick Co., Raleigh,
    N.C., F21
Cherry, Kathryn E., G1947
    portrait, 1947
Chesapeake Pottery Company,
    Baltimore, Md., G1034-
    1035, G1037. See also
    Haynes, D. F., & Co.
Chicago Art Institute. See
    Art Institute of Chicago
Chicago Ceramic Art Associa-
    tion, G592, G1022, G1376-
    1381, G1390, G1459,
    G2259-2261, G2296-2297
Chicago Ceramic Art Club,
    G1241
Chicago Historical Society,
    Chicago, Ill., A73, G880
Chicago (Ill.) potteries, A73,
    G880

Chicago (Ill.) terra cotta
    companies, A73
Chicago Public Library
    (Tiles), G2150
Chicago Sewer Pipe Co.,
    Brazil, Ind., G694
Chicago Terra Cotta Co.,
    Chicago, Ill., G17-18
Child, Edwin B. Charles
    Volkmar at Work (Sketch,
    1903), G2200
Chimney tops, G969
China painters' supplies,
    F20, F70, F95, F99
China painting, A6, A30, A44,
    A49, A52-53, A87, A90,
    A92-94, A99, A106, A113,
    A128-A136, A151, A157-164,
    A170-171, A181, A183-184,
    A186, A188, A194, A214,
    A239, A242, A251, A255,
    G189, G223-225, G247-250,
    G370, G983, G1030, G1201,
    G1248-1254, G1312, G1543,
    G1554, G1727, G1920,
    G2109, G2174, G2296. See
    also Decoration of pot-
    tery
Chinese influences. See
    under Influences
"Christ on the Rockies"
    (Denver Terra Cotta Co.),
    G507
Christ, Rudolf (1750-1833),
    Bethabara and Salem, N.C.,
    B9, B69, B85
Chryso-Ceramics, G572
Cincinnati Art Museum, G953,
    G1548
"Cincinnati Faïence," G1001,
    G1178
Cincinnati (Ohio) potteries,
    C5, D1, G1001, G1360,
    G1404, G1578, G1734,
    G1745
Cincinnati Pottery Club, G36,
    G60, G157, G219, G953,
    G1001, G1178, G1202,
    G1578, G1673-1674, G1734,
    G1745, G1984
Clark family potters, Mill-
    ville, Concord, N.H.,
    G1039
Clark, John Farmer
  portrait, G1039

Clark, N., and Co., Lyons,
    Mount Morris, and Roches-
    ter, N.Y., G570-571
Clark, Nathan, apprentices
    and branches, G569-571
Clark, Nathan, Jr. (1819-?),
    Athens, N.Y., G569, G1546
Clark, Nathan, Sr. (ca.1787-
    1880), Athens, N.Y., G547,
    G569-571, G1546
Clark potteries in New York
    State, G571, G1546
Clark potteries, Lyndeboro,
    N.H., G435
Clarke, William R., G338
    portrait, G338
Classical influences. See
    Influences, Greek and
    Roman
Clay and clays, A75-77, A152-
    153, A227, E38, E41, G294,
    G306-307, G387, G1933
  Alabama, E26, G2045
  Albany Slip, G1348
  analysis of, G1477-1478,
    G2323
  Arkansas, G415
  bibliographies, G1929
  California, G1497
  Connecticut, E13
  Delaware, G2148
  drying, G388. See also
    Clay dryers
  Eastern States, E24
  Florida, G595, G1174, G2014
  Fuller's earth, G977
  Georgia, E12, E15, G1227,
    G1540, G2053, G2117,
    G2182
  Idaho, G2064, G2287
  Indiana, E44, G279, G385-386
  Indianola, G2323
  Iowa, E3
  Kansas, G2145
  Kentucky, G593, G1337, G1932
  Louisiana, G790
  Massachusetts, G2275
  Missouri, G432-433
  New England States, G1680
  New Jersey, E27, G1362,
    G2015
  New York State, G1930
  North Carolina, E23, G847,
    G984, G2114-2115
  Ohio, E3, E28, E36, G1700-
    1702, G1704-1705, G1997,
    G2098

Clay and clays (cont'd)
  Oklahoma, E33, G1147
  Pennsylvania, E6-8, G1025,
      G1237, G1492, G1997
  preparation of, G2116
  South Carolina, G268-269,
      G456, G1074, G2241
  Southern States, G2240
  Tennessee, G797
  Texas, E22, G425, G1185
  Vermont, G1958
  washing, G1192, G1490
  Washington, G1114, G2287
  West Virginia, G2266
  Wisconsin, E2, G2237
Clay dryers, F61, G1531
Clay, Henry, letter to Tucker
    & Hemphill, G238
Clay House, Panama-Pacific
    Exhibition, G420, G615,
    G697
Clay industry. See Pottery
    industry; Pottery and
    clay products
Clay modeling in schools,
    G1049, G1573, G1880
Clay products, value of. See
    Pottery and clay products
Clay Products Co., Brazil,
    Ind., G729
The Clay-Worker, G92, G1865
Clayworkers' Tree of Knowl-
    edge, G644
Cleopatra Bust (I. Broome,
    Ott & Brewer), G850,
    G1317, G1605, G1644
Cleveland Museum of Art, G513
Clewell, Walter C., Canton,
    Ohio, G2132
Clews, James (1790-1861),
    Troy, Ind., G239, G2089
  portrait, G2089
Clifton Art Pottery, Newark,
    N.J., G1787
Clifton Ware (Chesapeake Pot-
    tery Co.), G1034-1035,
    G1037
Cloudland Vase (A. A.
    Robineau), G1899
Colanders, G1271, G1936
Cole family potters, North
    Carolina, G176
Collective bargaining. See
    Labor-Management rela-
    tions; Working conditions
    and wages

Colonial potteries, B17, B22,
    B34, B63, B67, B94, B100.
    See also Histories,
    general
Colono wares, B1
Color in pottery, G317, G1085,
    G1160, G1252, G1747, G2058
Columbian Art Pottery, Trenton,
    N.J., G254
Columbian Exposition. See
    under Exhibitions and ex-
    positions
Commemorative panels, G1105
Commerau, Thomas, New York
    City, N.Y., G1731
Commercial wares, A3, A244,
    E11, E39. See also
    Dining car china
Common Clay, G668
Condensing coils, G387
Conestoga Pottery, Wayne, Pa.,
    G877
Congress Pottery, S. Amboy,
    N.J., G1696
Conkling-Armstrong Terra
    Cotta Co., Philadelphia,
    Pa., F22, G645, G1500,
    G1504-1505, G1508, G1510
Connecticut potteries, B74,
    C2. See also Norwalk,
    (Conn.) potteries; Pottery
    industry, Connecticut
Cook, Charles Howell (1856-
    1926), G34, G858, G1523
  portrait, G34
Cook, Mary ("May") Elizabeth
    (1863-?), G49, G68, G1907
  portraits, G68, G1907
Cooper, Henry Alexander (1886-
    1959), G720. See also
    North State Pottery
Cooper, Rebecca Palmer (1886-
    1954), G720. See also
    North State Pottery
Cooper-Hewitt Museum, New
    York, N.Y., G171
Coors Porcelain Co., Golden,
    Col., F23, G932
Corliss Pottery, West Wool-
    wich, Maine, G1334
Cornelian Ware (Roseville),
    G451
Cornelison Pottery, Bybee,
    Ky., G889
Corson, Leon W., G2104
  portrait, G2104

Cortland (N.Y.) potteries,
    G522, G907
"Country" pottery, A209, B52.
    See also Folk pottery
Cowan Pottery Studios, Cleve-
    land, Ohio, and Rocky
    River, Ohio, A216, B15,
    G424, G817, G1597
Cowan, R. Guy (1884-1957),
    A216, B71, G424, G513
Cowden & Wilcox, Harrisburg,
    Pa., G1195
Cowden potteries, Harrisburg,
    Pa., G1195
Coxon Belleek China, G1563
Coxon, Charles, G221
  portrait, G221
Coxon, Jonathan, Jr. (1843-
    1911), G1835
  portrait, G1835
Crab Vase (A. Robineau), G375
Crackleware (Dedham), G1941,
    G2037
Cracqule Ware (Dedham). See
    Crackleware
Crafts Pottery, Nashua, N.H.,
    G1681
Craig, Burlon B. (1914-),
    Vale, N.C., B13, G423
  portrait, G423
Crane, Walter, G888
Crematory vases, G651
Crescent China Co., Alliance,
    Ohio, G700
Crolius, Clarkson (1773-1843),
    New York, N.Y., G1693,
    G2180
  portrait, G2094
Crolius, Clarkson, Jr. (1806-
    1887), New York, N.Y.,
    G2029, G2180
Crolius family potters, New
    York, N.Y., G1879, G2094
Crolius, John, New York, N.Y.,
    G883-884
Crolius ware, G2180
Crolius, William, G1879
Crook, Russell G., designs
    for tiles at "Dreamwold,"
    G421
Crooksville China Co., Crooks-
    ville, Ohio, G609, G742
Crossley Machine (Manufactur-
    ing) Co., Trenton, N.J.,
    F24-25

Crowley's Ridge Pottery,
    Crowley's Ridge, Mo., G882
Crown Point Pottery, Corona,
    N.Y., G2269
Croxall & Cartwright, East
    Liverpool, Ohio, G1094
Crucibles, F16, G1286, G1486
Cupid and psyche patterns,
    G1449
Cups, G362
Curtis, Edmund DeForest,
    portraits, G477, G529, G875
Cushman, Paul (1767-1833),
    Albany, N.Y., G878
Cuspidors. See Spittoons

D.A.R. Museum, Washington,
    D.C., G1308
Dallas Pottery, Cincinnati,
    Ohio, G1178
Dalquist, Edward, Billerica,
    Mass., and Mason City,
    Iowa, G1426
Dalquist, (Mrs.) Edward,
    Billerica, Mass., and Mason
    City, Iowa, G1426
Danvers (Mass.) potteries,
    G1559
Davies, Thomas J. (Col.),
    Aiken County, S.C., G218
Davis, George W., & Co.,
    Rochester, N.Y., G574
Davis, Nathan, G1222
Davis, Theodore R., designer,
    White House porcelain
    service, F44
Debolt & Atchison, New Geneva,
    Pa., G192
Debolt, George, New Geneva,
    Pa., G192
Decalcomanias, G108, G185-186,
    G1045, G1517, G1822. See
    also Transfer printing
Decker, Charles Frederick, Sr.
    (1832-?), Chucky Valley,
    Washington County, Tenn.,
    G434, G1592
  portrait, G434
Decker family potters, Chucky
    Valley, Washington County,
    Tenn., G434, G1592

Decoration of pottery, A55,
    A163, A181, A188, A248,
    G4, G311, G454, G581,
    G853, G1248-1254, G1256,
    G1453, G1516, G1519,
    G1524, G1527, G1572,
    G1892-1894, G1910-1912,
    G2306-2308, G2320. See
    also Color in pottery;
    Design; Influences;
    Motifs; Shapes of pottery
  under the glaze, G1611-1613,
    G1896-1898, G2096,
    G2185
Decorators' marks. See Marks,
    decorators'
Dedham Historical Society,
    Dedham, Mass., A110,
    G2078
Dedham Pottery, Dedham, Mass.,
    A110, B77, F26-28, G12,
    G931, G1011, G1046-1048,
    G1125, G1143, G1154,
    G1556, G1891, G2034,
    G2037, G2078, G2126. See
    also Chelsea Keramic Art
    Works; Chelsea Pottery,
    U.S.; Crackleware
De Dou Ceramic Studio, Oak
    Park, Ill., G1243
Dedouch, Joseph A., Oak Park,
    Ill., G1243
Delaware Art Museum, G1358
Deldare Ware (Buffalo Pot-
    tery), A3, G1115, G1525
Dell, William, Cincinnati,
    Ohio, G996
Del Turco, L., & Brothers,
    Harrison, N.J., G491
Denny-Renton Clay and Coal
    Co., Renton, Wash., G2198
Denver Fire Clay Co., Denver,
    Col., F26
Denver Terra Cotta Co.,
    Denver, Col., G507
Design. See also Decoration
    of pottery; Influences;
    Motifs; Shapes of pottery
  need for improvement in,
    A169, A249, G180, G293,
    G476-477, G529, G826,
    G875, G1078, G1593-1594,
    G2297
  piracy, G1078, G1797
  sources, G369, G372, G1571

Despondency Vase (Artus Van
    Briggle), G211, G583,
    G1465
Dessert molds. See Molds,
    dessert
Detroit Institute of Arts,
    Detroit, Mich., G1221
Diana (M. E. Cook), G1907
Diaper work, G322
Dickens Ware (Weller), G1232
Dickey W.S., Clay Manufactur-
    ing Co. Kansas City, Mo.,
    F30.
Dilliner family potters,
    New Geneva, Pa., G198
Dilliner, Samuel R., New
    Geneva, Pa., G198
Dining car china, E39, G1099.
    See also Commercial wares
Dinnerware, A100, A149, A156,
    E42, F47, G4, G6, G236,
    G692, G1690, G1988, G2228.
    See also Whitewares
Dipping baskets, G1172
Directories. See Trade
    directories
Doat, Taxile (1851-1938), A80,
    G990, G1333, G1985, G2183
  portraits, A80, G990
Dobbins, Murrel(l), G661,
    G772
  portraits, G661, G1506
Dobbins, Murrel, Sanitary
    Wares, Camden, N.J.,
    G1506
Dodd, W. J., G1603
Dodge Pottery, Portland,
    Maine, G408
Dogs, G1863. See also Animal
    figures
Dogwood Pottery (Hilton),
    G801
Dolls, G383, G1590, G1763,
    G1923
Donatello (Roseville), A230
Donovan, John, Peabody, Mass.,
    portrait, G1679
Dorchester Pottery Works,
    Boston, Mass., B56, G1016,
    G1963
Doremus, Carrie B., G1848
  portrait, G1848
Dovey, Arthur, G1008
  portrait, G1008
Dow, Arthur W., G1382, G1568

Dragonfly vase,(A. Robineau),
    G1628
Drakenfeld & Co., New York,
    N.Y., G129
"Dreamwold," Scituate, Mass.,
    (Tiles), G421
Dreps, Hildegarde Fried, G934
  portrait, G934
Duché, Andrew, Savannah, Ga.,
    G1122-1123, G1264-1267,
    G1269, G2242
Duché family potters, G1263
Duquesne Ceramic Club, G289,
    G1383
Durand, Asher B. The Capture
    of Major André, G1364
Durant Kilns, Bedford Village,
    N Y., G898
Duschek, Mary. Chicago, Ill.
    G730
DuVal, Benjamin, Richmond,
    Va., G1869

Eagle Tobacco Pipe Manufac-
    tory, Rouses Point, N.Y.,
    B90
Earthenware Association of
    Boston, Mass., A85
East Birmingham (Pa.) pot-
    teries, G1207
East Greenwich (R.I.) pot-
    teries, G1785
East Liverpool (Ohio) pot-
    teries, E35, G580, G1460,
    G1606, G1859-1861, G2184
Eddy, Mary Baker, medallion
    (Grueby), G1534
Edgerton (Wisc.) potteries,
    G1867
Education for ceramics and
    clayworking, A169, A249,
    D13, E20, G187, G301,
    G328-329, G346, G393,
    G480, G567, G816, G1107,
    G1239, G1292, G1350,
    G1520, G1537, G1593,
    G1598, G1647, G1699,
    G1707-1708, G1850, G1913,
    G2021, G2151. See also
    under names of individual
    schools and colleges
Edwin Bennett Pottery Co.
    See Bennett, Edwin, Pot-
    tery Co.

Egg Shell. See Belleek
Egyptian influences. See
    under Influences
Eighteenth-century potteries,
    A62, A178, D12. See also
    Histories, general
Eiler, P., East Birmingham,
    Pa., G1207
Election souvenirs. See
    Presidential campaign
    souvenirs
Elizabethtown (N.J.) potteries,
    G1300
Ellsworth, Ephraim Elmer
    Pitcher (Bennington),
    G1244
Enameled brick. See Brick,
    enameled
Enameling, A183
Enfield Pottery and Tile
    Works, Laverock, Pa.,
    F31, G1188
English ceramists' research
    tour, G658
Engobes. See Slips
Equipment. See Machinery and
    equipment
Eskesen, Eckardt V. (d.1943),
    G1695
Etruria Works (Ott & Brewer),
    Trenton, N.J., G1605,
    G1764
Etruscan Majolica (Griffen,
    Smith & Co.), D22, G202-
    204, G206, G214, G233,
    G288, G1588, G1758, G2043,
    G2091, G2238-2239
European influences. See
    under Influences
Evans, J. B. (decorator),
    G1364
Evans, Randal, G882
Everson Museum of Art, Syra-
    cuse, N.Y., A57, G2041
Excelsior Terra Cotta Co.,
    New York, N.Y., G763, G766
Excelsior Works, Rices Landing,
    Pa., G1992
Exeter (N.H.) potteries, G1682
Exeter Pottery Works, Exeter,
    N.H., A143, G1682
Exhibitions and expositions
  Centennial (Philadelphia,
    1876), G850, G2103
  Columbian (Chicago, 1893),
    A84, G592, G1981, G2234

Exhibitions and expositions
    (cont'd)
    Industrial (Indianapolis,
        1924), G662, G761
    International (London, 1871),
        A31
    International (Paris, 1900),
        F80, G401, G1405, G1425
    International (Paris, 1925),
        G565, G1950, G2020
    Louisiana Purchase (St.
        Louis, 1904), G172,
        G617, G633, G656, G759,
        G1097, G1113, G1406-
        1410, G2313-2314
    Panama-Pacific Internation-
        al (San Francisco,
        1915), C43, G420, G615,
        G697, G704, G1806,
        G2111,
    Pan-American (Buffalo,
        1901), G1413, G1415,
        G1455, G1544, G1615
    Sesquicentennial Inter-
        national (Philadelphia,
        1926), F6
Expositions. See Exhibitions
    and expositions

Factory or pottery design and
    construction, A96, G1315,
    G1781-1783, G2229
Fair Hill Terra Cotta & Lava
    Works, Philadelphia, Pa.,
    F87
FAR Gallery, New York, N.Y.,
    G1744
Farmingdale (Maine) potteries,
    G409
Farrar, William H., G892
Favrile Pottery (Tiffany),
    G975
Federal Terra Cotta Co.,
    Woodbridge, N.J., G520
Feldspar industry, G947
Fenton, Christopher Webber
    (1806-1865), G1120,
    G1962, G2070, G2300
    portraits, G1287, G2300
Fenton family potters, Ben-
    nington, East Dorset, and
    St. Johnsbury, Vt., G1120,
    G1287, G2071. See also
    Bennington (Vt.) potteries

Fenton, Jonathan (1766-?),
    Boston, Mass. and Dorset
    Hollow, Vt., G2222, G2300
Fenton Potteries, Bennington,
    Vt., G1163. See also
    Bennington (Vt.) potteries
Ferargil Galleries, New York,
    N.Y., G812
Ferguson family potters,
    Georgia, G437
Ferneries, G462
Feustal, Walz & Co., East
    Palestine, Ohio, F32
Figural bottles, see Bottles
    (pottery), figural
Fire company pitchers, G1696
Fire-painted ware (T. A.
    Brouwer, Jr.), G999
Fireplaces. See Mantels
Firing, A106, A132, A144,
    A152, G2-3, G300, G313,
    G925-926, G970, G1566,
    G1815, G1906, G2042,
    G2264. See also Kilns;
    Production and manufac-
    ture
Fischer, Benedict
    portrait, G2155
Fish molds. See Molds, fish
Fiske, J. Parker B. (1865-?),
    G95
    portrait, G95
Flame Ware (T. A. Brouwer,
    Jr.), G999
Flesh painting, G2174
Flint Faience & Tile Co.,
    Flint, Mich., G1434
Flometa Ware (Warner-Reffer
    China Co.), G1788
Floral arrangement in pottery
    containers, G2111
Florence Pottery Co., Mount
    Gilead, Ohio, G515
Florida potteries, B12
Florida State Museum, B12
Flower motifs. See under
    Motifs
Flower pots, G266, G450,
    G515, G1458. See also
    Garden pottery
Foell & Alt, East Birmingham,
    Pa., G1207
Folk pottery, A104-105, A193,
    A229, A264, B7, B50, C2,
    C6, C11, C14, C26, C52, D2,
    D7. See also "Country
    pottery"

Fonthill (H. C. Mercer),
    Doylestown, Pa., A48,
    G286, G1051, G1579
Footwarmers, G1463
Fords Porcelain Works, Perth
    Amboy, N.J., G672, G749
"Forms from the Earth: 1000
    years of Pottery in Amer-
    ica," G930
Forst, Arthur D., G82
  portrait, G82
Fort Dodge (Iowa) potteries,
    A23
Fort Pitt Hotel, Pittsburgh,
    Pa., Norse Room (Tiles),
    G718
Fountains, F34, G1213
Four Winds Summer School,
    Ceramic Class, G579,
    G1400
Frackelton, Susan Stuart Good-
    rich (1848-1932), Milwau-
    kee, Wisc., C22, G541,
    G835, G1401, G1405,
    G2099, G2206
  portrait, 2099
Franciscan Ware (Gladding,
    McBean & Co.), G79
Franzheim, Charles W. (1853-
    1912), G35
  portrait, G35
Frederick, Frank Forrest,
    G1837
  portrait, G1837
Frit furnaces, G2092
Frog mugs. See Mugs, frog
Fruit motifs. See under
    Motifs
Fry, Laura Anne (1857-1943),
    G543, G986, G1024, G2049
  portrait, G2049
Fry, Marshal(1), G1382,
    G1394-1395, G1397, G1408
Fry, William H.
  portrait, G2049
Fuller's earth. See Clays,
    Fuller's earth
Fulper Pottery Co., Fleming-
    ton, N.J., C17, F33, F86,
    G165, G383, G546, G933,
    G1790, G1806-1808, G1923,
    G2111, G2113, G2191
Fulper, William Hill (1872-
    1928), G89
  portrait, G89
Fulper, William Hill, II, G383

Funds (Industrial) for
    research in ceramics, G341

Galena (Ill.) potteries, A117,
    G1273
Galloway & Graff Co., Phila-
    delphia, Pa., F34-35
Galloway Terra Cotta Co.,
    Philadelphia, Pa., F36-39,
    G843-844, G1513, G2127
Galloway, William. See Gallo-
    way Terra Cotta Co.
Garden pottery, F15, F34-39,
    F41, F96-97, F100-101,
    G840, G843-844, G980,
    G1296, G1825, G1870, G1881,
    G2127. See also Bird
    baths; Jardinieres
Gardiner (Maine) potteries,
    G409
Gates Potteries, Terra Cotta,
    Ill., G866, G880, G962-
    963, G1053, G1055, G1872,
    G2112. See also American
    Terra Cotta and Ceramic
    Co.; Teco Ware
Gates, William Day (1852-1935),
    G77, G95, G630, G667-668,
    G1132, G1151-1152, G1324
  "The Manufacturer's Depend-
    ence on Ceramic
    Research," G655, G1107
  portraits, G77, G630, G655,
    G668
Gates, William Paul "Pat,"
    (1879-1920), G780
Geijsbeek, Samuel (d.1943),
    G95
  portrait, G95
Gelatin molds. See Molds,
    dessert
General Ceramics Co., Keasby,
    N.J., G2265
General Porcelain Co., Parkers-
    burg, W.Va., G845
George Ohr Pottery. See
    Biloxi Art Pottery; Ohr,
    George E.
George, Vesper, designs for
    tiles at "Dreamwold," G421
George Washington Bicentennial
    Center, Alexandria, Va.,
    G140

Georgia Art Pottery, Carters-
    ville, Ga., G1145
Georgia Kaolin Co., Macon,
    Ga., G2182
Georgia potteries, C11, D2,
    G437, G2054. See also
    Pottery industry, Georgia
Gilman, C. C., Eldora, Iowa,
    G21
Girard, Stephen, Vase (R. B.
    Beech), G1743
Gladding, A. J. (1858-1929),
    G726
Gladding, McBean & Co., Los
    Angeles, Calif., F40-41,
    G79, G1146, G1760
Glaes (Glase), John G., Pass-
    more, Pa., A33, G123
  portrait, A33
Glase, John G. See Glaes,
    John G.
Glaze formulae, A34, A144,
    B64, G873, G1072-1073,
    G1137, G1477
Glazes and glazing, A80, A144,
    A153, G127, G314-316,
    G340, G920, G928-929,
    G1065-1067, G1482, G2191
  alkaline glazes, B39, B64,
    G1169. See also Alka-
    line-glazed stoneware
  lead glazes. See Lead
    poisoning in potteries;
    Lead-glazed pottery
  matt glazes, G345, G1325
  salt glazes, G208, G748
  tin glazes, G365-368, G1868
Glebe Harbor (Va.) potteries,
    G577
Glen Tor Studio, G836
Glossaries. See Terminology
Godfrey, Lydia, G836
Gold decoration, G1402-1403
  etched, G1895
  in china painting, G1171
  Roman, G1402
  underglaze, G2187
Golding, Moses (1819-?), G71
Goodman, Helen Hastings,
    G1718
Gonzalez, Juanita, G830
Goodwin, Charles Fawcett
    (1874-1941)
  portrait, G820
Goodwin, George (d.ca.1932)
  portrait, G820

Goodwin, James F. (d.1896)
  portrait, G820
Goodwin, John (1816-1875),
    East Liverpool, Ohio, and
    Trenton, N.J., G284, G820
  portrait, G820
Goodwin, John Smith (1872-
    1909), G118
Gordy, William J., G1145
Gorton, E. E., G95
  portrait, G95
Grainger, Ella Ström, G812
Grand feu wares, A80, G913-
    929, G1057-1061, G1969.
    See also Grès; Porcelain
Grand Ledge Clay Products Co.,
    Grand Ledge, Mich., B54
Grand Ledge (Mich.) potteries,
    B54
Grand Ledge Sewer Pipe Co.,
    Grand Ledge, Mich., B54
Grave markers. See Tombstones
Greatbach, Daniel, G222,
    G1326, G1809
Greaves-Walker, Arthur
    Frederick (1881-1954), G29
Greek and Roman influences.
    See under Influences
Greenland, Norman, Cassville,
    Pa., G1194
  portrait, G1194
Greenpoint Porcelain Works.
    See Cartlidge, Charles &
    Co., Green Point, N.Y.
Greensboro (Pa.) potteries,
    A102-103, A221, E16, G1,
    G190, G195-196, G1314,
    G1590-1591, G1991
Greensboro Tile Roofing Co.,
    Greensboro, Pa., G1989
Greenwich House Pottery, New
    York City, N.Y., G147
Greenwood Pottery Co., Trenton,
    N.J., G791, G1518
Greer, Georgeanna, G2065
Gregory, M. E., Corning, N.Y.
  portrait, G758
Grès, A80, G295, G917, G1057-
    1061
Gridley, Oliver, Newburgh, N.Y.,
    G547
Griebel, H., G2202
Griffen, Henry Ramsay (1857-
    1907)
  portrait, G232

Griffen, Smith & Co., Phoenix-
    ville, Pa., D22, F42-43,
    G233, G2043, G2091, G2238-
    2239. See also Etruscan
    Majolica
Griffen, Smith & Hill Co.,
    Phoenixville, Pa., G214,
    G1588, G1758. See also
    Etruscan Majolica
Grog, G7
Groundhog Kilns. See Kilns,
    "groundhog"
Grueby Faience and Tile Co.,
    Boston, Mass., G377,
    G838, G974, G1284, G1534
Grueby Faience Co., Boston,
    Mass., G166, G377, G401,
    G838, G852, G896, G974,
    G997, G1150, G1279-1280,
    G1284, G1347, G1407,
    G1545, G1749, G1967,
    G1970, G1987, G2193
Grueby Pottery, Boston, Mass.,
    G112, G280, G377, G838,
    G852, G948, G974, G1126,
    G1545
Grueby, William Henry (1867-
    1925), G974
Grunewald & Busher. See
    Western Decorating Works
Grunewald, Frederick L., G535
    portrait, G535
Guastavino, Rafael, G179
Guernsey Earthenware Co.,
    Cambridge, Ohio, G1801
Guldin, Mahlon, Berks County,
    Pa., G1198

Haeger, David H. (d.1900),
    G58
    portrait, G58
Haeger Pottery, Dundee, Ill.,
    G58
Haig Pottery, Philadelphia,
    Pa., G239
Hall China Co., East Liver-
    pool, Ohio, A83, G59
Hamilton and Jones pottery,
    Greensboro, Pa., G1989
Hamilton family potters,
    Greensboro, Pa., G194
Hammerschmidt, William, G770
    portrait, G770

Hammerslough, Philip H., col-
    lection, G149
Hampshire Pottery (J.S. Taft),
    A127, A189, G1003
Hanlon, Bernard (ca.1748-1823),
    Trenton, N.J., G1776
Hanscom, Lena
    portrait, G1212
Hansen, Abel, G672, G749
    portrait, G672, G749
Harker, George S. (ca.1824
    1864), G818
    portrait, G818
Harker Pottery Co., East
    Liverpool, Ohio, G818
Harrison, John, G446
Harrison Log Cabin Money Bank,
    G239
Harrison Pitcher (Jersey City
    Pottery), G221, G1741
Harrisonburg Steam Pottery,
    Harrisonburg, Va., C9
Hartford Faience Co., Hartford,
    Conn., G617
Hartford Keramic Art Club,
    G1386
Hartsoe family potters,
    Lincoln County, N.C., G2047
Hatfield, Nina, G1218
    portrait, G1218
Haviland & Co., New York, N.Y.,
    F44
Hawthorne Beaker, G1915
Haydenville Mining and Manu-
    facturing Co., Haydenville,
    Ohio, G969
Haynes, D. F., & Co., Balti-
    more, Md., G122, G1034-
    1035, G1838. See also
    Chesapeake Pottery Co.
Haynes, David Francis (1835-
    1908), G1034-1035, G1795,
    G1800
Healey, Emily, G572
Healey, Mary, G572
Health conditions, pottery
    industry, E4, G1473, G1853.
    See also Lead poisoning in
    potteries; Working condi-
    tions and wages
Heatwole, John D. (1826-1907),
    Rockingham County, Va.,
    C9
Helton, John Wesley, Catawba
    County, N.C., G879
    portrait, G879

Henderson, David, Jersey City, N.J., G1549, G2219

Henne, Joseph K., Shartlesville, Pa., A45

Hennessey, Arthur Irwin, G1871

Hester, Jacob, Trenton, N.J., G1770

Hewell family potters, Georgia, G437

Hewitt, Isaac, Jr., Rices Landing, Pa., G1992
portrait, G1992

Hews Pottery, Cambridge, Mass., G1557

Hilton, Clara Maud Cobb, G38
portrait, G38

Hilton, Ernest Auburn (d.1948), North Carolina, G38, G801
portrait, G38, G801

Hilton family potters, Catawba County, N.C., G879

Hirzel, William, Rochester, N.Y., G1182

Hissong. See Hyssong

Historic Deerfield, Deerfield, Mass., G141

Histories, general, A13-17, A57, A61, A63, A81, A206-208, A233-235, A244, B25, B32, B40, B103, C32, D6, D25, G216, G252, G255, G586, G811, G1329-1330, G1856, G1858, G2321

Hoagland, Jane, G10

Hofman, Caroline, G1398

Hogged fuel, G970

Hokusai, Katsushika. Manga, G2156-2157

Holland Tunnel, G491, G533

Hollow tile, A240, G422, G677-678, G728, G1293, G1565

Holmes, Frank G., G179

Homer Laughlin China Co. See Laughlin, Homer, China Co.

Homer (N.Y.) potteries, G522, G907

Hotel china. See Commercial wares

Hotel Radison, Minn. (Teco Inn), G757

Hottinger, Gustav (1848-1929), G50-51
portrait, G51

Hound-handle pitchers, G1326, G1809

Hubbard, Elbert (1856-1915), G1098

Hughes, Albert S.
portrait, G2030

Hull Pottery Co., Crooksville, Ohio, G1041, G1291

Huntington (N.Y.) potteries, A219, G1976-1977

Hyssong, Charles S.
portrait, G1973

Hyssong, Elizah
portrait, G1196

Hyssong potteries, Bloomsburg, Pa., G1196, G1973

Hyssong potteries, Cassville, Pa., G1196

Hyten, Charles Dean (1887-1944), G1344. See also Niloak Pottery
portrait, G1007

Ice cream molds. See Molds, dessert

Illinois Clay Manufacturers' Association, G746

Illinois Clayworkers Association, G680

Illinois potteries, B55, G753, G1560. See also Chicago (Ill.) potteries; Chicago (Ill.) terra cotta companies; Galena (Ill.) potteries; Peoria (Ill.) potteries; Ripley (Ill.) potteries

Immigration of potters, G1042, G2146

Imports. See Tariffs and imports

Indian influences. See Influences, American Indian

Indian Vase (A. A. Robineau), G1899

Indiana potteries, C15. See also Pottery industry, Indiana

Indiana Pottery Co., Troy, Ind., G2089

Indianapolis Terra Cotta Co., Brightwood, Ind., G614, G618, G662, G760-761, G764

256   SUBJECT INDEX

Industrial Exposition. See
   under Exhibitions and ex-
   positions
Industry. See Pottery indus-
   try
Influences
  American Indian, G454,
     G1667, G1787
  British, D22, G800, G2239
  Chinese, C17, G339, G442,
     G576, G1903, G1979
  Egyptian, C17
  European, D1, G800, G973,
     G1667
  Greek and Roman, A248,
     G1983
  Italian, G795
  Japanese, B92, G442, G576,
     G1639, G1667, G2156
  poetic, G2190
  Swiss, A58
Inglis, Thomas, G896
Ink-blot design. See Motifs,
   Ink-blot
Inkstands and inkwells, G458,
   G1590, G1868, G1936
Insect motifs. See under
   Motifs
Insulators, porcelain. See
   Porcelain insulators
International Clay Products,
   Inc., Alhambra, Calif.,
   G523
International expositions.
   See under Exhibitions and
   expositions
Investment in pottery. See
   Pottery as an investment
Iowa potteries, G512. See
   also Fort Dodge (Iowa)
   potteries; Pottery
   industry, Iowa
Iowa State College, Depart-
   ment of Ceramic Engineer-
   ing, Ames, Iowa, E3,
   G479, G611, G629, G825
Irelan, Linna, G1012, G1423
Irvine, Sadie (1887-1970),
   G382
Italian influences. See
   under Influences
Ivory (Buffalo Pottery),
   G2081

Jackson, Andrew, letter to
   William Ellis Tucker,
   G238
Jacobus, Pauline (1840-1930),
   Chicago, Ill. and Edgerton,
   Wisc., B75, G1319, G2276
  portrait, B75, G1319
Jalan, G1004
Jalanivich, Manuel E., G1004
Jamestown (Va.) potteries,
   G188, G1290, G1676
Japanese influences. See
   under Influences
Jardinieres, F38-39, G844,
   G1811. See also Garden
   pottery
Jasperware (W. Stephen), G1873
Jeffords, J. E., & Co., Phila-
   delphia, Pa., F45
Jeppson, John, G56
  portrait, G56
Jersey City Pottery, Jersey
   City, N.J., G221, G239,
   G246, G464, G1326, G1741
Jersey Porcelain and Earthen-
   ware Co., Jersey City,
   N.J., G246
Jervis, William Percival
   (1849-1925), G855, G1019,
   G1325
  portraits, G855, G1325
Jewel work, G343
Jewelry, parian or porcelain,
   G1166, G2300
Johnson, Annette. See St.
   Gaudens, Annette Johnson
Joiner, Joseph, G2136
  portrait, G2136
Jones, Josiah (1801-1887),
   G230
  portrait, G230
Jones, McDuffee & Stratton Co.,
   Boston, Mass., A67
Jones, Morgan, Glebe Harbor,
   Va., G577, G1361
Judd, Norman L., Burlington,
   Vt., G2068
Jugs, A187, B76, G221, G822,
   G2033. See also Ollas;
   Pitchers; Sample jugs;
   Toby jugs
"Jugtown" pottery, A71, G1608,
   G1697, G2054

"Jugtown" pottery (cont'd)
  Georgia, G2054
  Illinois, B55, G1560
  New York, G1697
  North Carolina, A71, G38,
      G417, G443-445, G848-
      849, G1139, G1141,
      G1203, G1242, G1608,
      G1684, G1728-1729,
      G2301. See also North
      Carolina potteries

Kaolin (S.C.) potteries,
  G2246
Kemple family potters, East
    Amwell Township, Hunter-
    don County, N.J., B88
Kendrick, George Prentiss,
    G1150, G1749
Kennedy Pottery Co., Wilkes-
    boro, N.C., G959
Kenny, W. F., G677
Kentucky potteries. See
    Louisville (Ky.) potteries
Keramic Society of Greater
    New York, G5, G897, G967,
    G1142, G1388, G1691
Kersey, Jesse (1768-1846),
    A137
Ketcham residence, Santa
    Monica, Calif. (Roof
    tiles), G1180
Ketchum, O. W., Terra Cotta
    Co., Crum Lynne, Pa.,
    G725
Keystone Pottery, Chucky
    Valley, Washington County,
    Tenn., G434, G1592
Khayyam Pottery. See Omar
    Khayyam Pottery
Kilns, A75-77, A152-153, B37,
    F1, F29, G313, G921-922,
    G1361, G1921. See also
    Firing
  Broome's Improved, G1644
  Didier-March Tunnel Kiln,
      G387
  Dressler, G387, G942, G1288,
      G1457
  Excelsior, G129
  Fitch Charcoal Kiln, G2042
  Grath, G709
  "Groundhog," B38, E14,
      G423, G1169

Haigh, G628
Harrop Tunnel Kiln, G845,
    G1291
Harper Electric, G1031
Hawleys, F58
  Revelation, G162, G1733
  Tunnel Kilns, G472, G526,
      G944-945, G1209, G1318,
      G1662-1663, G1922, G2280
  Wilke Gasoline Kiln, G1566
  Zwermann Tunnel Kiln, G2326
Kirbee Kiln, near Montgomery,
    Texas, E14
Kirkpatrick, Cornwall (1814-
    1890), B21, D5, G1026.
    See also Anna Pottery
  portrait, G1026
Kirkpatrick, Wallace V. (1828-
    1896), Anna, Ill., B21,
    D5, G148, G1026. See also
    Anna Pottery
Knight, Maurice A., Co., East
    Akron, Ohio, G1172
Knowles, Edwin M., China Co.,
    East Liverpool, Ohio, and
    Chester and Newell, W.Va.,
    G564, G2253
Knowles, Homer H., Pottery,
    Santa Clara, Calif., G1005
Knowles, Isaac Watts (1819-
    1902), G685, G819
  portrait, G685
Knowles, Taylor & Knowles Co.,
    East Liverpool, Ohio, G13,
    G254, G854, G939, G1005,
    G1093, G1100, G1116, G1862
Koch, Fritz, Hollow Building
    Block, G683, G687
Kochs, Theodore A. Co.,
    Chicago, Ill., G2202
Koken Barber Supply Co., St.
    Louis, Mo., A199, G1843,
    G2057
Kokomo Keramic Club, G1971
Krause, George H.
  portrait, G48
Kromeich, Joseph Anthony (ca.
    1793-1838), Trenton, N.J.,
    G1771
Kurlbaum & Schwartz, Kensing-
    ton, Philadelphia, Pa.,
    G259, G1742
Kushequa (Pa.) potteries,
    G634

Labor unions, D19, G2030
Labor-Management relations,
    A154, G1363, G1620, G2030.
    See also Labor unions;
    Strikes
Lacey, George H., G1111
  portrait, G1111
Lady of the Lily Vase (Artus
    Van Briggle), G211
Lafayette jug (Jersey City
    Pottery), G246
La Fountain, Mark, collection,
    G469
Lakeware (Cowan), G424
Lamb Tavern Pottery, Trenton,
    N.J., G1768
Lamberton China (Scammell
    China Co.), B30, G1099
Lamps and Lighting fixtures,
    F100-101, G497, G836,
    G1271, G1590, G1790,
    G2113, G2166, G2212. See
    also Chandeliers
Lamson & Swasey Pottery, Port-
    land, Maine, G410
Lamson Pottery, Exeter, N.H.,
    G1475, G1682
Lancaster Iron Works, Lancas-
    ter, Pa., F46
Lancaster (Pa.) brickyards,
    G1224
Lancaster (Pa.) potteries,
    G1223
Landsun (Zane Pottery Co.),
    F100-101
Langenbeck, Karl (1861-1938),
    G65, G95, G832
  portrait, G95
Lantern (A. A. Robineau),
    G1899
Larkin Soap Co., Buffalo,
    N.Y., A3, G1098. See
    also Buffalo Pottery
Latona (Taylor, Smith &
    Taylor), G1788
Laughlin, Homer (ca.1841-1913)
  portrait, G2030
Laughlin, Homer, China Co.,
    Newell W.Va., F47, G174,
    G692, G1526, G1662,
    G2030, G2170, G2245
Laughlin, Shakespeare M.,
    F72

Lava Ware, F45
Lawson, Thomas W., residence,
    "Dreamwold," Scituate,
    Mass. (Tiles), G421
Layden, Harry
  portrait, G2030
Lead poisoning in potteries,
    E5, G1183-1184, G2084.
    See also Health conditions,
    pottery industry
Lead-glazed pottery, B3
Lee, M. J., Drain Tile Co.,
    Colfax, Ind., G628
Leidy, John, Montgomery County,
    Pa., G244
Lenox China, B49, G117, G119,
    G2080
Lenox, Inc., Trenton, N.J.,
    A5, A114-115, A199, A215,
    B30, F48, G120, G138, G179,
    G439, G447, G497, G815,
    G972, G978-979, G1043-1044,
    G1204, G1246, G1522, G1553,
    G1690, G1960, G1986, G2129,
    G2164, G2248. See also
    Ceramic Art Co.
Lenox, Walter Scott (1859-
    1920), A114-115, G117,
    G978, G1043, G1259-1260
  portraits, G1043, G1260
Leonard, Anna B., G1397-1398,
    G1846
  portrait, G1846
Le Prince, Sarah Elizabeth,
    G1493, G1846
  portraits, G1493, G1846
Lewis, Edward Gardner, G990
Lewis, H. A. (Boston Architec-
    tural Terra Cotta Works),
    F19
Lewistown (Pa.) potteries,
    G1196
Leykauf, George, G1748
  portrait, G1748
Library of Congress, Washing-
    ton, D.C. (Mosaics), G1050
Lighting fixtures. See Lamps
    and lighting fixtures
Limerick Pottery, Neiffer,
    Pa., G2256
Lincoln, Abraham, commemorative
    terra cottas at University
    of Illinois, G715
Linderoth, Sven, G407, G1365
  portrait, G407
Link, Christian, Stonetown
    Village, Pa., G1198

Lithophanes, G232, G1262
Loeb, Sophie Irene
  portrait, G1520
Lombard Brick and Tile Co.,
  Lombard, Ill., G770
Lombardic Mosaic (American
  Encaustic Tiling Co.),
  F3
London International Exposi-
  tion. See under Exhibi-
  tions and expositions
Lorelei Vase (Artus Van
  Briggle), G211, G1465
Lorimer, George Burford col-
  lection, G2002
Los Angeles City Hall (Tiles),
  G2304
Los Angeles Pressed Brick Co.,
  Alberhill, Los Angeles,
  and Santa Monica, Calif.,
  G678
Losanti Ware (M. L. McLaugh-
  lin), G69, G1551-1552,
  G1610, G1984
Lotus Ware (Knowles, Taylor
  & Knowles Co.), D16, G13,
  G819, G939, G1093, G1100,
  G1862
Louisiana Purchase Exposition.
  See under Exhibitions and
  expositions
Louisville (Ky.) potteries,
  G684
Louisville Pottery Co.,
  Louisville, Ky., G703,
  G1487
Lovejoy, Ellis (1860-?), G95
  portrait, G95
Low Art Tile Works, Chelsea,
  Mass., A75, A77, G887,
  G1596, G1632-1641, G1643-
  1645, G1981-1982, G2220
Low family potters, Chelsea,
  Mass., G1641
Low, J. and J. G., Chelsea,
  Mass., F49
Low, J. G. and J. F., Chel-
  sea, Mass., F50
Low, John Farnsworth, F49-51
  portrait, G1641
Low, John Gardner (1835-1907),
  F49-F51, G1596, G1609,
  G1636-1638, G1640, G1982,
  G2220
  portraits, G1637, G1640-
  1641

Lowestoft (Mercer), F52
Loy-Nel-Art vases, G1002
Ludowici-Celadon Roofing Tile
  Co., Alfred, N.Y., Chicago
  Heights, Ill., Ludowici,
  Ga., New Lexington, Ohio,
  G338, G609, G641, G663
Lumbard, Nina E., G542
  portrait, G542
Lumber, terra cotta. See
  Terra cotta, lumber
Lunaware (Buffalo Pottery),
  G2081
Lustre ware, G2123
Lycett, Edward C., New York
  and Atlanta, Ga., G235,
  G247-250, G1535
  portraits, G247, G249-250
Lycett family china painters,
  G250, G1535
Lycett, William, Atlanta, Ga.
  G1535
Lyle, William, Rochester, N.Y.,
  G1182
Lyndeboro (N.H.) potteries,
  G435

McAfee, W. Keith
  portrait, G1537
McAlpin Hotel, New York,
  N.Y. (Tiles), G689, G705
McBean, Athol(1), G79
  portrait, G79
McBean, Peter McGil(1) (1844-
  1922), G79, G736
McCoy, J. W., Pottery Co.,
  Roseville, Ohio, A118-119,
  G664, G1002, G1811
McCoy, Nelson, Putman and
  Zanesville, Ohio, A65-66,
  A119
"McCoy" pottery, A65-66, A118-
  119, G1002
McCully family potters, Tren-
  ton, N.J., G1772
McCully, John Stiles, Trenton,
  N.J., G1769
  portrait, G1769
McCully, Joseph, Trenton, N.J.,
  B83, G1768
McCully, Joseph II, Trenton,
  N.J., G1769

260   SUBJECT INDEX

McCully Pottery, Trenton,
    N.J., G1768
McDade Pottery, near Austin,
    Tex., G1302
Machinery and equipment, A59,
    A70, A75-77, A96, A153,
    E13, F1, F21, F24-25, F46,
    F61, G677, G1781-1783,
    G2229. See also Clay
    dryers; Frit furnaces;
    Kilns; Potter's wheels;
    Saggers; Seger cones;
    Tools
McKearin, George S., collec-
    tion, C16
McLaughlin, Mary Louise (1847-
    1939), C5, G28, G69, G219,
    G582, G1001, G1187, G1408,
    G1550-1552, G1578, G1610,
    G1734, G1984
  portraits, G582, G1187,
    G1610
McNicol, D. E., Pottery Co.,
    Clarksburg, W.Va., G2249
McQuate, Henry, Myerstown,
    Lebanon County, Pa.,
    G1462
  portrait, 1462
Maddock, Archibald M. (ca.
    1856-1910), G1829
  portrait, G1829
Maddock, John (1848-1938),
    G63
Maddock Pottery Co., Trenton,
    N.J., G1099
Maddock, Thomas (1818-1899),
    G94
Maddock, Thomas & Sons Co.,
    Trenton, N.J., G439, G527,
    G2165
Madison (N.J.) potteries,
    G2040
Maine potteries, A42-43,
    G1335, G2194. See also
    Farmingdale (Me.) pot-
    teries; Gardiner (Me.)
    potteries
Majolica, B53, F42-43, G427,
    G1034-1035, G1037, G1474,
    G1724, G1775, G1855,
    G1905, G2267, G2278-2279,
    G2291. See also Etruscan
    Majolica
Mantels, F17, F71, F90-91,
    G421, G909, G981
Manufacture. See Production
    and manufacture

Maratta, Hardesty Gillmore,
    G1053
Marblehead Pottery, Marble-
    head, Mass., G169, G982,
    G1128, G1179, G1189,
    G1398, G1558, G1972
Markham, Herman C., Ann Arbor,
    Mich., G1320
Markham Pottery, Ann Arbor,
    Mich., G1320
Marks, A22, A166, A206-208,
    A233-235, G1353
  decorators', A10-12, A111,
    A120, A140, A142, G263,
    G943, G1006
  potters', A10-17, A42-43,
    A46, A88, A100, A111,
    A125, A140, A142, A149-
    150, A178, A180, A215,
    A241, B43
Marsh, Fred Dana, designs for
    tiles, McAlpin Hotel, G689,
    G705
Marsh, R. A., residence, Los
    Angeles, Calif., (Roof
    tiles), G1180
Maryland potteries, B67-68,
    C20. See also Baltimore
    (Md.) potteries; Shenan-
    doah Valley potteries
Maryland Terra Cotta Co.,
    Baltimore, Md., G696,
    G1501
Mason, Elizabeth, G1396,
    G1398, G1847
  portrait, G1847
Mason, Maud M., G1142, G1382,
    G1391, G1396-1398, G1533,
    G1847, G1945
  design class, G1569
  portraits, G1847, G1945
Mason, William A.
  portrait, G1573
Massachusetts potteries. See
    Ashfield (Mass.) potteries;
    Danvers (Mass.) potteries;
    North Orange (Mass.) pot-
    teries; Peabody (Mass.)
    potteries; Pottersville
    (Mass.) potteries; Somer-
    set (Mass.) potteries;
    South Ashfield (Mass.)
    potteries; Sterling (Mass.)
    potteries; Whately (Mass.)
    potteries
Mathiasen, Karl (1860-1920), G724
  portrait, G724

Mayer, Ernest (1857-?), G95
  portrait, G95
Mayer, Joseph (ca.1849-1930),
  G64
  portrait, G64
Mead, Abraham, Greenwich,
  Conn., G2101
Mead, Henry, G2181
Meaders, Cheever, Cleveland,
  Ga., G813
  portraits, G813
Meaders family potters, Mossy
  Creek, Ga., C12, G834
Meaders, Lanier (1917-   ),
  B13
Mear, Frederick, East Boston,
  Mass., G1102
Meat tenderizers, G1590
Mechanization in potteries,
  G2170
Medals with potter-at-the-
  wheel motif, G1014
Medinger family potters,
  Neiffer, Montgomery
  County, Pa., G2255
Medinger, Jacob (1856-1932),
  Neiffer, Montgomery
  County, Pa., B96, G1886,
  G2255-2256
  portraits, G1886, G2256
Medinger, William S., Mont-
  gomery County, Pa., G1886
Mehwaldt, Charles August,
  Bergholtz, N.Y., G458
Meiere, Hildreth, G1489
Memorial wreaths. See
  Wreaths, memorial
Menzel, Earl
  portrait, G1212
Mercer, Henry Chapman (1856-
  1930), A25, A47-48, A167-
  168, B70, G182-183, G286,
  G378, G431, G794, G796,
  G896, G950, G1051, G1175,
  G1247, G1277, G1642,
  G1759, G1994, G2086,
  G2097, G2247. See also
  Moravian Pottery and Tile
  Works
  portraits, A48, G431, G794,
  G950, G2247
Mercer Museum, A48
Mercer Pottery Co., Trenton,
  N.J., F52, G2161
Merrimac Pottery, Newburyport
  Mass., G1342, G1983, G2127

Methods of production. See
  Production and manufacture
Metropolitan Museum of Art,
  New York, N.Y., G177,
  G478, G494, G1141, G1809,
  G1823
Meyer family potters, Atascosa,
  Tex., A101
Meyer, Joseph Fortuné (1848-
  1931)
  portrait, G828
Miami Pottery (Society of
  Arts and Crafts, Dayton,
  Ohio), G1421
Miami Tile and Marble Co.,
  Miami, Fla., G2121
Michigan potteries. See
  Grand Ledge (Mich.) pot-
  teries
Mid-Atlantic potteries, B62
Middle Lane Pottery, East
  Hampton, L.I., N.Y., G846,
  G999. See also Brouwer,
  Theophilus Anthony, Jr.
Middleton, Matilda, G291
Mid-West potteries, G142
Milk coolers, G635
Miller, William J. (1876-?),
  G91
  portrait, G91
Mills, Elizabeth Bennett
  (d.1910), G2016
Millville Pottery, Concord,
  N.H., G1039
Milwaukee (Wisc.) potteries,
  G471
Mineral Art League, Boston,
  G158
Minerva mosaic (E. Vedder),
  G1050
Miniature pottery, G462, G1299,
  G1446, G1774, G1824. See
  also Tea sets, toy
Minneapolis Keramic Art Club,
  G1411
Minnesota potteries, G2046.
  See also New Ulm (Minn.)
  potteries; Red Wing (Minn.)
  potteries
Minnesota Stoneware Co.,
  Redwing, Minn., A253-254
Minton, LeRoy H. (1882-1931),
  G552, G733
  portraits, G552, G733, G1670
Mirror Ware (Zane Pottery Co.),
  F100-101

Mississippi potteries, C26
Missoula Brick and Sewer Pipe
     Works, Missoula, Mont.,
     G1720
Missouri potteries, G2176
Molds, G222, G312
  cake, B80, G786
  candles, G266
  cookie, G1936
  dessert, B80, G266, G786
  fish, G1271
  jelly, B80
  jugs, G822
Monitor China (E. Lycett),
  G235
Montclair Art Museum, Mont-
     clair, N.J., G500
Moravian potteries
  at Bethlehem, Pa., A91,
     G1689
  at Winston-Salem, N.C.,
     A37, B9, B69, G987,
     G1075, G1082. See also
     Salem (N.C.) potteries
Moravian Pottery and Tile
     Works, Doylestown, Pa.,
     A25, A48, A78, A167-168,
     B70, F53-57, G167, G182-
     183, G378, G794, G796,
     G837, G899, G909, G1051,
     G1086, G1137, G1175,
     G1247, G1307, G1412,
     G1580, G1642, G1759,
     G2128. See also Mercer,
  Henry Chapman
Morgan, A. R. Co., New York,
     N.Y., F58
Morgan Belleek China Co.,
     Canton, Ohio, G1563
Morgantown (W.Va.) potteries,
     E9, G193, G1276, G2298
Morris, John T., collection,
     G1739
Morton, John, Trenton, N.J.,
     G1770
Mosaic Tile Co., Zanesville,
     Ohio, A265, C36, F59,
     G217, G237, G1439, G1648,
     G2294
Moses, Howard B. (1866-?),
     G858
Moses, John
  portrait, B61
Moss Aztec (Zane Pottery Co.),
     F100-101

Motifs. See also Decoration
     of pottery; Design; Influ-
     ences
  bird, G290, G1217
  Cupid and Psyche, G1449
  flower, A90, A133
     cornflower, G1754
     daisies, A87, G2026
     forget-Me-Not, A87
     poppy, G1948
     rose, A87, A129, A136,
        G1219
     sunflower, G1643
     tulip, G1952
     violet, G1719
     wild rose, A87
  fruit, A134
  ink-blot, G1453
  insect
     cicada, G1084
  "Rebekah-at-the-Well," G588-
     591, G1094
Mount Clemens Pottery Co.,
     Mount Clemens, Mich.,
     G1209, G1318
Mount Shepherd Pottery, near
     Asheboro, Randolph County,
     N.C., G2257
Moyer, William, Pottery,
     Harrisburg, Pa., G1195
Mueller, Herman Carl (1854-
     1941), C36, G55, G95, G782
  portraits, G55, G95, G782,
        G1647, G1649, G1651-1654
Mueller Mosaic Co., Trenton,
     N.J., C36, F60, G489,
     G525, G624, G649, G2159
Mugs, B76, G1013, G1454, G2033.
     See also Cups; Steins
  frog, G1026
  shaving. See Shaving mugs
  Sunbonnet Babies, G574
Museum of Art, Ogunquit,
     Maine, G1261
Museum of Contemporary Crafts,
     G930
Mycenean Ware (D. F. Haynes
     & Co.), G122

Napoleon at the Burning of
     Moscow (Tucker), G149
National Arts Club, G1413-1414

National Brotherhood of Oper-
ative Potters, A82, A154,
D19, G121, G124, G612,
G738, G1473, G2030
National Drain Tile Co.,
Summittville, Ind., G756
National League of Mineral
Painters, G159, G370,
G835, G867, G1305, G1381,
G1389, G1415, G1615,
G1717, G1750-1753
National Museum of History
and Technology (Smith-
sonian Museum), C33, G2221
National Sewer Pipe Co.,
Barberton, Ohio, G674
National Society of Crafts-
men, Ceramic Guild, G1384,
G1391
Nebraska State Capitol (Tiles),
G1489
New England potteries, A257-
259, B22, B26, B56, G937,
G955, G1679, G2074,.
G2217-2218, G2221
New Erection Pottery, Harri-
sonburg, Va., C9
New Geneva (Pa.) potteries,
A102-103, A221, E16, G1,
G191, G195-196, G1314,
G1590-1591, G1990-1991
New Hampshire potteries, B102,
G2223. See also Exeter
(N.H.) potteries; Lynde-
boro (N.H.) potteries
New Jersey Ceramic Research
Station, G87
New Jersey Clay Workers'
Association, A177, G496,
G501-504, G509, G549-550,
G557-560, G566, G711-714,
G783, G1599, G1670
New Jersey Porcelain and
Earthenware Co., Bergen,
N.J., B30
New Jersey potteries, A22,
A60, A64, A178, B51, B98,
C34, C37-38, C40-42, G486,
G500, G505, G789, G1311,
G1657, G1659, G2179. See
also Bloomsbury, Trenton
(N.J.) potteries; Cheese-
quake (N.J.) potteries,
Elizabethtown (N.J) pot-
teries; Madison (N.J.)
potteries; Old Bridge
(N.J.) potteries; South
Amboy (N.J.) potteries;
Trenton (N.J.) potteries;
Pottery industry, New
Jersey
New Jersey State Museum, Tren-
ton, N.J., C47, G1604
New Lexington High Voltage
Porcelain Co., New Lexing-
ton, Ohio, G690
New Orleans Art Pottery Club,
G828
New Ulm (Minn.) potteries, D21
New York and New Jersey Clay
Products, Inc., South
River (Sayreville), N.J.,
G677
New York Architectural Terra
Cotta Co., Long Island
City, N.Y., G1309, G2137
New York Blower Co., Bucyrus,
Ohio, and Chicago, Ill.,
F61
New York City (N.Y.) potteries,
B34-36, G1445, G2180,
G2281
New York Society of Keramic
Arts, G10, G160-161, G163,
G350, G966, G1142, G1220,
G1313, G1382, G1392-1394,
G1396, G1398, G1416-1417,
G1493, G1533, G1570
New York State potteries,
A138, B41, C30, C49, G570-
571, G2011, G2262. See
also Albany (N.Y.) potter-
ies; Athens (N.Y.) potter-
ies; Brooklyn (N.Y.) pot-
teries; Buffalo (N.Y.)
potteries; Cortland (N.Y.)
potteries; Homer (N.Y.)
potteries; Huntington (N.
Y.) potteries; New York
City (N.Y.) potteries;
Poughkeepsie (N.Y.) pot-
teries; Rochester (N.Y.)
potteries; Utica (N.Y.)
potteries; Pottery indus-
try, New York State
Onondago County, C10, G475
Ontario County, B41, C49
Wayne County, B41, C49
New York State School of Clay-
Working and Ceramics,
Alfred University, Alfred,
N.Y., A182, G303, G328-329,

New York State School of Clay-
    Working and Ceramics
    (Cont'd)
    G349, G521, G679, G716,
    G1088
  summer school, G1429-1430,
    G1432
Newark Museum, Newark, N.J.,
    G505, G789, G1311, G1657,
    G1805
Newark (N.J.) School of Fine
    and Industrial Arts, G485
Newark Society of Keramic
    Arts, G904-906, G971,
    G1070, G1399, G1418,
    G1541-1542, G2173
Newcomb Pottery, H. Sophie
    Newcomb Memorial College,
    Tulane University, New
    Orleans, La., A185, D10,
    D24, G155, G200, G283,
    G379, G382, G428, G829,
    G831, G868, G896, G1006,
    G1054, G1129, G1154,
    G1229, G1282, G1303,
    G1409, G1419, G1956-1957,
    G1978, G2017-2019, G2038,
    G2050, G2309, G2311
Newton, Clara Chipman (1848-
    1936), G36, G69
  portrait, G69
Nichols & Alford, Burlington,
    Vt., G2068
Nichols, Maria Longworth
    (later Storer), G72, G953,
    G1038, G1215, G1405,
    G1456, G1734, G2156. See
    also Rookwood Pottery
  portraits, G582, G1033,
        G1038, G1215, G1547,
    G1734
Nickerson, Thomas S., G1342,
    G1983. See also Merrimac
    Pottery
Niloak Pottery, Benton, Ark.,
    F62-63, G399, G1007,
    G1344, G1589
Nineteenth-century pottery,
    A33, A38, A109, A117,
    A145-147, A155, A178, B14,
    B17, B32, B61, C5, C39,
    C52, D3, D11-12, G266,
    G471, G793. See also
    Victorian ceramics; His-
    tories, general

Noble, W. Clark. Mary Baker
    Eddy medallion (Grueby),
    G1534
Nonconnah Pottery, Skyland,
    N.C., and Shelby County
    near Memphis, Tenn., C24,
    G1346, G1873. See also
    Stephen, Walter Benjamin
North American Manufacturing
    Co., Newell, W.Va., G719
North Carolina potteries, A37,
    A68, A71, A225, B18, B104,
    C23, G38, G585, G801, G813,
    G959, G1205, G1452, G1627,
    G1728, G1730. See also
    Bethabara (N.C.) potteries;
    Jugtown pottery, North
    Carolina; Pottery industry,
    North Carolina; Salem
    (N.C.) potteries
  Moore County, A71
  Union County, D7
North Carolina State University,
    Department of Ceramic En-
    gineering, Raleigh, N.C.
    G958
North Dakota School of Mines.
    See University of North
    Dakota, School of Mines
North Orange (Mass.) potteries,
    G406
North Star Stoneware Co., Red
    Wing, Minn., A254
North State Pottery, Sanford,
    N.C., A226, F64, F66-68,
    G720
Northwest Architectural Ar-
    chives, University of
    Minnesota, A98
Northwestern Terra Cotta Works,
    Chicago, Ill., F69, G598-
    599, G619, G646, G701, G721-
    722, G743, G1118, G1309,
    G2048
Norton & Fenton pottery, Ben-
    nington, Vt. See Benning-
    ton (Vt.) potteries
Norton, F. B., Pottery, Wor-
    cester, Mass., C56, G56
Norton, Julius, Bennington,
    Vt., G1665
  portrait, 1665
Norton potteries, Bennington,
    Vt. See Bennington (Vt.)
    potteries

Norwalk (Conn.) potteries,
    G2292-2293
Norwich Pottery, Norwich,
    Conn., G151, G2178

Occupational shaving mugs.
    See Shaving mugs, occupa-
    tional
Oconee Clay Products Co.,
    Milledgeville, Ga., G2299
Odell & Booth Brothers, Tarry-
    town, N.Y., G1364
O'Hara, Dorothea Warren,
    G1142, G1385, G1391,
    G1398, G1538, G1668,
    G1946, G1964
  portrait, 1946
Ohio Ceramic Industries Assoc-
    iation, G561
Ohio potteries, A1, A150, B15,
    E35, G1359, G1463, G1597,
    G1814, G2093, G2232. See
    also Cincinnati (Ohio)
    potteries; East Liverpool
    (Ohio) potteries; Point
    Pleasant (Ohio) potteries;
    Sebring (Ohio) potteries;
    Zanesville (Ohio) potter-
    ies; Pottery industry,
    Ohio
  Hocking County, G793
  Jackson County, B60
  Muskingum County, G1124,
    G1463
  Stark County, A155
  Summit County, A38
  Vinton County, G793
Ohio Pottery, Zanesville,
    Ohio, G998
Ohio State University, School
    for Ceramics, Columbus,
    Ohio, G37, G646, G735,
    G806, G1711-1713
Ohio Valley Clay Co., Steuben-
    ville, Ohio, G1288
Ohr, George E. (1857-1918),
    A39, B16, C25, G137, G285,
    G584, G829, G1304, G1470,
    G1491, G1692, G2036,
    G2044, G2199
  portraits, G137, G584, G828-
    829, G1304, G1692, G2199

Oklahoma Agricultural and
    Mechanical College, Still-
    water, Okla., (College
    Pottery), G2055
Old Bridge (N.J.) potteries,
    B81
Old Sturbridge Village, G2074
Olive Jar (S. Frackleton),
    G583
Ollas, G785
Olsen, Ingvardt, G1004
Omar Khayyam Pottery, Luther,
    Buncombe County, N.C., G38,
    G459, G801, G1345. See
    also Bachelder, Oscar
    Lewis
Ombroso Ware (Rookwood), G168
Onondago Pottery Clay Shop
    Elementary Apprentice
    Training School, G1725
Onondago Pottery Co., Syracuse,
    N.Y., B30, G815, G1416
Orchard Potteries, Cornish,
    G470. See also St. Gaudens,
    Paul
Orcutt & Crafts Pottery, Port-
    land, Maine, G411
Oriental influences. See
    Influences, Chinese; Influ-
    ences, Japanese
Orton, Edward, Jr. (1863-1932),
    E19, G40, G46, G74-75, G87,
    G95, G101, G488, G550,
    G554, G669-670
  Portraits, E19, G46, G75,
    G87, G95, G101, G488, G550,
    G554, G670, G1707, G1713
Orton, Edward, Sr. (1829-1899),
    G741
Osborn family potters, New
    Hampshire, G1585-1586
Osborne, Arthur, G1596, G1630-
    1631
Osbourne Pottery, Gonic, N.H.,
    G1683
Osgood Art School, New York,
    N.Y., A186, F70
Osgood, (Mrs.) Worth, G1848
  portrait, G1848
Otis & Gorsline, Rochester,
    N.Y., G1182
Ott & Brewer, Trenton, N.J.,
    B103, C35, F95, G419, G1605,
    G1764
Ouachita Pottery, Hot Springs,
    Ark., G1008

Overbeck, Elizabeth Gray
    (1875-1936), A197, G41
  portraits, G41, G76
Overbeck, Hannah B. (1870-
    1931), A197
Overbeck, Margaret (1863-1911),
    A197
Overbeck, Mary Frances (1878-
    1955), A197
  portrait, G76
Overbeck Pottery, Cambridge
    City, Ind., A197, G76,
    G1779
Owen China Company, Minerva,
    Ohio, G1017
Oyster plates, G1755

Pacific Clay Products Co.,
    Los Angeles, Calif., G785
Paige, M. B., Pottery, Pea-
    body, Mass., G450
Paist, Henrietta Barclay,
    G1394
Palestine Pottery, F32
Palm, Fechteler & Co., New
    York, N.Y., G108
Pamplin Smoking Pipe and
    Manufacturing Co., Pam-
    plin, Va., G1186
Pamplin (Va.) potteries,
    G1186
Panama-Pacific International
    Exposition. See under
    Exhibitions and exposi-
    tions
Pan-American Exposition. See
    under Exhibitions and ex-
    positions
Pardee, C., Tile Co., Perth
    Amboy, N.J., G1440, G1715
Pardee-Matawan Tile Co.,
    Perth Amboy and Matawan,
    N.J., G1433
Parian, B53, G446, G1160-1166,
    G1499, G2144, G2288
Paris International Exposi-
    tions. See under Exhibi-
    tions and expositions
Parmelee, Cullen Warner (1874-
    1947), G39, G682
  portrait, G682
Pass, James (1856-1913), G95,
    G1726, G1804
  portrait, G95

Passmore Pottery, Passmore,
    Berks County, Pa., A33,
    G123
Pastoral Vase (A. Robineau),
    C43, G1899, G1942
Patent medicine bottles, G1655
Pâte-sur-Pâte, G1892-1894
Patina (Clifton Art Pottery),
    G1787
Patterson, J. B., Fire Clay
    Ware Manufacturers, Potts-
    ville, Pa., G1199
Paul Revere Pottery, Boston,
    Mass., and Brighton, Mass.,
    G152-153, G380, G548, G1190,
    G1284-1285, G1678, G1738,
    G1763, G1974-1975, G2095,
    G2318. See also Saturday
    Evening Girls
  School of Ceramic Art, G152
Pauline Pottery, Chicago, Ill.,
    and Edgerton, Wisc., B75,
    G1319, G2276
Peabody (Mass.) potteries,
    G1559
Peacock, Emily F., G1395
Pencil leads, G181
Pennsylvania Academy of Fine
    Arts Clay-working Depart-
    ment, G1507
Pennsylvania Capitol Building,
    Harrisburg, Pa., A167-168,
    G286, G1247
Pennsylvania Museum. See also
    Philadelphia Museum of Art
  School of Industrial Art,
    G841-842, G873, G1528,
    G2189
Pennsylvania potteries, A58,
    A145-147, A198, B50, G292,
    G1614, G2082. See also
    Bethlehem (Pa.) potteries;
    Bloomsburg (Pa.) potteries;
    East Birmingham (Pa.) pot-
    teries; Greensboro (Pa.)
    potteries; Kushequa (Pa.)
    potteries; Lancaster (Pa.)
    potteries; Lewistown (Pa.)
    potteries; New Geneva (Pa.)
    potteries; Philadelphia
    (Pa.) potteries; Phoenix-
    ville (Pa.) potteries; Pot-
    tery industry, Pennsylvania;
    Pottsville (Pa.) potteries;
    Shenandoah Valley potteries;
    Waynesboro (Pa.) potteries;

Pennsylvania potteries (cont'd)
    Moravian potteries, at
    Bethlehem, Pa.
  Berks County, A45, G1198,
      G1883, G1887
  Bucks County, G1994
  Chester County, A123-124,
    B72, G201
  Clinton County, A228
  Fayette County, B57
  Greene County, B57
  Washington County, B57
Pennsylvania-German potteries,
    A18-21, B50, B89, B95,
    B97, C44, G139, G220,
    G234, G240-241, G244,
    G908, G954, G960, G1096,
    G1235, G1528, G1581-1582,
    G1587, G1616-1618, G1664,
    G1756, G1823, G1842,
    G1883, G1887-1889, G2002,
    G2088, G2096, G2102,
    G2302
People's University, Ceramic
    Division, University City,
    St. Louis, Mo., G990,
    G1422, G1469
Peoria (Ill.) potteries, G1962
Peoria Pottery Co., Peoria,
    Ill., G938, G1962
Pereco (Zane Pottery Co.),
    F100-101
Perkins, Annie F., G578, G792
Perkins, Lucie Fairfield,
    G578, G792, G2127
Perry, Mary Chase. See
    Stratton, Mary Chase Perry
Perth Amboy Terra Cotta Co.,
    Perth Amboy, N.J., A247,
    F71, G1117, G1510, G1687,
    G2048, G2127, G2134
Peters and Reed Pottery, South
    Zanesville, Ohio, G1340
Petruscan artware (Ohio Pot-
    tery), G998
Pewabic Pottery, Detroit,
    Mich., A40, A46, A112,
    A190, A192, B11, G1040,
    G1221, G1257, G1471,
    G1530, G1732-1733, G1761,
    G2106. See also Stratton,
    Mary Chase Perry
Pfaltzgraff Pottery, York,
    Pa., G1197
Philadelphia China and Tile
    Works, Philadelphia, Pa.,
    F72

Philadelphia City Pottery,
    Philadelphia, Pa., F45
Philadelphia Museum of Art,
    G1322, G1739. See also
    Pennsylvania Museum
  Barber, E. A., collection of
    American pottery and por-
    celain, C44
  terra cotta decoration, G530,
    G2062
Philadelphia (Pa.) potteries,
    B67-68, D11, E18, G956,
    G1121
Phillips, (Mrs.) Vance, Chau-
    tauqua, N.Y., G1375
Phoebe West Pitcher (Tucker),
    G149
Phoenixville majolica. See
    Etruscan Majolica
Phoenixville (Pa.) potteries,
    G214, G232-233, G1262
Pickard china, Chicago, Ill.,
    A195, G2052, G2109, G2153
Pickard, Henry Austin (1902-
    1966), A195
Pickard, W. A., Studios, Ravens-
    wood, Chicago, Ill., G2109.
    See also Pickard china
Pickard, Wilder Austin (1857-
    1939), A195, G2153
Pickling crocks, G1271
Pine Cone (Roseville Pottery
    Co.), G1995
Pipes
  drainage. See Tiles, drainage
  sewer. See Sewer pipes
  smoking. See Tobacco pipes
  water. See Water pipes
Pisgah Forest Pottery, Arden,
    N.C., C24, G38, G1346,
    G1873. See also Stephen,
    Walter Benjamin
Pistols, G412
Pitchers, B82, G2226. See
    also Hound-handle pitchers;
    Jugs
Pitkin, Albert Hastings, col-
    lection, A193
Pittsburgh Clay Pot Co., Pitts-
    burgh, Pa., G691
Plastic Sketches (A. Osborne,
    Low), F49, F51, G1631
Plates. See Calendar plates;
    Dinnerware; Presidential
    campaign souvenirs, Cam-
    paign plates; Oyster plates

Plumbing fixtures. See Sanitary wares
Plumbism. See Lead poisoning
Poetic influences on pottery decoration, G2190
Poetry about clays and pottery, A227, C40, G952, G1323, G1957, G2022
Poillon, Clara L. (1850-1936), Woodbridge, N.J., G107, G784, G857, G2127
Poillon Pottery, Woodbridge, N.J., G1675
Point Pleasant (Ohio) potteries, B91, G1222, G2147
Pollard Clay Co., Burnsville, N.C., G556
Pomona Tile Manufacturing Co., Pomona, Calif., G946
Poole, Joshua (d.1928), G819, portrait, G819
Poor, Henry Varnum (1888-1971), G461, G798, G1176
"Poor Potter" of Yorktown, Va., B4, E37, E40, G1289
Pope Pius IX (I. Broome), G1499
Pope-Gosser Co., Coshocton, Ohio, G1800
Poppy (Steubenville Pottery), G1798
Poppy vase (A. Robineau), G1294, G1942
Porcelain, A62, A80, A139, A196, A224, B10, C39, C47, F98, G352, G917, G921, G1021, G1116, G1298, G1604, G1802, G1815, G1942, G1954, G2181. See also Belleek; Grand feu wares; Parian
  insulators, G2231
  painting. See China painting
  translucency of, E21
Porcelain League, Cincinnati, Ohio, G60, G80, G1674
Potters' Joint Stock Emigration Society and Savings Fund, G1042
Potters' marks. See Marks, potters'
Potter's wheels, G1323, G2186
  use of, G309
Pottersville (Mass.) potteries, G267

Pottersville (Wisc.) potteries, G1042
Pottery and clay products
  value of, E17, G514, G637-639, G732, G739, G775, G2005, G2010, G2168
Pottery industry, A84, A154, A156, A165-166, A179, A212, B58, B61, D20, E20, E25, G113, G252, G255, G332, G387, G439, G586, G1621 G1698, G1777, G1844, G1924, G2009, G2105
  Arkansas, G416
  Connecticut, E13. See also Connecticut potteries
  Georgia, E15. See also Georgia potteries
  Indiana, G621-623. See also Indiana potteries
  Iowa, E43, G823-824. See also Iowa potteries
  New Jersey, B19, C38, E27, G1600, G1657. See also New Jersey potteries
  New York State, G1584, G1930. See also New York State potteries
  North Carolina, E23, G951-952, G1156. See also North Carolina potteries
  Ohio, A155, B60, E35, G1703-1706, G2031, G2232-2233. See also Ohio potteries
  Oklahoma, E33
  Pennsylvania, E6-8, E29. See also Pennsylvania potteries
  Tennessee, G777, G2270-2273. See also Tennessee potteries
  Texas, E22. See also Texas potteries
  Wisconsin, E2. See also Wisconsin potteries
Pottery as an investment, G1136, G2076
Pottery Club of Cincinnati. See Cincinnati Pottery Club
Pottsville (Pa.) potteries, G1199
Poughkeepsie (N.Y.) potteries, G1697, G1841, G1890
Powder Valley (Pa.) Pottery. See Stahl's Powder Valley Pottery

Presidential ceramics
  campaign souvenirs,
      Harrison campaign, G221,
        G239, G1741
     plates, G2023
  china (White House), A5,
     B49, F44, G138, G1246,
     G1368, G2129
  commemorative,
     Lincoln, G715
     Washington, G246, G492,
     G1644
Price guides, A23, A102-104,
  A126, A215, A256
Price (Mrs.) S. Evannah, G965
Prince of Wales vases (Ben-
  nington), G1159
Production and manufacture,
  A34-36, A70, A75-77, A80,
  A96, A100, A109, A114-115,
  A144, A153, A166, A196,
  A198, A211, A218, A246,
  A260, A263, B44, B65, E3,
  E11, E13, F1, F23, F29,
  G174, G304-315, G351,
  G353, G355, G363, G395,
  G439, G677, G777, G831,
  G856, G877, G913-929,
  G1090-1091, G1138, G1205,
  G1343, G1349, G1458,
  G1551, G1596, G1603,
  G1682, G1803, G1842,
  G1889, G2037, G2051,
  G2170, G2172, G2188,
  G2208-2209, G2234, G2245
Profession of ceramics, G1598.
  See also Education for
  ceramics and clayworking
Providence Pottery, South
  Amboy, N.J., G412
Pruden, Keen, Elizabethtown,
  N.J., G1300
Purdy, Ross Coffin (1875-
  1949), G84-85, G517, G603
  portraits, G84-85, G517,
    G603, G699

Radford, Albert (1862-1904),
  A205
Radford, A., Pottery, Tifflin
  and Zanesville, Ohio, and
  Clarksburg, W.Va., A205
Ramsay, Barnet, Linn County,
  Ore., G1211

Randall, Theodore Amasa (1857-
  1926), G14, G92, G1866
  portraits, G14, G1866
Raymond, C. W., Clay Machinery
  Co., Dayton, Ohio, G710
"Rebekah-at-the-Well" teapots,
  G588-591, G1094
Red Wing (Minn.) potteries,
  A180, A253-254, G935
Red Wing Potteries, Inc., Red
  Wing, Minn., A253
Red Wing Sewer Pipe Co., Red
  Wing, Minn., A254
Red Wing Stoneware Co., Red
  Wing, Minn., A253-254,
  G2046
Red Wing Union Stoneware Co.,
  Red Wing, Minn., A253
Redlands Art Pottery, Redlands,
  Calif., G1009
Redware, A139, A245, E31, G940,
  G1272, G1864, G1937, G1998
  New England, G2218
  New Jersey, E31
  Pennsylvania, G1936, G2312
Reidinger and Caire, Pough-
  keepsie, N.Y., G1841
Reinhardt family potters, North
  Carolina, G2003
Rekston Ware (Stockton Art Pot-
  tery), G1015
Remensnyder, John Paul, collec-
  tion, C33
Remmey family potters, New York,
  N.Y., G1875
Remmey family potters, Phila-
  delphia, Pa., G1876
Remmey, Henry (ca.1770-?),
  Philadelphia, Pa., G1876
Remmey, Henry Harrison (1794-?)
  Baltimore, Md. & Philadel-
  phia, Pa., G1876
Remmey, John, New York, N.Y.,
  G1879
Remmey, Joseph Henry, South
  Amboy, N.J., G1877
Remmey, Richard C., & Son,
  Philadelphia, Pa., G1509
Remmey, Richard Clinton, Phila-
  delphia, Pa., G1876
Remmey ware, New York City,
  N.Y., G2180
Repair of ceramics, G1686,
  G1918. See also Architec-
  tural terra cotta, restor-
  ation

Revere, Paul, Pottery. See
    Paul Revere Pottery
Rhead, Frederick Hurten (1880-
    1942), G45, G78, G827
  portraits, G45, G1019
Rhode Island potteries, G802-
    803. See also East Green-
    wich (R.I.) potteries
Rhodes, James, "Pot-Works,"
    Bloomsbury, Trenton, N.J.,
    G1771
Rice, A. H., collection, C48
Rice, Jean(ne) Durant, G1142
Richards, William, Lamberton
    (Trenton), N.J., G1765
Richardson, Willard Durant
    (1857-?), G95
  portrait, G95
Riddle, Frank H.
  portrait, G754
Ridgway, William G227
  portrait, G227
Ries, Heinrich (1871-1951),
    G52, G54, G95
  collection of ceramics, G93
  portraits, G52, G95
Ringoes Pottery, East Amwell
    Township, Hunterdon
    County, N.J., B88
Ripley (Ill.) potteries, G2140
Risley, George L., G151
Risley, Sidney, G151
Ritchie, Robert David (1862-
    1929), Corinth, N.C.,
    B104
Ritchie, Thomas (1825-1909),
    Corinth, N.C., B104
Rittenhouse, Evans & Co.,
    Trenton, N.J., F95
Roach traps, G1271, G1721
Robertson, Alexander W. (1840-
    1925), G1012, G1015
  portrait, G1012
Robertson Art Tile Company,
    Morrisville, Pa., and
    Trenton, N.J., G82, G492,
    G2063, G2162-2163
Robertson, Cadmon, A127
Robertson family potters,
    Chelsea, Mass., and Ded-
    ham, Mass., A110, B77,
    G991, G1214, G1941, G2034
Robertson, Hugh Cornwall (1844-
    1908), Chelsea, Mass. and
    Dedham, Mass., G896, G931,
    G1010, G1127, G1214, G1940

  portraits, G397, G1127,
    G1940
Robertson, William A., Dedham,
    Mass., G1048
Robineau, Adelaide Alsop (1865-
    1929), B16, C21, C43, C53,
    F88, G25, G112, G175, G297-
    298, G375, G900-901, G1294,
    G1298, G1382, G1394, G1410,
    G1494, G1628, G1694, G1953,
    G1955, G1967, G1980, G2032,
    G2295
  portraits,
    G25, G175, G375, G900-901,
      G1294, G1494, G1872,
      G1953, G1955, G2032
Robinson Clay Product Co.,
    Akron, Midvale, and Canal
    Dover, Ohio (factories)
    and New York, N.Y. (office),
    F73, G745
Roblin Art Pottery, San Francis-
    co, Calif., G1012. See
    also Irelan, Linna; Robert-
    son, Alexander W.
Roblin Ware [L. Irelan], G1423
Rochester (N.Y.) potteries,
    B41, C49, G1182
Rockingham, A139, C50, F32,
    F45, G412, G1677, G1857,
    G1999
Rodgers Tile Co., Seattle,
    Wash., G1436
Roman influences. See Influ-
    ences, Greek and Roman
Roofing Tiles. See Tiles,
    roofing
Rookwood Pottery, Cincinnati,
    Ohio, A50, A54, A72, A140-
    141, A191, B45, B78, B92,
    C5, C18, F75-81, G36, G83,
    G112, G168, G263, G398,
    G400, G440, G516, G538,
    G543, G632, G747, G838-839,
    G863, G868, G890, G896,
    G943, G953, G981, G1023-
    1024, G1033, G1036, G1038,
    G1056, G1077, G1143, G1153,
    G1212-1213, G1215, G1279-
    1280, G1297, G1306, G1404,
    G1425, G1456, G1466, G1544,
    G1547-1548, G1578, G1734-
    1736, G1839, G1967, G2024,
    G2027-2028, G2035, G2130,
    G2140-2142, G2156-2157,
    G2171, G2177, G2190, G2313,
    G2319

Rookwood Pottery, Cincinnati,
Ohio (cont'd)
architectural ceramics, F74,
G718, G997, G1424
Rorabeck, Eleanore, G2107
portrait, G2107
Roseville Pottery, Zanesville,
Ohio, A2, A51, A120-121,
A201, A230, F82-83, G48,
G451-452, G665, G949,
G1230-1231, G1341, G1574
G1780, G1995
Rose Valley Association, Rose
Valley, Pa., G807, G1331-
1332
Roseville Creamware (Roseville
Pottery), G1341
Rozane (Roseville), F82-83
Rumble, Larry
portrait, G1991
Russell, H. B., collection,
G576
Rutgers, State University of
New Jersey, Ceramics De-
partment, New Brunswick,
N.J., G426, G486, G520,
G553, G708, G1599, G1669,
G1723

S.E.G. See Saturday Evening
Girls
Safford family potters, Mon-
mouth, Maine, G413
Safford, Sara Wood, G1396-
1398, G1535
Saggers, G278, G391-392, G923-
924, G2025
St. Gaudens, Annette Johnson,
G891, G1539
St. Gaudens, Paul (1900-),
G470, G891
portrait, G891
St. Paul's Cathedral, Detroit
(Tiles), G1530
St. Regis (Globe Pottery Co.),
G1800
Salem (N.C.) potteries, B86,
G9, G374
Sales manuals, A213
Salmagundi Club, New York,
N.Y., G1013, G1427-1428,
G1454
Salt-glazed stoneware. See
Stoneware; Stoneware,
salt-glazed; Glazes and

glazing, salt glazing
Sample jugs, G1299
Samson Brothers & Co., Edger-
ton, Wisc., G1867
San Jose State Normal School,
Calif. (Tiles), G626
Sanchez, J. B., residence,
Miami, Fla. (Tiles), G2121
Sanctuary bird bath (A. J. St.
Gaudens), G1539
Sanitary wares, A165-166, F18,
F84-85, G57, G511, G518-
519, G749, G772, G881,
G893, G1601-1602
Saturday Evening Girls, A220,
G548, G1140, G1678, G1738,
G2318. See also Paul
Revere Pottery
Sax, Sara, G1212
Scammell China Co., Trenton,
N.J., B30, G492, G1099
Scarab Vase (A. Robineau), C43,
G25, G375, G583, G1294,
G1494, G1872, G1899, G1942,
G1955, G1980
Schmidt, Herman, G939
Schneider, Karl. Life of
Lincoln terra cottas, G715
School of Industrial Arts,
Trenton, N.J., G104, G134,
G771
School of Mines, University of
North Dakota. See Univer-
sity of North Dakota,
School of Mines
School of Pottery and Painting
on Porcelain, Museum of
Fine Arts, Boston, Mass.,
G19
Sculpture, B7, C31, G1261
Seagle, Daniel, Lincoln County,
N.C., G1658
Seagle, James Franklin, Lincoln
County, N.C., G1658
Sebring, Frank A. (1865-1936),
G43
portrait, G43
Sebring (Ohio) potteries, G768
Sebring Pottery Co., Sebring,
Ohio, G768
Seger cones, G750
Selden-Bybee Pottery Co., Lex-
ington, Ky., G889
Serpent Bowl (A. A. Robineau),
G1220
Seven-Foot Vase (Gates), G762,
G1132

Sewer pipe art, A1, B54,
    G1182, G1646
Sewer pipes, A75-77, G674,
    G693-694
Sgraffito ware, A18-21, G220,
    G940, G1664, G1756, G2102,
    G2104. See also Pennsyl-
    vania-German potteries
Shaker pottery
    tobacco pipes, G1656
Shape books, A54, G1018
Shapes of pottery, A54, A181,
    A248, C14, E34, G125-126,
    G236, G310, G576, G1255,
    G1328, G1607, G1672,
    G1908, G1910-1912, G1983,
    G2305-2308. See also
    Design
Shaving mugs, A199, G2204
    coal scuttle, G2204
    emblem, A256, G1460, G1843
    fraternal, A200
    occupational, A199-200,
        A256, G210, G404, G1245,
        G1351, G1451, G1460,
        G1495, G1685, G1843,
        G1993, G2056-2057,
        G2125, G2202-2203, G2205
Shaw, Leon Irwin, G66
    portrait, G66
Shawsheen Pottery (Dahlquist),
    G1426
Shearwater Pottery, Ocean
    Springs, Miss., G830
Sheerer, Leonard F., G2055
    portrait, G2055
Shenandoah Valley potteries
    (Md., Pa., Va.), A264,
    C48, G15, G2316
Shenango China Co., New
    Castle, Pa., G61
Shively, R. R., G552
    portrait, G552
Shoes, B76, G2033
Sicard, Jacques, A217, G1961
Sicardo Ware (Weller), A217,
    G127, G1233, G1564, G1961
Sighs of the Pond (Campagna),
    G2296
Single shot kilns. See Kilns,
    "groundhog"
Sipe & Sons, Williamsport,
    Pa., G1200
Skeel, Albert E.
    "Expressing the Purpose of
    a Building by Its En-
    trance," G659

Slip-decorated ware, A18-21
    A58, B28-29, G940, G1177,
    G1281, G1452, G1664, G1823,
    G1842, G1889, G2102. See
    also Pennsylvania-German
    potteries
Slips, G2008
Sloane, W. and J.
    exhibit, G1310
Smith, Asa E., G2293
    portrait, G2293
Smith, Charles H. L. (1848-
    1908), G115
    portrait, G115
Smith, David (1839-1895)
    portrait, G2238
Smith, Fife & Co., Philadel-
    phia, Pa., G259, G2303
Smith, James Macmath, Sr.
    (1862-?), G61
Smith, Joseph, Wrightstown,
    Bucks County, Pa., G1177
Smith, Willoughby, Womelsdorf,
    Pa., A45
Smithsonian Museum. See
    National Museum of History
    and Technology
Smoking pipes. See Tobacco
    pipes
Snow & Coolidge, West Sterling,
    Mass., G809
Society of Decorative Art, G19
Soda fountains, G1637-1638
Soderholtz, E. E., West Goulds-
    boro, Maine, G1283
Soini . . . [potter, fl.ca.
    1925], G1176
Soldiers' Monument, Indianap-
    olis, Ind., G1119
Solitude beaker (Tucker),
    G1757
Solon, Leon Victor, G67, G530,
    G1561
    portrait, G67
Somerset (Mass.) potteries,
    G267
Somerset Potters Works, Pot-
    tersville, Somerset, Mass.,
    G267
South Amboy (N.J.) potteries,
    G1696, G2040
South Ashfield (Mass.) potter-
    ies, G2227. See also
    Ashfield (Mass.) potteries
South Carolina potteries, B67-
    68, B86, C13. See also
    Bethune (S.C.) potteries;

South Carolina potteries
(cont'd)
     Kaolin (S.C.) potteries
South Zanesville Sewer Pipe
     and Brick Co., Zanesville,
     Ohio, G642
Southern Porcelain Co., Kao-
     lin, S.C., G218, G2144,
     G2246
Southern potteries, A69, B27,
     B87, G218, G436, G438,
     G788, G1169, G1447
  Gulf states, G828-830
Southwark China Works, Phila-
     delphia, Pa., B30
Souvenir ceramics, G1000
Spark plugs, G695
Sparta Ceramic Co., East
     Sparta, Ohio, G1439
Spiers Landing Site, Berkeley
     County, S.C., B1
Spinner, David, Bucks County,
     Pa., G242-243, G1823
Spitting out, G361
Spittoons, G1590
Spongeware, B48, G1158
Spotting, G1453
Stahl family potters, Powder
     Valley, Upper Milford
     Township, Lehigh County,
     Pa., B42, G418, G1235
Stahl's Powder Valley Pottery,
     Upper Milford Township,
     Lehigh County, Pa., G47,
     G418, G1889, G2088
Staley, Homer F., G552
  portrait, G552
Standard Dry Kiln Co., Louis-
     ville, Ky., G597
Standard Floor and Wall Tile
     Co., Zanesville, Ohio,
     G2051
Standard Sanitary Manufactur-
     ing Co., Pittsburgh, Pa.,
     F84
Stangl Pottery, Flemington and
     Trenton, N.J., A210, F86,
     G933. See also Fulper
     Pottery
Star Pottery, Greensboro, Pa.,
     G1989
Star Stoneware Co., Crooks-
     ville, Ohio, G1830
Star Tiling Co., Pittsburgh,
     Pa., G1438
Statuary, F34, F38-39, G231

Steavenson & Cassel, Philadel-
     phia, Pa., F87
Steins, G1234, G1427-1428,
     G1986. See also Mugs
  football, G1234
Stephen, Walter Benjamin (1876-
     1961), Tennessee and North
     Carolina, C24, G38, G801,
     G1346. See also Nonconnah
     Pottery; Pisgah Forest Pot-
     tery
  portraits, C24, G38, G801,
     G1346
Stephens, Cooper & Co., Terra
     Cotta Works, Philadelphia,
     Pa., G643
Sterling (Mass.) potteries,
     G809
Steubenville Pottery Co.,
     Steubenville, Ohio, G1789
Stevens family potters, Georgia,
     G2299
Stevens, Henry (1813-1883),
     G2299
  portrait, G2299
Stevens, Walter Crawford (1845-
     1916), G2299
  portrait, G2299
Steward, Florence Pratt (Mrs.
     Leroy T.), G178, G964
  portraits, G178
Stewart, Gerald (1917-), B13
Stockton Art Pottery Co.,
     Stockton, Calif., B79,
     G1015
Stockton Terra-Cotta Company,
     Stockton, Calif., G1015
Stoneware, A107, A139, A243,
     A245, A261, B2, C1, C33,
     G209, G547, G575, G581,
     G1314, G1441-1443, G1445,
     G1476, G1607, G1744, G1776,
     G1874, G1938, G1990, G2087,
     G2131, G2180, G2274. See
     also Grès
  alkaline glazed. See Alka-
     line-glazed stoneware
  condensing coils, G387
  Ohio, G903
  Illinois, G2140
  Indiana, C15
  Massachusetts, G2222
  Minnesota, A180
  New England, G2217
  New Jersey, C27, E30
  New York, B41, G1208

Stoneware (cont'd)
  Pennsylvania, A146-147, B57,
    E16, G1591
  shapes. See Shapes of pot-
    tery
  salt-glazed, B2, G209, G547,
    G2131. See also Glazes
    and glazing, salt glaz-
    ing; Stoneware (above)
  Vermont, G976
Storer, Maria Longworth. See
    Nichols, Maria Longworth
Storer, (Mrs.) Bellamy. See
    Nichols, Maria Longworth
Storm, Nicholas
  portrait, G2096
Stover, Edward C., G95
  portrait, G95
Strasburg (Va.) potteries, C48
Stratton, Mary Chase Perry
    (1867-1961), A40, A112,
    A190, G1257, G1407, G1732-
    1733, G1761. See also
    Pewabic Pottery
  portraits, G1471, G1732-
    1733, G1761, G2106
Streator Drain Tile Co.,
    Streator, Ill., G737
Strikes, G495, G738, G2030.
    See also Labor-Management
    relations
Studio pottery, A35-36, A57,
    A70, A81, A211, D6, G304-
    316, G1782-1784. See
    also Art pottery; Produc-
    tion and manufacture; and
    under names of individual
    studio potters
Stull, Ray Thomas (ca.1876-
    1944), G81
  portrait, G81
Subway decoration, G135, G717,
    G1279-1280, G2133
Sullivan, Louis, G734
Summit China Co., Akron, Ohio,
    G745
Sunbonnet Babies mugs, G574
Sun-Worshippers (Hartford
    Faience Co.), G617
Suter, Emanuel (1883-1902),
    Harrisonburg, Va., C9
Swastika Keramos (Owen China
    Co.), G1017
Swimming pools (Tiles), F9,
    F11, G1437
Swiss influences. See under
    Influences

Synan Brothers Pottery, Potters-
    ville, Somerset, Mass.,
    G267
Syracuse China (Onondago Pot-
    tery Co.), B65
Syracuse Museum of Fine Arts,
    G1694
Syracuse University, G1943-
    1944, G1949-1951

Tablewares. See Commercial
    wares; Dinnerware
Taft, J. S., and Co., Keene,
    N.H., A127, A189, G1003
Taft, James Scollay, A127
Tams, James (1845-1910), G62,
    G791, G1833-1834
  portraits, G1833-1834
Tanware (New Geneva, Pa.),
    G195
Target Brick and Tile Co.,
    Cleveland, Ohio, G707
Tariffs and imports, A74, A86,
    A249-250, D20, E41, G116,
    G130, G596, G713, G1130-
    1131, G1496, G1822, G1914
  Tariff of 1894, G2030
Taylor, James (ca.1838-1898),
    G686
  portrait, G686
Taylor, John Nessly (1842-1914),
    G1794
  portrait, G1794
Taylor, William Watts (1847-
    1913), G654. See also
    Rookwood Pottery
  portrait, G654
Tea sets, toy, G1824
Teco Inn (Hotel Radison), G757
"Teco" Military-Band, G1110
Teco Ware (Gates), G866, G880,
    G962-963, G1029, G1055,
    G1132, G1151-1152, G1407,
    G1603, G1872, G2022, G2108,
    G2112, G2314. See also
    Gates Potteries
Tennessee potteries, C54, E32.
    See also Pottery industry,
    Tennessee
  DeKalb County, G2235
  Putnam County, G2235
  White County, G2235
Tepeco Ware (Trenton Potteries),
    F92

Terminology, A7-8, A59, E42,
    G323-326, G2230
Terra cotta, A97, G279, G473,
    G833, G1105, G1275, G1825,
    G2284, G2315. See also
    Architectural terra cotta
  animal heads, G232
  architectural. See Archi-
        tectural terra cotta
  columns, G1338-1339
  defects, G8
  lumber, G21
  polychrome, G2152, G2286.
        See also Architectural
        terra cotta, polychrome
Texas potteries, C51. See
    also Pottery industry,
    Texas
Therapeutic uses of pottery,
    G376, G1959
Thirst Panel (Low), G1981
Thomas China Co., Lisbon,
    Ohio, G688
Thompson family potters,
    Morgantown, W.Va., G193
Thompson, John Wood,
    portrait, G193
Tiffany & Co., F88
Tiffany Pottery, Corona, N.Y.,
    G975
Tile Club, G1472, G1536, G2322
Tile industry, A84, G1654,
    G2058, G2155. See also
    Pottery industry
  Missouri, D17
  Ohio, A155
Tiles, C44, E11, F10, G1644
  drainage, G266, G628, G727,
        G737, G770, G1083,
        G1157
  hollow. See Hollow tile
  mosaic, F3, G217, G237,
        G1050, G1301. See also
        Tiles, ornamental
  ornamental, A24, A48, A75-
        78, A111, A167-168,
        A190, A204, A244, B53,
        C36, C55, F2-4, F7, F12,
        F31, F49-51, F55, F57,
        F58-60, F90-91, G150,
        G182-183, G260, G363-
        364, G378, G532, G794,
        G837, G888, G894, G899,
        G981, G1020, G1137,
        G1257, G1277, G1284,
        G1357, G1484, G1489,

    G1576, G1579, G1596,
    G1609, G1629-1630, G1635,
    G1637-1640, G1642, G1645,
    G1732-1733, G1759, G1796,
    G1928, G1982, G2012,
    G2059, G2110, G2112,
    G2122, G2128, G2220,
    G2234
  suggestions for framing,
        G1634
  roofing, A75-77, E45, F40,
        G265-266, G395, G430,
        G594, G641, G769, G1180,
        G1760, G1989, G2149
  setting, F53
  stove, G1075, G1583, G1632-
        1633, G1644, G1689,
        G1935, G2176
  subway. See Subway decora-
        tion
  swimming pool. See Swimming
        pools
  tunnel. See Holland tunnel
Tin glazes. See Glazes and
    glazing, tin glazes
Tioughnioga Pottery, G522,
    G907
Tobacco pipes, A196, B90-91,
    B93, C44, E34, G9, G814,
    G1026, G1186, G1222, G1238,
    G1656, G2066, G2085, G2147
Toby jugs, G256
Tombstones, G264, G969, G1206,
    G1991
Tools, A198, G1276. See also
    Machinery and equipment;
    Production and manufacture
Topping, Helen M., G539
  portrait, G539
Trade directories, A59, A79,
    A172
Transfer printing, G221, G261,
    G2157. See also Decalco-
    manias
Tree labels, F54
Trent Tile Co., Trenton, N.J.,
    F89-91, G2160
Trenton (N.J.) potteries, A109,
    A215, G133, G419, G481,
    G484, G506, G524, G740,
    G859, G1090-1091, G1577,
    G1765-1773, G1791, G1840,
    G2100
Trenton Potteries Co., Trenton,
    N.J., F92
Trippet, Wesley H., G1009

Troxel, John, Berks County,
     Pa., G1198
True, Brunkhorst & Co., Chi-
     cago, Ill., F69
Tucker & Hemphill, Philadel-
     phia, Pa., C45, G238,
     G262, G895, G1274, G1316
Tucker & Hulme, Philadelphia,
     Pa., C45, G73, G105,
     G238, G895
Tucker china, B20, B30, C45,
     D4, G73, G149, G202, G212-
     213, G226, G238, G262,
     G449, G587, G956-957,
     G961, G988, G1274, G1308,
     G1316, G1322, G1595,
     G1619, G1757, G1927,
     G2167, G2289, G2303
Tucker family potters, B20
Tucker, Thomas (1812-1890),
     Philadelphia, Pa., G238,
     G1321-1322, G1619
  portrait, G1321
Tucker, William Ellis (d.1832),
     G73, G106, G238
Twin City Brick Co., St. Paul,
     Minn., G683
Twin City Keramic Club, G1431
"Two Brothers" punch bowl (C.
     Paulus), G787

Underglaze decoration. See
     Decoration of pottery,
     under the glaze
Union Porcelain works, Green-
     point, Brooklyn, N.Y.,
     B10, B103, G1116, G1832
Union Pottery Works, Point
     Marion, near Greensboro,
     Pa., G199, G1989
Union Stoneware Co., Redwing
     Minn., A253-254
Unions. See Labor unions
Unitarian Church, Ithaca,
     N.Y. (Tile roof), G769
United States Bureau of Stand-
     ards, G2006
United States Encaustic Tile
     Co., Indianapolis, Ind.,
     G457, G1301
United States Housing Corpor-
     ation, G1565
United States Potters' Associ-
     ation, A154, A169, A250,
G131-132, G390, G568, G586,
     G647, G738, G860, G1133,
     G1817-1821, G1831, G1837
United States Quarry Tile Co.,
     Parkersburg, W.Va., G1439
University City Pottery. See
     People's University, Cer-
     amic Division
University of Illinois, Depart-
     ment of Ceramic Engineering,
     Urbana, Ill., G336-337,
     G630, G655, G682, G1107,
     G1722
  Heinrich Ries collection, G93
University of Illinois, Lincoln
     terra cottas, G715
University of Minnesota, North-
     west Architectural Archives.
     See Northwest Architectural
     Archives
University of North Dakota,
     School of Mines, Grand
     Forks, N.Dak., A26, G453-
     454, G528, G934, G936
University of Washington,
     Ceramic Engineering De-
     partment, Seattle, Wash.,
     G681, G2283
Upjohn, Charles Babcock (1866-
     1953), G1232
Upton, Isaac, G1785
Upton, Samuel, G1785
Ussery's Pottery, Water-Valley-
     Banner, Miss., G1181
Utica,(N.Y.) potteries, C28

Valentien, Albert (1862-1925),
     G1352
  portrait, G1352
Valentien, Anna (1862-1947),
     G1352
  portrait, G1352
Valentien Pottery Co., San
     Diego, Calif., G1018, G1352
Value of pottery and clay
     products. See under Pot-
     tery and clay products
Van Briggle, Ann Lawrence
     Gregory, (1868-1929),
  portrait, G1278
Van Briggle, Artus (1869-1904),
     A41, G211, G1095, G1465,
     G1979
  portraits, G211, G1278

Van Briggle Pottery, Colorado
    Springs, Col., A41, C7,
    F93, G211, G276, G752,
    G754, G776, G1095, G1134,
    G1278, G1421, G1925, G2172
Vance Faience Co., Wheeling,
    W.Va., G1019
Vance, J. Nelson, G1019
Van Heusen, Charles, Albany,
    N.Y., G1368
Vasekraft (Fulper Pottery Co.),
    G165, G1790, G1807-1808,
    G2113
Vases, G1328. See also Seven-
    Foot Vase
Vedder, Elihu, mosaics in
    Library of Congress,
    G1050
Vermont potteries. See Ben-
    nington (Vt.) potteries;
    Burlington (Vt.) potter-
    ies
Vestals (Campana), G1554,
    G2297
Veyon, Samuel, Milford, Ill.,
    G281
  portrait, G281
Vickers Pottery, Lionville,
    near Downingtown, Pa.,
    B28-29
Victorian ceramics, A24, B8,
    B53, B76, C3, G2001. See
    also Nineteenth-century
    pottery
Viking Ships Vase (A. Robi-
    neau), G583, G1294, G1494
Virginia potteries. See
    Alexandria (Va.) potter
    ies; Glebe Harbor (Va.)
    potteries; Jamestown
    (Va.) potteries; Pamplin,
    (Va.) potteries; Shenan-
    doah Valley potteries;
    Strasburg (Va.) potter-
    ies; Yorktown (Va.) pot-
    teries
Virginia Pottery Co., Har-
    risonburg, Va., C9
Virginian (Lenox), G1204
Vitrified china. See Com-
    mercial wares; Dinner-
    ware
Vitrified wares (plumbing).
    See Sanitary wares
Vodrey Pottery Co., East
    Liverpool, Ohio, G1824

Volkmar, Charles (1841-1914),
    Tremont, N.Y. and Corona,
    N.Y., A251, G862, G1013,
    G1295, G1398, G1408, G1428,
    G1792, G1845, G2200-2201,
    G2269
  portraits, G778, G1845,
    G2200-2201
Volkmar Kilns (C. Volkmar &
    Son), Metuchen, N.J., G778
Volkmar, Leon G. (1879-1959),
    G154, G1176
Vulcan (H. Madsen), G723

Wabash Keramic Club, G1971
Wachusett Pottery, West Ster-
    ling, Mass., G809, G2277
Wages. See Working conditions
    and wages
Wagner, Fritz (ca.1857-1920),
    G653
  portrait, G653
Wahl Co., Chicago, Ill., G181
Walker, Francis William (1855-
    1933), G44, G95
  portrait, G95
Walker-Gordon Laboratories,
    Inc., Plainsboro, N.J.
    (Tiles), G489
Walrath, Frederick E., G303
Walters, Carl (1883-1955),
    C31, G405, G1176, G1261
  portrait, G405
Wanamaker, John, Co.
  china sale, G1826
Wareham, John Hamilton Delaney
    (1871-1954),
  portrait, G1212
Warren, Dorothea. See O'Hara,
    Dorothea Warren
Wartime uses of ceramic prod-
    ucts, G1210, G1565, G1931
    G2207
Warwick China Co., Wheeling,
    W.Va., G2254
Washington, George, commemora-
    tive ceramics, G492
  Washington jug (Jersey City
      Pottery), G246
  Washington teaset (I. Broome),
    G1644
Washington-Wakefield (Lenox),
    G1553

Water coolers, G257
Water Panel (Low), G1981
Water pipes, G1590
Watts, Arthur Simeon (1876-?),
    G30
"Way of the Cross," Allegany,
    N.Y., G731
Waynesboro (Pa.) potteries,
    C48
Webster, Daniel Dolbeer, Ply-
    mouth, N.H., G2075
Weeks, A. J., Chemical Stone-
    ware Plant, Akron, Ohio,
    G745
"Welcome La Fayette" Jug
    (Jersey City Pottery),
    G246
Weller, S. A. Pottery Co.,
    Zanesville, Ohio, A122,
    A202, G127, G487, G808,
    G1101, G1232-1233, G1564,
    G1787, G1811, G1961
Weller, Samuel A. (ca.1851-
    1925), A217, G86, G1124
    portraits, G86
Wells, W. E. (1863-1931),
    G88, G495, G531, G779,
    G2244
    portraits, G88, G495, G531,
        G692
Wellsville China Co., Wells-
    ville, Ohio, F94, G781
Wendel, Edgar, G1843
West Virginia potteries, E11,
    G1112, G1467. See also
    Morgantown (W.Va.) pot-
    teries
Western Decorating Works,
    Chicago, Ill., F95, G537,
    G544
Westinghouse Electric and
    Manufacturing Co., Derry,
    Pa., G660
Whately (Mass.) potteries,
    G141, G2224-2225
Wheatley Pottery, Cincinnati,
    Ohio, F96, G462
Wheeler, Herbert A.,(1859-?),
    G53, G95
    portrait, G95
Wheeling Pottery Co., Wheel-
    ing, W.Va., G35, G1135
Whistles, G810
White, Dennis, Glebe Harbor,
    Va., G577, G1361

White House (Washington, D.C.)
    china. See Presidential
    ceramics, China (White
    House)
White Water Brick and Tile
    Co., White Water, Wisc.,
    G702
White's pottery, Utica, N.Y.,
    C29, G1069
Whitewares, A79, A139, A179,
    G90, G394, G1734, G1988,
    G2158, G2229. See also
    Commercial wares; Dinner-
    ware
    cost of producing, G1562
Whitman, J. Franklin, Co.,
    Philadelphia, Pa., F97
Wilcox, Alvin, West Bloomfield,
    N.Y., G266
Willets Manufacturing Co.,
    Trenton, N.J., F95, F98
Willette Corporation of New
    Jersey, Pottery Plant at
    New Brunswick, N.J., G511
Williams, Robert T., New
    Geneva, Pa., G197
Williams, Roger (d.1739), E40.
    See also "Poor Potter" of
    Yorktown, Va.
Wilse Blue (Zane Pottery Co.),
    F100-101
Wilson Bill, G596
Wilson, Samuel, Pottery, Troy,
    Ind., A108
Wimer, Thomas, Trenton, N.J.,
    G1769
Wingender, Charles & Brothers,
    Haddonfield, N.J., G258
Winkle, Joseph, G173
    portrait, G173
Winkle Terra Cotta Co., St.
    Louis, Mo., G173, G666
Winslow Pottery, Portland,
    Maine, G414
Wisconsin Clayworkers' Associ-
    ation, G773
Wisconsin potteries, D9, G1042.
    See also Edgerton (Wisc.)
    potteries; Milwaukee
    (Wisc.) potteries; Potters-
    ville (Wisc.) potteries;
    Pottery industry, Wiscon-
    sin
Women in ceramics, G219, G573,
    G799. See also Cincinnati
    Pottery Club and under
    names of individual women
    ceramists

Women's Clubs of New Jersey,
    A178
Women's Pottery Club. See
    Cincinnati Pottery Club
Woodbridge Ceramic Corp.,
    Woodbridge, N.J., G1191
Woodlands beaker (Tucker),
    G1757
Woodward, Ellsworth (1861-
    1939), G42, G829
Woodward, William, G829
  Painting of George Ohr and
      Joseph F. Meyer at
      Potter's Wheel, G829
Wooton, Joseph, South Amboy,
    N.J., G412
Working conditions and wages,
    A154, D20, G121, G124,
    G673, G1622-1624, G1791,
    G2030-2031. See also
    Health conditions, pot-
    tery industry
World War I, effects of, E41.
    See also Wartime uses of
    ceramic products
Wreaths, memorial, G458
Wright, Henrietta Barclay,
    G534, G544, G1226
  portraits, G544, G1226
Wright, (Mrs.) E. Schofield,
    Pueblo, Col., G2068
Wright, Tyndale & Van Roden,
    Philadelphia, Pa., F99
Wrigley, William Jr., Cata-
    lina, Calif., G2122
Wyllie China Co., Huntington,
    W.Va., G1799, G2251

Yale University,
    exhibit, G545
Yellow ware, A139, F32, F45,
    G1448
York, Henry F., Lake Butler,
    Fla., G1076
Yorktown (Va.) potteries,
    B4-5, E37, E40, G270,
    G1289
Young, Anna M., G48
  portrait, G48
Young, George F. (1863-1920),
    G48, G102
  portrait, G48

Young Women's Christian
    Association Art School,
    New York, N.Y., G1827,
    G2195-2197

Zane Pottery Co., South Zanes-
    ville, Ohio, F100-101,
    G1340
Zane Ware (Zane Pottery Co.),
    F100-101
Zanesville (Ohio) potteries,
    A203-204, A222, G604
Zanesville (Ohio) tile compan-
    ies, A265
Zimmer, Werner Hermann
    (1857-?), G95
  portrait, G95

ABOUT THE COMPILER

RUTH IRWIN WEIDNER is a Librarian and Associate Professor at West Chester State College in Pennsylvania, where she specializes in the arts in nineteenth-century America. She is coeditor of *Essays on Mannerism in Art and Music,* and is in the process of writing a work on the Callowhills, Anglo-American ceramists and illustrators.